Gertrude Hoyt Memorial

UNEQUAL TREATMENT:
A STUDY IN THE NEO-
CLASSICAL THEORY OF DISCRIMINATION

Unequal Treatment

A Study in the Neo-Classical Theory of Discrimination

Mats Lundahl
and Eskil Wadensjö

NEW YORK
UNIVERSITY
PRESS

CROOM HELM
London & Sydney

©1984 M. Lundahl and E. Wadensjö
Croom Helm Ltd, Provident House, Burrell Row,
Beckenham, Kent BR3 1AT

Croom Helm Australia Pty Ltd, First Floor,
139 King Street, Sydney, NSW 2001, Australia

British Library Cataloguing in Publication Data

Lundahl, Mats
   Unequal treatment: a study in the neoclassical
   theory of discrimination.
   1. Discrimination in employment
   I. Title   II. Wadensjö, Eskil
   331.6   HD 4903

ISBN 0-7099-16175

New York University Press, Washington Square,
New York, New York 10003

Library of Congress Cataloging in Publication Data

Lundahl, Mats, 1946-
   Unequal treatment.

   Includes index.
   1. Discrimination in employment. 2. Discrimination –
Economic aspects. 3. Race discrimination – South Africa.
I. Wadensjo, Eskil, 1944-   . II. Title.
HD4903.L86   1984   331.13'3'0968   84-11544
ISBN 0-8147-5012-5

Printed and bound in Great Britain

CONTENTS

Preface	ix
1. INTRODUCTION	1
Points of Departure	1
The Approach of the Present Study	4
Notes	6
2. ECONOMIC THEORIES OF DISCRIMINATION	8
The Theory of Discrimination Prior to Becker	8
Becker's Theory of Discrimination	20
Development and Criticism of Becker's Theory	26
Alternative Theories of Discrimination	37
Summary and Conclusions	57
Notes	72
3. THE BECKERIAN APPROACH TO DISCRIMINATION	81
The Becker Model	83
The Flaw in the Becker Model: Changing Preferences	89
A Reformulation of the Becker Model: Constant Preferences	91
The Case of Nepotism	94
The Interpretation of the Discrimination Coefficient	97
Conclusions	103
Notes	104
4. THE PECUNIARY BECKER MODEL	109
Problems with the Taste Approach	109
The Krueger Approach	113
An Alternative Approach: Labor Market Segregation	117
Conclusions	127
Notes	129
Appendix 1: Tastes for Discrimination among White Labor	130
Appendix 2: The Madden Model	131
Notes to Appendix 2	133
5. A TWO-GOOD MODEL WITH COMPLETE SPECIALIZATION	134
The Limitations of the One-Good Model	135
Capital Market Segregation	137
Labor Market Segregation	147

Conclusions	158
Notes	160

6. A CROWDING APPROACH TO LABOR MARKET SEGREGATION — 161
Integration of the Economy, Disaggregation of the Labor Force	162
A One-Good Model	166
A Two-Good Model	168
Conclusions	180
Notes	181

7. A MORE REALISTIC CROWDING MODEL — 183
The Extended One-Good Model	185
The Extended Two-Good Model	187
Conclusions	195
Notes	196
Appendix: The Development of Relative Commodity Prices	196
Notes to Appendix	208

8. AN APPLICATION OF THE THEORY: RACIAL DISCRIMINATION IN SOUTH AFRICA — 209
A Brief History of South African Discrimination	209
A Model of South African Discrimination	226
Conclusions	242
Notes	245
Appendix 1: Mathematical Solutions	249
Appendix 2: The Porter Model of the South African Economy	255
Notes to Appendix 2	259

9. SUMMARY AND CONCLUSIONS — 261
Main Conclusions	261
Theories of Discrimination and Anti-Discrimination Policies	268
Ending Discrimination: The First Best Solution	278
Economic Effects of a Trade and Investment Boycott against South Africa	280
Notes	293
Appendix: Mathematical Solutions	295

BIBLIOGRAPHY	297
INDEX	309

LIST OF FIGURES AND TABLES

Figures

2:1	Discrimination with a Variable Supply of Labor	35
2:2	Discrimination with a Negative Supply Elasticity of Labor	36
2:3	Predictions of Productivity by Race and Test Score	45
2:4	Monopsonistic Wage Determination	46
2:5	Monopsonistic Wage Determination with Organized Male Labor	48
2:6	A Radical Model of Wage Discrimination	50

Tables

2.1	Causes and Economic Effects of Discrimination in the Labor Market	60–5
3.1	Welfare Effects of Discrimination in the Becker Model	87
3.2	Welfare Effects of Discrimination in the Constant Preference Becker Model	94
3.3	Welfare Effects of Discrimination Caused by Nepotism in the Constant Preference Becker Model	97
3.4	Welfare Effects of Discrimination Caused by Tastes with a Specific Discrimination Coefficient	101
3.5	Welfare Effects of Discrimination Caused by Nepotism with a Specific Discrimination Coefficient	102
4.1	Welfare Effects of Discrimination in the Krueger Model	116
4.2	Welfare Effects of Labor Market Segregation with Uniform Negro Wages	121
4.3	Welfare Effects of Labor Market Segregation with Uniform Wages in the White Sector	126

viii List of Figures and Tables

5.1	Welfare Effects of Capital Market Segregation in the One- and Two-Good Models	146
5.2	Welfare Effects of Labor Market Segregation in the One- and Two-Good Models with Uniform Negro Wages	153
5.3	Welfare Effects of Labor Market Segregation in the Two-Good Model with Uniform Wages in the White Sector	158
8.1	Impact of White Policy Instruments on Target Variables and on African Incomes. Stage I	228
8.2	Impact of White Policy Instruments on Target Variables and on African Incomes. Stage II	231
8.3	Impact of White Policy Instruments on Target Variables and on African Incomes. Stage III	234
8.4	Number of Temporary African Migrants Absent from the Rural Areas of South Africa on the Census Day	235
8.5	Secondary Effects of Discrimination on Target Variables. Stage III. Changes in Capital Stocks	238
9.1	The Impact of a Trade and Investment Boycott on the South African Economy	285
9.2	Probable Secondary Effects of a Trade and Investment Boycott and of Reduced Racial Discrimination on the South African Economy	289

PREFACE

The present book is the result of a project which, with many interruptions for other duties, has been going on since 1976.

This project had several sources of inspiration, ranging from Gary Becker's theoretical work in *The Économics of Discrimination* via a general interest in questions related to income distribution to applied research on problems connected with the economic attainment of migrants in Western Europe and with the South African Apartheid system.

Part of the material in Chapters 8 and 9 has been published in *Economy and History*, *The American Economic Review* and the *Scandinavian Journal of Economics*. This material is reprinted by permission. Arne Bigsten, Helen Ginsburg and Karl-Gustaf Löfgren read the entire or virtually the entire manuscript and improved its quality by a number of constructive criticisms. Bengt Assarsson, Gary S. Becker, Jan Ekberg, Ulf Hannertz, Göte Hansson, Peter Högfeldt, Christina Jonung, Lennart Jörberg, Anne O. Krueger, Gunnar Myrdal, Richard C. Porter and Gabriele Winai-Ström contributed to the discussion and clarification of different draft chapters. Göte Hansson checked our algebra. Carole Gillis and Alan Harkess struggled with improving our English. Many people, but in particular Eleanor Rapier, had to suffer the ordeal of typing innumerable versions of the manuscript. To all these people we are in deep gratitude for their efforts.

The study was financed by a grant from the Swedish Council for Research in the Humanities and Social Sciences, which is gratefully acknowledged.

As usual, we take the sole responsibility for the final product. Chapters 6–8 were written by Mats Lundahl. The remainder constitutes a joint product.

Mats Lundahl, Eskil Wadensjö
Lund and Stockholm

1 INTRODUCTION

Points of Departure

A substantial part of the welfare economics which emerged after World War II was for a long time concentrated on the analysis of situations that are Pareto optimal and of changes that are Pareto sanctioned. In this way the problem of interpersonal comparisons of utility was avoided.

The theory of international trade provides an excellent illustration. The major theorem – the one proving the superiority of trade to autarky from a welfare point of view – rests on the assumption that lump-sum redistribution is feasible, so that no group is hurt when trade is opened. In practice, it is difficult to find examples of situations where such redistribution takes place. Rather, the introduction of trade puts one group of producers (exporters) and consumers in a better position, while those producers who work in the import-competing sector will find themselves in a situation where their profits have shrunk and where they may have to go out of business if they cannot cut their costs or switch into export production instead. This discrepancy between what the theory states and what happens in practice is usually forgotten in the debate on trade policy. Instead of facing the real issue – that of comparing group interests – trade is advocated as a measure which is to everybody's advantage. The qualification 'potentially' is left out of the picture.[1]

This type of approach to economics has of course met with criticism in many quarters. In Marxian economics with its stress on classes and class conflicts, the tendency has always been to highlight the differential impact of economic and political measures. The majority of Western economists, however, have never been Marxists. By and large, neoclassically inclined economists have preferred not to become involved with class analysis. Some non-Marxist economists have, however, been critical. In *The Political Element in the Development of Economic Theory*[2] Gunnar Myrdal dealt at length with the futility of analyzing economic life in terms of social harmony or some 'common good' and took a firm stand against such purely academic exercises which he felt were devoid of empirical content. Instead he stressed the importance of concentrating the analysis of economic policy on how different policies affect different groups with conflicting interests:

> If there is reason to believe that in a particular case interests are identical, this would have to be ascertained and proved. As a major premise it should not be concealed by an *a priori* principle or a basic concept. The political conclusions are valid only in so far as this premise has been established as a factual basis for analysis. It is certainly not self-evident.
>
> But in most questions of economic policy there are conflicts of interests. This in fact should not be concealed by obscure talk of *a priori* principles. In those cases neither an economist nor anybody else can offer a 'socially' or 'economically correct' solution. No service is rendered to a rational conduct of politics by misusing scientific method for attempts to conceal conflicts. They continue to exist, however vehement the barrage of categorical principles and basic concepts.
>
> It should be one of the main tasks of applied economics to examine and to unravel the complex interplay of interests, as they sometimes converge, sometimes conflict. This ought to be done by economists because the intricacies of the price system are such that interests often run along different lines from those suggested by a superficial examination. It would be of great practical importance to reconstruct precisely the social field of interests. In the first place, we should want to know where interests converge, for in these cases we could make at once generally valid recommendations. We should also want to ascertain where lines of interests intersect. In these cases we could offer alternative solutions, each one corresponding to some special interest. Both types of solution can claim objectivity, not because they express objective political norms, but because they follow from explicitly stated value premises which correspond to real interests. The solutions are of practical interest to the extent to which their value premises are relevant to political controversies, i.e. in so far as they represent the interests of sufficiently powerful social groups.[3]

For a long time, however, Myrdal's message was ignored. Most theoretical economists continued to be fascinated by the Paretian type of analysis.[4] Game theory never quite managed to be incorporated into the mainstream of economic analysis, and it was by and large not until the late fifties and early sixties, when research was begun on public choice[5] and economic discrimination, that conflicting interests were explicitly analyzed by more traditionally inclined economists.

The point of departure for the present work is Gary Becker's analysis in *The Economics of Discrimination*.[6] After decades of neglect,[7] this book reopened discrimination as a field for modern economic analysis. In Chapter 2 we will survey the attempts to analyze discrimination in economic terms which preceded the publication of Becker's book in 1957. With a few limited exceptions none of these efforts managed to draw other contributors into the field. On the other hand, Becker not only triggered off research along the lines indicated in his book but also — and what is equally important — provoked criticism and discussion among dissenting economists who found themselves compelled to advance alternative theories as to why discrimination arises in economic life and what the effects of such discrimination are for different groups in society.

Recently, the trend has been to break away from the Beckerian analysis rather than to use it as a point of departure or a source of inspiration for further theoretical and empirical work. Contemporary economists have tended to favor other approaches and the discussion of Becker's work has been mostly based on pointing out the weak points rather than building on Becker's theory of discrimination, i.e. it has been one which has not used the Beckerian theory in any constructive way.

We feel that such a 'negative' approach to Becker's work unduly obscures the fact that — if not interpreted too literally — his theory contains many more building blocks than is commonly realized. Thus, the present book has a twofold aim. In the first place, it seeks to provide a critical discussion of some selected aspects of Becker's theory of discrimination in order to establish clearly its weaknesses. In addition, once these points have been elucidated, it attempts to pursue a positive analysis of discrimination which contains elements from the Beckerian approach as well as material from other theories of discrimination.

A second point of departure stems from an interest in questions related to the role of institutions — presently the legislature and employer and employee organizations — for determining the distribution of income and wealth in society. The framework of the analysis of the present work is neo-classical. For some reason, neo-classical economics has not been able to come up with a theory of distribution which comes anywhere close to the degree of acceptance of most other parts of neo-classical theory. One possible, and plausible, reason for this failure is that most neo-classical analysis has remained essentially devoid of an explicit institutional framework, while the shape of the institutions is highly important when it comes to determining the distribution of income and wealth. In neo-classical economics the institutional setting has generally been taken for granted — to the point where it has been more or less ignored in the analysis.

Yet, neo-classical analysis can be amended so as to accomodate the role of institutions as well. In fact, there is no reason why it should not perform even better in an explicit institutional setting than in one where institutional features are not dealt with. At any rate, an analysis of discrimination is incomplete without institutions. As Chapter 8 of the present volume will show, discrimination is often institutionalized in a series of legal sanctions which serve to uphold the economic supremacy of one group in society against another. Institutions are present in a second sense as well since one would expect those groups that can be shown to gain from discriminatory practice to attempt to form collective pressure groups that could be used for advocating discriminatory measures.

The Approach of the Present Study

The point of departure for Becker's study of economic discrimination is the existence of preferences for discrimination, that is discrimination is practiced since people have preferences concerning with whom they want to have economic relations. They are prepared to incur costs for being allowed to deal with one particular category of economic agents instead of another.[8] This readiness to pay for avoiding contact with some groups in society is expressed analytically by means of a discrimination coefficient which states the extent to which one group is favored over another. Formally, the coefficient is treated in the same way as a tax which is proportional to the extent of economic relations with the non-preferred group. The existence of this taste for discrimination serves to explain the *act* of discrimination, i.e. the act whereby people who in some economic sense are equal (equally productive in a given job, equally well-off as buyers, or sellers of the same product, etc.) do not receive the same treatment in economic transactions.

Starting from the taste for discrimination, Becker carries out a macroeconomic analysis using a model from the theory of international trade: a model with two economies and two production factors — capital and labor — where one of the economies (the discriminating one) exports capital to the other. This model will be subject to discussion in the present volume. Becker, however, also employs a microeconomic approach where he assumes that employers, employees or consumers discriminate against one particular group of employees (called Negroes in Becker's analysis), that is they are prepared to pay a price for not having to deal with the members of the latter group. Becker compares the analytical results obtained with the economic conditions that typically prevail for ethnic minorities in the United States (blacks, Indians) and also points out that the model can be used to shed some light on the situation of women in the labor market.

It is thus possible to view Becker's book as a work where the emphasis is laid on the deduction of results from the premise that certain groups in society have a taste for discrimination. Given this view, the importance of the Beckerian approach lies in its ability to generate interesting results, and the applications are made mainly to illustrate this fact. It is, however, also possible to discuss Becker's book from another point of view: as an attempt to explain why persons or groups in the same type of occupations receive different wages and why groups with common economic characteristics are found in different labor markets (labor market segregation). With regard to this latter interpretation the Beckerian theory is but one of several attempts to explain wage differentials and labor market segmentation.

Chapter 2 will be devoted to a survey of economic theories of discrimination, in order to place the Beckerian analysis in its proper context. This survey will cover both of the interpretations outlined above. We will review both the results generated from a given notion of what causes discrimination and the relative strength of different theories to explain why discrimination exists.

In *Chapter 3*, the (macroeconomic) Becker model and the welfare implications derived from it by Becker are presented. The major flaw in Becker's formulation — that of changing preferences — is discussed and the model is reformulated in a way which allows preferences to remain constant. The case of nepotism, preferences in favor of a particular group, as opposed to preferences for discrimination against another group, is taken up, both within the original Becker approach and with the amended model. Finally, Becker's formulation and interpretation of the discrimination coefficient are scrutinized. It is pointed out that this formulation has some undesirable properties. Alternative formulations are suggested and their implications for the Beckerian type of analysis are investigated.

In *Chapter 4*, the notion of preferences or tastes for discrimination among the discriminating group is dropped and an alternative analysis, along the lines originally suggested by Anne Krueger, is pursued. It is assumed that discrimination takes place for purely economic reasons, as a result of a desire to increase pecuniary incomes. The case when labor (and not capital, as assumed by Becker) is the mobile factor, and when discrimination takes the form of labor market segregation (exclusion of Negro labor from the white sector) is analyzed.

The models in Chapters 3 and 4 are all one-commodity models. In *Chapter 5*, a second good is introduced to increase the realism of the model. The analysis is carried out within the framework of a traditional trade model with two goods, two factors and two (completely specialized) 'economies', both for the case of capital withdrawal from the Negro sector and for that of labor market segregation.

The Beckerian approach to discrimination makes the somewhat unrealistic assumption that the economy may be divided into two 'sectors' which, excepting factor movements, operate more or less independently of each other. Discrimination takes the form of a regulation of factor movements. In real life, however, discrimination also takes place within integrated economies with complete freedom of factor movement as between sectors. It often shows up as a reservation of certain jobs — the best paid ones — for a particular group. This type of discrimination (crowding) is analyzed in *Chapter 6*, both in a one-good model à la Becker, with skilled and unskilled labor, and in a two-by-two framework for a closed economy.

In *Chapter 7*, a further specific production factor is introduced for each sector in order to increase the degree of realism. It is shown that, as a result of this change, the results obtained in Chapter 6 no longer necessarily hold.

In *Chapter 8*, elements from the discussion of labor market segregation in Chapters 4 and 5 and from the analysis of job reservation in Chapters 6 and 7 are combined in the application of the methodology to the discussion of discrimination in a particular country: South Africa.

Chapter 9 summarizes and evaluates the results of the study and discusses different measures to end discrimination.

Notes

1. Compensatory schemes exist in many countries but these schemes as a rule do not fully compensate those who are injured by free trade. See Baldwin (1980).
2. Myrdal (1929). Originally published in Swedish, the work was translated into English 24 years later. See Myrdal (1953).
3. Myrdal (1953), p. 193.

4. See, however, e.g. Little (1957), Nath (1969) or Sen (1980) for criticisms of Paretian welfare economics. Sen explicitly mentions the principle of non-discrimination as one of the principles of social judgement that requires non-utility information and which is 'typically not very much discussed in traditional welfare economics' (Sen (1980), p. 29).

5. A survey of public choice theories is made in Mueller (1979).

6. Becker (1957), second edition; Becker (1971:2). All references in the present work are to the second edition.

7. Maybe the fact that conflicting interests must be analyzed explains why discrimination remained for so long a neglected field in economics (cf. Reich (1981), p. 76).

8. This means a break with Jevons' 'Law of Indifference' which states that 'sellers will sell to the highest bidder and buyers buy from the source with the lowest offer-price '(Leijonhufvud (1976), p. 75, note 17).

2 ECONOMIC THEORIES OF DISCRIMINATION

Since discrimination is an old phenomenon, a great deal of speculation regarding its causes and effects has naturally taken place over the centuries. In the present chapter we will survey the twentieth-century discussion as carried on by economists, starting with the British Equal Pay Controversy which began during the 1890s and continued until after World War II. Special attention will be paid to the work of Gary Becker, since this constitutes one of the most important points of departure of the present book. While a fairly extensive debate had already taken place prior to the publication of Becker's *The Economics of Discrimination* in 1957, the Becker book undoubtedly was the beginning of modern, formalized economic theorizing on the subject.

In the first section, an account is given of pre-Beckerian theories: the British Equal Pay Controversy and the crowding hypothesis, the application of the monopsony theory in the 1930s and Gunnar Myrdal's cumulative process approach in *An American Dilemma*. The second section surveys Becker's different concepts and models. In the third section, reference is made to later developments and criticisms of the Beckerian theory. Finally, an overview is given of contemporary theorizing not steeped in the Beckerian tradition.

The Theory of Discrimination Prior to Becker

The Early Debate[1]

The majority of the early analyses of discrimination in the labor market are based on a discussion of the reasons for the differences between the wages of men and women. One of the first contributions to the debate was Sidney Webb's study of 1891, 'The Alleged Differences in the Wages Paid to Men and to Women for Similar Work'.[2] Webb made a survey of available statistics for four different types of work — manual work, routine mental work (office work), artistic work and intellectual work — with the emphasis on the first two. In both of these groups, wage differences existed even when men and women did the same job.[3]

Webb ascribed the differences to:

(1) customs and public opinion,

(2) lower demands from women due in part to lower standards of living ('Might not women do more work, and better, if they learned to

eat more?')[4], in part to their family situation, being economically supported by family or husband,

(3) lower productivity by women, caused by several factors: insufficient training, lack of strength, institutional restrictions,

(4) '. . . lack of protective power, through failure to combine want and adaptability, limited number of alternatives and greater immobility.'[5]

Thus, Webb does not limit his analysis to the labor market but examines institutional conditions such as legislation, traditions, educational systems and family structure as well. Two of the four arguments can be considered as labor market discrimination in a narrow sense, that is, differences in treatment in the labor market not arising from differences in productivity. This is valid for customs and public opinion which can be viewed as employer discrimination due to preferences or prejudices (to use concepts from recent theory). Both the lack of protective power and lower wage demands due to economic support from husband and family may be interpreted in terms of a low elasticity of the female labor supply. The principal factors here which combine to produce lower wages for women are their lesser dependence on wage incomes, lower geographic mobility than men, and the monopsonistic position of firms in the labor market.

During the First World War, the female participation rate increased in England. To a larger extent than previously, women also performed the same or similar work as men. Their wages, however, were still considerably lower than the male ones. The economists agreed on the fact that wage differences existed. They disagreed, however, on the reasons for the differences. The decisive question was, to quote Gustav Cassel:

> How can female labour generally and permanently receive a lower wage than it is worth — that is to say, a price below that which equilibrium between supply and demand would fix in the pricing process, and would therefore represent the valuation of this labour on the part of the demand?[6]

Some of the contributions to this debate came from female economists. Eleanor Rathbone[7] stated that the lower wages for women, apart from differences in productivity, which she believed were of importance, could be explained by four different factors:

(1) that women lack trade unions,
(2) that women's wages are only pocket money or to be regarded as supplementary to the family income,

(3) that women have a low standard of living, and
(4) that wages are set according to individual subsistence requirements: the woman is not normally the family wage-earner.

Rathbone concentrated on the fourth factor in her analysis, but it is not clear from her work why wages are lower in practice. Her argument can be interpreted as stating that employers pay men and women different wages for the same job due to social convention.

In two articles from 1917 and 1918,[8] Millicent Fawcett presented a point of view which was different from Rathbone's regarding the causes of the wage differences between men and women. Fawcett argues that Rathbone overemphasizes possible differences in productivity and that the mechanism of discrimination is not what Rathbone alleges it to be. According to Fawcett, the male-dominated trade unions, which in many cases refuse to accept women as members, are the cause of discrimination. Men have succeeded in various ways in excluding women from certain jobs. This has created an occupational segregation which has confined women to a few jobs, and has led to higher wages in male than in female jobs.[9]

Fawcett's analysis is interesting from two points of view. In the first place, it stresses the role played by the unions, something which reappears in many of the later analyses. In the second place, it emphasizes the connection between discrimination and segregation, by indicating that segregation is a way to achieve discrimination.

The question of relative wages for men and women became an important political issue during the First World War, when women were increasingly allowed to enter occupational areas that had been traditionally reserved for men. A War Cabinet Committee on Women in Industry was set up which, on the completion of its work after the end of the war, recommended the principle of equal pay for equal work.

If men and women did not make the same work contribution and equal wages could therefore not be paid, the employer had to prove this difference in work contribution. The Committee's suggestion was never acted upon, but it is interesting as an early example of how anti-discrimination legislation can be formulated.[10] Among other things, the Committee sent out a questionnaire to economists.[11] The questions were concerned above all with what effects a transition to the principle of equal pay for equal work would have on the economy. In their answers, however, two of the economists also analyzed why women received lower wages for the same jobs.

Edwin Cannan[12] believed that the explanation lay in the fact that due to — among other things — different types of restrictions, women were concentrated within a few occupations. The supply was therefore large and the wages low in those occupations where women could get work. Cannan also suggested that the limitation of the female labor market could be due in part to the preferences of the consumer, above all in certain service occupations. In common with Sidney Webb and Eleanor Rathbone, he stressed the lower standard of living for women which resulted in lower productivity as a reason for the differences in wages.

Arthur Cecil Pigou was the other economist who considered the reasons for women receiving lower wages. Pigou mentioned, as Cannan had done, that certain occupations were closed to women and discussed the occurrence of what current terminology would label monopsonistic elements in the labor market:

> There is reason to believe that the general tendency of competition is also obstructed by quasi-monopolistic pressure. Women's wages in certain occupations are depressed below the level which economic competition tends to bring about, because, owing to their strategic weakness, unscrupulous or unthinking employers are able to pay them less than they are worth (in technical terms less than the value of their marginal net product).[13]

The Interwar Period

Two articles from the interwar period drew certain parallels with Rathbone's and Fawcett's discussion. Francis Edgeworth[14] stressed the productivity differences but believed that wage differences existed that did not correspond to differences in productivity. There were several different reasons for these wage differences. He said in answer to Cassel's question that the latter's paradox could be explained by the fact that the labor market was not in a state of perfect competition.[15] He then emphasized, as Fawcett had done, the role of the trade unions. The male trade unions excluded women from certain occupations, leaving fewer opportunities for them. Thus, women were drawn into the remaining occupations, a fact which depressed wages.[16] Like Rathbone, Edgeworth presented differences in the burden of support as a motive for wage differences. It is not clear from his presentation, however, whether he meant that this type of difference in the burden of support actually influenced the wage structure as well.[17]

Sargant Florence[18] criticized the advocates of the 'crowding' hypothesis, that is those who thought that wage differences depended on the fact that women were concentrated into just a few occupations. He believed that wage differences which were not due to productivity differences (Cassel's paradox) could be explained instead with reference to:

(1) that the firms have a monopsonistic position in the labor market,
(2) that women are less mobile in the labor market (exhibit a lower elasticity of supply than men),[19] and
(3) that a certain type of indivisibility exists concerning decisions to employ female labor.

The last point meant that men would not agree to perform the same occupational tasks as women at the same place of work. This can be viewed as a form of discrimination by the (male) employees. The firm therefore must have either a completely male or a completely female work force in any one occupation. This 'indivisibility' combined with the lower female supply elasticity is, in Florence's opinion, the explanation of the fact that companies that are monopsonists in the labor market will set higher wages for men than for women. Hence, Florence's model of discrimination includes both employer discrimination (monopsony) and discrimination by a group of employees (men refusing to perform the same work as women at the same place of employment).

During the interwar period, a British governmental study[20] examined another possible reason for the differences in occupational distribution and wages between men and women, namely legislation which limits women's working hours (weekend work, night work, overtime work) and work tasks (for example, working with lead). Only a few examples of this were found. The investigation, however, was primarily an overview and the hypothesis that the legislation had had no effect was not subjected to any stringent tests.

Florence's monopsony explanation for discrimination recurs in a much more elaborate form in Joan Robinson's classic work, *The Economics of Imperfect Competition* (1933). In her analysis of a firm with a monopsonistic position in the labor market, Robinson took as an example a division of the labor supply into one male and one female component. She considered both the case where men and women have different supply elasticities and therefore receive different wages, and the case where the men, but not the women, are organized in trade unions and have successfully obtained a minimum wage for themselves. In the latter case, the wage differences are dependent both on discrimination by the employer and on the fact that one of the two groups is organized in unions. The discrimination in this instance lies in the fact that everyone does not belong to (or is not allowed to belong to) the unions.

In a much later article,[21] Martin Bronfenbrenner has further developed the case of monopsony. His point of departure is that employers are, as a rule, satisfied with less than the entire monopsony profit. Wages are instead held at a level between what would have arisen in the case of perfect competition and what the result would have been in the case of complete exploitation of the monopsonistic position. The supply of labor would then exceed the demand, giving a certain freedom to the employers in their choice of employees. This could lead, for example, to a situation where blacks are not allowed into those occupations where wages are relatively high but instead must take jobs with employers who make more use of their monopsonistic position.

Several of the works referred to above discuss the role of the trade unions. Fawcett and Edgeworth emphasized the importance of the trade unions in the concentration of women in certain occupations, while Robinson showed how the difference in the degree of organization between different groups can contribute to the establishment of wage differences between them. In an article published in 1939,[22] Bronfenbrenner concerned himself with how the existence of trade unions can influence conditions for organized and non-organized workers respectively. Given wages that are equal for the two groups and given trade unions that follow a policy of preferential treatment for their members (preferential shop treatment, closed-shop system), differences in unemployment arise between the organized and the non-organized, thus producing different incomes.[23]

Bronfenbrenner also discussed discrimination by employers. In one of his cases the employer considers the wage, w, for a union member the equivalent of the wage, w_N − dw, for a non-union member. This formulation is very similar to the one Becker was to use later on but the rationale is different. For Bronfenbrenner, dw was the expected higher expense for labor conflicts,[24] and thus was not based on preferences for contacts with one group over another, as is the case with Becker. The wages were assumed to be equal for the organized and the non-organized even in this case where non-organized are hired before organized and the total volume of employment of the firm is lower.

Finally, Bronfenbrenner analyzed cases covering differences in wages for the same work; for example, where white employees but not black ones are organized in a trade union which sets wages in such a way as to maximize the total white incomes, given the total demand for labor.

Employers can then hire black workers who are non-organized, and who receive lower wages than they would obtain under perfect competition throughout the whole labor market. Bronfenbrenner's case can be viewed as a specific example of Joan Robinson's monopsonistic employers. It is also worthwhile to note the difference in the choice of examples. For a long time, the discussion in the United States was primarily concerned with racial discrimination, while in Britain the central topic for debate and analysis was discrimination against women.

The Second World War

The Second World War led to a continued discussion concerning wages for men and women in Britain. A new commission, the Royal Commission on Equal Pay, was set up during the last years of the war to examine the question of equal wages. The Commission asked a number of researchers, primarily economists, to reply to three questions about male and female wages. The first question was as follows:

> It has usually been argued that the failure of industrial employers in normal times to substitute women's for men's labour in cases in which, at the prevailing relative rates of wages, it would apparently pay them to do so, is due to conventions and pressures of various kinds. It has however also been suggested that it is due to a limitation in the number of women available for industrial employment, coupled with a superiority of bargaining power on the part of employers, which prevents the women from obtaining the higher wages which, if competition were perfectly free, they would in these conditions be able to secure. Which of these two explanations (if either) do you favour?[25]

The Commission wanted the researchers to state whether the low female wage rate was due to conventions and pressures or to low supply elasticity together with the existence of monopsonistic companies.

Replies were received from ten researchers, of whom nine were economists.[26] All based their opinions on the fact that differences between male and female wages exist for a given work contribution. Many of the eight male researchers who responded believed, however, that productivity differences exist as well.[27] Neither of the female economists, Joan Robinson or Barbara Wootton, dealt with the question of productivity differences.

Of the ten, only Sargant Florence chose the second alternative. Referring to his article of 1931, he was of the opinion that the inelastic labor supply of women was the decisive factor underlying wage differences and emphasized how women's inferior bargaining power allows firms to take advantage of a monopsonistic position. The others placed the emphasis on 'conventions and pressure', even though some at the same time pointed out the importance of monopsonistic elements combined with a low degree of union organization among women.[28]

However, 'conventions and pressure' mean different things to different economists. Roy Harrod stressed the convention that the man in the family is the main wage-earner and that, because of this, firms pay higher wages to men. Others, like Wootton, polemicized against this way of thinking and believed that wages are not set according to need: 'There is no such thing as a living wage for either sex.'[29] Several emphasized that pressure from the male employees limit the women's labor market and, as a result, their wages remain lower. Such is the case with Hubert Henderson, for example:

> The most important of the 'pressures' is, of course, the fear that the introduction of women would cause serious friction with the male employees; but, as the word 'conventions' suggests, this inhibition may often be reinforced by a feeling in the minds of employers that it would be socially undesirable to replace men by women on an extensive scale.[30]

Conventions and pressure can thus be viewed partly as ideas (mainly among employers) about what is socially desirable, partly as discrimination from a group of employees against another group. However, a uniform theoretical treatment of how conventions and pressure influence female work conditions is lacking among the economists who responded to the Commission.

Henry Phelps Brown[31] commented upon the Commission and the statements of the researchers in an article in the *Economic Journal*. He considered three questions:

(1) What does equal pay for equal work imply?

(2) To what extent does unequal pay for equal work exist in Great Britain?

(3) In so far as unequal pay exists today, what is the reason for this?

Phelps Brown did not take up the issue of why men and women as a rule do not have the same jobs. He divided up the causes for wage differences into those which arise from the fact that men and women are not of equal value to the employers (productivity differences, differences in personnel turnover) and those which are due to other factors. Regarding the latter, he emphasized the role of the trade unions and conventions with regard to male and female wages.

A union pamphlet about the question of equal wages,[32] written as a sequel to the Commission's report, dealt with, amongst other questions, the reasons as to why women have lower wages. In addition to customs and prejudices, the lower degree of women's union bargaining power was presented as an explanation.

Like its predecessor, the committee which was set up during the First World War, the Royal Commission on Equal Pay recommended that the Government should eliminate the differences between the wages for men and women in the public sector. In both cases, the Government turned down the recommendations as being too costly to carry out.[33]

Myrdal's Dynamic Analysis

A radically different approach to the problem of discrimination is to be found in Gunnar Myrdal's book *An American Dilemma*[34] — a book which surprisingly made very few ripples in the subsequent literature on discrimination.[35] In contrast to Edgeworth, for example, who followed the neo-classical tradition with its emphasis on static and comparative static analysis, and Joan Robinson, who built upon Marshallian foundations and partial equilibrium analysis to criticize the assumption of perfect competition, the starting point for Myrdal was that the racial discrimination problem — and socio-economic problems in general — must be analyzed with the help of dynamic theory and that variables other than the narrowly economic ones must be included.[36]

Myrdal was well prepared. In *Monetary Equilibrium*, he had discussed and criticized in depth Wicksell's analysis of the cumulative process in the credit market.[37] In *An American Dilemma* he made a bold analogy and sketched how the principle of a circular, cumulative causation could, and should, be used instead of the neo-classical equilibrium concept. Myrdal distinguished three components as being of strategic importance in the cause-and-effect relation that created a 'Negro problem' in the United States:[38] (1) the prejudices of whites and their discrimination of blacks, (2) the standard of living of the blacks, (3) the blacks' intelligence, ambitions, health, education, decency, manners and morals.

These three components interact and reinforce each other in a circular causal relationship, and every change in one or more of these three components leads to a secondary change in all other components in the same direction. Assume, for example, that white prejudices against blacks increase autonomously. This leads to more discrimination, which subsequently results in increased difficulties for blacks in obtaining employment and causes the average standard of living of blacks to decrease. Worsened economic conditions lead in turn to a decline, for example, in health standards and education. The behavior of blacks (decency, manners, morals) is then influenced in a negative direction.

However, the process does not stop here: the worsening of the standard of living of the blacks and their behavior is interpreted by the whites as a confirmation of their ideas of blacks. By this process, the prejudices are reinforced. Discrimination of blacks increases again, etc. The process becomes not only circular but cumulative as well. Each (hypothetical) state of equilibrium in the Myrdalian analysis thus becomes unstable and as soon as the system is exposed to an exogenous shock, this shock will be reinforced in the manner we have just described. Instead of returning to the old state of equilibrium or converging towards a new one, the system is set in motion away from every form of equilibrium, and this motion does not stop unless the system is exposed to new, opposing, exogenous shocks.

It should be noted that the system can move 'upwards' as well as 'downwards'. Myrdal prefers the expression 'principle of cumulative causation' to 'vicious circle',[39] since, given a positive shock, the circular causal relation will give rise to a 'good' spiral instead of a 'bad' one. In principle, one can thus attack the racial discrimination problem by attacking any one of the three factors comprising the complex. Myrdal emphasizes, however, that a rational policy whose purpose is to abolish discrimination cannot expect to concentrate measures on a single factor. Instead, all three ought to be attacked simultaneously.

Myrdal's analysis of the problem of discrimination was couched in much more general terms than that of the majority of the British economists. He stressed the importance of analyzing how discrimination altered gradually in combination with other factors, and did not limit himself to the traditional 'economic' factors. His work was wholly problem-oriented and contained all the categories and tools of analysis which could aid in shedding light on the 'Negro problem' and its solution. The closest parallel to the breadth of his methodology is Webb's study of 1891, which, however, is less of a coherent analysis and more of an enumeration of the economic and non-economic factors that could be relevant.

Myrdal's method for analyzing discrimination is not, however, free from criticism. The most important objection to *An American Dilemma* came from Trevor Swan[40] and was based on the view that one seldom observes in any existing society the type of cumulative motion that Myrdal describes in his book. Strictly speaking, in its final phase this motion is explosive. After a negative external shock, the three components in the Negro problem would set the system in such motion that increasing white prejudices and discrimination on the one hand and a decreasing black standard of living on the other would cumulate unceasingly until the whole system would finally reach such a level of instability that it would collapse.

According to Swan such explosions are rare phenomena. Even in practice, if a cumulative process gets underway in one way or another and accelerates for a certain time, opposing forces of sufficient strength will sooner or later bring the process to a halt.[41] The causal relations do not necessarily need to be unequivocally reinforcing, as Myrdal implies, but can proceed in both directions. This is of special importance for the possibilities of solving the 'Negro problem' through economic-political measures. One cannot simply start a positive cumulative process: it is likely that a number of obstacles or threshold values for certain strategic variables exist which must be overcome before cumulative causation can start to take effect. Perhaps, to borrow a couple of terms from development economics,[42] some type of 'big push' or 'critical minimum effort' is required.

Conclusions

As can be seen from our survey of the discrimination literature prior to Becker, there are several different competing or complementary explanations from that period for the existence of discrimination. These explanations may be grouped in several ways — for example, according to the motive for discriminatory behavior. Two primary reasons are mentioned in the literature: one is that employers or employees discriminate in their own economic interest, while the other is that the employers discriminate because of conventions.

The most developed theory is that which shows how an employer who has a monopsonistic position can derive a gain by setting different wages for different groups of employees. The prime advocates of this point of view are Florence, Robinson and Bronfenbrenner, all of whom have, moreover, shown how monopsonistic discrimination can be combined with other forms: with employee discrimination (Florence), with the existence of discriminating trade unions (Robinson and

Bronfenbrenner) and with the occurrence of preferential treatment for one group of labor over another (Bronfenbrenner).

One group of employees can discriminate against another group of employees in order to receive economic advantages. This can take place in relatively unorganized forms. For example, the employees (whites, men) may quit their jobs if the company hires persons belonging to another group (blacks, women) (primarily Florence). Discrimination can also occur in more organized forms through trade unions which are controlled by the discriminating groups. Through the unions, one group can prevent another group from getting employment in certain occupations, with 'crowding' and lower wages for the other group as a result (amongst others, Fawcett and Edgeworth). It may also get preferential treatment when decisions concerning hiring and firing are made and thus create differences in, among other things, unemployment risks (Bronfenbrenner). Finally, it may promote a wage policy which accepts wage differences for organized and non-organized workers (Robinson and Bronfenbrenner).

An alternative explanation of discrimination is that employers by convention set different wages for different groups even when these have the same jobs (several of the contributions to the Royal Commission on Equal Pay). In order for such a convention to give a stable solution, however, all employers must follow it. In any other case, the non-discriminatory employers would receive economic advantages and would expand at the expense of the discriminatory ones. If all the employers use the same convention, we have a case that resembles monopsonistic collusion (though not necessarily in the manner which yields the highest possible profits). One reason for such a convention which is often cited (e.g. Edgeworth, Rathbone and Harrod) is the difference in the burden of support between men and women, while others lean towards the explanation that the convention originated rather from the pressure from other groups of workers, that is, that discrimination actually began with the employees.

There are also those who try to see discrimination in a larger perspective and include the educational system, family structure, consumption standards, etc., in their analysis. Among these are Sidney Webb (discrimination against women) and Gunnar Myrdal (discrimination against blacks), but other economists as well have pointed out that discrimination must be seen in a larger perspective. Barbara Wootton gives an example of this:

> . . . . I think we get nearest to the truth of the matter if we simply say that both the relatively low level of women's wages, and the

relatively restricted scope of their employment, are merely reflections of the general position of women in contemporary society.[43]

The majority of the economists mentioned here focus their interest on the causes of discrimination. Few analyze the effects. One reason for this is that they start with an analysis of wage differences, in which discrimination may be one of many causes, and then analyze what caused them. The only pure exceptions are those who deal with monopsonistic behavior and its effects, i.e. chiefly Robinson and Bronfenbrenner. In this area, Becker would break with the tradition by starting with a given cause of discrimination and then analyzing the effects.

Becker's Theory of Discrimination

What sets Gary Becker's *The Economics of Discrimination* apart from earlier works is the fact that Becker aims at a general theory for the analysis of the effects of discrimination in a market economy.[44] He makes a sharp distinction between the *causes* and the *act* of discrimination and between the *act* and the *effects*.

The emphasis in Becker's analysis is placed on the effects while relatively little notice is taken of the causes. His point of departure is that individuals may have a taste for discrimination which can vary in strength from person to person. According to Becker, this taste is due to the fact that individuals have preferences for making transactions with certain persons rather than with others. Those individuals who discriminate because of these preferences are willing to abstain from incomes in order to avoid certain transactions.

The Discrimination Coefficient

In order to analyze the effects of the taste for discrimination, Becker employs the concept *discrimination coefficient*. It can be used when analyzing the discrimination of a certain group from other factors of production, the employers or the consumers. Assume that the wage for a group against whom an employer discriminates is w and that the employer acts as if the wage is $w(1 + d)$, due to his preferences *vis-à-vis* members of that group. Hence, the discrimination coefficient is d while wd represents the non-monetary costs for the employer which are connected with the transaction. Using the discrimination coefficient as a tool, Becker analyzes the economic effects of discrimination on, for instance, wage differences. In order to measure the effect of discrimination on wages, he employs the concept 'market discrimination coefficient', which is defined as the difference in wage rate between the discriminated and the non-discriminated groups divided by the wage rate for the discriminated group.

The tastes for discrimination are exogenously determined in Becker's model. In several places in his study, however, there is a discussion of the causes of a taste for discrimination. Becker relates discrimination to the degree of contact: if contact with members of a certain group is completely lacking, there is no taste for discrimination. Tastes will also be weak or non-existent if contacts are very common and intensive. For all the cases that fall between these two poles, the probability exists that a taste for discrimination will arise. According to Becker, contact has several different dimensions. It is dependent upon the size of a certain group (in Becker's example, the number of Negroes as compared with the number of whites),[45] the group's economic significance and the duration and level of the contact.[46] Becker does not develop this, nor does he build on any elaborate theory for the determination of the taste for discrimination of a group. One can, however, see the beginning of a dynamic system similar to Myrdal's in which the contacts between different groups influence the degree of discrimination and the discrimination affects segregation and thereby the extent and direction of the contacts. Still, the lack of an elaborate theory of the causes of discrimination is one of the problems with Becker's approach.

Another problem is that Becker bases his theory on the idea that people discriminate because they dislike having contact with members of one group as compared to another, not because they like having contact with the latter rather than with the former. The basis, thus, is 'negative' and not 'positive' discrimination (nepotism). Becker comments briefly on the problem and argues that it is difficult empirically to differentiate between theories based on hatred for one group and those building on love for another group. He believes that the positive economic analysis will yield the same result regardless of which of the two emotions that causes a difference in treatment, while on the other hand the normative conclusions will differ between the two cases.[47]

The Macroeconomic Model

In order to analyze the effects of discrimination, Becker works with two different approaches, one macroeconomic and the other microeconomic. The former is of the type commonly used within the theory of international trade. In this model there are two 'societies', two production factors (labor and capital), but only one commodity. The societies thus do not trade commodities but 'export' production factors. In the main text of the book,[48] there is a non-mathematical model where each society exports its relatively abundant factor. Society W exports capital and society N, labor. In a state of equilibrium without discrimination, the reward to a particular production factor is not dependent on whether it is employed in community N or community W. If the members of W then develop a taste for discrimination, this leads to lower capital exports from W which results in turn in a lower export of labor from N, according to Becker.

In the Appendix to Chapter 2 of Becker's study, the form of the macroeconomic model is slightly different.[49] Capital is the only mobile factor of production. In this model, the existence of a taste for discrimination in the capital exporting society makes capital exports lower than in a situation with equilibrium without discrimination. Becker's primary result from the macroeconomic model is that both the discriminated and the discriminating groups lose. It is also important to note that for the latter group, a comparison is made between a situation with preferences for discrimination and discrimination (reduced exports of capital), and a situation without such preferences and discriminated and the discriminating groups lose. It is also important loss, relatively speaking, from discrimination. It turns out not to be possible to obtain a clear-cut result unless an assumption is made about the communities' relative incomes before discrimination compared with the relative size of their labor forces.

Even given the point of departure that Becker has chosen for his analysis of discrimination, there are certain undesirable limitations with regard to his use of the macroeconomic model. In the first place, it builds on the idea that the discrimination coefficient does not vary between different capital owners.[50] Secondly, the analysis is limited to the case where the capital owners in one community discriminate against labor from the other community. The model is not employed to analyze the discrimination of one group of laborers by another. Further, it cannot be used to analyze discrimination on the part of the consumer against goods which are produced through the efforts of the labor force of one of the communities. Employee and consumer discrimination are dealt with in terms of microeconomic theory.[51]

The Microeconomic Model

In the microeconomic analysis, Becker utilizes the same concepts as in the macroeconomic one, namely the discrimination coefficient, in order to derive a measure of the intensity of the taste for discrimination, and the market discrimination coefficient to measure the effect of discrimination on wages. First, he treats different types of discrimination by employers, employees, consumers, tenants and government separately, and then he merges the effects of the various forms of discrimination. As in the macroeconomic analysis, there is only one commodity in the model.

In the case of employer discrimination, the simplest case analytically is that in which all employers have the same discrimination coefficient. With perfect substitutability between the discriminated and the non-discriminated labor, the market discrimination coefficient becomes equal to the discrimination coefficient regardless of the size of the discriminated group and the degree of competition in the commodity market. When there is incomplete substitutability, the market discrimination coefficient becomes lower than the discrimination coefficient. The discriminated group is protected to a certain extent by the lack of substitutability.

Of greater interest are the complications that arise when the discrimination coefficient varies among different employers. The discriminated group will then be employed by the employers with the lowest discrimination coefficient. Discrimination leads to segregation. The market discrimination coefficient is in this case determined not only by the distribution of the discrimination coefficients but also by the size of the discriminated group: the larger the group, the higher the market discrimination coefficient.

One problem which Becker touches briefly upon and which is of great significance for the theory is the stability of this form of discrimination. Firms with low or no discrimination coefficients will produce more due to lower labor costs and receive higher profits than firms with high coefficients. This leads to a further expansion of firms with low coefficients, and to a gradual elimination of the firms with a strong taste for discrimination.

By definition, firms that have a monopoly in a commodity market do not run the risk of being driven out of the market if they discriminate. On the other hand, a monopolistic company will be worth more for the employer who does not discriminate than for the one who does. If there is competition in the capital market, entrepreneurs without a taste for discrimination will consequently buy up monopoly companies (when the monopoly is transferable). Competition in the capital market will have the same effect as competition in the commodity market in the previous case. Hence, the market discrimination coefficient will be zero in the long run. According to Becker, however, this limitation of the possibilities of discrimination does not exist for non-transferable monopolies such as federal and municipal ones.

Thus, increased competition works against employer discrimination. If the aim is to decrease discrimination, attempts should be made to increase competition in different markets.[52]

The effects of employee discrimination depend on the extent to which the discriminating and discriminated groups can be substituted for each other in production. If they are perfect substitutes, the result will be segregation. Each firm that chooses to have a work force consisting of people from both the discriminated and the discriminating groups will have higher costs than the firm whose employees come from only one of the groups. With non-discriminatory employers the wage rate will be the same for both groups. The market discrimination coefficient will thus be zero.

If the groups are not perfect substitutes, the results will be different. Assume that we have three groups, for example white foremen, white workers and black workers. Further, let us assume that the foremen and the workers are perfect complements in the production process and that white foremen discriminate against black workers. In this case, the market discrimination coefficient will not be zero. Black workers will receive a lower wage than white workers. In the case where the groups are neither perfect substitutes nor perfect complements, the market discrimination coefficient falls somewhere between these two cases. Even in the case of perfect substitutes, according to Becker, we may get a market discrimination coefficient which is greater than zero. This is valid if trade unions discriminate, for example, by not allowing members of a certain group to join. However, the assumption that the unions do not allow everyone to become a member is insufficient by itself. It is also necessary that the unions have control over the employment policy of the firms, for example through a closed shop clause, or that they can influence the wage setting for their members, and that these members are given preference in employment.[53]

Consumers can discriminate against commodities and services which are produced or otherwise handled by a certain group, for example, by refusing to buy commodities when the sales staff belong to this group. The size of the market discrimination coefficient is then determined by the discrimination coefficient and the relative importance of the discriminated group in the production process. Variations in the discrimination coefficient yield similar results as variations in the employer discrimination coefficient, that is segregation — in this case, segregation in consumption. Whites shop in white stores, blacks in black ones. Discrimination between different groups of consumers, for example tenants in the housing market, also leads to (residential) segregation.

Becker provides a brief analysis of government discrimination. Under certain simplified conditions, it is the median voter's discrimination coefficient which will be valid for government policy. In connection with this[54] Becker discusses certain problems which arise with the application of the median voter theorem in this area, for example, the occurence of logrolling.

The various forms of discrimination are not independent of each other. According to Becker, the combined effect of employer, government and trade union discrimination, that is the market discrimination coefficient, will be equal to the sum of the different discrimination coefficients multiplied by the relative importance of the group in the production process. If consumer discrimination is added, it is possible (with an approximation) to include it with the other discrimination coefficients and then once again multiply by the relative economic importance of the discriminated group in the production process. This presupposes that the different types of discrimination coefficients do not vary within the groups of employers, consumers, etc.

The following conclusions of Becker's microeconomic analysis ought to be stressed: (1) Discrimination does not lead only to wage differences but also to segregation, (2) different types of discrimination can have additive effects and (3) there are forces in the economic system which tend to reduce wage differences among employers, if preferences vary between different employers and commodity markets are competitive or monopolies transferable.

Conclusions

Despite the objections that were subsequently raised to Becker's book, his work still represents a large advance in the theory of discrimination. For the first time, a coherent theoretical account of economic discrimination existed in monograph form. Becker analyzed the effects of discrimination in the labor market using neo-classical economic theory. He showed that the result is not necessarily wage differences but that under certain conditions, segregation might result instead. The theoretical analysis also pointed to measures which could be effective against discrimination. Becker provided an analysis based on an assumption of the causes of discrimination. This coherent analysis was useful both for those who chose to expand Becker's analysis and for those who were critical of his theory. The level of the theoretical debate in the field was raised. Becker's analysis also contained certain implications that could be used as points of departure for empirical investigations. Thus, his contribution inspired both theoretical and empirical work.

There are two elements in Becker's analysis which can be viewed as theoretical innovations. One is the use of the theory of international trade in the analysis of the effects of discrimination. The other is the discrimination coefficient as a measure of the taste for discrimination. Both of these elements were also later used by economists who started with causes of discrimination that differ from Becker's.

Becker's achievements in the development of the theory of discrimination must not, however, blind us to the fact that there are problems inherent in his analysis. He lacks, for example, an elaborate theory of the causes of discrimination. The dynamic characteristics in his model are incompletely analyzed, questions can be raised concerning his normative analysis, and empirical tests on the implications of his theory in many cases have not verified them. (We will return to some of these problems later on in this work.)

Development and Criticism of Becker's Theory

During the latter half of the 1960s and 1970s, a large number of studies on economic discrimination were published. Many of these works are relevant to an evaluation of the theoretical development in the area. Some of them are basically a continuation and further development of Becker's theory, others offer primarily a criticism of the theory, while a third category consists of different alternatives to the Becker theory.

In the presentation of the theoretical contributions, it is possible to make a distinction between the theories that are based on Becker and those that are not. A clear-cut grouping cannot be made, however, between the extensions of Becker's theory and the alternatives to it: any subdivision depends on which issues are considered to be of central importance in Becker. Here we will deal with those contributions where the cause of discrimination takes the form of preferences for making transactions with one group rather than another. We will also consider the case where these preferences take a form which differs from Becker's,[55] as well as those cases where discrimination is analyzed with the aid of trade theory, even though the preference approach is dropped, and where the production functions of the individual firms are identical and linearly homogeneous. The section 'Alternatives Theories of Discrimination' deals with theories that are not concerned with any of these elements.

Dynamic Characteristics of Becker's Theory

One of the central problems with Becker's theory of discrimination is that it cannot explain why wage differences between the discriminating and the discriminated groups remain in the long run, when the commodity and labor markets are characterized by competition. In this case, the firms that have the lowest discrimination coefficient will hire all the members of the discriminated group. If there is at least one employer who does not have a taste for discrimination, the wage differences will disappear.

If, on the other hand, it is the industries and not the firms that exhibit constant returns to scale, 'unit costs would rise with output, and the firm with the smallest DC would not produce everything.'[56] The existing non-discriminatory firms would not then necessarily drive the discriminators out of the market altogether.[57] Free entry may, however, put an end to discrimination. Provided that entrepreneurship is not a scarce resource, firms with lower discrimination coefficients enter and firms with higher coefficients are forced out. Only in the case where there are systematic differences in the level of entrepreneurship that may act as a barrier to entry should we expect the discriminatory firms to remain in the long run. This case is, however, less likely to occur in practice, excepting such 'monopolies based on personal ability'[58] as are exemplified by singers, tennis players, etc.[59] It must also be the case that the taste for discrimination is held by the person or persons who simultaneously command the personal ability monopoly and not by the owners only of the firm. In the latter case, other people, without discriminatory preferences, could easily buy up the monopoly, provided that there is competition in the capital market. The same is true when a monopoly exists in the commodity market and this monopoly is transferable. 'The highest bids would come from those having the smallest DCs.'[60]

The Becker results are thus contrary to the empirical picture, which shows permanent wage differences in competitive industries between blacks and whites in the United States and between women and men in many countries. Kenneth Arrow has tried to reconcile this observation with Becker's theoretical point of departure.[61]

In Arrow's analysis, all employees belong initially to a single group (for example whites). A new group (for example blacks) then enters the labor market. The former group has preferences for discriminating against the latter. According to Becker's analysis, we should at this point get a segregated labor market with whites in certain firms and blacks in others. Discrimination produces non-convexities in the cost function so that marginal adjustments are not optimal. Arrow assumes, however, that adjustment costs exist, for example due to costs in connection with hiring and firing. These costs can be partly of an administrative character, partly connected with training expenses. It may be extremely costly to substitute quickly one group of workers for another. Instead of segregation with equal wages, the result is partial segregation and wage differences. The newly-arrived group will be hired by certain firms, which also retain employees from the previous group.[62] Those members of the discriminating group who are employed in integrated firms will receive higher wages and the employees from the new, discriminated, group will receive lower wages than those paid by the firms that are still segregated.[63]

Arrow shows how adjustment costs in conjunction with employee discrimination can lead to persisting wage differences for a certain time period. Even in this case, however, there are market adjustment mechanisms working towards equalization of wages. New firms are constantly being established, and, when differences in wages exist, they will hire the group with the lowest wage. This will lead to a leveling-out of wage differences and to segregation with the discriminated group employed in certain of the newly-established firms. With the high turnover of firms characteristic of industrialized market economies, the wage differences ought not to have survived for such long periods as they actually have done.

According to Becker, competition in the capital market will even cause firms who have a monopoly position to pursue a non-discriminatory policy. A monopoly is worth more for someone who does not discriminate than for someone who does. People without preferences for discrimination will buy the monopoly firms. There are, of course, monopolies which are not transferable, e.g. federal or municipal ones, in which competition in the capital market does not lead to wage equalization. Moreover, the administrators of such a monopoly cannot themselves usually take the entire profit in the form of dividends and salaries. The cost of discrimination thus becomes low for the administrator in such a case.[64] Thomas Sowell gives as an example:

> Perhaps the classic examples were the railroad occupations, where blacks in the South were generally *over*represented in the nineteenth-century *before* federal regulation and widespread unionization, and then *totally excluded* from most railroad occupations afterwards. When railroads were unconstrained profit-maximizers, the

opportunity cost of discrimination was high. Later, as a regulated utility, high union pay scales created a chronic surplus of applicants, and the costs of discrimination were virtually zero.[65]

Armen Alchian and Reuben Kessel[66] have pointed out that it is not self-evident that competition in the capital market works in the way indicated by Becker, even for private monopolies. According to these economists, private monopolies cannot maximize their profits either. If they do, they run the risk of receiving negative attention from the general public and of being subject e.g. to government action. Consequently, firms do not dare to use their monopolistic position to its full extent. Thus, in this case a monopolist who has preferences for discrimination can continue discriminating.[67] The monopolist who does not possess these preferences can do something else instead (a more expensive office building, higher entertainment expenses, etc.), but this does not make it more profitable for a non-discriminating person to own a monopoly than for a discriminating one. However, this does not have to result in wage differences between the discriminated and the discriminating groups in the case of monopolies either. Segregation can arise instead if the monopolistic sector constitutes only a small share of the labor market. The discriminated group will then work in the sector with competitive firms.

Harold Demsetz has extended the analysis of the monopoly case to other types of monopolies[68] — for example, craft unions and professional associations. If there is no market for entrance to these associations, the cost of discrimination for those people who regulate entrance to these associations is zero. (It is, however, possible that a black market exists.)

Employer discrimination and employee discrimination of a group of workers who constitute a perfect substitute for the discriminating group in production can explain segregation but not wage discrimination in the long run. On the other hand, employee discrimination of a group that is complementary in production — for example, discrimination by white foremen against black workers — implies that lasting wage differences arise between white and black workers. Whether segregation results depends on the substitutability of the two groups and on the strength of the preferences for discrimination.[69] The problem thus becomes a question of whether segregation without wage differences would not also arise here, so that, for example, white foremen and workers are employed together in one type of workplace and black foremen and workers in another. The question to be answered is why a certain group is not represented in all occupations, in this case both among workers and foremen.[70]

Unemployment. Variable Labor Supply

Becker's model assumes a fixed labor supply and full employment. In his formulation, it cannot directly explain differences in unemployment between different groups. Harry Gilman has shown how Becker's method can be extended so as to be applicable even to analyses of how discrimination can lead to differences in unemployment.[71] His starting-point is that wage rigidity prevails. This means that excess demand arises in some cases, and excess supply in others — queues for available jobs — which make it possible for the employer to discriminate between different groups. The discriminated group will then suffer from more unemployment than the non-discriminated group:

> Given a preference for discrimination, the greater the pressure in an occupation or region for nonwhite-white wage equality, the greater will be the gap between equilibrium and actual wages, and the greater will be the reduction in employment opportunities for nonwhite relative to white workers.[72]

Demsetz analyzes this problem as well.[73] He maintains that fair employment laws, minimum wage laws and agreements concerning minimum or equal wages, pushed through by trade unions, result in the effect described above. The cost of discrimination will be zero when wage differences are not allowed and there is an excess supply of labor:

> The cost to employers of a continuance of the degree of discrimination they have been practicing is increased by allowing non-preferred workers to offer their services for lower wages. Prohibiting an employer from employing workers at wages lower than the legal minimum prohibits the offering of this wealth compensation to ... discriminating employers. These employers will then choose from among competing applicants solely on the basis of personal characteristics.[74]

The result of the discrimination can partly be that the discriminated group has to accept to work to a greater extent within areas that are not covered by the minimum (or equal) wage principle, and partly that it has to face a higher rate of unemployment.

If the total labor supply of the discriminated group varies with the wage rate, this means that the relation between the discrimination coefficient and the market discrimination coefficient derived by Becker is no longer valid.[75] How the relation is altered depends on the wage elasticity of the labor supply.[76] If this is positive, the effect on the wage level of the discriminated group will be less than in Becker's case, where the wage elasticity is zero. This means that it is not possible to measure directly, via wage differences, the intensity in the preferences for discriminating:

> The point to be made is that the effect of labor market discrimination against a particular group of workers is not, in general, adequately measured (is understated) by a function of the difference between their equilibrium wage rate and the equilibrium wage rate of (otherwise) comparable workers not victimized by discrimination. This is because the potentially adverse effect of discrimination on the wage rate is likely to be masked in part by a reduction in the quantity of labor supplied.[77]

Neither the assumption of wage rigidity nor the assumption that the size of the labor supply is dependent upon the wage level implies any fundamental criticism of Becker's theory; they mean only that the theory is applied to an economic model with somewhat different characteristics.

Nepotism

The basis of Becker's analysis is that people who discriminate do so out of preferences *against* having contact with a certain group, and that group membership is not determined by economic characteristics. Becker states that nepotism, i.e. the case in which people discriminate due to preferences *for* having contact with a certain group, could be analyzed in the same way. He notes that the welfare-economic conclusions in such a case could be different.[78] Richard Toikka, using Becker's international trade model, has made an analysis of nepotism and shown that Becker's presumption that the welfare-economic conclusions are changed is correct.[79] It is important, however, to note that Becker's and Toikka's welfare-economic assessment of the effects of discrimination on a group are at the same time an evaluation of the preferences for discrimination (or nepotism) and of the effects of the act of discriminating. The welfare-economic analysis thus includes an evaluation of a certain set of preferences as compared with another.[80]

One of the conclusions above was that discriminating firms will in the long run tend to be driven out of the commodity market, or sold to non-discriminating owners. In a recent article, Matthew Goldberg shows that this result may not be valid if the cause of unequal treatment is nepotism towards white workers.[81] In this case, the discriminating employer also receives a lower profit, but is compensated by the utility of nepotism. The sell-out price of the firm is not determined by the profit but by the utility level, taking nepotism into consideration. The nepotistic firm must, however, at least break even to be able to survive. This implies that it is possible for nepotistic firms to survive in the long run with low or zero profits.

A problem not discussed by Goldberg is whether the conditions for entry and growth of firms with zero or low profits are the same as for firms with normal profits. His analysis is confined to the survival of already established firms.

Alternative Formulations of the Utility Function

Kenneth Arrow uses a somewhat different formulation than Becker of the preferences for discrimination.[82] When analyzing employer discrimination, he starts with two utility functions: one where the utility for the employer depends upon the profit and the number of persons in two groups employed, $U(\pi,B,W,)$, and one where the utility depends on the profit and the share of the employees who belong to one of the groups, $U(\pi,B/W)$. Thus in the latter case, it is only the *distribution* between the two groups and not the absolute number which is decisive.

In the first case, Arrow assumes that the discrimination coefficient is negative against W, i.e. nepotism exists, and positive towards B, that is preferences for discrimination exist against this group. This can be seen as a generalization of Becker's theory in so far as employer discrimination is concerned. In the first of Arrow's two cases, the result for the employer will depend on the strength of the preferences for discrimination as compared with the preferences for nepotism. With the second formulation of the utility function, the result will be that the employer neither gains nor loses by discriminating. In that case the discriminated employee group loses while the group favored by nepotism makes a gain equal to the former group's loss. The welfare-economic differences become significant even with these seemingly small changes in the preference functions.

Becker's and Arrow's models lead to approximately the same result regarding wage differences and segregation. When variations in the discrimination coefficient among different firms occur, the short-term equilibrium conditions are somewhat different. Arrow's first formulation of the utility function, like Becker's, makes segregation complete, while his second utility function tends to produce partial segregation. Regardless of which of the three preference functions (Becker's or Arrow's two) that is used, in the long-run equilibrium, both groups receive equal pay.

Other alternative formulations of utility functions are possible. One example is given by Marcus Alexis.[83] In addition to preferences for having contact with one group as opposed to another, Alexis points to envy or malice as a supplementary reason for treating the groups differently. He assumes that the utility functions are interdependent. Higher utility for one's own group and lower utility for other groups has a positive effect on the individual's utility. Alexis has added an income distribution term in the employers' utility function $U=U(\pi,B,W,Y^1)$, where Y^1 is the white workers' share of the wage income. The results that Alexis obtains by using this model do not differ in any fundamental way from those obtained by Arrow's formulation $U=U(\pi,B,W)$. The wages of the black workers can be either lower or higher in Alexis' case as compared with Arrow's. More information about the form of the utility functions is necessary in order to decide which gives the lower wages.[84] Alexis' motivation for the alternative formulation of the utility function is that it is more realistic especially with respect to discrimination by absentee capital owners. However, one can raise the same objections to its ability to explain persistent long-term differences as to Becker's theory. Firms that do not discriminate will reap greater profits and outcompete those which do discriminate.

Becker assumes that those who discriminate do it because they have preferences for not having transactions — contacts — with members of a certain group. Several economists have criticized this general formulation, arguing that discrimination does not refer to all types of contacts but only to some, and that the decisive factor for the occurrence of discrimination is occupational status. An example of this type of criticism is given by Ray Marshall: 'Clearly, discrimination is more a status or caste phenomenon, a concept which makes the theory more general because the physical phenomenon surely cannot be applied to sexual discrimination.'[85]

Discrimination is not directed against persons from a certain group who have jobs of equal or lower status, only against those whose jobs entail higher status. White workers do not have preferences for not working with black workers, only with black foremen; men have preferences for not working with women in supervisory positions, but none against women in inferior jobs. By using this specification, attempts have been made to explain the occurrence of crowding.[86] Nevertheless, this qualification, that is that the prejudices against a group vary with the relative status of the group, only leads us back to the case with discrimination of a complementary production factor. In order for the effects of this type of discrimination to remain in the long run, other factors must exist which prevent the group from having the same occupational distribution, a distribution which would have enabled complete segregation to occur.[87]

The International Trade Model

In several of the following chapters we will concentrate on the analysis of discrimination with the aid of the theory of international trade, 'the theoretical innovation in the first edition of [Becker's book] that has had the greatest influence.'[88] In this survey, therefore, we will deal only briefly with the criticism of this part of Becker's theory.

A number of economists have accepted international trade theory as a point of departure for the analysis of economic discrimination, but have chosen a reason other than preferences for discrimination to explain it. This is true, for example, of Anne Krueger,[89] who assumes instead that the white sector, or the capital owners in the white sector, seek to maximize their pecuniary incomes and choose the size of capital exports (and thus the degree of discrimination) which achieves this goal. The extent of the discrimination as well as the welfare-economic interpretations differ from those of Becker's analysis.[90] We will take up this contribution in more detail in Chapter 4.

Krueger, like Becker, postulates that the labor supply of both groups is fixed, that is, that the wage elasticity is zero. Lester Thurow has shown how the economic gains of discrimination of the white society depend on the elasticities of supply of the discriminated group. He takes up three typical cases with different wage elasticities of the labor supply[91] (see Figure 2.1). In all of the cases, a situation without discrimination is compared to a discriminatory case.[92] The discrimination implies that the white employers' demand for labor from the discriminated black group decreases. The changes in demand are assumed to be equal in all three cases. In the first case, the labor supply is completely inelastic (Becker's case), in the second case, infinitely wage elastic; and in the third case, the elasticity has a value somewhere in between these extremes. In the first case the white society will gain economically by discrimination. In the second case, it loses, as the supplied quantity of labor decreases with a given wage. The result in the third case is

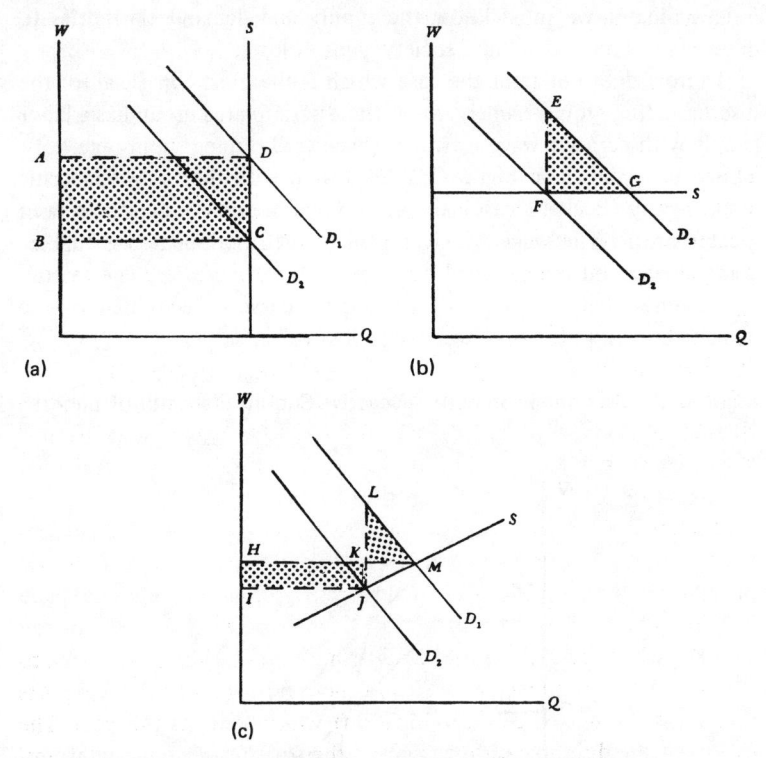

Figure 2.1: Discrimination with a Variable Supply of Labour

(a) Completely inelastic labor supply
ABCD = gains to the white society

(b) Infinitely elastic labor supply
EFG = losses to the white society

(c) Elastic labor supply
HIJK = gains to the white society
LMK = losses to the white society

Notations: W = wage rate, Q = quantity of labor, S = supply of labor, D_1 = demand for labor without discrimination, D_2 = demand for labor with discrimination.

Source: Reprinted by permission of the Brookings Institution from Thurow (1969), p. 114.

indeterminate: we must know the supply and demand elasticities to determine whether the white society gains or loses.

Thurow does not treat the case which is the most beneficial for the discriminating group, namely when the discriminated group has a labor supply with negative wage elasticity (backward-sloping supply curve.)[93] This case is shown in Figure 2.2. Compared with the case of inelastic labor supply (Becker's case), the discriminating society makes an even greater profit. The wage which is paid to the discriminated group becomes lower and the supplied quantity of labor increases. The reasoning assumes that the slope of the supply curve exceeds that of the demand curves. In the opposite case, a loss will arise.

Figure 2.2: Discrimination with a Negative Supply Elasticity of Labor

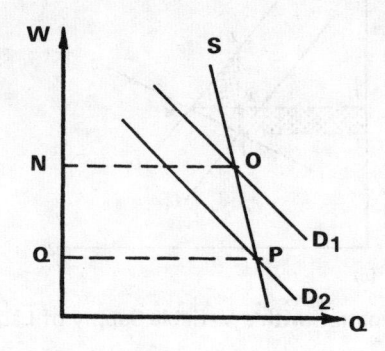

NOPQ = gains to the white society

Becker employs a model taken from international trade theory. No commodity trade occurs, though, only factor export. The discrimination consists in less capital being exported (less labor being allowed to immigrate) than is necessary in order to create factor price equalization. It is well-known from international trade theory that trade in commodities under certain conditions (incomplete specialization, constant returns to scale, etc.) can lead to an equalization of factor prices even when there is no factor mobility across the borders. Joseph Stiglitz has presented this as an important objection to Becker's use of the foreign trade model in explaining wage differences: 'Our point is that even with infinite aversion to working with members of other groups, there may be complete factor-price equalization.'[94] In Chapter 5, we will treat this issue in more detail and examine the effects of discrimination in a case where there is trade and, at the same time, complete specialization in production.

Alternative Theories of Discrimination

As we have seen, both Becker's assumption regarding the causes of discrimination and his use of the neo-classical economic theory in the analysis have met with sharp criticism. As a result, alternative theories of economic discrimination have been developed.

Several of these can be connected with the debate that took place during the first decades of this century. A good example is George Akerlof's theory of social customs, which is employed in an attempt to explain, among other things, racial discrimination.[95] In the early British discussion, customs and tradition were two of the most frequently advanced explanations for the existence of discrimination, even though no analytically satisfactory explanation was given to clarify how these customs could exist. There are also certain similarities between Akerlof's theory of discrimination and Becker's. For example, preferences for transaction with one group rather than another are included in the utility function. However, the motivation, the form and the implications differ to some extent between the two theories.

The majority of opponents to Becker's theory have rejected the assumption of preferences as the cause of discrimination. They have attempted to explain discrimination with theories based on profit-maximizing firms and utility-maximizing individuals who do not include the group affiliation of the persons with whom they have transactions in the utility functions, and where either the employer or some group of employees discriminate to obtain an economic gain.

There are three main categories of this type of discrimination theory:

(1) The first category is based on the notion that the employers possess incorrect or incomplete information about the productivity of those hired (and that information gathering cannot take place at zero cost). The most commonly used term for this type of theory is 'discrimination under uncertainty', with 'statistical discrimination' as the most important subgroup.

(2) A second category builds on the idea that the firms have a monopsonistic position in the labor market and that different groups of employees have different elasticities of supply. Apart from the pure monopsony model, well-known since the 1930s, this group includes

theories which in addition make special assumptions about the way the firm or the labor market functions. Two examples are the 'dual' and the 'radical' labor market theories. The latter is based on the idea that the employers, by dividing the labor force according to e.g. ethnic affiliation, can improve their bargaining position and depress the wage level.

(3) The last group deals with a bargaining economy in which different groups of firms and employees take part. A coalition between firms and certain groups of workers directed against other groups of workers can lead to wage differences between those workers who are part of the coalition and those who are not.

We will briefly survey these theories of discrimination in the remainder of this chapter.

Discrimination as a Social Custom

In the early British debate regarding discrimination of women in the labor market, one of the most frequently alleged reasons for lower wages for women than for men in the same jobs or for exclusion of women from certain occupations was traditions or customs.[96] From this early literature, however, it is difficult to see how customs or traditions could explain long-term discrimination. Firms that do not follow tradition but instead hire (lower-paid) women in male occupations or only employ the lower-paid female labor force in mixed occupations thus ought to make greater profits than other firms. These firms could then expand until the differences in wages and employment possibilities between men and women disappear. The criticism against Becker's theory with respect to the stability of discrimination in the long run in a competitive economy is thus relevant here as well.

George Akerlof has shown in various articles how social customs, despite this type of objection, can possess characteristics which make them stable.[97] In two of these articles, he applies the theories to racial discrimination, amongst others to the extreme form of discrimination represented by caste systems.

A fundamental assumption in most economic theory is that a transaction between two parties does not influence the transactions that one or both of the parties might have in the future with a third party. Akerlof, however, argues that it is precisely this influence which is characteristic of a caste system,[98] and that the same mechanism also can appear in other forms of discrimination. If someone in a caste system breaks the transaction rules, for example by hiring an untouchable for a job reserved for a certain caste, the employer himself becomes an untouchable. This means that the economic opportunities for someone who does not adhere to the rules of the caste system are drastically reduced. It can be economically profitable for the individual to follow the rules.

The discrimination which exists in a caste system can in this way be compatible with a stable equilibrium. For such an economy, there is also an equilibrium without caste rules, with a higher output than a caste system, but there is no mechanism whereby a transition from one equilibrium to another can be achieved with marginal changes.[99] The model does not rule out, however, that a transition to an equilibrium without caste rules can be made in stages. The minimum coalition necessary to break the rules of the caste system is a coalition of an economic size that is sufficient to allow all the coalition members to be at least as well off as they would be through adherence to the rules of the caste society.[100] The smaller this minimum rule-breaking coalition is, the more unstable is the equilibrium with caste rules. The caste model presents the same problems when it comes to explaining the long-term stability of discrimination as Becker's analysis: the economic incentives and competition tend to make discrimination disappear.

Akerlof's model does not require *per se* that people have preferences for discriminating against a non-discriminating person. It suffices that everyone believes or fears that the other will do so.[101] Thus we are, as Robert Klitgaard has shown, dealing with the situation which in game theory is known as the prisoner's dilemma: 'Therefore, thinking that others are racists can make it economically rational to take actions which seem to be those of an irrational racist . . . Notice here that what matters are the players' *perceptions* of . . . the pay-offs and choices, not the real facts.'[102]

In another article,[103] Akerlof has tried to solve the problem with small coalitions breaking the 'sanction equilibrium'. He bases this model on the notion that there are codes of behavior in every society and that a certain percentage, although not necessarily 100 per cent, of the population supports this code. Akerlof assumes that people's utility depends not only on consumption but also on prestige in society. This prestige, in turn, is assumed to depend in part on whether the person follows the code of behavior or not, in part on the percentage of the population which supports it. In addition to consumption and personal preferences, three arguments are included in the utility function: (1) the person's prestige, (2) a dummy variable for if the person follows the code of behavior or not and (3) a second dummy variable which shows if the person believes in the code or not.[104]

Opposing a norm can be economically advantageous but may at the same time lead to diminished prestige. The percentage supporting a norm is assumed to be endogenously determined in the model. The change in this percentage depends on the difference between the percentage that follows and that which supports the norm. If this difference is positive, the percentage supporting the norm increases; if negative, it decreases. Akerlof indicates that with a certain given norm, the economy can end up in one of two equilibria. In the first equilibrium almost everybody believes in and follows the norm. In the other, almost nobody does. In a system having many different norms, there can be many different equilibria. In this way, Akerlof's model can contribute to an explanation of enduring discrimination:

> As a result, if the major features of the model accurately reproduce the major features of reality, Becker's marginal analysis of customs, while correct (at the margin) also misses the important point. Marginal methods are appropriate for comparative static analysis of a single equilibrium. However, with more than one equilibrium, marginal analysis of a single equilibrium fails to analyze the causes for movement from one equilibrium to another.[105]

The analysis is not, however, exempt from objections. In the same way that Becker lacks an elaborate theory of the origins of preferences for discrimination, Akerlof lacks a theory for the origins of (and changes in) social customs:

> ... the community's code of behavior was taken as exogenous, and the number of believers in the code considered endogenous. A full explanation of social customs and economic equilibrium must describe not only how the system works with existing conditions, but also how such codes themselves evolve.[106]

Social anthropologists have advanced various explanations of the caste system. The main dividing line is between those arguing that the system is unique to India[107] and those looking at it as an example of a larger class of phenomena of inequality.[108] One of the few economists who deal with the caste system is Mancur Olson.[109] He sees it as an example of a distributive coalition. The caste furthers its interests by excluding others from entry to the group (through the rule of endogamy).

In this way, the gains of the distributive coalition will not be diluted:

> Traditionally . . . caste groups were not only mainly occupational, but also exhibited all the features of cartels and other special-interest organizations. They controlled entry into occupations and lines of business, kept craft mysteries or secrets, set prices monopolistically, used boycotts and strikes, and often bargained on a group rather than on an individual basis.[110]

The underlying explanation of caste in Olson's analysis is not preferences or prejudice, but economic gain made possible by the caste acquiring monopoly and monopsony power. The main differences in relation to the standard theory in that area are the stress on the coalition formation process and on the use of power to keep the coalition intact.

The emergence of the caste system is an area of conflict among social anthropologists. The traditional explanations have emphasized either a combination of invasion and racism or occupational monopolies. A survey and criticism is given in a recent book by Morten Klass.[111] Klass' own explanation builds on the evolution of castes from 'equalitarian' clans when the techniques of agricultural production became known in Southern Asia. The position of a class in the emerging caste system was mainly determined by the acquisition of agricultural land during this period.

> In classic South Asia, then, redistributive exchange is the economic integrative system in a stratified society in which the differential access to basic resources is *solely* by the representatives of corporate groups . . . able to maintain control over its members because the body was in principle occupationally homogeneous and invariably endogamous.[112]

Theories of Discrimination under Uncertainty

Is it possible to explain discrimination by employers even in the case where the firms are profit-maximizing, non-monopsonistic and without preferences for one group over another? One theory based on these assumptions builds on the idea that firms have incomplete information about the productivity of the workers. An employer cannot measure a person's productivity when he makes the hiring decision and wages are not directly related to individual productivity, and/or there are employment and training costs which make the profits dependent on whether the firm hires someone with a high or with a low productivity.

The easiest explanation is that the employers have incorrect information, prejudices, about the productivity of different groups.[113] The reasons for the occurrences of prejudices can vary greatly: in addition to different psychological and socio-psychological theories, judgements based on obsolete information may be mentioned. A group's productivity can be influenced by the degree of discrimination outside the labor market, for example in the school system. If the extent of such discrimination changes, a previously correct assessment of the productivity differences can become incorrect. In this situation, if the wage is set for a certain position without taking group affiliation into account and the firms have prejudices about the productivity of different groups, those who belong to the group that the firms believe has the lowest productivity will be hired last.

This explanation of economic discrimination suffers from the same weakness as Becker's theory: it is difficult to explain enduring discrimination. The firms who do not discriminate make larger profits and will expand at the expense of the discriminating firms and new non-discriminatory firms may enter. In this case, there should also be an effect via dissemination of information among the firms about the actual productivity of different groups:

> Information-dispensing institutions — personnel conventions, journals and associations, employment agencies and public and private civil rights organizations — will bring this information to the attention of other personnel managers. Misperceptions should not endure, for they can be corrected by simply examining the experience of other firms.[114]

Discrimination is affected by the state of the market; it will be lowest during times of prosperity and highest in a recession.[115] The discriminated group will be hired to a greater extent during periods of low unemployment, which enables the firms to acquaint themselves more readily with the actual productivity of the group. Prejudices ought to disappear more rapidly during periods of prosperity. However, prejudices can also influence the behavior of the discriminated group. If, for example, a group's productivity is subject to prejudice in certain occupations but not in others, this can result in a lack of interest from the members of the discriminated group in acquiring the skills necessary for the former type of jobs.[116] Or, they will not make investments which indicate that they are suitable for these jobs, investments that produce 'signals', according to Michael Spence's terminology.[117] These types of investments are naturally less profitable for the discriminated group than for others. Such a feed-back mechanism can delay an equalization between different groups, but it is doubtful whether it can be permanently prevented. As long as some individuals within a discriminated group educate themselves and get a job in a specific occupation, the information-dispensing mechanism ought to work, and if the decisive factor is differences in signal expenses, there ought to be economic incentives to establish a better-functioning market in that area.[118]

There are other ways as well for this type of discrimination in the labor market (based on incorrect notions of productivity differences) to influence productivity. Lower wages can lead to lower productivity via a lower standard of living.[119] This case is perhaps of relevance primarily when analyzing underdeveloped economies. The possible effects of low wages on work motivation are more interesting for industrial economies.[120] The lower wages and inferior working conditions can also perhaps influence the preferences for work in relation to other activities. Endogenously determined preferences could result in lasting differences in productivity. We will return to this in the analysis of dual labor markets.

Of greater theoretical interest than the case with incorrect information is perhaps the one where the employers are assumed generally to possess correct expectations regarding the productivities of different groups but uncertainty concerning each separate individual. This case was analyzed for the first time in the beginning of the 1970s by Kenneth Arrow and Edmund Phelps,[121] and has been characterized by the latter as statistical discrimination. The basis for this theory is that firms have an idea about the productivity of different groups which is on the average correct, but that they do not know the productivity of each individual. Group affiliation, on for example sex or racial grounds, thus becomes an inexpensive aid for the firms when making employment decisions. A distinction can be made between two cases here: (1) when the expected productivity is equal for the different groups and (2) when the expected productivity differs between groups (for example due to discrimination outside the labor market). The first of these is of greater interest in the present context.

Edmund Phelps' point of departure in 'The Statistical Theory of Racism and Sexism'[122] is that the employer uses some sort of test in the employment decision which measures productivity but not with precision; only sufficiently for the results to vary with the productivity. There will be a random variation, given the test value. By assumption, the variations in productivity and the random variation in the test value, given the productivity, can differ between groups. This means that the expected productivity for a person with a certain test result will vary according to his or her group affiliation. The relationship between the test and expected productivity depends on the variance in productivity as compared with the variance in the random term: the greater the variation in productivity, the better the test will perform. A hiring procedure based on this type of decision criterion does not mean that on the average discrimination will result. The groups receive equal average wages if their expected average productivity is equally high.

A specific explanation for the differences in the variance of the random term is that the efficiency of the test instrument depends on the group tested, as it is devised and tried out on one group and measures the performance of other groups less accurately.[123] Dennis Aigner and Glen Cain give a concrete example of this idea: 'The Scholastic Aptitude Test has been found, for example, to be a *less* reliable indicator of college grades for blacks than for whites.'[124]

Assuming that the actual variations and the average productivity are equal for white and black groups, a steeper slope is obtained for the relation between test results and productivity for whites than for blacks (see Figure 2.3). Whites with high test values should receive higher wages than blacks with the same values, while the opposite should be valid for low test values. Even here it is doubtful whether it is appropriate to talk about economic discrimination, as the average wage will be equal for both groups, assuming that they have equal average productivity. In any group, those with high productivity lose if the test is unable to provide an accurate measurement of this fact. However, this must be weighed against the gains of those who have low productivity in the group.[125]

So far, we have assumed that, given a certain expected value, differences in the variance in productivity is cost-free for the firms. The firm is therefore risk-neutral. If there are costs connected with the uncertainty, the variance of employees' expected productivity will be included in the profit function. The employer has risk aversion. Given that two groups have the same expected productivity, discrimination occurs against the one with the most uncertain productivity. In accordance with the previous example, blacks in the United States would be discriminated against as compared to whites because the uncertainty for the former is greater given the expected productivity.

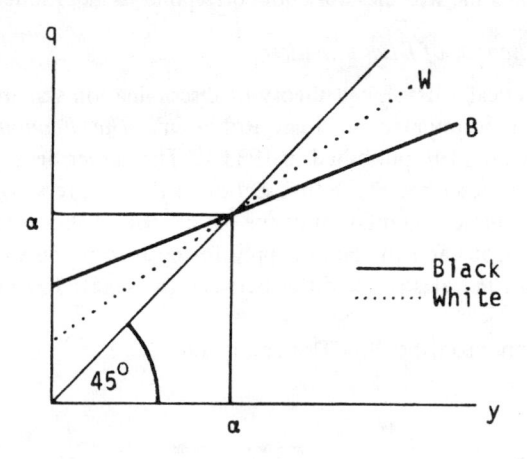

Figure 2.3: Predictions of Productivity by Race and Test Score

Notations: q = predictions of productivity, y = test score, α = average ability (equal for the two groups).
Source: Reprinted with permission from Aigner & Cain (1977), p. 180. © 1977 by Cornell University.

In this way, the theory of statistical discrimination should be able to explain wage differences between groups that do not depend on differences in productivity. As long as differences exist in the ability of firms to measure the productivity of different people by the use of tests, and as long as firms have risk aversion, discrimination will continue. The differences which can be explained in this way should, however, not be overestimated.[126] If the wage differences are considerable, there will also be a greater economic incentive to improve test instruments and to organize the firms so that the variation in the difference between actual and expected productivity becomes of lesser importance for production.

All this requires that the groups have equal average productivity. The conclusions will be somewhat different if the average productivities of the groups differ. A person whose productivity is greater than could be expected from the test results and from group affiliation could be said to be discriminated against as a person if tests and group affiliation are used as selection mechanisms in hiring.[127] In a competitive labor market with non-rigid wages, however, the group as a whole cannot be labeled 'discriminated'. The average wage in a certain group corresponds to the average level of productivity. With long-term wage rigidity, an excess supply of labor and job competition, discrimination may, however, exist. The expected productivity of the lowest-ranking group may fall short of the minimum a person must reach in order to be hired.[128] The group's labor income will therefore not correspond to its productivity.

Monopsony Theories of Discrimination

The first analytically developed theory of discrimination was the monopsony model formulated in Joan Robinson's *The Economics of Imperfect Competition*, published in 1933.[129] The earlier development of this theory is described in the first section of this chapter. Figure 2.4 gives a diagrammatic presentation of the basic model. Labor is assumed to be homogeneous and the labor supply for both men and women is wage-elastic but the elasticities differ between the sexes. The profit of

Figure 2.4: Monopsonistic Wage Determination

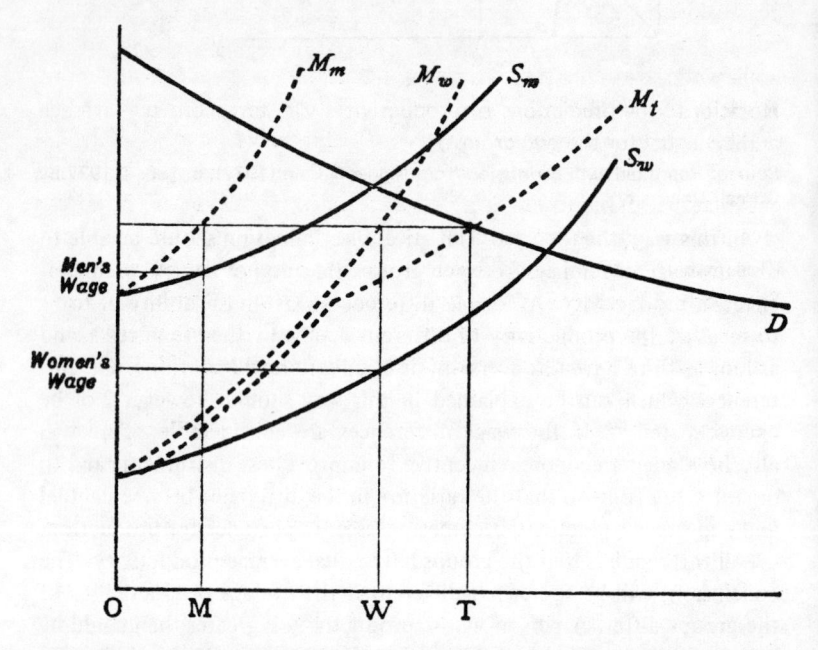

Notations: D is the demand curve for labor. S_m is the supply curve of male labor. M_m is the marginal cost curve of male labor. S_w is the supply curve of female labor. M_w is the marginal cost curve of female labor. M_t is the marginal cost curve of total supply of labor, obtained by summing ($M_m + M_w$) laterally. OT (total amount of labor employed) = OM (number of men employed) + OW (number of women employed).

Source: Reprinted by permission of Macmillan, London and Basingstoke from Robinson (1933), p. 302.

the monopsonist is at its maximum when the marginal cost of the total and of each type of labor is equal to its demand price. The wage rates will be equal to the supply price of the number employed for men and women, respectively.

A profit-maximizing monopsonistic firm will offer a higher wage to men than to women in Robinson's model, due to the fact that the elasticity of the male labor supply to the firm is higher than the female one. The fact that different econometric investigations have indicated a higher over-all female than male supply elasticity can *per se* be consistent with the fact that the women's labor supply to every *firm* is more inelastic than the men's labor supply. One reason for the female supply elasticity's being lower is that women are more locally tied due to the traditional division of labor within the family.[130] The residential location of women is often determined by the husband's job and wives usually avoid jobs with long commuting times because of housework responsibilities. Both factors make for a lower female supply elasticity to the *firm*.[131]

This simple monopsony model can hardly explain racial discrimination; most probably, the only thing it can do is to provide a partial explanation of discrimination against women.[132] There are, however, several developments of the monopsonistic model. First of all, there are those which add different assumptions to those of the basic model. Secondly, there are other theoretical traditions where the assumption about monopsony is included as one of several important elements. This applies to the radical and dual labor market theories.[133]

Already in the earlier contributions referred to above, a few amendments of the simple monopsony model are found. Joan Robinson herself discusses one case where men but not women are organized in trade unions and where therefore the male wage rate is fixed for the individual firm. The labor supply becomes infinitely elastic for the firm. (This is depicted in Figure 2.5.)

We have also dealt with another special case in the survey of the earlier literature in the area, namely Bronfenbrenner's monopsonist firm that makes only limited use of its monopsony position. The monopsonist employs this position instead in order to allow a certain freedom in the choice of employees. Bronfenbrenner's model comes very close to being a combination of monopsony and discrimination because of preferences (Becker's cause of discrimination).

Several economists have dealt with another combination of monopsonistic firms and preferences for discrimination, namely the simultaneous existence of monopsony and employee discrimination. Sargant

Figure 2.5: Monopsonistic Wage Determination with Organized Male Labor

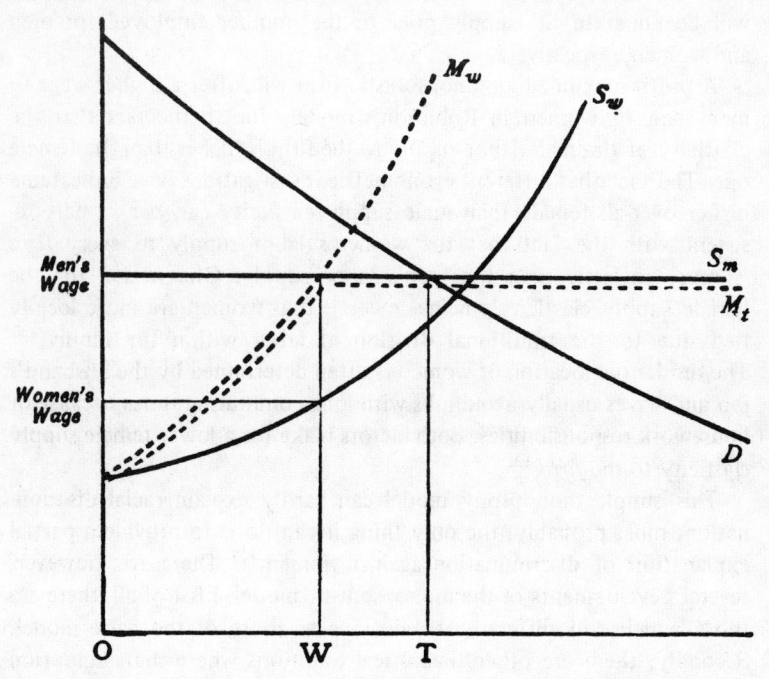

Notations: D is the demand curve for labor. S_m is the supply curve and marginal cost curve of male labor. S_w is the supply curve of female labor. M_w is the marginal cost curve of female labor. M_t is the marginal cost curve of total supply of labor. OT = total amount of labor employed. OW = number of women employed. WT = number of men employed.

Source: Reprinted by permission of Macmillan, London and Basingstoke from Robinson (1933), p. 304.

Florence's article of the beginning of the 1930s can be interpreted in this way.[134] Later Duncan Bell[135] as well as Nancy Gordon and Thomas Morton[136] have presented this combination with explicit reference to both elements of the theory. Bell discusses a case in which whites have preferences against working with blacks, while Gordon and Morton deal with the case where men have preferences against working with women. In both cases, the two groups are assumed to be perfect substitutes for each other in production. The labor supply of the discriminated group depends on the wage level (positive wage elasticity), while the labor supply of the discriminating group depends on the wage level and the proportion of employees who belong to the discriminated group. In contrast to Becker's case, a profit-maximizing firm can employ an integrated labor force, but at different wages for the discriminated and discriminating groups.

The resulting segregation or integration depends on the supply elasticities and the strength of the preferences for discrimination.[137] It is of interest to note that wage differences can occur in this case even if the groups have the same wage elasticity. Together with employee discrimination, monopsony could possibly explain differences in wages between ethnic groups, and not only between the sexes. However, the actual strength of the monopsony position held by firms is of crucial importance for the explanatory value of this theory.

The basis of both the radical and the dual labor market theories is the existence of significant monopolistic or oligopolistic elements in the commodity market and monopsony in the labor market. According to these theories the large monopolistic or oligopolistic firms dominate the economy despite the presence of other types of firms. The existence of internal labor markets is emphasized in the dual theory as well as in some formulations of the radical labor market theories. Characteristic for an internal labor market is that an individual can be hired only for certain positions or ports of entry in the firm and that he can start making a career in a (hierarchical) promotional system from such recruiting stations. The firms then have a monopsonistic position except in relation to persons in the recruiting positions.[138]

On the other hand, the employees have a monopolistic position *vis-à-vis* the employers because of skills specific to the firm. In this way, the wage level is indeterminate. This is emphasized in the dual as well as in the radical labor market theory. The monopsonistic power that the firms possess can be counteracted by e.g. the formation of trade unions. Within the radical theory, discrimination is viewed as a means for the employers to decrease the bargaining power of the employees in any given firm. In the dual theory, discrimination is found in the pattern of recruitment to the internal labor markets. This determines who remains outside in the secondary labor market. We will account for the main features of both these theories below.

The Radical Labor Market Theory

The basis of the radical labor market theory (sometimes called neo-Marxist) is profit-maximizing firms with a monopsonistic position in the labor market.[139] By dividing, i.e. by pitting different ethnic groups against each other, the employer rules, that is he can lower wages. The theory is formulated in several different ways. John Roemer[140] assumes that the workers' bargaining power is greatest when the labor force is ethnically homogeneous (completely white or completely black). In any other case, the bargaining power is lower and the lowest wage the employer can establish is higher. Roemer discusses two different relations between ethnic composition and wage level: (1) where the lowest accepted wage is a continuous function of the ethnic composition, and (2) where the wage becomes lower only between certain threshold values. This is shown in Figure 2.6. Roemer demonstrates that

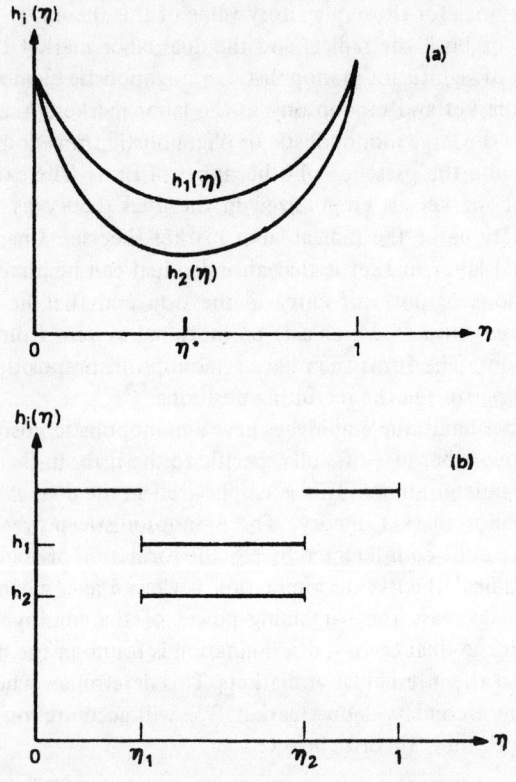

Figure 2.6: A Radical Model of Wage Discrimination

Notations: $h_i(\eta)$ = workers' minimal wage functions; 1 = white, 2 = black. η = share of the workforce that is white.

Source: Reprinted by permission of *Bell Journal of Economics* from Roemer (1978), p. 697.

equilibrium with discriminatory wage differences is possible. (There is no other possible wage combination which yields positive profits for a firm.)

According to the figure, Roemer has assumed that when integration occurs, white workers receive higher wages than black. The possibility that equal but lower wages could be the case in integrated firms is not to be excluded: '... the absence of discriminatory wages cannot be taken as evidence of the absence of the divide-and-conquer effect.'[141] Wage differences are, however, the rule.

It ought to be feasible for a coalition between a firm and a discriminated black labor group to reach a solution more advantageous to both. Roemer remarks, however, that the employers in these segregated firms are always at the mercy of a militant work force, whereas employers in integrated firms have insurance against being 'held up' by the workers. Big firms, it can be argued, might opt for the strategy with insurance.[142]

In Roemer's model, there is a wage level (the minimum wage accepted) for every given ethnic composition. Michael Reich[143] has formulated a model in which one wage, the minimum hourly wage, is set by the market, but where the firms themselves can decide the ethnic composition and the hourly wage for one of the groups (in practice the white group) which exceeds the minimum wage. The major feature in Reich's model is that the work contribution does not only depend on the size of the labor force, but on the bargaining power of the workers as well, which in turn depends on the ethnic composition and the relative wages in the firm.

As in Roemer's model, the bargaining power for the workers is strongest when the labor force is segregated, and at any given degree of integration, the greater the degree of wage equality between the various ethnic groups, the greater the degree of bargaining power held by these groups. Employers can increase their bargaining power by opting for an integrated labor force and by increasing the wage spread (raising the wages for the white workers). The primary result is the same as in Roemer's case. An equilibrium with wage differences between ethnic groups can be obtained. If the wage level in Reich's case is reformulated in terms of wage per unit of output (rather than wage per hour), it is possible to obtain the same result as Roemer for the white wage level as well. In other words, the wage for whites will be lower in the integrated firms than in the segregated ones.

There are a few unclear points in the radical theory. For a model built on power and especially bargaining power, it gives the trade unions a very small part to play. In Reich's model, for example, the bargaining power of the workers influences only the work effort made per unit of time, not the hiring (the ethnic composition), the wage level or the wage structure in the firm.[144] Just as Becker does not explain why prejudices against a certain group exist and Akerlof does not elucidate the reasons behind the existence of certain social traditions, the exponents of the radical theory do not explain why employers can divide and rule using ethnic affiliation.

The Dual Labor Market Theory

The best known example of a segmented labor market theory is the dual labor market theory.[145] The major assumption in the theory is that the labor market is divided into two parts. One of these parts, the primary labor market, consists of jobs within different internal labor markets. Recruitment from the outside to these markets is limited to certain ports of entry. A position in an internal labor market provides significant employment security, there are definite mobility chains from one station to another, and the jobs are set up so that the more a person works, the more automatic, incidental learning he acquires. The other, secondary, part of the labor market consists of jobs with low employment security and with a short training period. There are no mobility chains between the jobs in the secondary labor market and the mobility between the two markets is strictly limited.

Further divisions of the labor market have also been made in the dual labor market theory. Michael Piore, who perhaps more than anyone else has contributed to the development of the dual labor market theory, in several articles,[146] divides the primary labor market into an upper and a lower tier. Craft jobs are difficult to classify in the dual labor market theory and female clerical workers represent a second group who do not fit into the typology. Why, then, according to this theory, is a division of the labor market obtained?

One way of explaining the existence of a dual labor market is through the level of technology and degree of uncertainty in the economy.[147] Given certainty of demand, the optimal production structure is characterized by high capital intensity and specialized labor. With this type of technology, production on any level other than that which gives the lowest costs implies sharply rising average costs, especially as the labor force has become an increasingly fixed production factor. Trade unions in different countries have forced the creation of laws and agreements which make it hard for the firms to vary their labor force.[148] According to Piore, this makes the larger oligopolistic firms plan for balanced production growth using the production factor combination which has the lowest average cost. Short-run variations in demand lead to changes in production, but the permanent employees in the larger firms are not affected. It is the employees in the secondary sector who have to meet the variations in demand. The institutional set-up can differ from sector to sector and from country to country. In some cases, employees in the secondary labor market work in the same firms as those in the primary labor market, but have a more insecure position.[149] In other cases, variations in production emanate from smaller firms that are either subcontractors for larger firms or wholly independent firms, or from variations in work done at home. The character of the secondary labor market differs but the problem of uncertainty in the economy remains the same.

In Piore's early work, the supply side is treated as an independent determinant of the existence of a dual labor market: '. . . heavy emphasis has been placed on the historical importance of changing individual attitudes as a primary source of the emergent dualism.'[150] According to Piore, attitudes towards work are largely class-determined. As a result, certain groups have work attitudes which make them less suitable for jobs within the primary sector. The composition of the labor supply should to some extent determine the division between the primary and the secondary markets. In his early work, Piore also emphasized how jobs in the respective sectors influence people so that they not only acquire different skills but also different preferences for work as compared to other activities and that these preferences do not alter with a change to a job in the primary sector. Hence, preferences are endogenously determined in this formulation of the dual labor market theory, which is thus very reminiscent of the one Gunnar Myrdal developed in *An American Dilemma*.[151]

It is difficult to move from a secondary job to a primary one. Once a person lands in the secondary labor market, he or she tends to stay there, according to the dual theory. As a result, recruitment to the primary labor market assumes paramount importance. The occurrence of employer discrimination (preferences, prejudices, statistical discrimination) together with preferences that are endogenously determined (in the labor market) can lead to wage differences between groups, differences that do not disappear even if the discrimination ceases to exist.[152]

The dual labor market theory should, however, not be seen as a separate theory of discrimination:[153] on the contrary, viewed *together with* a theory of discrimination, it can yield an explanation of long-term discrimination. The objections to theories of discrimination based on preferences, prejudices or statistical discrimination remain, however, even when these features are combined with a dual labor market. In the long run, competition in the commodity and capital markets should lead to the disappearance of discrimination.

In Piore's later work, more explicit emphasis is placed on the demand side. A combination of variations in demand, technology and institutional relations (laws, trade unions) lead to a division of the available jobs into a primary and a secondary labor market. Instability is concentrated in the secondary sector where jobs are taken by people who for one reason or another have less permanent ties to the labor market and therefore look for (or accept) this type of work. In certain countries, this category primarily consists of women, whose main work tasks lie outside the labor market. Youths, whose first jobs are often in the secondary labor market, can be included, as can immigrants (or migrants within a country) who are recruited or move by themselves to another country. As a rule, young persons leave this type of work, while immigrants return to their home country or work their way up to jobs within the primary sector (perhaps in its lower tier). As a result, there is a constant need to recruit new people to the secondary labor market. This recruitment does not occur, however, because certain groups are rejected from jobs in the primary sector due to discrimination:

> . . . the capitalist system *finds* these classes and *does not create* them. . . The migrants (foreign and domestic), the rural workers, and the women are attractive precisely because they belong to another socioeconomic structure and view industrial employment as a temporary adjunct to their primary roles. They are willing to take temporary jobs because they see their commitment to these jobs as temporary, and they are able to bear the flux and uncertainty of the industrial economy because they have traditional economic activities upon which to fall back.[154]

In this later version of the dual labor market theory, the size of the two labor markets is determined from the demand side. Different groups are represented to widely different degrees in the primary and secondary labor markets respectively, but this fact is not explained with reference to discrimination. Nor is it the case in this version that those who work within the secondary sector develop characteristics which make them unsuitable for work within the primary sector:

> We have been impressed with how easily the skills required for moving from one segment to another are acquired by most people

and how little constraining are intrinsic intelligence or initial values and orientations when economic expansion and social change make mobility possible. The same people who once worked in the unstable segment of industry and had poor work habits, little discipline, and low skills move into regular industrial work requiring disciplined, conscientious endeavor when possibilities open for such a shift.[155]

In this form, the dual labor market theory is not a theory which analyzes discrimination in the labor market. The differences in the occupational distribution of various groups in the labor market are to be sought outside that market. This change in theory can be seen as an answer to the criticisms of the assumption of deficient mobility between the secondary and the primary labor markets,[156] the assumption in the dual labor market theory which has been subject to most scrutiny and discussion.

Bargaining Models

Characteristic for the majority of discrimination theories is that they place great importance on the individual agents in the economy but little on organizations and various institutional arrangements. The behavior of individual employers and employees occupies the major position, while unions, employer organizations and public authorities are placed on the periphery. Wages are set by the market, not through bargaining.

This is not to say, of course, that trade unions and bargaining play no part at all in the theories that we have discussed so far. In the early British debate, the trade unions played a central part. Fawcett[157] and Edgeworth,[158] for example, contended that the dominance of men in the unions was a decisive factor when explaining why women were concentrated in just a few low-wage occupations. Robinson[159] and Bronfenbrenner[160] analyzed how the trade unions could influence relative wage positions by using a discriminatory policy. Even Becker discussed how the labor union could affect the incomes of different groups by controlling hiring decisions.[161]

In the radical and dual labor market theories, bargaining is treated more explicitly than in the other models. In the former, the employer can influence the result of wage bargaining through the choice of composition of the employees, and in the dual theory, trade unions and bargaining have great significance for the formation of the internal labor markets.

There have also been a few attempts to design models that place greater direct importance on bargaining. The simplest variety views the economy as three-part bargaining with, for example, employers, white workers and black workers as the three parties. Two of the parties — employers and white workers — are assumed to join forces at the expense of the third party — the black workers. The decisive question is how a coalition is established between these two parties. David Swinton assumes that white workers are the dominant group which forces employers by means of pressures and threats to reserve the best-paid positions for them.[162] Blacks get the lower positions; moreover, their bargaining power is weakened, which reduces wages in these positions. In this way, according to Swinton, employers make a higher profit. The model is reminiscent of the radical theory in that it also assumes that only one party, although a different one than in the radical theory, is active in the bargaining. White employees are the active party in the bargaining and profit by discrimination. Swinton's formulation of the theory is, however, too imprecise to be testable.

A more elaborate bargaining model has been presented by Ray Marshall.[163] His point of departure is that there are five protagonists in the economy: managers, white workers, black workers, trade unions and different governmental organizations responsible for anti-discrimination measures or labor market relations. Basic to Marshall's theory is the idea that those who discriminate do so not out of a general dislike for another group but out of opposition to hiring the group in certain positions. Discrimination is thus to be seen as an attempt to reserve certain advantageous positions for one's own group. It is a question of status, and not of like or dislike for another group.

According to Marshall, managers behave as in the neo-classical theory. They attempt to maximize profits and have no preferences for discrimination, with the possible exception of blacks in managerial positions. The management's employment policy, however, is not only influenced by the wage levels that are established for different groups; it is also affected by the risk of losing federal contracts because of discrimination and by the risk of aggressive actions on the part of the different labor groups. White workers strive to retain certain jobs for themselves and are prepared to take certain actions to do so. Trade unions, which as a rule are dominated by whites, have the same goal. Here policy can differ between the local and the central levels — the former being more prone to discriminate. The bargaining power of the black workers grows in proportion to the size of the group. If the black group is large, the employer has a stronger position in bargaining with the white workers. If whites quit their jobs in protest at blacks being hired in positions previously reserved for whites, the firms can hire blacks to replace them.

The governmental anti-discrimination policy can influence the position of employers in relation to the white workers and thereby lead to diminished discrimination. When dealing with the white workers, the firms can blame the government if they hire blacks in positions previously held by whites.

The above description indicates that there are features in Marshall's model which can also be found in other theories of discrimination. This is especially true of the analysis of employers who have a monopsonistic position in the labor market which is combined with employee discrimination.[164] The position of the discriminated group thus becomes dependent both on the strength of employee discrimination and on the group's own elasticity of supply. If this elasticity is high the effect of employee discrimination will be limited. What is new in Marshall's approach is the attempt to take several forms of discrimination into consideration and at the same time include the governmental authorities in the analysis. Basically, however, Marshall's theory is not so much an elaborate model, but rather a program for determining in which direction a theory of discrimination that includes organizations and institutional relations might be developed.

Summary and Conclusions

The basis for the theoretical discussion about discrimination is that the position of certain persons or groups in the labor market is determined not only by their productive capacity but also by group affiliation. In particular, the treatment of women in various countries and of blacks in the United States initiated research in the area. Discrimination has been a 'paradox' for economists, to use Cassel's term. In a market economy which fulfils the conditions for perfect competition, wages are equal to the value of the marginal product of labor, and two equally productive persons receive the same wages.

The theories of economic discrimination dealt with in this survey have certain features in common even though they are basically different:

(1) They are based almost without exception on a microeconomic foundation. The microeconomic base, however, differs from that of the

general equilibrium model: either, more arguments than goods and services are included in the preference function, or, there are market failures such as monopsony, uncertainty or incorrect information.

(2) All the theories take up the existence of wage differences between groups not caused by differences in productivity. In many cases, this is obvious, since these divergences are the starting point for the formulation of the theory.

(3) A person's income is not determined by the hourly wage alone. Another important factor is the rate of employment or unemployment. In many cases, there is an attempt to explain the differences in unemployment between, for example, women and men or blacks and whites by means of a theory of discrimination.

(4) The implicit or explicit treatment of segregation is common to the majority of discrimination theories. The treatment, however, differs between the various theories. In some, segregation is a result of discrimination, while in others, it is a means of discrimination. In one theory, integration — i.e. the opposite of segregation — is a means by which employers can achieve lower wages. It is important to note that segregation can possess several dimensions — among others, workplace and occupation — and that different theories may be concerned with different dimensions of segregation: occupational integration can be combined with workplace segregation and vice versa.

In certain cases, the theories yield conflicting results. The theory of employee discrimination due to preferences for discrimination leads to workplace segregation, while the radical discrimination theory results in workplace integration. Different theories provide different implications concerning the stability in the wage differences caused by discrimination. In such cases, the validity of the discrimination theories can be corroborated via empirical studies. It should be emphasized there that there is no reason at all to expect that any single discrimination theory has the greatest explanatory value for all cases: a certain form of discrimination may be dominant in one case, a second in another.

Nor should one anticipate that there is only one form of discrimination in each individual case: combinations of most of the forms are quite possible, such as e.g. simultaneous monopsony and employee discrimination. In this connection, it is of importance to note that the effects of the simultaneous existence of two forms of discrimination are not necessarily the same as the sum of the effects of each form. Each combination must be analyzed separately.

Table 2.1 summarizes some of the basic elements of the various discrimination theories, especially the causes of discrimination, and the effects on wages, unemployment and segregation. It is important to observe that in addition to being an effect of discrimination, segregation can be a means of discrimination. We will compare briefly below the different theories regarding causation and economic effects and also touch upon the welfare economic conclusions in the different cases.

Two of the major contributions to the discrimination theory cannot satisfactorily be represented in such a table: namely, the works of Sidney Webb and, even more so, those of Gunnar Myrdal. The reason is that their explanations for discrimination can be related to several different theories. Furthermore, they take up discrimination not only in the labor market but also in other facets of life. We must also leave out Anne Krueger's model from the table, since it lacks a microeconomic foundation and the reasons for discrimination are therefore unclear.

Causes

None of the different discrimination theories provide a complete explanation for the causes of discrimination within the framework of the model. Each theory contains a central element which is not explained within it. Additional economic or other theories are necessary. This can be seen by putting the following questions to the theories:

(1) Why do the members of one group have *preferences* for discriminating against another (Becker's discrimination theory)?

(2) Why does the social tradition of treating a certain group in a specific way arise (Akerlof's theory of *social customs*)?

(3) Why do the labor supply elasticities of different groups as viewed by the firms differ in a systematic way (*monopsony* theory)?

(4) Why do incorrect ideas about the relative productivity of different groups occur (*prejudices*)?

(5) Why is it more difficult to estimate in advance the productivity of individuals from some groups than from others (*statistical discrimination*)?

(6) Why is it possible to weaken the employees' bargaining power by pitting different ethnic groups (or men and women) against each other (the *radical discrimination* theory)?

The various answers to the question of why discrimination exists do

Economic Theories of Discrimination

Table 2.1: Causes and Economic Effects of Discrimination in the Labor

Type of discrimination	Motive for companies to include sex or race in wage-setting/employment decisions	Complementary (alternative) assumptions	Wage differences Short term
Employers have *preferences* for discrimination	Own preferences		Yes
See above	See above	Wage rigidity (minimum wage & equal wage laws or similar agreements); job-competition models'	No (if effective equal wage laws or agreements exist)
See above	See above	Monopoly in the commodity market. Competition in the capital market	Yes
See above	See above	Monopoly in the commodity market. No competition in the capital market (non-transferable monopolies; alt. not possible to realize monopoly profits)	Yes
A worker group has *preferences* for discrimination	Higher costs for employees from the discriminating group if the firm also employs members of the discriminated group	The discriminated and discriminating groups are perfect substitutes in production	No
See above	See above	The discriminated and discriminating groups are not perfect substitutes in production	Yes

Market

Wage differences Long term (stability properties)	Unemployment differences	Segregation	References
No (unless all employers have preferences for discrimination)	Neo-classical model with full employment	Yes (unless all firms have the same tendency to discriminate). The discriminated group will be employed in firms with little or no tendency to discriminate	Becker (1957)
No	Yes, differences will vary with market fluctuations (greater difference in times of recession)	See above	Gilman (1965) Demsetz (1965) Thurow (1969)
No	Neo-classical model with full employment	Yes; the discriminated group will be employed in firms with little or no tendency to discriminate	Becker (1959)
Yes (depends on the size of, in part the discriminated group, in part the non-monopoly sector)	See above	The discriminated group will be over-represented in the competitive sector of the economy	Alchian & Kessel (1962)
No	See above	Yes	Becker (1957)
Yes	See above	Depends on the strength of the preferences for discrimination in comparison with the possibilities for substitution	von Furstenberg (1972)

Table 2.1 (*continued*)

Type of Discrimination	Motive for companies to include sex or race in wage-setting/employment decisions	Complementary (alternative) assumptions	Wage differences Short term
See above	See above	The discriminated and discriminating groups are complements in production	Yes
See above	See above	The discriminated and discriminating groups are perfect substitutes in production. Hiring costs (costs for substituting employees)	Yes (if there is an increase in the size of the discriminated group)
A worker group has *preferences* for discrimination	Higher cost for employees from the discriminating group if the firm also employs members of the discriminated group.	Monopsony in the labor market. The discriminated and discriminating groups are substitutes in production	Yes (even if the groups have the same supply elasticity)
A worker group attempts to exclude another from certain jobs (due to *preferences* or own economic interests)	Conflicts with the discriminating group (higher costs) if members of the discriminated group are employed in reserved jobs		Yes
A consumer group has *preferences* for discrimination	Lower prices must be set in order to sell goods and services if members of the discriminated group are employed		Yes
Discrimination as a social custom	Influences other transactions negatively, influences employer's social prestige		Yes

Wage differences Long term (stability properties)	Unemployment differences	Segregation	References
Yes	See above	No	Becker (1957)
No (unless there is a constant increase in the size of the discriminated group)	See above	Some firms segregated, others integrated (new firms segregated with only employees from the discriminated group)	Arrow (1972:1 1972:2 and 1973)
Yes	See above	Depends on the strength of the preferences for discrimination in relation to supply elasticities for the discriminated and discriminating groups	Bell (1974) Gordon & Morton (1974)
No (unless exclusion is effected with the help of laws or sanctions from authorities not directly involved in the transaction)	See above	Yes, in the short run in certain jobs (*crowding*); in a longer perspective, the discriminated group is represented in all occupations but segregated to certain work places	Cannan (1914) Fawcett (1918) Edgeworth (1922) Bergmann (1971, 1974)
No (if there is a possibility of segregation between different groups of consumers)	See above	Yes (by occupation or restriction to selling within one's own group)	Becker (1957)
Yes	See above	In those cases where social custom decrees that certain jobs are reserved for certain groups	Akerlof (1976, 1980)

64 *Economic Theories of Discrimination*

Table 2.1 (*continued*)

Type of discrimination	Motive for companies to include sex or race in wage-setting/employment decisions	Complementary (alternative) assumptions	Wage differences Short term
Statistical discrimination (cannot gauge productivity exactly when employment decisions are made, use sex, race, etc. as criteria)	Increased uncertainty in estimated productivity involves costs	The groups are considered to have the same producitivy (mean and variance) but the variance of the estimate for a person before hiring differs	Yes
Monopsonistic discrimination	Profit maximization, if there are differences in wages between different groups	Groups have different supply elasticities	Yes
The radical theory of discrimination	Lower wage level if integrated work force; wage differences	The bargaining power of the labor force in a firm depends on its composition; the greater the homogeneity the greater the power	Yes (lower wage level for the non-discriminated group in segregated firms than in integrated ones)
Negotiation theories (bargaining game with different parties in-involved)	Costs for labor conflicts, interference by authorities; wages vary according to employment policy	Influence from different worker groups (discriminated, discriminating) unions and authorities within the firm	Yes
Prejudices (an incorrect perception of different groups' productivity)	Profit maximization (where there is incorrect information)		Yes

Wage differences Long term (stability properties)	Unemployment differences	Segregation	References
Yes	Yes (if wage rigidity exists e.g. in the form of mimimum wages)	No	Phelps (1972:2) Aigner & Cain (1977) Borjas & Goldberg (1978)
Yes	Full employment assumed	No (possibly segregation to certain tasks if laws or agreements on equal pay for equal work exist)	Robinson (1933) Bronfenbrenner (1956)
Yes (lower wage level for the non-discriminated group in segregated firms than in integrated ones)	See above	No (the discriminated group will be found in integrated firms)	Roemer (1977) Reich (1981)
Yes (the result is influenced by changes in bargaining power)	See above	Yes (if any worker group negotiates the right to reserve certain jobs for itself)	Marshall (1974, 1977) Marshall & Christian (1978)
No (economic advantage for firms with employees from the discriminated group, dissemination of information about actual productivity)	Yes, short-term if there is wage rigidity	Yes (the discriminated group does not work in firms with the more prejudiced employers; i.e. those who learn less quickly)	McCall (1972, 1973)

not stem from a common cause. It is however, possible to trace a pattern in the answers.

(1) Becker discusses to a certain extent why preferences for discrimination exist. His explanatory factor is the degree of contact between different groups: when contact is lacking or is very intensive, there are no preferences for discrimination, but in all the cases between these poles, such preferences can arise. The weakness of this theory is that it cannot explain the occurrence of all types of discrimination, for example that between the sexes. Nor does the pattern for racial discrimination seem to agree with the one that Becker describes. Extensive contact can exist simultaneously with extensive discrimination.

(2) Akerlof indicates clearly that he deals only with the stability of social customs and not their origin or why certain traditions arise rather than others. In this respect, the British economists writing between the end of the nineteenth century and the end of the 1940s are more explicit. They state among other things that social conventions can build on income distribution arguments — a wage sufficient to support a family must be higher for men than for women due to the different family roles. In turn, the differences in family roles were explained partly by the characteristics of work at home, partly by earlier conditions (traditions). Above all, it is the factors that determine the division of labor within the family that require explanation. For this purpose, we require a theory with an historical perspective.

The prevailing explanation of conventions for work for men and women cannot be applied directly to racial discrimination. Even here it is not unreasonable to seek historical explanations for the existence of discrimination, for example, in the appearance of other forms of discrimination in earlier periods.

(3) The explanation as to why women have a lower labor supply elasticity than men in relation to individual firms, is also based on the division of labor in the family. Women have a labor market which is more geographically restricted due to the greater extent of their work in the home. However, in order to explain this phenomenon, it is, necessary to explain how this unequal division arose.

Attempts have also been made to explain the wage differences between blacks and whites by referring to the existence of monopsony and differences in supply elasticity. In this case, the explanation could be that blacks are discriminated against in the housing market and segregated in certain housing areas, which in turn leads to a more limited labor market. (Blacks cannot move about as freely as whites in order to be closer to their places of work.) This does not, however, solve the problem of the actual cause of discrimination. It merely shifts the question from the labor market to the housing market.

(4) Why do prejudices (incorrect ideas) against a certain group arise? Theories which work with this type of explanation lie essentially outside the area of economic theory. One explanation for prejudice, however, could be that the productivity of a group changes – for example, if the discrimination in education diminishes or if there is a change in traditional sex roles. A certain amount of time can be required for knowledge of productivity changes to spread. Even in such a case, the analysis must be conducted in approximately the same way as in the theories mentioned above. Why is there a certain division of labor within the family? Why does this division change? Why is there discrimination in education? Why does it decrease?

(5) There is one kind of statistical discrimination which does not solely concern individuals but groups as well. It builds on the assumption that the firms have greater difficulties in ascertaining in advance the productivity of members of one group than of another, and that divergences from anticipated productivity cause increased costs. This may be explained by divergent cultural traditions: the employers, belonging to a tradition different from that of the discriminated group, have difficulties in judging the latter; general tests are originally designed for persons from a certain ethnic background. Even this explanation leads to further questions: why are the employers from one group and not from another? Why were the tests designed for one group and not for another?

(6) Regarding the radical discrimination theory, the question which lies outside the theory is: why is it possible to divide and rule along certain lines? (and, implicit in this question, why is it not possible to do so along others?). Even here it is probably necessary to go back to earlier relations between the groups.

From the preceding discussion of the causes of discrimination, two conclusions can be drawn: (1) that it is necessary to use knowledge from areas other than discrimination in the labor market and from theories other than economic ones, and (2) that the analysis ought not to be ahistorical. However, given a specific cause, this does not preclude an economic analysis of the effects of discrimination from being of significant interest.

Effects

Many of the theories that we have taken up here explain wage differences that arise when a group begins to discriminate against another (or if a newly-arrived group is discriminated against). There are, however, some exceptions. For example, discrimination by a group of employees due to prejudices against another which is a perfect substitute for it in production results in workplace segregation, but not in wage differences. Hiring costs can, however, explain why wage differences exist at least temporarily. Wage differences may also be the outcome if the discriminating and discriminated groups are imperfect substitutes or if employee discrimination is combined with a monopsonistic position in the labor market for the firms. It is important to observe in this case of monopsony that it is not necessary for the groups to have different supply elasticities. Employee discrimination between two groups which are perfect substitutes combined with monopsony with the same supply elasticity for both groups, can explain wage differences, while neither of the two forms can do so separately. This illustrates that it is not possible to add the effects of two independently existing forms of discrimination to determine what effect a combination of both of them would have.

Another exception to the conclusion that discrimination implies wage differences is found in the radical discrimination theory. The central element here is that integration makes it possible to divide and rule. Wage differences can be an aid in pitting the different groups against each other but is not a necessary prerequisite in the theory.

A third exception occurs when effective laws or agreements against wage discrimination exist. Such laws can in turn lead to other effects, for example, differences in unemployment in Becker's theory and increased employment for the discriminated group in the case of monopsony.

An issue that has been greatly discussed in the literature concerning discrimination is the stability of the wage differences caused by discrimination. Can the discrimination theories explain a wage difference continuing over a long period of time or merely short-term deviations? Among other things, it has been claimed that Becker's discrimination theory can only explain short-term differences, which disappear after a longer period of time due to the influence of competition. Nor can the prejudice theory explain long-term stable wage differences. Other theories can explain them, however, such as the social customs, the monopsony, the statistical and the radical discrimination theories. In all these cases, there is still a problem concerning the explanation of stability of very large wage differences. The use of better test instruments or systems with trial employment should cause the elimination of large wage differences based on statistical discrimination, and labor market mobility should do the same to differences caused by monopsony. In the radical and the social customs theories, the incentive to build coalitions which oppose discrimination increases with growing wage differences. The research position in this area is quite unclear, however, and there are strong motives for continued analysis of the stability characteristics of the different models.

In the neo-classical model, all production factors are fully employed. There is no unemployment. The problem of differences in unemployment rates thus becomes irrelevant in this model. If some form of wage rigidity due to collective wage agreements, laws or transaction costs is appended to it, on the other hand, the neo-classical model can explain the existence of unemployment. If there is unemployment and at the same time job competition exists, discrimination can cause unemployment differences. This is the case regardless of whether the discrimination depends on preferences or prejudices or whether it is 'statistical'. Also the theory of social customs can explain both the origin of unemployment and differences in its incidence. On the other hand, there are two theories which cannot be expanded as easily to treat differences in unemployment: monopsony and radical discrimination.

Segregation is of central importance in the majority of the theories. Its position, however, differs from theory to theory and its form is not always the same. In Becker's theory, workplace segregation is a result of discrimination, whether it be by employees, consumers or employers — in the latter case, when tastes for discrimination vary between different employers. On the other hand, the radical theory considers workplace integration as a means for employers to lower the wage level. Here we have one of the areas in which different theories of discrimination have yielded diametrically opposed hypotheses.

The Becker theory is also applicable to occupational segregation, for example in cases where discrimination is only employed against a group when it holds a certain occupation, such as when male personnel discriminate against females in supervisory positions. Under certain conditions, this type of discrimination can lead to occupational segregation. The discriminated group is excluded from some occupations. Under other conditions, the result can be wage differences or workplace segregation.

In other theories, occupational segregation is a means to achieve discrimination (wage differences, differences in unemployment). A group can use different methods to exclude another group from certain occupations. Laws and trade union agreements are two forms of institutional arrangements. The result is 'crowding', a concentration of the discriminated group into the remaining occupations, which leads to a lowering of the wage level. Such an exclusion of a group from certain occupations can also occur indirectly through discriminatory regulations within the educational system.

Several of the remaining theories can be formulated to imply occupational segregation. The social norm can be such that persons from a group are not employed in certain jobs. The prejudices can apply to a group's capacity in certain but not all occupations, and the uncertainty concerning the capacity of different persons can be greater for some jobs than for others. The fact that a group may have a slight chance of getting a job in some occupations may cause differences in wage levels and unemployment rates between groups. The size of the differences depend among other things on the substitutability between different occupations in production.

Job segregation as a means of discrimination is a central issue in many discrimination theories. The effects of this type of discrimination have inspired surprisingly few studies. In Chapters 6 and 7, we attempt an analysis of this type of effects.

Welfare Economic Effects

In addition to the labor market effects of discrimination which were discussed above, the more comprehensive questions about the effects of discrimination on resource allocation and the welfare of different groups are of great interest.

It seems intuitively clear that total production will be lower with discrimination than without — in other words, that discrimination leads to inferior resource allocation. There is one type of discrimination, however, which may involve higher production than would otherwise have occurred without discrimination (assuming the existence of the same market failure). This exception is statistical discrimination due to differences in uncertainty in estimating productivity for people from different groups and in which deviations from anticipated productivity imply actual costs. Consequently, refraining from discrimination could lead to lower production.

The welfare economic conclusions concerning the existence of discrimination are similarly uncertain when there are other preferences than just for goods and services. This is true with preferences for a group (nepotism), or against a group, as well as when the income distribution between different groups or social reputation is included in the utility function. A decreased quantity of goods in such a case can be weighed against the benefit (given the preferences) resulting from being able to act according to the preferences. When discrimination caused by preferences of the type described above exists, a summation of the gains or losses of different groups is, however, not meaningful. On the other hand, though, it can be of great interest to analyze which groups gain or lose through discrimination.

Becker employs the theory of international trade to investigate the welfare economic effects of discrimination arising from preferences. The discrimination takes the form of diminished capital exports from the discriminating society. According to Becker, both societies lose while one group in each society wins: the workers in the discriminating society and the capital owners in the discriminated. This conclusion is crucially dependent, however, on the fact that the preferences for discrimination change. In Chapter 3 below, we will show that with fixed preferences for discrimination, the discriminating group as a whole stands to gain from discrimination due to preferences for discrimination and that the discriminating capital owners can do so if one specific condition is fulfilled. If preferences are ignored and attention is only paid to the change in money income (we deal with this case in Chapter 4), the capital owners in the discriminating society lose from discrimination.

According to Becker's analysis, the group which suffers the largest loss is, however, the discriminated worker group. The only exception is employee discrimination between groups that are perfect substitutes in production. This case results only in segregation, and the welfare of the different groups is not affected.

In Akerlof's theory of social custom, it is possible to have an equilibrium with the social custom of discriminating against a certain group. This equilibrium involves lower production than the equilibrium without this social custom. In order to determine the distributional consequences, however, the form of the discrimination must be specified.

In the case of discrimination due to prejudices (incorrect information), a non-optimal employment of resources arises. The losers are the firms and the discriminated employee group. If certain conditions (wage rigidity, job competition) are fulfilled, the non-discriminated employee group can gain by discrimination.

Monopsony is also an imperfection which leads to an incomplete utilization of resources. Here, the monopsonistic firm gains while the employee groups with a not completely elastic labor supply to the firm lose in comparison with the case of perfect competition. Groups who have different supply elasticities lose by different amounts. The radical labor market theory also concludes that firms gain while the employee groups lose. One group (the discriminated one) loses more than the other.

The results of discrimination are more indeterminate in the bargaining model. This is due to the fact that the relative bargaining power of the parties involved is not determined *a priori*. One of the examples given is when white workers have the stronger position and force a solution in which both the black workers and the firm lose.

From the summary above, certain more general conclusions can be drawn: (1) discrimination contributes to a non-optimal resource allocation (possible exception: statistical discrimination), (2) the discriminated worker group loses through discrimination (exception: employee discrimination between groups that are perfect substitutes in production), (3) according to some theories, the discriminating firms (capital owners) lose, according to others they gain, (4) the workers who do not belong to the discriminated category (that is, the group having higher wages than the discriminated one, productivity being equal) gain according to some theories and lose according to others.

As can be seen from the last two points, the distributional consequences of discrimination are the subject of disagreement. Once again this indicates that it is important to establish the cause of discrimination, but it also points toward certain testable implications. In the next chapter we will deal with the welfare and distributional effects of discrimination according to the Beckerian approach.

Notes

1. For other surveys of the early British debate see Madden (1973) and Phelps Brown (1977).
2. Webb (1891).
3. Women and men very infrequently held the same job at the same place of employment. Thus, Webb had difficulties in obtaining complete comparability. See also Collet (1891), who, when investigating female labor in Leeds, found only two smaller firms in which men and women did the same job.
4. Webb (1891), p. 661, footnote 1. This reasoning bears a striking resemblance to that which has lately been put forward concerning the relationship between the amount of food eaten and working capacity in developing countries. See e.g. Leibenstein (1957), Ch. 6, Shoup (1965), Oshima (1967), Berg (1973), Bliss & Stern (1978), Lundahl (1979), Ch. 9.
5. Webb (1891), p. 661.

6. Cassel (1923), pp. 314-15. This quotation is from the first English edition but the same question may be found in earlier German editions: in the first German edition (Cassel 1918), pp. 292-3.

7. Rathbone (1917).

8. Fawcett (1917 and 1918). The latter article is a direct polemic against Rathbone.

9. Fawcett had dealt with the same question twice before in the *Economic Journal*. A gradual change can be observed in her opinion concerning the issue. In the first article (Fawcett, 1892) she emphasized insufficient education as a cause of the concentration of women within certain occupations. In a review twelve years later (Fawcett, 1904) she placed great importance on the fact that women were not granted entrance to technical schools due to resistance from the trade unions. In the articles of 1917 and 1918, Fawcett stressed that the trade unions limited the choice of occupation for women in several different ways. Her altered opinion can be due to actual changes at the time – an increased degree of union organization among men and a different union policy.

10. There is an elaborate minority report to the Committee by Beatrice Webb, one of its members. See *War Cabinet Committee on Women in Industry* (1919:2) and also Webb (1919), in which the minority report is reprinted with a special introduction but without the section concerning the wages for those women who replaced men in industry during the war. According to Beatrice Webb, the reason for the wage differential is a difference in union power between men and women. Webb believed that the suggested measures were based on erroneous concepts. Instead of equal pay for equal work, she suggested standard wages – hourly or piecework rates – for each occupation regardless of who was doing the work (principle of occupational rate). Furthermore, as opposed to the majority of the Committee, she rejected the idea that wages should be related in any way to family obligations.

11. The following economists answered the questionnaire: Edwin Cannan, Arthur Cecil Pigou, A.L. Bowley, Henry Clay, J.H. Jones and E.C.K. Gonner.

12. Cannan in part replied with a long quotation from an earlier work (Cannan 1914).

13. *War Cabinet Committee on Women in Industry* (1919:3), p. 176.

14. Edgeworth (1922).

15. Edgeworth is referring to a German edition of Cassel's work.

16. In Anglo-Saxon literature, this has been dubbed 'crowding', with Edgeworth as the alleged originator of the term. (See, e.g. Chiplin & Sloane 1976). However, the phenomenon is well described by, amongst others, Fawcett (1918), p. 2. She describes how the occupations due to this type of restriction can become 'overcrowded'. Madden (1973), p. 30, also names Fawcett as the first person to present the hypothesis of 'overcrowding'. Even Cannan in *War Cabinet Committee on Women in Industry* (1919:3) used the terms 'crowding' and 'overcrowding' before Edgeworth and also described the phenomenon, without however using the term itself, in *Wealth*, which was published in 1914. John Stuart Mill had described the female occupations as overcrowded already in *Principles of Political Economy*, first published in 1848: 'It must be observed, that as matters now stand, a sufficient degree of overcrowding may depress the wages of women to a much lower minimum than those of men' (Mill 1848, Book 2, Chapter XIV, § 5).

17. Janice Madden (1973), pp. 30-2, states that Edgeworth incorrectly concluded that, under perfect competition, males will earn more than females in occupations where the two sexes are equally efficient. She shows diagrammatically how under perfect competition the two sexes earn the same wage, if they are equally efficient and employed in the same industry.

Edgeworth's point of departure is, however, that men and women do not have the same efficiency in most occupations. Men are more efficient in some occupations and women in others. The demand for labor is higher with a given supply in the male occupations than in the female ones, which implies that the average male wage is higher than the average female wage. 'It may be expected that there are some branches of industry into which women only will enter, others into which they will never, or hardly ever, enter.' The average weekly earning in the former is less than in the latter, according to Edgeworth. The integrated occupations will be such, where male efficiency is greater than female: 'There remain occupations that are entered by both sexes: say G, H, I, K, L. For any one of these, e.g. occupation, I, the (rate of) pay, say t, for unit of work . . . is to be the same for men and women; but the weekly earnings will not be the same, say i_1, for the female and i_2 for the male workers: i_1 less than i_2.' (Edgeworth 1922, p. 443).

18. Florence (1931).
19. The first two points are in agreement with one of Webb's (1891) explanations for differences in wages.
20. *Women in Industry* (1930).
21. Bronfenbrenner (1956).
22. Bronfenbrenner (1939).
23. The two extreme cases are 'open shop' where non-union members are not discriminated against as compared with union members, and 'closed shop — closed union': outsiders are not hired and they cannot become union members, the prerequisite for gaining employment, either.
24. In a much later paper, Welch (1967) uses almost the same explanation for the existence of discrimination, '. . . under integrated conditions, some of a laborer's time may be wasted because of his disgruntlement' (Welch 1967, p. 229).
25. *Royal Commission on Equal Pay* (1946), p. 86. The other two questions were related to the effects of the raising of the women's wage and to the causes of the differences between the wages of male and female teachers. This last question concerns a case often referred to in the British debate. Millicent Fawcett included it as an exercise for students in her textbook, *Political Economy for Beginners* (1876), already in the 1870s.
26. They were Sargant Florence, Roy F. Harrod, Hubert Henderson, John R. Hicks, D.H. MacGregor, Arthur Cecil Pigou, Joan Robinson, David Ross, Hamilton Whyte and Barbara Wootton. Harrod's memorandum is also published in Harrod (1952) and Pigou's in a slightly revised version in Pigou (1952).
27. A typical phrase is the following by Hicks: 'I should therefore be willing to accept the view that the wage-gap tends to be somewhat wider than is justified by relative efficiency though it does not follow that it is very much wider' (*Royal Commission on Equal Pay* 1946, p. 100).
28. In an expert report to a Swedish Governmental Committee the economist Karin Kock (1938) stressed the same factors as her British colleagues: (1) traditions both regarding occupations '(male and female occupations) and wages in integrated occupations (male and female wages) and (2) the higher degree of unionization among the male workers.
29. Wootton in *Royal Commission on Equal Pay* (1946), p. 114.
30. Henderson in *Royal Commission on Equal Pay* (1946), p. 96. Henderson here anticipates the reasoning which would be put forth later on by Welch (1967) and Arrow (1972:1).
31. Phelps Brown (1949).
32. *Q & A on Equal Pay* (1947).
33. Phelps Brown (1949), p. 384, footnote 2. The Chancellor of the Exchequer declared in Parliament on 11 June 1947: 'The Government do not consider that this is the time when it would be in the national interest for these additional burdens to be taken' (438 H.C DEB. 5s p. 1070).
34. Myrdal (1944).

35. Becker's (1971:2) only reference is a footnote on p. 123: 'Of the literally hundreds of sources that can be cited [on ill feeling in the South against Negroes caused by slavery and the losses suffered from the Civil war], see Gunnar Myrdal, *The American Dilemma.*' Marshall (1974) does not include Myrdal in his survey of racial discrimination. Masters (1975) on the other hand, allots a relatively large space to Myrdal as an example of the liberal tradition within this research area (cf. also Reich 1981).

36. It should be stressed here, however, that even the early British economists included other than economic relationships in their analyses. This is true chiefly of Sidney Webb, who took up the effect of laws as well as traditions, family patterns and living conditions. Even later authors like Fawcett, Florence and Robinson emphasized institutional relationships and especially the role of the trade unions, but they did not employ a dynamic theory as Myrdal did.

37. Myrdal (1939).

38. Myrdal (1944), especially Chapter 3.7 and Appendix 3. In Appendix 5, 'A Parallel to the Negro Problem', a comparison with the status of women is made.

39. Myrdal (1944), footnote, p. 75.

40. Swan (1962).

41. Myrdal admits that this criticism is a just one. In *Asian Drama*, which also builds methodologically upon the principle of circular, cumulative causal chains, he writes, 'The great bulk of historical, anthropological and sociological evidence and thought suggests that social stability and equilibrium is the norm and that all societies, and underdeveloped societies in particular, possess institutions of a strongly stabilizing character' (Myrdal 1968, p. 1871). A short summary of Myrdal's views on economic analysis and cumulative causation is given in Myrdal (1978).

42. See Rosenstein-Rodan (1961) and Nelson (1956) plus Leibenstein (1957), respectively.

43. *Royal Commission on Equal Pay* (1946), p. 114.

44. '. . . a framework has been proposed for analyzing discrimination in the marketplace because of race, religion, sex, color, social class, personality, or other non-pecuniary considerations' (Becker 1971:2, p. 153).

45. Becker consistently uses the designation W ('whites') for the discriminating group and N ('Negroes') for the discrimated group. (We will employ the same convention in this work.) He does, however, analyze other types of discrimination — among others the discrimination against American Indians in the United States.

46. Becker (1971:2), p. 155.

47. Ibid, p. 160. The distinction is not without importance. Becker uses the conclusions from the normative analysis to reject economic causes for discrimination. The results from the normative analysis, however, build on the assumption that the difference in preferences depends on hatred against a certain group (see Becker 1971:2, p. 21, especially footnotes 3 and 4).

48. Ibid, p. 20.

49. Becker's formulations are such that it is not evident that there are two different macroeconomic models: a non-mathematical one and a mathematically formulated one, with different assumptions. In the presentation of the non-mathematical model, for example, he refers to results drawn from the mathematical model (see also Madden 1973, p. 44, note c).

50. In the Appendix to Chapter 2, Becker (1971:2) touches briefly upon the consequences that a variation of the values of the discrimination coefficient would have on the results. The conclusion is that net income would be greater for the discriminating group if there was a variation of the discrimination coefficients than if all had the same coefficient, given the degree of discrimination.

51. It is easy to expand the model in the main text to a case where the labor force is mobile between the sectors, so that discrimination by employees in one society against the capitalists in the other can also be included.

52. Cf. also Friedman (1953).

53. In the first edition of Becker's book, union discrimination is taken up only in passing. In the second edition, the section is greatly expanded through the inclusion of the text in Becker (1959) as an addendum to Chapter 4. The case of discrimination by the unions is more extensively treated by Bronfenbrenner (1939) even if Bronfenbrenner does not use the same nomenclature (see the first section of this chapter, 'The Theory of Discrimination Prior to Becker').

54. This is a neglected area in later research. On exception is Borjas (1982) who relates the degree of wage discrimination in the governmental sector to the racial and sexual composition of the constituencies and the nature of the agency's output.

55. We will in this section, however, not deal with cases where people have preferences concerning transactions *between other persons*. This will be dealt with in the section on alternatives to Becker's theory.

56. Becker (1971:2), p. 44.

57. We are grateful to Gary Becker for stressing this point to us (personal communication, 12 October 1982).

58. Becker (1971:2), p. 46.

59. Traditionally, entrepreneurial efficiency is considered a random attribute (cf. Koutsoyiannis 1979, p. 159).

60. Becker (1971:2), p. 46.

61. Arrow (1972:1, 1972:2 and 1973).

62. Partial segregation will also be the result in models that are based on employee discrimination in combination with differences and variations over time in the wage elasticity of the labor supply of different groups, i.e. in the case of a combination of employee discrimination and monopsonistic behavior (see Bell 1974).

63. From this follows that the wage dispersion in a labor market will vary with the size of the discriminated relative to the discriminating group (see Chiswick 1973).

64. See Alchian & Kessel (1962). When discrimination exists in federal or municipal monopolies, the ones who shoulder the higher expense are the inhabitants in the country or the municipality via higher taxes.

65. Sowell (1981), p. 48.

66. Alchian & Kessel (1962).

67. Compare with Bronfenbrenner (1956), who deals with the case of a monopsonist who does not realize the entire monopsonistic profit.

68. Demsetz (1965). See also Sowell (1981).

69. Furstenberg (1972). In a model which contains more than one commodity there is also the possibility of factor-price equalization through trade. See Stiglitz (1973 and 1974) and Madden (1973).

70. See Freeman (1974), p. 37.

71. Gilman (1965).

72. Ibid., p. 1091.

73. Demsetz (1965). See also Landes (1967 and 1968), Kosters & Welch (1972) and Sowell (1981), Chapter 3.

74. Demsetz (1965), p. 276.

75. Reder (1974).

76. Here we are dealing with the supply for the labor market, not with the

labor supply facing a specific firm. If the supply of labor for a single firm is not infinitely elastic, the firm is monopsonistic. If the supply elasticity differs between groups, it is profitable for the firm to pursue a monopsonistic policy of discrimination.

77. Reder (1974), p. 35. If the labor supply is negatively elastic (backward bending supply curve), the market discrimination coefficient constitutes an overestimation of the discrimination coefficient. For a further elaboration, see Butler (1982), who proposes the use of structural instead of reduced form estimates of the discrimination coefficient.

78. Becker (1971:2), p. 160.

79. Toikka (1977). This case is analyzed in Chapter 3 below.

80. See Thurow (1969), p. 116, for a criticism of Becker and see also Chapter 3 below for a closer criticism of this condition.

81. Goldberg (1982).

82. See Arrow (1972:1, 1972:2 and 1973). Becker does not make an explicit formulation of the utility function in *The Economics of Discrimination*. In a later textbook (Becker 1971, p. 71) he states that the assumed utility function for the study of discrimination is $U = I - dw_i q_i$, where I denotes profits, w_i the wage rate, q_i the number of black employees, and d the firm's discrimination coefficient.

83. Alexis (1973 and 1974). Alexis sees it as a model to explain racism as opposed to models which only explain discrimination. 'Racism, as distinct from mere discrimination, necessarily implies $du_j/du_i<0$,' that is, j's utility is higher the lower i's utility is (Alexis 1973, p. 297).

84. The same undetermined conclusion is arrived at for employer discrimination between complementary production factors (see Alexis 1973, pp. 299-301).

85. Marshall (1974), p. 859. See moreover Bergmann (1971), among others.

86. Bergmann (1971 and 1974).

87. The case of discrimination against one's own group (women having prejudices against female bosses, etc.) is an exception. We ignore this type of discrimination in the following discussion.

88. Becker (1971:2), p. 6.

89. Krueger (1963).

90. See also Madden (1973), Appendix A, and Thurow (1969).

91. Thurow (1969), pp. 112-16.

92. Thurow, like Becker, compares a situation without tastes for discrimination with one where such tastes exist, but only investigates what happens to the monetary income of the white group (ibid., p. 113). However, he also points to an alternative comparison: the case where the white society has constant preferences for discrimination but where in the initial position no discrimination takes place (ibid., p. 116).

93. See e.g. different articles about labor supply in the United States in Cain & Watts (1973) which demonstrate that different groups may display backward-sloping curves (the income effect dominates the substitution effect). According to these studies, men (regardless of race) have a backward-sloping supply curve while the supply curve of married women (regardless of race) is forward-sloping. (See in particular Boskin 1973.) When discrimination of e.g. black men occurs, the case in Figure 2.2 ought to be relevant, while the case in Figure 2.1 ought to be suitable for the analysis of discrimination of women.

94. Stiglitz (1974), p. 8. See also Stiglitz (1973).

95. See Akerlof (1976 and 1980).

96. See e.g. Webb (1891) and several of the contributions in *Royal Commission on Equal Pay* (1946).

97. See primarily Akerlof (1976 and 1980).

98. This type of analysis does not have to be viewed only as an analysis of the Indian caste system but can also be applied to other economic systems with social stratification where a person's position is birth-ascribed. Berreman (1960) is of the opinion that the Indian caste system and the race relationship in the US South, for example, possess basically the same characteristics.

99. A leading anthropologist specializing in caste systems, Gerald Berreman, regarding the possibilities for changes in a caste system, states: 'If change occurs, it must be either through a major change in the power of a single caste . . . or through a change of the total socio-cultural environment . . . Then people may be able to combine forces across the traditional caste lines or to mobilize themselves for certain purposes without regard to caste at all.' (Berreman 1979, p. 104).

100. Cf. ibid., p. 105: 'If the system were to be challenged or altered, however, it would be likely to become advantageous or even necessary for some groups to join forces.'

101. Klitgaard (1972).

102. Ibid., p. 42.

103. Akerlof (1980).

104. In a recent article, Akerlof (1983) discusses in more detail how values, e.g. class loyalty, are transferred from one generation to another.

105. Akerlof (1980), p. 751.

106. Ibid., p. 773.

107. See e.g. Dumont (1970).

108. See e.g. Berreman (1979).

109. Olson (1982). Olson extends his analysis to other extreme forms of discrimination, e.g. the South African Apartheid system.

110. Ibid., p. 157.

111. Klass (1980).

112. Ibid., p. 133.

113. There are different designations for this type of discrimination. Arrow (1972:1), p. 97, labels if 'prejudice', while Zellner (1972) calls it 'erroneous' discrimination.

114. Reich (1981), pp. 106-7.

115. See McCall (1972 and 1973), Chapter 2. One gets similar results with a 'job-competition' model — see e.g. Thurow (1975).

116. Arrow (1972:1), p. 98.

117. Spence (1974).

118. For a criticism of Spence regarding this point, see Aigner & Cain (1977), pp. 183-4.

119. See Stiglitz (1974), pp. 18-20 and in the early British debate, Webb (1891) and Rathbone (1917).

120. Stiglitz (1974).

121. Arrow (1972:1, 1972:2 and 1973) and Phelps (1972:1 and 1972:2). The first to use the term 'statistical discrimination' was probably Michael Piore (1970).

122. Phelps (1972:2). For a development and criticism of Phelps' model, see Aigner & Cain (1977) and Borjas & Goldberg (1978).

123. '. . . the score differential is due to a "cultural bias" in the test: since intelligence tests are prepared by members of the "ruling" white middle class, it is inevitable that the test questions will be loaded in favor of experiences familiar to this group.' (Borjas and Goldberg 1978, p. 919).

124. Aigner & Cain (1977).

125. If all workers are not employed in the firms (e.g. because all positions demand a certain minimum level), this compensation mechanism does not need to work (see Borjas & Goldberg 1978).

126. See e.g. Aigner & Cain (1977), p. 186.
127. See e.g. Blau & Jusenius (1976), p. 194, who define statistical discrimination as 'a situation in which decisions regarding individuals are based on group-derived probabilities.' For a criticism of this definition see Aigner & Cain (1977).
128. See Aigner & Cain (1977), p. 184, and Thurow (1975), pp. 173-5.
129. This form of discrimination is often called 'exploitation of labor'. See e.g. Bloom (1941).
130. See Madden (1977:1 and 1977:2) and Siebert & Sloane (1980), p. 245.
131. See Madden & White (1980). Schlicht (1982) explains monopsonistic discrimination by a search-theoretic approach. In his model the probability of finding an applicant for a job with a specified wage rate differs between groups.
132. See e.g. Blau & Jusenius (1976) for a criticism of this point.
133. Both these theories are often called institutional while the rest of the theories are often collectively referred to as neo-classical. The classification method varies greatly, however.
134. See the section on 'The Discrimination Theory Prior to Becker', pp. 11-12.
135. Bell (1974).
136. Gordon & Morton (1974).
137. Compare with Furstenberg's (1972) case − a combination of incomplete substitutability and employee discrimination.
138. The employers can have a monopsonistic position even *vis-à-vis* those in recruiting positions, but in that case because of reasons other than the existence of an internal labor market.
139. For surveys of the radical theory, see Gordon (1972) and Reich (1981). Gordon, Edwards & Reich (1982) deal with the historical development of segmentation. There are other versions of radical models that emphasize discrimination as a remnant from earlier phases of capitalism. According to these explanations capitalists do not necessarily gain from discrimination, nor are they necessarily in favor of racial discrimination. See e.g. Baron (1975) and for a survey Cherry (1977).
140. Roemer (1979).
141. Ibid., p. 702.
142. Ibid.
143. Reich (1981), pp. 204-15.
144. For criticism, see e.g. Rubery (1978).
145. The major work is Doeringer & Piore (1971). See Gordon (1972) for a survey of the early theory development. A later version which deviates on several points is found in Berger & Piore (1980).
146. See among others Piore (1974 and 1975).
147. As e.g., Berger & Piore (1980) have done. See also Bluestone (1970).
148. Berger & Piore (1980) have investigated the development in France, Italy and the United States.
149. It is assumed that the firms use another, less capital intensive and more flexible technology to meet the fluctuations.
150. Gordon (1972), p. 52.
151. Myrdal (1944).
152. If there is a 'social inheritance' of preferences, the effect of an earlier discrimination can be retained for several generations, even if the degree is gradually decreased. See e.g. Sowell (1975 and 1981) who in this way tries to explain wage differences between blacks and whites in the United States that also remain in the long run.
153. Cf. Sloane (1980), p. 128.
154. Berger & Piore (1980), p. 50.
155. Ibid., p. 11. To be sure, the preferences are determined by the job, but they change with a change in job.

156. See e.g. Cain (1976) and Wachter (1974).
157. Fawcett (1918).
158. Edgeworth (1923).
159. Robinson (1933).
160. Bronfenbrenner (1939).
161. Becker (1971:2), Addendum to Chapter 4.
162. See Swinton (1977).
163. Marshall (1974 and 1977) and Marshall & Christian (1978). Marshall (1977) contains a somewhat more detailed presentation.
164. Cf. e.g. Gordon & Morton (1974).

3 THE BECKERIAN APPROACH TO DISCRIMINATION

Modern interest in the theory of economic discrimination began only recently. It was not until after the publication in 1957 of Gary Becker's *The Economics of Discrimination* that extensive research on the topic was initiated — and then only after a lag of a decade or more. 'Current knowledge about the theory of discrimination rests almost entirely on the work of Gary Becker', wrote Lester Thurow in 1969.[1]

Becker's work is founded in the neo-classical tradition of economics with its emphasis on fixed institutions, perfect competition (excepting discrimination), linearly homogeneous production functions, equality of factor rewards and marginal value products, etc. In fact, it is the first fully fledged analysis within this tradition. The efforts of Edgeworth and others in the 1920s were but a sketchy beginning in tackling the problem. It remained for Becker to develop a model which makes full use of the neo-classical apparatus, giving a formalized treatment of the problem.

Perhaps it is the very fact that Becker integrated the treatment of economic discrimination with the dominating paradigm of modern economics that best accounts for the later success of his book, perhaps not. At any rate, the book was widely read and with time, as we found in Chapter 2, triggered off a number of studies either progressing along the same lines as Becker himself or criticizing the Becker approach. However, a reading of the literature that has developed in the Beckerian tradition gives rise to certain confusions. This is not a casual result: Becker's original book is itself hard to interpret. Several different interpretations are given, and it is often not clear what the premises of the analysis are. This is reflected clearly in the subsequent literature.

The aim of the present chapter is to discuss one particular aspect of Becker's analysis, that which has received most attention in the subsequent theoretical literature in the Beckerian tradition. This is Becker's model for analyzing the welfare effects of discrimination for different groups in society, and especially the astonishing result that the group which is supposedly behind discrimination — white capitalists or white society as a whole — makes a loss from discrimination. By scrutinizing this model, it is hoped that at least some of the haze surrounding the Becker analysis may be dissipated so that a clearer understanding of the model and its workings can be arrived at. In this process some attempts will be made to revise and extend the model.

We will begin with a presentation of the Becker model and the welfare conclusions that can be derived from it. The second section points out the major flaw in Becker's analysis: that his model contains preferences that do not remain constant but change when discrimination is introduced. In the third section, the model is reformulated so as to allow for constant preferences, and it is shown that this reformulation reverses Becker's main welfare conclusion: that the discriminating group loses from discrimination. With constant preferences, an unequivocal gain accrues to this group.

Becker's formulation of the discrimination problem builds on the notion of a taste for discrimination against a particular group, that is the discriminating group acts as if it is willing to incur a cost for not associating with this particular category of people. (This is 'discrimination' or, 'negative discrimination'.) It may, however, also be the case that the unequal treatment takes place because the discriminators put a premium on associating with their own kind. (This is 'positive discrimination', 'nepotism' or 'favoritism'.) The differences between these two approaches have been explored before, within the framework of the original Becker model, with changing preferences, and it has been shown that the welfare implications of nepotism are exactly the opposite of those of discrimination in that the discriminating group makes a gain in the former case. It will be demonstrated shortly that this result does not necessarily hold when the constant preference approach is used.

The final section deals with the interpretation of Becker's discrimination coefficient (the taste for discrimination). In Becker's formulation, the white group discriminates because of a dislike of contact with Negroes. It is shown that under certain circumstances this formulation implies that the psychic costs for the discriminating group of associating with Negroes remain constant even if the extent of association is reduced. A reformulation of the discrimination coefficient is presented which assumes that the taste for discrimination arises from *the very fact* that white capital is handled by Negroes and not from *the extent* of the association. This type of 'perverse' result is thereby excluded from the analysis. The welfare implications of the reformulation are derived subsequently. It is especially evident that with this reformulation, whites always gain by discriminating in the case of nepotism.

The Becker Model[2]

Becker divides society into two groups, a majority (whites) and a minority (Negroes). Each of these two groups is treated as a separate entity or society with its own endowments of labor and capital. The supply of labor is given in both sectors. So is the supply of white and Negro capital. The white group is assumed to have a larger relative endowment of capital than the Negro group so that

$$\frac{\bar{K}_W}{\bar{L}_W} > \frac{\bar{K}_N}{\bar{L}_N}. \qquad (3:1)$$

A single commodity is produced in both sectors (white and Negro) with the aid of both labor and capital:

$$Q_W = f_W(\bar{K}_W - K_E, \bar{L}_W), \qquad (3:2)$$

$$Q_N = f_N(\bar{K}_N + K_E, \bar{L}_N), \qquad (3:3)$$

where K_E denotes the amount of capital exported from the white to the Negro sector. The production functions are taken to be linearly homogeneous and identical, with $f_W^K > 0$, $f_W^L > 0$, $f_W^{KK} < 0$, $f_W^{LL} < 0$ and $f_W^{KL} = f_W^{LK} > 0$ (analogous for f_N).

Perfect competition prevails in all markets before discrimination is introduced.

Before we allow for the possibility of factor movements from one sector to another, according to (3:1) and the assumption of linear homogeneity, we have a situation in which the marginal productivity of capital in the Negro sector exceeds that in the white sector while the reverse is true with regard to the marginal productivity of labor. Now, Becker assumes that labor is immobile[3] between the two groups or sectors while capital is mobile. Hence the white group will export capital (K_E) to the Negro sector until the returns to capital are equal in the two sectors. The exported capital will thereby fetch a return which is equal to the return earned by the white capital that remains in the white sector. This occurs, with linearly homogeneous production functions, when the capital-labor ratio is the same in both sectors:

$$\frac{K_R}{\bar{L}_W} = \frac{\bar{K}_W - K_E}{\bar{L}_W} = \frac{\bar{K}_N + K_E}{\bar{L}_N}. \qquad (3:4)$$

The easiest way to define *discrimination* in Becker's model is by presenting a non-discriminatory situation. This is a situation where the return on capital is equal in all sectors of the economy as above. Discrimination (unequal treatment) occurs when white capital owners demand a return per unit of exported capital which exceeds the unit return on capital that is left working in their 'own' sector. Such a divergence in rates is created by a reduction of the volume of capital exported as compared to the situation where rates are equalized.

To introduce discrimination into the model, Becker assumes that all capital owners in the white group have an identical taste for discrimination so that '[if] members of W develop a desire to discriminate against labor and capital owned by N, they become willing to forfeit money income in order to avoid working with N. This taste for discrimination reduces the net return that W capital can receive by combining with N labor, and this leads to a reduction in the amount of W capital exported.'[4] The taste for discrimination is tantamount to a psychic cost for the white capitalists equal to $d_W^K > 0$, so that when white capital is put to work in the Negro sector, the white capitalists require a higher pecuniary return than on the capital employed in the white sector:

$$f_N^K(1 - d_W^K) = f_W^K. \qquad (3:5)$$

Thus, the discrimination coefficient in Becker's model plays a role which is analogous to that of a tariff in international trade theory. It lowers the return to the white-owned capital employed in the non-preferred ('protected') Negro sector and thereby reduces capital exports.[5]

The Welfare Effects of Discrimination

The main point of Becker's analysis is the investigation of the welfare effects of discrimination. With tastes for discrimination present, (3:4) no longer holds. Less capital than K_E will now be exported, and this in turn will have repercussions on

(a) the net income of the white community as a whole,
(b) the net income of the Negro community as a whole,
(c) the net incomes of workers and capitalists in both communities.

By 'net' income, Becker means the income which takes psychic costs or benefits into account.

Net white incomes are given by the sum of monetary capital and labor incomes at home and incomes from the capital exported to the

Negro sector, minus the psychic costs of letting export capital be handled by Negroes:

$$Y_W^{net} = K_R f_W^K + \bar{L}_W f_W^L + K_E f_N^K (1 - d_W^K). \tag{3:6}$$

Substituting (3:5) into (3:6) gives

$$Y_W^{net} = (K_R + K_E) f_W^K + \bar{L}_W f_W^L. \tag{3:7}$$

To find out what happens to these incomes when capital exports are reduced as a result of discrimination, we may differentiate (3:7) with respect to K_E. This yields

$$\frac{dY_W^{net}}{dK_E} = [(K_R + K_E) f_W^{KK} + f_W^K + \bar{L}_W f_W^{LK}] \frac{dK_R}{dK_E} + f_W^K, \tag{3:8}$$

or, since

$$K_R = \bar{K}_W - K_E, \tag{3:9}$$

$$\frac{dY_W^{net}}{dK_E} = -K_R f_W^{KK} - \bar{L}_W f_W^{LK} - K_E f_W^{KK}. \tag{3:10}$$

Expression (3:10) may be simplified. Since the production function (3:2) is assumed to be linearly homogeneous, Euler's theorem applies so that

$$K_R f_W^{KK} + \bar{L}_W f_W^{LK} \equiv 0. \tag{3:11}$$

Then,

$$\frac{dY_W^{net}}{dK_E} = -K_E f_W^{KK}, \tag{3:12}$$

or in Becker's formulation:

$$\frac{dY_W^{net}}{dK_E} = -K_E f_W^{K_E K_E}, \tag{3:13}$$

since, according to (3:9),

$$f_W^K = -f_W^{K_E} \tag{3:14}$$

and

$$f_W^{KK} \frac{dK_R}{dK_E} = -f_W^{K_E K_E}. \tag{3:15}$$

Expression (3:12) is positive — assuming diminishing marginal returns to capital. In other words, the net income of the white community as a whole is reduced when capital exports decrease as a result of discrimination.

Net Negro incomes[6] are given by

$$Y_N^{net} = (\bar{K}_N + K_E)f_N^K + \bar{L}_N f_N^L - K_E f_N^K. \tag{3:16}$$

Employing the same methodology as above, it may be shown that

$$\frac{dY_N^{net}}{dK_E} = -K_E f_N^{KK}, \tag{3:17}$$

which is positive, meaning that Negro incomes will fall as a result of discrimination.

Capital and labor incomes in the two sectors are given by

$$Y_{K_W}^{net} = (K_R + K_E)f_W^K, \tag{3:18}$$

$$Y_{L_W}^{net} = \bar{L}_W f_W^L, \tag{3:19}$$

$$Y_{K_N}^{net} = \bar{K}_N f_N^K, \tag{3:20}$$

$$Y_{L_N}^{net} = \bar{L}_N f_N^L, \tag{3:21}$$

and

$$\frac{dY^{net}_{K_W}}{dK_E} = -(K_R + K_E)f^{KK}_W > 0, \qquad (3:22)$$

$$\frac{dY^{net}_{L_W}}{dK_E} = -\bar{L}_W f^{LK}_W < 0, \qquad (3:23)$$

$$\frac{dY^{net}_{K_N}}{dK_E} = \bar{K}_N f^{KK}_N < 0, \qquad (3:24)$$

$$\frac{dY^{net}_{L_N}}{dK_E} = \bar{L}_N f^{LK}_N > 0. \qquad (3:25)$$

White capital owners and Negro labor lose by the imposition of discriminatory treatment while white labor and Negro capitalists gain.

A summary of Beckers' results concerning the welfare effects of discrimination is given in Table 3.1. The results are all neat and clear-cut

Table 3.1: Welfare Effects of Discrimination in the Becker Model

Effects on net incomes of:	
Whites	loss
White capitalists	loss
White labor	gain
Negroes	loss
Negro capitalists	gain
Negro labor	loss

and most of them lend themselves to simple economic interpretation. Beginning with Negro incomes, it is easy to understand that when export capital leaves the Negro sector as a result of discrimination, the resultant fall in the capital-labor ratio reduces the wage rate and increases the return on capital. Thus, Negro workers lose and Negro capitalists gain from discrimination. To account for the reduction of total Negro incomes, we note that equation (3:17) expresses the difference between the change of output in the Negro sector,

$$\frac{dQ_N}{dK_E} = f_N^K, \tag{3:26}$$

and the change in the share of output in that sector accruing to white capitalists:

$$\frac{d(K_E f_N^K)}{dK_E} = f_N^K + K_E f_N^{KK}. \tag{3:27}$$

Had the return on capital been given, a loss of export capital would have led to a reduction of payments to white capitalists corresponding exactly to the reduction of output and would hence not have affected total Negro incomes. The decrease of the capital stock in the Negro sector caused by discrimination also leads, however, to an increase in this return so that any white capital remaining in the Negro sector has to be paid more per unit than before. Thus, total Negro incomes must fall.

It is also easy to understand why white labor incomes must increase. The transfer of capital from the Negro sector to the white economy leads to an increase in the marginal productivity of labor in the latter.

Following the reasoning employed by Becker, the change in white capital incomes can be understood by noting that increasing the capital stock in the white sector leads to a fall in the return to capital there. In order to establish a new equilibrium, this reduction must correspond to a reduction of equal magnitude in the net return to white capital in the Negro sector (that is the return including the psychic costs connected with having the capital work in that sector). Finally, having established this equilibirum, the increase in white output can be shown to correspond exactly to the changes in factor payments within the white sector.[7] Hence, the change in total white net incomes corresponds to the reduction in payments to the white capital remaining in the Negro sector. In order for production to continue to take place in the white sector when K_E changes, average costs must remain constant at a given product price. Thus, the change in the value of production must equal the change in total costs.

However, the reasoning in the preceding paragraph is dubious, since it may be shown that the premises upon which this part of Becker's analysis rests are such that they violate some basic postulates of welfare economics. As a result any interpretation of the parts concerning white capitalist incomes and total white incomes in Table 3.1 tend to become somewhat artificial. We will now turn to this issue.

The Flaw in the Becker Model: Changing Preferences

The most fundamental criticism to be raised against the Becker model is that it contains changing preferences.[8] The procedure employed is a comparison of two equilibrium situations; one where there are no tastes for discrimination and one where the white sector has developed such tastes. This may be seen with the aid of condition (3:5), the equilibrium condition for the capital market:

$$f_N^K(1 - d_W^K) = f_W^K. \tag{3:5}$$

In equilibrium, net returns to white capital must be the same in both sectors.

Solving (3:5) for d_W^K yields

$$d_W^K = \frac{f_N^K - f_W^K}{f_N^K} \tag{3:28}$$

and differentiating (3:28) with respect to K_E gives

$$\frac{d(d_W^K)}{dK_E} = \frac{f_N^K f_W^{KK} + f_W^K f_N^{KK}}{(f_N^K)^2}. \tag{3:29}$$

In (3:29), $f_N^K > 0$, $f_W^K > 0$, $f_W^{KK} < 0$ and $f_N^{KK} < 0$. The marginal productivity of capital is positive and diminishing in both sectors, as is usually assumed in neo-classical models. Thus, $d(d_W^K)/dK_E$ is negative. A decrease of capital exports from the white to the Negro sector always goes hand in hand with an increase in the taste for discrimination. Changes in capital exports could only be triggered by a change in the discrimination coefficient. The latter cannot be kept constant when we allow for changes in capital exports if we are to retain the usual assumptions of neo-classical analysis with respect to the signs of the first and second derivatives of the production functions.[9]

Hence Becker's analysis contains changing preferences, and this violates one of the basic postulates of traditional welfare theory, namely that it is not possible to determine whether one set of preferences in any sense is 'better' than another set. By the same token, it is not possible to pass any judgement on the relative welfare of the white group or on that of white capitalists as their 'net incomes' change, since the underlying preferences are not held constant:

> Indeed, the question becomes *meaningless. Welfare comparisons are defined only for given fixed orderings*: an increase in welfare is defined as a shift to a preferred position (*preferred according to that ordering*), and a decrease in welfare is defined as a shift to a position which is, *in that ordering*, inferior. There is no meaningful way, in terms of the concept of welfare that is the basis of the new welfare economics, in which the well-being of a given individual or of a society at time t_0 can be compared to the well-being at time t_1 when the preference map at t_1 is *not* the same that it was at t_0.
>
> It is meaningless, to take an extreme example, for the reader to ask himself whether he is more or less happy now than he was when he was four years old. It is equally meaningless to ask, for much the same reason, whether people were more or less happy thirty years ago than they are now. If, thirty years ago, people had had the same preference maps that people have today, they clearly would have been much less happy in those days — they would have missed their television sets terribly. Fortunately for them, however, their preference maps were different. But unfortunately for the modern welfare economist he has, as a result, no way at all of comparing, in this conceptual scheme, the welfare then and the welfare now. And the same fact holds for any lesser degree of change in the preference maps of individual persons — as long as there is *any change at all* welfare comparisons are undefined and therefore meaningless.[10]

However, the results with respect to white labor income and total Negro incomes as well as Negro factor incomes, are not affected by this discovery, since in neither case do 'net' incomes differ from monetary incomes. Neither labor nor Negroes are assumed to have any taste for discrimination.

A possible solution to the problem of changing preferences is to use a double test, that is to make two separate analyses, one for each set of preferences. Thus, one test could be made of the case with preferences for discrimination (the case analyzed below) while another dealt with the case without preferences for discrimination (the Krueger approach analyzed in Chapter 4). Only if both comparisons yield the same result can anything be said about the welfare effects of a change in discriminatory behavior.[11]

A Reformulation of the Becker Model: Constant Preferences

To escape the problem of changing preferences while still retaining the 'tastes' approach, it is possible to give a different interpretation to discrimination caused by tastes. It can be shown that *given* certain tastes for discrimination (a *constant* d_W^K), it pays for the white group to act according to these tastes, that is it increases white net incomes to withdraw capital from the Negro sector. This can be seen in the following way.

Net incomes from export capital (K_E) equal the net value of the marginal product of capital in the Negro sector, so that total white net incomes may be written as

$$Y_W^{net} = K_R f_W^K + \bar{L}_W f_W^L + K_E f_N^K (1 - d_W^K), \tag{3:6}$$

where $f_N^K d_W^K$ is the psychic cost per unit of export capital of letting white capital work with Negro labor.

Assume now, for the sake of argument, that the white group does not let its taste for discrimination guide its economic action. In that case, money, rather than net factor price equalization would prevail at the outset so that

$$f_W^K = f_N^K. \tag{3:30}$$

Now, what will happen to white net incomes if resort is made to discrimination, that is if capital is withdrawn from the Negro sector and put to use in the white sector instead, so that the return to capital in the former sector exceeds that in the latter? To find this out, we must differentiate (3:6) with respect to K_E, which gives us

$$\frac{dY_W^{net}}{dK_E} = -K_R f_W^{KK} - \bar{L}_W f_W^{LK} + K_E(1-d_W^K)f_N^{KK} - f_N^K d_W^K, \tag{3:31}$$

if money factor prices are equal at the outset, and the psychic cost d_W^K of letting white capital work with Negro labor remains constant.

Since f_W is homogeneous of the first degree, its partial derivatives are homogeneous of degree zero and Euler's theorem applies so that, as we already know,

$$K_R f_W^{KK} + \bar{L}_W f_W^{LK} \equiv 0 \qquad (3:11)$$

and

$$\frac{dY_W^{net}}{dK_E} = K_E(1 - d_W^K)f_N^{KK} - f_N^K d_W^K, \qquad (3:32)$$

which, in the presence of diminishing money returns to capital in the Negro sector, must be negative.

Equation (3:32) shows that white society gains from discrimination both in 'net income' and in 'money income' terms (that is disregarding psychic costs). Hence, it pays for the white group to act according to its tastes or prejudices. If the whites for some reasons attempt to disguise these tastes, they have to pay a price in terms of a net income which is smaller than it would have been, were overt discrimination resorted to. This is an important conclusion. It shows that *once the Becker model is amended so as to allow for constant preferences, Becker's conclusion that the discriminating group suffers a reduction in net income by discriminating is reversed. With a constant taste for discrimination, whites can increase their net income by discriminating against the Negro sector.*[12]

The economics behind this result runs as follows. Since output changes and changes in factor payments in the white sector cancel each other out (cf. the discussion of changes in total white incomes in the Becker formulation above, and note 7), as expression (3:32) shows, we have only to explain the changes connected with events in the Negro sector. Firstly, the reduction of the capital stock leads to an increase in the monetary return on capital equal to $-f_N^{KK}$. In net terms the increase is $-(1 - d_W^K)f_N^{KK}$. (Since $|d_W^K|$ is smaller than or, at most, equal to one, a reduction can never take place.) Thus, the net return on all white capital that remains in the Negro sector increases. White capitalists also make a second gain, since, at a given rate of return, the removal of some white capital from the Negro sector yields a psychic benefit equal to $f_N^K d_W^K$ per unit of the capital removed. Together, these two constitute the net gains from discrimination for white society as a whole.

Our reformulation of the Becker model will also affect the result with respect to white capital income. The latter is given by

$$Y^{net}_{K_W} = K_R f^K_W + K_E f^K_N (1 - d^K_W), \qquad (3:33)$$

and

$$\frac{dY^{net}_{K_W}}{dK_E} = -K_R f^{KK}_W + K_E f^{KK}_N - K_E f^{KK}_N d^K_W - f^K_N d^K_W, \qquad (3:34)$$

where the first and third terms on the right-hand side are positive and the other two negative (signs included). The first two terms express the monetary changes. When capital is withdrawn from the Negro sector, its marginal productivity in that sector increases, but at the same time the marginal productivity of capital in the white sector falls as the withdrawn capital is put to use in the latter sector. We will show later that with identical production functions in the two sectors (as postulated by Becker), the latter effect will dominate the former, that is that the sum of the first two terms is positive[13] (and hence also the sum of the first three terms on the right-hand side of (3:34)).

The last two terms together express the net psychic gain from discrimination. The first of these shows the gross psychic loss deriving from the fact that since the psychic cost (discrimination coefficient) is defined as a fraction of the monetary factor price, white capitalists suffer a psychic loss when the marginal productivity of capital (and hence the price of the latter) increases in the Negro sector as capital is withdrawn. Finally, the second of these terms shows that, as the number of capital units present in the Negro sector falls, white capitalists derive a gross psychic benefit. The sum of the two terms yields the net psychic gain (loss).

The conclusion to be drawn from (3:34) is that the effect of discrimination on white capital incomes is not clear-cut. White capitalists stand to gain from discrimination if the net psychic benefits derived from it are positive and large enough to outweigh the net monetary loss resulting from the inefficiency of resource allocation. Provided that this is true, Becker's original result — that white capital owners lose by discrimination — will be reversed.

Recalling that white labor incomes and Negro incomes are not affected by our reformulation, since neither of them involves any taste for discrimination, our results may be summarized in Table 3.2. This table may be compared to Table 3.1. One of the major difficulties with the original Becker results is that the agents of discrimination — white

Table 3.2: Welfare Effects of Discrimination in the Constant Preference Becker Model

Effects on net incomes of:	
Whites	gain
White capitalists	gain if net psychic effects are positive and outweigh monetary losses; otherwise loss
White labor	gain
Negroes	loss
Negro capitalists	gain
Negro labor	loss

capital owners — supposedly lose by applying discriminatory practices. In other words they ought to have no incentives to depart from the non-discriminatory equilibrium. Our reformulation of the Becker model provides one such possible incentive, namely that, if the psychic costs of letting white capital be handled by Negro labor are considered to be high enough, discrimination will pay. Even if the opposite situation applies, it is possible that white labor — and/or Negro capitalists — who always stand to gain from discrimination, by means of offering compensatory payments may be able to persuade the white capitalists to take discriminatory action. (In the original Becker formulation, white labor alone cannot accomplish this, since its gains are not large enough to offset the losses incurred by white capital owners.) Thus, the reformulated model provides a mechanism whereby the motives behind discrimination may be understood in economic terms.

The Case of Nepotism

In the foregoing section we have assumed that the coefficient of discrimination, d_W^K is positive. In *The Economics of Discrimination*, Becker, however, points out that this need not be the case. Nepotism (or favoritism) rather than discrimination is deemed to be the appropriate term when the unequal treatment is a result of preferences for working *with* one of the groups rather than of a taste for discrimination.[14]

Becker does not analyze the case of nepotism explicitly, but in a later article, employing the same methodology as Becker — that is one of changing preferences — Richard Toikka has shown that if discrimination is a result of psychic benefits rather than of psychic costs, the net income of the white group as a whole will increase.[15] Hence, in a model employing the original Becker formulation 'tastes' and 'nepotism' differ with respect to their welfare effects.

This result does not, however, necessarily hold when the reformulated model is used. If it is assumed that white capital owners prefer their capital to be handled by white labor and hence put a premium on this, equal to $d_W^K(\text{nep})$, defined to be *less* than zero, the equilibrium condition for the capital market becomes[16]

$$f_W^K(1 - d_W^K(\text{nep})) = f_N^K \qquad (3:35)$$

and white net incomes may be written as

$$Y_W^{net} = K_R f_W^K(1 - d_W^K(\text{nep})) + \bar{L}_W f_W^L + K_E f_N^K. \qquad (3:36)$$

Discrimination (withdrawal of capital from the Negro sector) has an impact on white welfare equal to

$$\frac{dY_W^{net}}{dK_E} = K_E f_N^{KK} + (K_R f_W^{KK} + f_W^K)d_W^K(\text{nep}) \qquad (3:37)$$

when, at the outset, monetary (and not net) returns to capital are equalized between the two sectors.

The first term on the right-hand side of (3:37), which has a negative sign, shows the monetary gain from discrimination while the second shows the net psychic gain (or loss). The sign of the latter term is not unambiguous, but the gross gain arising from fewer units of capital being employed in the Negro sector must be weighed against the gross loss emanating from the falling marginal productivity of capital in the white sector. *Thus, the Toikka conclusion that whites always gain in net terms by employing discriminatory behavior does not necessarily hold when constant preferences are assumed to govern behavior.*

The reasons are analogous to those for the 'tastes' case when there were no pecuniary changes originating in the white sector, since output increases correspond exactly to changes in factor payments in the sector. Furthermore, the rate of return to white capital remaining in the Negro sector increases, as before, when capital leaves the sector. One difference between the case of nepotism and that of tastes for discrimination consists of the welfare effects. Corresponding to the gain made in the latter case by having some of the formerly exported capital avoid contact with Negroes, we now have a gain due to the benefits of increased association of capital with white workers.

Of even greater importance, however, is another difference. With discrimination caused by 'tastes', the increase in the return to capital in the Negro sector of $-f_N^{KK}$ leads to a corresponding increase in the psychic costs of those capital owners who retain capital in the Negro sector also in the discriminatory situation. However, as we have seen, this increase is always smaller than the pecuniary gain accruing to the same group. With discrimination caused instead by nepotism, that part of the white-owned capital stock which is used in the white sector regardless of whether discrimination takes place or not is valued less in pecuniary terms. Given the Becker-Toikka definition of psychic gains as a fraction of the return to capital in the white sector, the psychic gain of having white capital handled by white instead of Negro workers is hereby also reduced to a corresponding extent. Only if the net psychic effects are positive or if the monetary gains outweigh negative net psychic effects will the white sector as a whole gain from discriminatory practices in the reformulated model when nepotism is the cause of the unequal treatment.

As we should expect, the effects of discrimination on white capital incomes are not unambiguous either:

$$Y_{K_W}^{net} = K_R f_W^K (1 - d_W^{K \, (nep)}) + K_E f_N^K \tag{3:38}$$

and

$$\frac{dY_{K_W}^{net}}{dK_E} = -K_R f_W^{KK} + K_E f_N^{KK} + (K_R f_W^{KK} + f_W^K) d_W^{K \, (nep)}. \tag{3:39}$$

As with (3:34), the sum of the first two right-hand side terms of (3:39) (the monetary effects) is positive, and in the discussion of (3:37) we also found that the sign of the third term is not determinate. Thus, for white capitalists to gain from discrimination caused by nepotism, the net psychic effect must be positive and large enough to outweigh the monetary losses.

A summary of the effects of discrimination when the latter is caused by nepotism instead of by tastes for discrimination is given in Table 3.3. (As before white labor incomes and Negro incomes are not affected.)

Table 3.3: Welfare Effects of Discrimination Caused by Nepotism in the Constant Preference Becker Model

Effects on net incomes of:	
Whites	gain if net psychic effects are positive or monetary gains outweigh psychic losses; otherwise loss
White capitalists	gain if net psychic effects are positive and large enough to outweigh monetary losses; otherwise loss
White labor	gain
Negroes	loss
Negro capitalists	gain
Negro labor	loss

The Interpretation of the Discrimination Coefficient

The Becker analysis assumes that the psychic costs of exporting capital to the Negro sector (the discrimination coefficient) are due to the contact between Negroes and white capital, 'the frequency and regularity of "contact" with N in different establishments and firms'.[17] At the same time the discrimination coefficient is measured as a fraction of the monetary price of capital (marginal productivity of capital).[18] The simultaneous use of these two assumptions may, however, give rise to some perverse results. These cases may arise where the extent of contact between Negroes and white capital *decreases* and where yet the psychic cost of allowing a unit of white capital to be used in the Negro sector *increases*. This is due, in turn, to the fact that, as the price and marginal productivity of capital change and the discrimination coefficient remains constant, the psychic costs of letting Negro labor handle white capital (the psychic gains of letting white workers handle it), per unit of capital exported (employed in the white sector), will change. Let us examine the possible consequences.

We may begin with Becker's own interpretation of the discrimination coefficient: 'Discrimination is commonly associated with *dis*utility caused by contact with some individuals, and this interpretation is followed here', he writes.[19] 'If members of W develop a desire to discriminate against labor and capital owned by N, they become willing to forfeit money income in order to avoid working with N.'[20] One possible interpretation of this statement is that, given the level of capital exports from whites to Negroes, the marginal productivity of capital, and hence also the price of capital, will fall as the number of Negro workers decreases. The marginal productivity of capital is a function of the factor intensity in the sector. As the capital intensity rises, contact between Negro workers and white, exported capital will diminish since the more capital that has to be served by a given labor force, the less will be the attention that can be paid to each individual unit of capital. Thus, given this interpretation of the rationale it would seem that the tying of the psychic costs per unit of capital to the marginal productivity of capital is a sensible formulation.

Such an interpretation is, however, questionable, for there is at least one case where the neat one-to-one correspondence between unit costs and capital intensity does no longer apply, and that is in the case of technological progress. The Becker model tacitly assumes that no technological progress takes place. Once we allow for technological change, we either have to use an alternative formulation of the discrimination coefficient or allow for changes in the coefficient itself, that is for changing preferences.

In order to explain this finding let us use (3:28) as a point of departure:

$$d_W^K = \frac{f_N^K - f_W^K}{f_N^K}. \tag{3:28}$$

Assume now that technological progress takes place in the Negro sector so that the marginal productivity of capital increases in that sector, from f_N^K to f_N^{K*}. If the productivity increase does not spread to the white sector, this will lead to increased exports of capital, that is to a *higher* capital-labor ratio in the Negro sector, and also to a rise in the marginal productivity of capital in the white sector through a fall in the capital-labor ratio of the latter. We may differentiate (3:28) with respect to f_N^K:

$$\frac{d(d_W^K)}{df_N^K} = \frac{\left(1 - \frac{df_W^K}{df_N^K} \cdot \frac{f_N^K}{f_W^K}\right) f_W^K}{(f_N^K)^2}. \tag{3:40}$$

The second term within the parentheses in the numerator on the right-hand side of (3:40) is an elasticity: the elasticity of the marginal productivity of capital in the white sector with respect to changes in the same marginal productivity in the Negro sector. For the discrimination coefficient to remain constant, we see that this elasticity must be equal to one, that is the two marginal productivities must rise by the same percentage. In that case a situation has arisen in which the capital intensity of the Negro sector has increased due to increased capital exports while at the same time, as a result of the technological changes, the marginal productivity of capital in the sector is higher than before. This means that the psychic costs per unit of export capital have increased from $f_N^K d_W^K$ to $f_N^{K*} d_W^K$, in spite of the fact that Negro labor now has less contact with each unit of capital (including export capital) than before. Such a development is obviously not compatible with the interpretation of tastes (and nepotism) which stresses contact with the despised (favored) group.[21]

This, in turn, suggests a different interpretation of the discrimination coefficient and of the quotation from Becker above. What we want is a discrimination coefficient which represents the tastes for discrimination. Moreover these tastes should not be affected by technological change. Hence it is natural to choose a coefficient defined as 'per unit of export capital' rather than one expressed as a percentage of the marginal productivity of capital in the Negro sector. Let us call the latter type an 'ad valorem' coefficient, and the former type a 'specific' coefficient (d^A and d^S, respectively).

From the foregoing we have:

$$d^S = f_N^K d^A. \qquad (3{:}41)$$

Assume now that we wish d^S, which represents the *tastes* for discrimination, defined per unit of export capital, that is the psychic cost of letting one unit of export capital be handled by Negroes, to remain constant when technological progress takes place in the Negro sector. Consequently, d^A, which represents the psychic cost of letting Negroes handle white capital, calculated as a percentage of the return to capital in the Negro sector, must be allowed to change. Assume furthermore that d^S is the specific coefficient equivalent of d_W^K of (3:5), so that

$$f_N^K - d^S = f_W^K. \qquad (3{:}42)$$

For d^S to remain constant when the marginal productivity of capital increases due to technological progress in the Negro sector, the following must hold:

$$\frac{d(d^S)}{df_N^K} = 1 - \frac{df_W^K}{df_N^K} = 0, \qquad (3:43)$$

that is that

$$df_W^K = df_N^K. \qquad (3:44)$$

Since $f_N^K > f_W^K$ with discrimination present at the outset, f_W^K must increase more than f_N^K in percentage terms. Returning to (3:40), we find that this implies that the *ad valorem* coefficient must fall (cf. also (3:41)). However, it does not mean that the taste for discrimination changes as well — only that the psychic costs as a percentage of the return to capital do so. What it does mean is that, with technological change that does not automatically spread to the white sector, we cannot retain the interpretation of taste (d^S) which relates to the ratio of export capital to Negro labor. In that case, this ratio increases as a result of technological change, since the latter serves to pull white capital into the Negro sector. It is only when the transfer of technology is effected automatically that the ratio remains constant.

Hence, unless we want to assume that new technologies are adopted without delay by both sectors, we must choose an interpretation of d^S which contends that it is the *very fact* that white capital is being handled by Negroes which generates discrimination and that the white capital owners dispense with the more sophisticated computations as to the intensity of contact between white capital and Negro labor.[22]

This also suggests that it is preferable to work directly with specific coefficients in the analysis. Substituting the new specific discrimination coefficient for the *ad valorem* one used hitherto in the case of tastes gives the equilibrium condition (3:42) instead of (3:5) (with corresponding changes in the case of nepotism). We then find that if discrimination is a result of tastes,

$$\frac{dY_W^{net}}{dK_E} = K_E f_N^{KK} - d^S < 0. \qquad (3:45)$$

and

$$\frac{dY_{KW}^{net}}{dK_E} = K_E f_N^{KK} - K_R f_W^{KK} - d^S. \quad (3:46)$$

These two expressions are to be compared with (3:32) and (3:34), respectively. Beginning with the net incomes of the white group as a whole, we find that the qualitative results are the same. In both cases, whites gain by discrimination. However, quantitatively the results differ. Given that the psychic costs vary with the price of capital, the monetary gain deriving from increased marginal productivity of capital must be weighed against a psychic loss emanating from the same source. As long as the discrimination coefficient remains below one, however, this psychic effect will always be less than the monetary gain.

A comparison of (3:46) with (3:34) yields the same type of conclusions. Here, as well, a psychic cost due to increased marginal productivity of capital enters the picture when these costs depend on the price of capital. Expression (3:46) is simple. The net psychic effects are always positive and for white capitalists to gain from discrimination, these gains must outweigh the net monetary loss.

These results are summarized in Table 3.4.

Table 3.4: Welfare Effects of Discrimination Caused by Tastes with a Specific Discrimination Coefficient

Effects on net incomes of:	
Whites	gain
White capitalists	gain if psychic gains outweigh monetary losses; otherwise loss
White labor	gain
Negroes	loss
Negro capitalists	gain
Negro labor	loss

As we proceed to look at the case of nepotism, the differences in formulation assume increased importance in terms of welfare effects. We find that

$$\frac{dY_W^{net}}{dK_E} = K_E f_N^{KK} + d^{S(nep)} < 0 \quad (3:47)$$

and

$$\frac{dY_{K_W}}{dK_E} = K_E f_N^{KK} - K_R f_W^{KK} + d^{S(nep)}. \tag{3:48}$$

These expressions can be compared with (3:37) and (3:39). We now find that with a specific discrimination (nepotism) coefficient, the white group in its entirety will always gain by resorting to discrimination. *Reinterpreting nepotism in 'specific' terms re-establishes the Toikka conclusion in the model with constant preferences.* The psychic loss connected with the fall of the marginal productivity of capital in the white sector is no longer present. The same is true with respect to white capital incomes. With this effect removed, the sufficient condition for a gain is that the psychic gain outweighs the monetary loss.

The results are summarized in Table 3.5.

Table 3.5: Welfare Effects of Discrimination Caused by Nepotism with a Specific Discrimination Coefficient

Effects on net incomes of:	
Whites	gain
White capitalists	gain if psychic gains outweigh monetary losses; otherwise loss
White labor	gain
Negroes	loss
Negro capitalists	gain
Negro labor	loss

So far, we have analyzed the case where whites do not differ in their reaction regardless of the rate of contact between exported capital and Negro labor. On the other hand, if we are to retain the idea that it is the very *amount* of contact between white capital and Negro labor that gives rise to prejudice, another formulation is to be preferred. We may define d^{S*} as the constant psychic cost per Negro worker per unit of export capital. Then the cost per unit of export capital becomes $\bar{L}_N d^{S*}$, and the total psychic cost for white capitalists is $K_E \bar{L}_N d^{S*}$. The cost per unit of capital varies directly with the number of Negro workers, that is with the amount of contact between these workers and the white capital employed in the Negro sector.

However, not much is gained by such a procedure. The only difference is that all terms in (3:45) to (3:48) which contain d^{S*} or $d^{S(nep)*}$

will have to be multiplied by $\bar{L}_N$ and $\bar{L}_W$, respectively. The conclusions otherwise remain essentially the same.

Conclusions

In this chapter, we have presented the Beckerian model of economic discrimination, where society is divided into two groups, whites and Negroes, and where whites discriminate against Negroes by withdrawing some of the capital 'exported' by them into the Negro sector so as to cause the return on capital to be higher in this sector than in the white one. Analogous with the Becker analysis, the welfare implications of this behavior have been determined for whites and Negroes as well as for capitalists and workers within the two groups.

The second section pointed out the main weakness of the Becker approach, namely that it contains changing preferences so that it becomes impossible to compare the discriminatory and non-discriminatory situations, at least if adherence is to be made to the principles of standard welfare theory.

The third section provided a reformulation of the Becker model. Even though changing preferences make the original version untenable, it is still possible to compare discriminatory and non-discriminatory situations in a specific sense. An analysis can always be made of the monetary and psychic gains and losses that arise from not allowing any actual tastes for discrimination to guide economic action. If this approach is taken, we find that one of Becker's main results — that the white community as a whole loses by discriminating against the Negro community — is reversed. Once changing tastes are removed from the analysis, whites are provided with a motivation to withdraw capital from the Negro sector.

The fourth section presented a reformulation for the constant preference case of Richard Toikka's analysis of welfare changes where discriminatory action is not caused by tastes for discrimination against Negroes, as in the case in the Becker formulation, but by nepotism — a desire to let white capital be handled by members of the white community — while no special feelings are connected with capital 'exports'. In the constant preference model whites do not necessarily gain from discrimination.

The fifth and last section provided a second criticism of the Becker formulation where the psychic cost per unit of capital export of allowing this capital to be handled by Negroes varies according to the return on capital. It was shown that in at least one case — that connected with technological change — such a formulation may lead to inconsistencies between the size of the psychic cost per unit of export capital and the intensity of contact between this capital and Negro labor. To remove these inconsistencies, a formulation was suggested whereby the psychic costs per unit of export capital remain independent of the extent of contact. It was also demonstrated that if the same formulation is employed in the analysis of nepotism, the white group as a whole will always stand to gain from discrimination.

Finally, a result which runs through the entire chapter should be stressed. One of the main problems with Becker's original formulation of the analysis of discriminatory situations is that the group that undertakes discriminatory action — white capitalists — is shown to incur a loss. Thus, this group hardly has any incentive at all to discriminate against Negroes. Disregarding the problem of the interpretation of changing preferences, white capitalists must be bribed by the group that gains from discrimination — white workers — if discrimination against Negroes is to take place at all. Such payments are, however, not possible in the Becker formulation, since the white community as a whole loses as well. Hence bribing the capitalists would mean that the white workers would lose. The model fails to point out any clear reasons for discrimination.

This problem has been solved in the present chapter. In all the reformulations of the Becker model, both those which run in terms of tastes and those which make nepotism the reason for discriminatory attitudes towards the two groups of workers, there is a possibility that white capitalists will make a gain. In the most realistic case, where a specific discrimination coefficient not related to the extent of contact between white capital and Negro (or with nepotism, white) labor is used, white capitalists can at least be certain of making a psychic gain. If this gain is larger than the monetary loss that capitalists incur from discrimination, their net income will rise as well. Since white workers and white society as a whole also make an unconditional gain, the possibility of side payments or bribes from white workers to white capitalists, to induce the latter to take discriminatory action, also exists.

Notes

1. Thurow (1969), p. 112.
2. Becker (1971:2), Appendix to Chapter 2.

3. Cf., however, the verbal exposition of ibid., Chapter 2, (and especially p. 20) where it is assumed that the Negro sector exports labor. Cf. also the Appendix, p. 35.

4. Ibid., p. 20.

5. As Chiplin & Sloane (1974) p. 386, as well as (1976) p.60 and note p. 148, have noted, Becker himself was of the opinion that the discrimination coefficient had more in common with transportation costs than with tariffs: 'If we compare discrimination with tariffs, we find that, although some of their effects are similar, other effects are quite different. Discrimination always decreases both societies' net incomes, while a tariff of the appropriate size can, as Bickerdike long ago pointed out, increase the levying society's net income. A tariff operates by driving a wedge between the price a society pays for imported goods and the price each individual member pays; it does not create any distinction between net income and total command over goods. Discrimination does create such a distinction and does not drive a wedge between private and social prices. Discrimination has more in common with transportation costs than with tariffs' (Becker (1971:2), note, p. 21).

In the preface to the second edition of *The Economics of Discrimination* he furthermore states: 'I was well aware from optimal tariff and general monopoly theory that a reduction in trade could increase the *money* incomes of say the majority group, but I considered this irrelevant if trade were reduced because of tastes for discrimination. It would become relevant if trade were reduced because of collective action by various members of the majority to benefit themselves at the expense of others, including the minority. These actions include price discrimination by firms with monopsonistic power in labor markets, restrictions on entry by strong trade unions, and the use of government power to further various interests' (ibid., p. 6).

6. Becker assumes that the Negro group has no taste for discrimination. Hence, net and money incomes do not differ in this sector.

7. The change in white production is given by

$$\frac{dQ_W}{dK_E} = f_W^K E,$$

the change in payments to capital in the white sector by

$$\frac{d(K_R f_W^K)}{dK_E} = -f_W^K + K_R f_W^{KK} E = f_W^K E - K_R f_W^{KK}$$

and the changes in wage payments by

$$\frac{d(\bar{L}_W f_W^L)}{dK_E} = \bar{L}_W f_W^{LK} E = -\bar{L}_W f_W^{LK},$$

so that, by (3:11), the three expressions cancel.

8. This point was first noted by Krueger (1963), note, p. 481. It is also implicit in Toikka (1976), p. 476: 'If we take the discrimination coefficient as measuring relative costs or benefits and do not use it as an index of absolute pleasure or pain, then we can conclude nothing about how discrimination . . . affects the

welfare of the group discriminating . . . We may conclude merely that they are maximizing utility and that the discrimination coefficient indicates how much discrimination is optimal from their private point of view.'

9. Becker (1971:2), p. 15, claims that a (positive) discrimination coefficient can take on any value up to plus infinity. For practical purposes, however, it must be considered to be below one. A value exceeding one would mean that the marginal productivity of capital in one of the sectors must be negative (cf. (3:5)).

10. Schoeffler (1952, pp. 883-84).

11. See ibid. and, for a comment, Rothenberg (1961).

12. This possibility was originally suggested by Thurow (1969), p. 116: 'If racial prejudice already exists among whites but they have not been able to act upon it, introducing discrimination can give them a clear gain in net utilities. Real incomes can increase . . . and reducing the number of Negroes with whom whites are forced to associate results in higher utility from the physical distance argument of the utility function. Fewer Negroes means less disutility from associating with them. The result is a clear white gain in net utility.' Thurow refers to the case when labor is mobile between the sectors, but an analogous result is obtained in the present case.

13. See Chapter 4, pp. 113-15, for a formal proof and for the economic explanation.

14. Becker (1971:2), p. 15.

15. See Toikka (1976). Toikka uses the term 'favoritism' instead of nepotism.

16. It is seen that in the case of nepotism $d_W^K(\text{nep})$ can take on any value between zero and minus infinity without requiring any marginal productivities to be negative.

17. Becker (1971:2), p. 16.

18. Toikka (1976) uses a different formulation. When discussing the Becker case, he employs the equilibrium condition (T for Toikka)

$$f_W^K(1 + d_W^{KT}) = f_N^K.$$

This equilibrium condition is difficult to interpret, however. Becker uses a similar formulation for the case where employers discriminate against a particular factor (Becker 1971:2, Chapter 3). However, what will be discussed presently is the case where factor owners — white capitalists — discriminate, and not employers. It is hard to give any other meaning to Toikka's condition than that of nepotism if the equilibrium condition is one of net returns.

Toikka's equilibrium condition is presented with a reference to Becker's definition of the market discrimination coefficient:

$$\text{MDC} = \frac{w_W - w_N}{w_N},$$

where the w:s represent equilibrium wage rates for whites and Negroes, respectively (see Becker 1971, pp. 17-18). In Toikka's paper, the equivalent of Becker's MDC is

$$d_W^{KT} = \frac{f_N^K - f_W^K}{f_W^K}.$$

However, the two are fundamentally different. The MDC is not identical to the discrimination coefficient d_W^K. The latter is a measure of the *taste* for discrimination of white capital owners – what causes them to discriminate against Negro labor – while the MDC is a measure of the *outcome* of the discriminatory practices. The factor being discriminated against in this case is Negro labor, and hence the MDC has to be defined in terms of wage differences, rather than differences in the return on capital:

$$MDC = \frac{f_W^L - f_N^L}{f_N^L}.$$

Toikka has not observed this distinction. Instead he defines the MDC in terms of a difference between the money returns to white capital used in the Negro and the white sectors, respectively, and thereafter equates his MDC with d_W^K. The correct procedure is to depart from the behavior of white capital owners, which leads to the equilibrium condition

$$f_W^K = (1 - d_W^K) f_N^K.$$

From the *practical* point of view it does not matter whether we use Toikka's or Becker's equilibrium condition. We have that

$$d_W^K = \frac{f_N^K - f_W^K}{f_N^K}.$$

and in Toikka's formulation,

$$d_W^{KT} = \frac{f_N^K - f_W^K}{f_W^K}.$$

Here,

$$d_W^{KT} = \frac{d_W^K}{1 - d_W^K},$$

i.e., d_W^{KT} is a monotonic transformation of d_W^K. Viewed in this manner (disregarding the misinterpretation of the MDC) the two measures are two different ways of describing the same preferences.

19. Becker (1971:2), p. 15.
20. Ibid., p. 20.
21. The reasoning assumes that the new technology is not transferred to the white sector. Even if this should be the case, however, the same type of conclusions apply. Capital exports from the white sector do not increase, while the psychic costs per unit of export capital increase in spite of the fact that the ratio between Negro labor and export capital remains constant.

22. An obvious analogy here is busing. White American parents presumably resent the fact for the most part that their children are bused into a black neighborhood and would not greatly change their views on this type of integration, whether the ratio of black to white children in 'black' schools were doubled or cut in half.

A third possible interpretation of tastes for discrimination is given by Thurow (1969), p. 117: 'Discrimination is not simply demanding a premium to associate with Negroes, as described by Becker. The discriminator may want to work with, buy from, or hire Negroes, but he insists on specifying the relationships under which the two parties will meet and how the Negro will respond. Perhaps it is more accurate to say that whites maximize a utility function with social distance rather than physical distance as one of its arguments. A desire for social distance can lead to a very different set of actions. The discriminator may prefer to hire Negro maids, Negro garbage collectors, or to work with Negroes if he can be in a position of authority. He may also prefer to hire Negro labor if it can be exploited to increase his own profits.' As seen, this type of interpretation calls for a completely different type of analysis than the one pursued in the present chapter.

4 THE PECUNIARY BECKER MODEL

The analysis of Chapter 3 removed two contradictory features from the Becker model, the changing preferences and the tying of the discrimination coefficient to the marginal productivity of capital in the Negro sector. In the present chapter, we will proceed to deal with a third difficulty in the Beckerian analysis: one which is due to the fact that the latter builds on tastes for discrimination.

We will begin with a discussion of why the introduction of tastes in the Becker model, assuming that everybody does not have identical tastes, leads to results which are not likely to be observed in real life: complete segregation of the labor force or absence of discrimination in competitive industries.

Given interpersonal differences in tastes for discrimination, discriminatory practices are not likely to survive in the long run. Consequently, in order to remove instability, tastes are eliminated from the model for the remainder of the chapter (and the book). With tastes for discrimination no longer present, discriminatory action is motivated solely by pecuniary economic gains. Within the framework of this model it can be shown that white capitalists can no longer be considered as the discriminating group, since they suffer a loss from discriminatory practices.

In the third section, we discuss the case when labor, rather than capital, is the mobile factor. The conclusion that white capitalists lose from attempting to discriminate against Negro labor by applying labor market segregation (as opposed to capital market segregation as in the Becker formulation) is shown to be not necessarily valid. Here, as in the case of capital market segregation, white workers emerge as the group which has an economic interest in maintaining discriminatory practices.

Problems with the Taste Approach

The rationale of the original Becker model (and the analysis of the present Chapter 3 as well), builds on the assumption that white capitalists — the discriminating group — who have a taste for discrimination (a dislike for associating their capital with Negroes) incur a psychic cost when some of their capital is put to work in the Negro sector of the economy. For several reasons, however, the introduction of tastes and psychic costs into the analysis of economic discrimination appears as a somewhat artificial approach. In the first place, the basic assumption made by Becker is that tastes for discrimination arise out of a desire on the part of white capital owners not to associate with Negro labor. However, in the approach where white capital is exported to the Negro sector (when labor is immobile between sectors) to be worked there by Negro labor without any active participation by white capitalists, the extent of contact between the two groups must be regarded as minimal. Consequently, this type of 'tastes' can hardly be said to provide a satisfactory explanation of the causes of discrimination.[1]

The same type of criticism applies to the variant which relies on nepotism instead of tastes. The comparison of a situation where white capitalists associate with labor from their own racial group (and derive a psychic benefit out of this association) with one where they export capital to the Negro sector without being involved in production operations — that is a situation of no association with the Negro community — strains the bounds of reality.

In both cases, the Becker model contradicts a common-sense approach. In common-sense terms we expect prejudice to arise when Negro labor is exported to the white sector so as to make physical association with white capitalists and laborers a necessity. By the same token, the case of capital export from the discriminating to the discriminated group is hardly the most likely source of discriminatory practices. Prejudice is likely to be rooted first and foremost among white workers rather than among the capital owners, since the former group may conceive of Negro workers as competitors who are felt to take 'white' jobs and to depress the going wage rate. Thus, with tastes, we should expect that it is white laborers rather than white capitalists who promote discriminatory measures.

Tastes for discrimination among white labor can be analyzed with the same methods as those used in Chapter 3. It can then be shown that, provided that Negro labor is paid the same pecuniary wage as white workers, the latter will derive a net gain from the exclusion of Negro competitors from working in the white sector (that is by segregating the labor market) while white capitalists would suffer a loss.[2] The results are, however, no different from what would be obtained if no tastes were present.

However, such an analysis does not solve our problem. At this stage an analysis which primarily attributes discriminatory practices to tastes runs into a fundamental obstacle of which Becker himself was very aware. If we assume that white labor and Negro labor are perfect substitutes for each other, we will never find a situation where a mixed labor force, with whites being paid higher pecuniary wages, is hired by employers displaying no prejudice of their own:

> Each employer must pay a higher wage rate to a member of W if he is to work with N rather than with other W. An income-maximizing employer would never hire a mixed work force, since he would have to pay the W members of this force a larger wage rate than members of W working solely with other W. He hires only W if W's wage rate is less than N's, and only N if N's is less than W's. He is indifferent between hiring them if and only if their wage rates are equal. Both N and W can be employed (in different firms) only if each employer is indifferent between them. Therefore, if a perfect substitute for N has a taste for discrimination against N, market segregation rather than market discrimination results: a firm employs either teams of N or teams of W; W and N are not employed in the same work force.[3]

It does not help to introduce tastes for discrimination among white employers because the analysis would then have to proceed on the unlikely premise that all employers have the same discrimination coefficient. Otherwise those with lower coefficients could always undersell their competitors due to the lower monetary costs incurred by a lesser degree of discrimination. The market discrimination coefficient would in the long run always equal the lowest individual coefficient.[4] The Becker employer discrimination model 'predicts the absence of the phenomenon it was designed to explain', concludes Kenneth Arrow, somewhat ironically, with reference to tastes for discrimination among employers.[5]

Other economists, of a more conservative bent, have, however, drawn other conclusions from similar premises. Thus, Milton Friedman, in *Capitalism and Freedom*, concludes that discrimination in economic life is a phenomenon which goes hand in hand with monopolistic tendencies rather than with competition. Competition in the market-place, with its insistence on economically efficient solutions, is the best guarantee that discrimination will not rear its ugly head. According to Friedman competitive capitalism, during the course of history, has done more than any other social force in eliminating differences in wages and employment along, for example, racial lines:

> It is a striking historical fact that the development of capitalism has

been acccompanied by a major reduction in the extent to which particular religious, racial, or social groups have operated under special handicaps in respect of their economic activities; have, as the saying goes, been discriminated against . . . The Southern states after the Civil War took many measures to impose legal restrictions on Negroes. One measure which was never taken on any scale was the establishment of barriers to the ownership of either real or personal property. The failure to impose such barriers clearly did not reflect any special concern to avoid restrictions on Negroes. It reflected, rather, a basic belief in private property which was so strong that it overrode the desire to discriminate against Negroes. The maintenance of the general rules of private property and of capitalism have been a major source of opportunities for Negroes and have permitted them to make greater progress than they otherwise could have made. To take a more general example, the preserves of discrimination in any society are the areas that are most monopolistic in character, whereas discrimination against groups of particular color or religion is least in those areas where there is the greatest freedom of competition.[6]

Still, in practice, discrimination takes place within competitive industries as well as in monopolies. The evidence for the assertion that more discrimination takes place in monopolistic than in competitive industries, quoted by Becker, is limited to the observation that proportionately fewer non-whites are employed in monopolistic industries than in competitive ones in the United States,[7] but, as Michael Reich has pointed out, this evidence is hardly convincing, since it is open to many different interpretations.[8] In addition, it may be pointed out that in a country like South Africa, where racial discrimination has characterized economic life since the very beginning of white colonization, it has hardly mattered at all whether the industry in question has been a competitive or a monopolistic one.[9]

To conclude, it seems as if the taste approach to economic discrimination is not a very realistic one, even when the Becker model is amended, as in Chapter 3, in order to remove the logical contradictions of the model itself. In practice, whites and Negroes work in the same firms, discrimination obviously takes place in competitive as well as in monopolistic industries, and discrimination based on employer tastes is inherently unstable under competitive conditions. We will therefore in the remainder of the book drop the assumption that tastes are the root of unequal treatment. Instead we will go on to examine the effects of discrimination in pecuniary income terms in different settings, in order to find out whether such an analysis can yield a more convincing explanation of the causes and effects of unequal treatment of different racial, sex or other groups.[10] We will begin with an examination of the model by Anne Krueger, which builds directly on Becker's approach.

The Krueger Approach

A formulation in Beckerian terms of a theory of economic discrimination that is not based upon tastes has been made by Anne Krueger.[11] The only difference between the Krueger and Becker models is that Krueger works exclusively in pecuniary terms. Apart from that, all the assumptions employed by Becker (stated in Chapter 3 above) are retained. This light difference, however, proves sufficient to reverse some of Becker's fundamental welfare conclusions.

This is most apparent in the case of the effect of discrimination on white incomes. In pecuniary terms, these are

$$Y_W = K_R f_W^K + \bar{L}_W f_W^L + K_E f_N^K, \qquad (4:1)$$

and when discrimination is applied, we find that (with equal factor rewards at the outset),

$$\frac{dY_W}{dK_E} = K_E f_N^{KK} < 0. \qquad (4:2)$$

When a strictly pecuniary approach is used, the white group as a whole stands to gain from applying discriminatory measures against Negroes. This runs contrary to the Becker theorem that there are no gains to be derived from discrimination for the white group but corresponds well with the result obtained in our reformulated Becker model (equation (3:45) in Chapter 3).

The same parallels are retained in the case of white factor incomes. The pecuniary incomes of white workers and capitalists respectively are given by

$$Y_{LW} = \bar{L}_W f_W^L \qquad (4:3)$$

114   *The Pecuniary Becker Model*

and:

$$Y_{K_W} = K_R f_W^K + K_E f_N^K. \tag{4:4}$$

Differentiating (4:3) with respect to K_E yields

$$\frac{dY_{L_W}}{dK_E} = \bar{L}_W f_W^{LK_E}. \tag{4:5}$$

White workers gain from discrimination, since this puts more capital at their disposal. Performing the same operation on (4:4) gives

$$\frac{dY_{K_W}}{dK_E} = K_E f_N^{KK} - K_R f_W^{KK}, \tag{4:6}$$

provided that returns on capital in the two sectors are equal in the absence of discrimination.

Here, the second term on the right-hand side (sign included) is positive, while the first one is negative, due to diminishing returns to capital in the two sectors. However, using the fact that the two production functions are identical and homogeneous of degree one, we may unequivocally determine the sign of expression (4:6). Then, f_W^K is a function of $K_R/\bar{L}_W$ and f_N^K is a function of $(\bar{K}_N + K_E)/\bar{L}_N$ and

$$f_W^K = f_N^K \iff \frac{K_R}{\bar{L}_W} = \frac{\bar{K}_N + K_E}{\bar{L}_N}. \tag{4:7}$$

The derivatives of the marginal product of capital may be written as

$$f_W^{KK} = \frac{df_W^K}{d(K_R/\bar{L}_W)} \frac{d(K_R/\bar{L}_W)}{dK_R} = \frac{df_W^K}{d(K_R/\bar{L}_W)} \frac{1}{\bar{L}_W} \tag{4:8}$$

and

$$\begin{aligned}f_N^{KK} &= \frac{df_N^K}{d[(\bar{K}_N + K_E)/\bar{L}_N]} \frac{d[(\bar{K}_N + K_E)/\bar{L}_N]}{dK_E} \\ &= \frac{df_N^K}{d[(\bar{K}_N + K_E)/\bar{L}_N]} \frac{1}{\bar{L}_N}.\end{aligned} \tag{4:9}$$

Equation (4:6) may thus be reformulated as

$$\frac{dY_{K_W}}{dK_E} = \frac{K_E}{\bar{L}_N} \frac{df_N^K}{d[(\bar{K}_N + K_E)/\bar{L}_N]} - \frac{K_R}{\bar{L}_W} \frac{df_W^K}{d(K_R/\bar{L}_W)}. \qquad (4:10)$$

The two derivatives are equal since

$$\frac{\bar{K}_N + K_E}{\bar{L}_N} = \frac{K_R}{\bar{L}_W} \qquad (4:11)$$

in the absence of discrimination.

Hence, substituting (4:11) into (4:10), we have that

$$\frac{dY_{K_W}}{dK_E} = \left(\frac{K_E}{\bar{L}_N} - \frac{K_R}{\bar{L}_W}\right) \frac{df_W^K}{d(K_R/\bar{L}_W)}. \qquad (4:12)$$

Furthermore, $df_W^K/d(K_R/\bar{L}_W) < 0$ and $K_E/\bar{L}_N - K_R/\bar{L}_W < 0$, since $K_R/\bar{L}_W = (\bar{K}_N + K_E)/\bar{L}_N$ and $\bar{K}_N > 0$.

Therefore $dY_{K_W}/dK_E > 0$. White capital owners lose on discrimination.[12] This is the result used without proof in Chapter 3.

The economic explanation of this result is that, for a given stock of white-owned capital, incomes will be maximized when returns are equal in the two sectors. (As long as this is not the case, a gain can be made by reallocating capital to the sector with the higher return.) With identical, linearly homogeneous production functions, equalization of returns takes place when the two sectors have the same capital-labor ratio. (Linear homogeneity ensures that returns depend only on factor intensities.) This is the situation in the absence of discrimination. When capital exports are subsequently reduced to obtain discrimination, a discrepancy in capital–labor ratios, and hence in returns to capital, arises between the sectors. White capital incomes consequently fall. (Adding the expressions for the changes in white labor (4:5) and capital (4:6) incomes yields the change in total white incomes (4:2) which is negative since, due to the linear homogeneity of the white production function, the terms $\bar{L}_W f_W^{LKE}$ ($= -\bar{L}_W f_W^{LK}$) and $-K_R f_W^{KK}$ cancel. Worker gains outweigh capitalist losses.)

When the impact of discrimination on Negro incomes is examined, we find that there is no difference between the pecuniary and the net model, as long as we do not allow for any tastes in the Negro sector. Hence, we still have our old expressions (here renumbered):

$$\frac{dY_N}{dK_E} = -K_E f_N^{KK} = -\frac{dY_W}{dK_E} > 0, \qquad (4:13)$$

$$\frac{dY_{L_N}}{dK_E} = \bar{L}_N f_N^{LK} > 0, \qquad (4:14)$$

and

$$\frac{dY_{K_N}}{dK_E} = \bar{K}_N f_N^{KK} < 0. \qquad (4:15)$$

The Negro sector as a whole and Negro workers lose, but Negro capitalists gain, by discrimination.

Table 4.1 summarizes the results of the Krueger model. The most

Table 4.1: Welfare Effects of Discrimination in the Krueger Model

Effects on pecuniary incomes of:	
Whites	gain
White capitalists	loss
White labor	gain
Negroes	loss
Negro capitalists	gain
Negro labor	loss

important point to make is that white capitalists lose by withdrawing their capital from the Negro sector.[13] The assumption that the discriminating white group attempts to raise the income of the group as a whole by discriminatory practices implies that consensus exists between workers and capitalists in the white sector. In the Krueger formulation, there are no incentives for white capitalists to begin to discriminate unless a redistribution of incomes in favor of the capitalist class can be arranged with the workers, the group who stands to gain. In practice such a redistribution is, however, less likely to take place. This also reduces the explanatory value of the model where capital is exported while labor is immobile, since it is hard to think of any good reasons why white capitalists should display not only benevolence towards the white labor group but also altruism in the sense that for the workers to reap the gains of discrimination, the capitalists must be prepared to face a loss.[14]

An Alternative Approach: Labor Market Segregation

The Krueger model follows the Becker approach in the sense that it assumes the supply of labor to be fixed in both sectors and holds white capital owners to be the agents of discrimination. In the first section of the present chapter, it was pointed out that such an approach violates common sense knowledge with respect to the circumstances under which discrimination takes place. We should expect labor rather than capital to be the mobile factor and look for discrimination where Negro labor is working side by side with white labor in the same sector. In this type of situation, a different form of discrimination, which may be labeled 'discriminatory labor market segregation' (henceforth shortened to 'labor market segregation'), may arise. The term 'labor market segregation' denotes a reduction (exclusion) of the inflow of Negro labor into the white sector as compared with the case of equal returns to labor in both sectors.

Becker has the following comment to make on his 'trade' approach to economic discrimination:

> Suppose labor enters the United States from abroad and that some United States capital (c_t) is employed with this labor. A well-known economic theorem states that United States citizens must (economically) benefit from immigration as long as there is diminishing marginal productivity of labor, since intra-marginal immigrants raise the productivity of American capital. The net income of United States citizens is an increasing function of the amount of immigration, which can be measured by c_t, the amount of capital employed with immigrants. This discussion shows that treating discrimination as a problem in trade and migration is far from artificial, since they are closely and profoundly related.[15]

The implication of this comment is that capital and labor market segregation should have identical effects. The validity of the comment, however, depends on the assumptions that are made about the labor market. Prior to the onset of labor market segregation, wages are equal in the white and Negro sectors. However, with segregation they will differ. Two possibilities then suggest themselves:

(1) Those Negro workers who remain in the white sector are paid according to their opportunity cost outside the sector, that is they receive a wage which is equal to the marginal value product of labor in the Negro sector.
(2) The workers are paid according to their marginal productivity in the white sector. (White and Negro workers receive the same wage when working in this sector.)

The implications with regard to gains and losses from labor market segregation differ depending on the assumption that is made. Becker's assertion is (approximately) true in the first case, if the quotation refers to the white community as a whole, whereas if it refers to white capitalists only the second assumption should be used.

Equal Negro Wages in Both Sectors

With equal renumeration of Negro labor in the two sectors and no capital exports ($K_R = \bar{K}_W$), white incomes are given by

$$Y_W = \bar{K}_W f_W^K + (\bar{L}_W + L_E)f_W^L - L_E f_N^L, \qquad (4:16)$$

where L_E and L_R denote the parts of Negro labor employed in the white and Negro sectors, respectively ($L_E + L_R = \bar{L}_N$). Differentiating (4:16) with respect to L_E, applying Euler's theorem (and since factor prices are equal at the outset), gives

$$\frac{dY_W}{dL_E} = -L_E f_N^{LL_E} \qquad (4:17)$$

which with diminishing returns to labor in the Negro sector is negative. Hence, the white group will gain from labor market segregation — a parallel to the Krueger result regarding the impact of discrimination on white money incomes.

Performing the same analysis with respect to Negro incomes

$$Y_N = \bar{K}_N f_N^K + (L_R + L_E)f_N^L, \qquad (4:18)$$

where

$$L_R = \bar{L}_N - L_E, \tag{4:19}$$

gives

$$\frac{dY_N}{dL_E} = L_E f_N^{LL_E}, \tag{4:20}$$

meaning that the Negro group as a whole will lose the same amount that the white group gains.

We will now study the effects on factor incomes of this type of discrimination. Assuming that the difference between the marginal product of Negro labor and its wage accrues to the capital owners (presently taken to be employers as well):

$$Y_{K_W} = \bar{K}_W f_W^K + L_E (f_W^L - f_N^L), \tag{4:21}$$

and

$$\frac{dY_{K_W}}{dL_E} = \bar{K}_W f_W^{KL} + f_W^L - f_N^L + L_E (f_W^{LL} + f_N^{LL}). \tag{4:22}$$

Starting from a situation without discrimination, with $f_W^L = f_N^L$, using Euler's theorem:

$$\bar{K}_W f_W^{KL} + (\bar{L}_W + L_E) f_W^{LL} \equiv 0, \tag{4:23}$$

we obtain

$$\frac{dY_{K_W}}{dL_E} = L_E f_N^{LL} - \bar{L}_W f_W^{LL}. \tag{4:24}$$

Expression (4:24) may be reformulated:

$$\frac{dY_{K_W}}{dL_E} = L_E \frac{df_N^L}{d(L_R/\bar{K}_N)} \frac{d(L_R/\bar{K}_N)}{dL_R} - \bar{L}_W \frac{df_W^L}{d[(\bar{L}_W + L_E)/\bar{K}_W]} \frac{d[(\bar{L}_W + L_E)/\bar{K}_W]}{dL_E}. \tag{4:25}$$

120 The Pecuniary Becker Model

Since the two production functions are identical and the marginal productivities of labor are equal at the outset,

$$\frac{df_W^L}{d[(\bar{L}_W + L_E)/\bar{K}_W]} = \frac{df_N^L}{d(L_R/\bar{K}_N)}, \qquad (4{:}26)$$

and we obtain finally

$$\frac{dY_{K_W}}{dL_E} = \left(\frac{L_E}{\bar{K}_N} - \frac{\bar{L}_W}{\bar{K}_W}\right) \frac{df_W^L}{d[(\bar{L}_W + L_E)/\bar{K}_W]}. \qquad (4{:}27)$$

It is not possible to tell whether white capital owners gain or lose from discrimination, since we do not know the sign of the expression within parentheses. However, since $\bar{K}_W > \bar{K}_N$, $L_E > \bar{L}_W$ is sufficient to ensure a gain.

Differentiating the expression for white labor incomes,

$$Y_{L_W} = \bar{L}_W f_W^L, \qquad (4{:}28)$$

yields

$$\frac{dY_{L_W}}{dL_E} = \bar{L}_W f_W^{LL} < 0 \qquad (4{:}29)$$

which means that white labor gains from labor market segregation.

Performing the same analysis on the Negro sector yields the following results:

$$Y_{K_N} = \bar{K}_N f_N^K \qquad (4{:}30)$$

and

$$Y_{L_N} = L_R f_N^L + L_E f_N^L, \qquad (4{:}31)$$

$$\frac{dY_{K_N}}{dL_E} = -\bar{K}_N f_N^{KL} < 0 \qquad (4{:}32)$$

and

$$\frac{dY_{L_N}}{dL_E} = -(L_R + L_E)f_N^{LL} > 0, \qquad (4:33)$$

that is Negro capital owners gain and Negro workers lose by labor market segregation.

The results of the present section are summarized in Table 4.2.

Table 4.2: Welfare Effects of Labor Market Segregation with Uniform Negro Wages

Effects on pecuniary incomes of:	
Whites	gain
White capitalists	indeterminate; gain if $L_E > \bar{L}_W$
White labor	gain
Negroes	loss
Negro capitalists	gain
Negro labor	loss

The easiest effects to explain are those on labor incomes. When Negro labor leaves the white sector, the marginal productivity of white labor, and hence the white wage rate, increases. By the same token, Negro wages must fall, since more Negro workers are pushed into the Negro sector, and the wage rate for Negroes in both sectors is determined by the marginal productivity of Negro labor in the Negro sector. Negro capitalists, in turn, gain by the same measure, since with more labor to handle their capital, the marginal productivity of the latter will increase.

The effects on white capital income are more complicated. In the first place, the marginal productivity of capital will fall in the white sector as Negro labor is made to leave. Against this, however, we must set the gain that white capitalists make by capturing the difference between the marginal productivities of labor in the two sectors, since the Negroes working in the white sector are paid according to the marginal productivity of labor in the *Negro* sector.

The latter effect can be split into two components. The first one consists of the change in the difference between marginal productivities multiplied by the change in the number of Negro workers in the white sector. This component equals zero since, at the outset, no discrimination takes place so that the marginal productivity of labor is the same in the two sectors. Thus, white capitalists always benefit from being able to acquire the difference in marginal productivities.

Whether this gain is large enough to outweigh the loss due to the falling marginal productivity of capital, as expression (4:27) shows, depends to a large extent on how many Negro workers were orginally employed in the white sector. If, as is reasonable to assume, the white capital stock, $\bar{K}_W$, is larger than the Negro one, $\bar{K}_N$, a sufficient condition for white capitalists to gain from labor market segregation is that the original number of Negro workers in the white sector, L_E, exceeds that of white workers, $\bar{L}_W$.

Finally, by adding the changes in white labor and capital incomes (expressions (4:29) and (4:22)), it can be seen that the linear homogeneity of the production function of the white sector ensures that the effect of labor market segregation on total white incomes is always positive.

If we compare Table 4.2 with Table 4.1, we find that the qualitative results of capital and labor market segregation differ only in the case of white capital incomes. In the Krueger analysis a loss is always incurred. Given that Negro workers in the white sector receive a wage equal to the marginal value product of labor in the Negro sector and labor markets are segregated, a gain might accrue to the white capital-owning class if the number of Negro workers in the white sector is high enough in comparison with the white labor force. Hence, the parallel drawn by Becker holds for the two groups as a whole but not necessarily for the functional distribution of incomes.

Uniform Wages in the White Sector

In the preceding section, it was assumed that Negroes earn the same wage irrespective of whether they work in the white or in the Negro sector, the wage level being determined by the marginal productivity of labor in the latter. Given the latter assumption, it was shown that the parallel between capital and labor market segregation suggested by Becker holds (but only approximately). If it is assumed instead that all workers, regardless of skin color, receive the same wage in the white sector, this conclusion no longer holds.

The possibility of equal pay for all workers in the white sector regardless of group membership is considerably more realistic than the one analyzed above — both from the empirical and from the theoretical point of view. Beginning with the former aspect, a good example is furnished by the immigration to Sweden from the Mediterranean area. Immigration is restricted (a case of labor market segmentation in terms of the present model) but the migrants who are permitted to enter Sweden receive approximately the same wages as Swedish workers and much higher wages than in their countries of origin.[16] In the United States, newly arrived immigrants have lower wages than non-immigrants[17] but higher wages than in their countries of origin. There is, however, a much wider discrepancy between their wages in the United States and what they would receive in their home countries, than between their wages in the United States and those of non-immigrants there. The case of uniform wages in the white sector combined with the restricted immigration of the discriminated group is more realistic than the case of equal wages for the discriminated group in both sectors.

The theoretical difficulties that beset an argument which maintains that the wages of Negroes working in the white sector are not determined by supply and demand in the labor market of that sector, but by what takes place in the Negro sector, are even greater. If the white sector is competitive, it is hard to understand why competition among white employers would not raise Negro wage rates to the level prevailing in the white sector. As long as the Negro wage rate in the white sector remains below the white one and the two types of labor are perfect substitutes, employers (capitalists in our model) will always gain by hiring Negroes instead of whites. Competition between employers would, however, ensure that all such gains would be only temporary. For the difference in wage levels to persist, some mechanism or institution that prevents competition from taking its course is required. The Negro workers must be distributed to white firms according to criteria other than competitiveness. Some type of centrally-directed economy would be called for. The United States — the example given by Becker in the quotation above — is hardly such an economy.

With this, let us turn to the implications of the case when Negroes and whites in the white sector have the same wage — one which is determined by the forces of demand and supply in that sector. Assuming this to be the case, we have the following expression for white incomes:

$$Y_W = \bar{K}_W f_W^K + (\bar{L}_W + L_E) f_W^L - L_E f_W^L, \tag{4:34}$$

and

$$\frac{dY_W}{dL_E} = -L_E f_W^{LL} > 0, \tag{4:35}$$

124 *The Pecuniary Becker Model*

while Negro incomes are given by

$$Y_N = \bar{K}_N f_N^K + L_R f_N^L + L_E f_W^L, \qquad (4:36)$$

and

$$\frac{dY_N}{dL_E} = L_E f_W^{LL} < 0. \qquad (4:37)$$

In this case the Negro group as a whole will gain the same amount that the white group loses.

Going on to factor incomes, the effects on white capital and labor incomes are given by:

$$\frac{dY_{K_W}}{dL_E} = \bar{K}_W f_W^{KL} > 0 \qquad (4:38)$$

and

$$\frac{dY_{L_W}}{dL_E} = \bar{L}_W f_W^{LL} < 0, \qquad (4:39)$$

which means that white capital owners lose and white workers gain on this form of segregation.

Negro capital incomes are given by

$$Y_{K_N} = \bar{K}_N f_N^K \qquad (4:40)$$

and

$$\frac{dY_{K_N}}{dL_E} = -\bar{K}_N f_N^{KL} < 0, \qquad (4:41)$$

which means that Negro capital owners gain from discrimination.

The expression for Negro labor incomes is

$$Y_{L_N} = L_R f_N^L + L_E f_W^L \tag{4:42}$$

and

$$\frac{dY_{L_N}}{dL_E} = L_E f_W^{LL} - L_R f_N^{LL}. \tag{4:43}$$

The marginal productivities of labor in the two sectors are equal at the outset which, with identical, linearly homogeneous production functions, implies that

$$\frac{df_W^L}{d[(\bar{L}_W + L_E)/\bar{K}_W]} = \frac{df_N^L}{d(L_R/\bar{K}_N)}. \tag{4:44}$$

As

$$f_W^{LL} = \frac{df_W^L}{d[(\bar{L}_W + L_E)/\bar{K}_W]} \frac{d[(\bar{L}_W + L_E)/\bar{K}_W]}{dL_E}$$

$$= \frac{df_W^L}{d[(\bar{L}_W + L_E)/\bar{K}_W]} \frac{1}{\bar{K}_W} \tag{4:45}$$

and

$$f_N^{LL} = \frac{df_N^L}{d(L_R/\bar{K}_N)} \frac{d(L_R/\bar{K}_N)}{dL_R} = \frac{df_N^L}{d(L_R/\bar{K}_N)} \frac{1}{\bar{K}_N}, \tag{4:46}$$

we get

$$\frac{dY_{L_N}}{dL_E} = \left(\frac{L_E}{\bar{K}_W} - \frac{L_R}{\bar{K}_N}\right) \frac{df_W^L}{d[(\bar{L}_W + L_E)/\bar{K}_W]}. \tag{4:47}$$

The initial equality of the marginal productivities of labor implies that

$$\frac{L_E + \bar{L}_W}{\bar{K}_W} = \frac{L_R}{\bar{K}_N}, \qquad (4:48)$$

which means that $L_E/\bar{K}_W < L_R/\bar{K}_N$, so that the expression within parentheses is negative and dY_{L_N}/dL_E is positive as $df_W^L/d[(\bar{L}_W + L_E)/\bar{K}_W]$ is negative. Negro workers lose from discrimination.

The effects of labor market segregation when Negro workers receive the same wages as white workers when employed in the white sector are summarized in Table 4.3.

Table 4.3: Welfare Effects of Labor Market Segregation with Uniform Wages in the White Sector

Effects on pecuniary incomes of:	
Whites	loss
White capitalists	loss
White labor	gain
Negroes	gain
Negro capitalists	gain
Negro labor	loss

When Negro labor is removed from the white sector, the marginal productivity of capital falls in this sector and rises in the Negro economy. Thus, white capital owners lose and their Negro counterparts gain. Moreover, the marginal productivity of labor rises in the white but falls in the Negro sector. This means that white workers are better off with labor market segregation. On the other hand, Negro workers lose. As long as wages differ between the two sectors, Negro workers can gain by a reallocation to the sector with the higher wage rate. Thus, Negro labor income is maximized when wages are equal in the white and in the Negro sector. With identical, linearly homogeneous production functions, this takes place when the capital-labor ratios are equal, i.e. in the absence of discrimination. With labor market segregation, this equality is lost. Hence, Negro labor incomes must fall. Finally, the changes in total income are derived from the addition of factor income changes for either group. The linearly homogeneous production functions allow us to use the identities derived from Euler's theorem. The results indicate that the white group incurs a loss while Negroes make an overall gain.

A comparison of these results with those presented in Tables 4.1 and 4.2 shows that the differences between the Krueger results and the results of labor market segregation with uniform wages in the white sector are larger than those between capital and labor market segregation when Negro wages are equal in both sectors. With a single wage rate in the white sector, the white group as a whole loses while the Negro group gains. These results are completely contrary to those of the capital market segregation case. Here, the parallel drawn by Becker holds only for capital and labor incomes. For white society as a whole the effects are opposite those of capital market segregation.

It should also be noted that when Negro labor receives a wage equal to that of white labor when working in the white sector, white capitalists lose by restricting the amount of Negro workers permitted in the sector. Hence, neither here nor in the Krueger case is it possible to find any mechanisms which from an egoistic point of view would induce these capitalists to advocate discriminatory measures directed against Negroes.

Conclusions

In the first section of the present chapter, the Becker approach to discrimination was criticized because it is based on tastes. It was shown that such an approach leads to predictions regarding the form and distribution of discrimination that are likely to run counter to what we find in the real world. It was concluded that tastes should be omitted from the analysis.

Thereafter the model by Anne Krueger, where discrimination is caused by a desire to maximize pecuniary incomes, was reviewed, and it was seen that the discriminating group — white capitalists — would incur a loss from discrimination. The analysis also extended the Krueger model to the case where discrimination takes the form of labor market segregation, that is exclusion of Negro labor from the white sector. Comparisons were made between this type of discrimination and that which is caused by withdrawal of capital from the minority sector (capital market segregation). It was possible to identify the groups that gained and lost in the white and Negro communities. As a result we now know which groups are likely to advocate discrimination and which are not. The results of the analysis are very clear on this point. In the original Becker formulation, it is the white capitalist group that decides the amount of capital to be exported to the Negro sector and hence also the extent of discrimination. In the introductory section of the present chapter, a criticism was raised against this assumption, and in the light of the findings of the rest of the chapter, this criticism may now be extended.

We have shown that it is only in the case where Negroes receive the same wage irrespective of which sector they work in that the possibility arises for white capitalists to gain from labor market segregation. This possibility must be considered a remote one, however, since the equality of Negro wages in both sectors in the presence of discrimination requires that Negro labor in the white sector must be distributed among firms according to criteria that are not related to competitiveness.

If the alternative assumption regarding the determination of wages is applied — that everybody regardless of skin color receives the same wage within the white sector — these results no longer hold. White capital owners will always lose: from capital market segregation, labor market segregation, or from a combination of the two. This in turn makes it difficult to see why white capital owners should be actively fighting for discrimination. Instead, the Krueger model and our extension of it points to labor as the group within the white community that stands to gain from discrimination. In every one of the cases analyzed, white labor makes a pecuniary gain. Hence we should expect lobbying for discrimination to come mainly from this group. Moreover, since white capitalists are likely to lose, discrimination can be expected to take the form of labor market segregation rather than capital withdrawal which may be harder for the white workers to control. Nevertheless there remains the possibility that it may be easier for white workers to persuade white capitalists to agree to capital market segregation since, in that case, white society as a whole will gain, whereas it will lose when labor market segregation is applied. In that case, the capitalists can be compensated for their losses, but if resort is made to labor market segregation, the gains made by the workers do not suffice to compensate the capitalists unless the workers themselves are to make a loss.

A final interesting conclusion to be drawn from the present chapter is that Negro labor — the group that always loses from discrimination — is in no position to retaliate or even to mitigate the impact of discriminatory measures. A group which is the victim of discriminatory practices can be expected to unite and apply whatever measures it can to avoid the undesirable consequences of discrimination. In the 'trade' model, the only thing that Negro labor could possibly do is reduce the number of Negro immigrants to the white sector. This, however, is tantamount to applying labor market segregation, and that, as we have seen, will always result in a loss for Negro workers.

Notes

1. Cf. Marshall (1974) p. 851.
2. See Appendix 1 to the present chapter for a demonstration.
3. Becker (1971:2), p. 56.
4. Ibid., pp. 43-5. Cf. also e.g. Marshall (1974), p. 852, and Reich (1981), pp. 85-6.
5. Arrow (1972), p. 192.
6. Friedman (1962), pp. 108-9.
7. Becker (1971:2), pp. 47-50.
8. Reich (1981), pp. 86-7.
9. South African discrimination is dealt with e.g. in Hutt (1964) and Horwitz (1967). Both these authors stress government interference with the free market as one of the main causes of racial discrimination in the labor market. This does, however, not mean that the South African economy is or has been characterized mainly by monopoly (of the nontransferable kind) in different branches of production. (Competition policy in South Africa is discussed e.g. in Beacham (1974) and Spandau (1975, 1977).) A completely different (neo-Marxist) treatment is offered in Johnstone (1976). For a criticism of this book, see e.g. Yudelman (1977).
10. As mentioned in Chapter 2, the long-run instability of discrimination does not apply with the same strength in the case of nepotism. Firms where employers favor white workers for extra-economic reasons may survive in the long run. Thus, the approach in terms of nepotism cannot be ruled out as easily as the taste approach. In the rest of the present work we will, nevertheless, drop the assumption of nepotism. The capital export case has already been covered and in the labor market segregation cases to be dealt with in the present chapter, the presence or absence of nepotism does not have any effect at all on white incomes. Labor market segregation means that the number of Negroes in the white economy are reduced, but this has no impact, since nepotism refers to the association with *whites* and the number of white workers is assumed to be constant.

We will also exclude nepotism in Chapters 5-9. In Chapter 5 only the capital market segregation model would be affected. The capitalists would receive an additional (psychic) gain equal to the size of the nepotism coefficient. This is, however, analytically trivial. All one has to do is to insert the additional term $-(\bar{K}_W - K_E) d\bar{w}^x(\text{nep})$ in the expressions for capitalist income (5:22) and (5:24). In Chapters 6 and 7, a formulation in terms of nepotism would have to deal with both sectors. Here, the interesting question would be whether white (skilled) labor moves into or out of the relevant sector. In neither chapter is this known with certainty. In the simple formulation of Chapter 6 the practice of discrimination leads to the movement of both skilled and unskilled labor into agriculture at constant prices. As a result, the relative price of agricultural goods falls, which in turn induces a movement in the other direction. The net effect of these changes cannot be determined with certainty. Besides, without further specification, we do not know whether the skilled workers moving from one sector to the other will be white or Negro. In Chapter 7, the situation becomes even more complicated since factor use at given commodity prices is indeterminate.

Finally, Chapters 8 and 9 provide an application of the theories in the context of South Africa. Here nepotism is not considered to be an adequate representation of reality. Besides, one of the very purposes of those chapters is to discuss whether economic (pecuniary) gains could be behind racial discrimination in that country.

11. Krueger (1963). A model along the same lines presented by Janice Madden (1973) is discussed in Appendix 2 to the present chapter.

12. The result stated in equation (4:12) differs from the one derived by Anne Krueger (Krueger 1963, pp. 482-3, note 6). Her result is that

$$\frac{dY_{K_W}}{dK_E} = f_N^K - f_W^K + K_E f_N^{KK} - K_E f_W^{KK},$$

which, she states, equals zero (Y_{K_W} reaches a maximum) when the marginal products of capital are equal in the two sectors. The last term on the right-hand side is, however, not correctly calculated: K_R should be substituted for K_E as in our equation (4:6). dY_{K_W}/dK_E equals zero when the marginal products of capital are equal in the two sectors only when $K_E/\bar{L}_N = K_R/\bar{L}_W$. This follows from equation (4:12). Equality of the marginal products, in turn, implies that $K_R/\bar{L}_W = (\bar{K}_N + K_E)/\bar{L}_N$. Thus, Krueger's result is valid only if the Negro sector has no capital of its own.

13. The main difference between the results of the Krueger model and the constant preference Becker model analyzed in Chapter 3 concerns white capitalists. They lose in the former case whereas the result is indeterminate in the second. Schoeffler's (1952) double test does not give any conclusive results for that group. For all other categories the outcome is the same in both models.

14. Cf. also Marshall (1974), p. 851, and Reich (1981), pp. 89-90, for critical views. Krueger (1963), p. 483, makes this assumption of possible consensus or benevolence on the part of white capitalists: 'There are several possible ways in which discrimination against exporting capital to the Negroes might occur even if white capitalists had no personal taste for discrimination. For example, white capitalists may aim at maximizing income of the whole white community rather than white capitalist income only. A welfare function of this kind would be quite similar to Becker's, except that discrimination would be directed at maximizing white real income rather than avoiding the distastefulness of working with Negro factors of production.'

15. Becker (1971:2), pp. 34-5.
16. See e.g. Wadensjö (1975), pp. 6-11.
17. Cf. Smith & Newman (1977), and Sowell (1975), Chapters 3-5.

Appendix 1: Tastes for Discrimination among White Labor

In the main text of Chapter 4 it was stated that if white workers have tastes for discrimination they will derive a net gain (equal to the pecuniary gain) on discriminating against Negro workers employed in the white sector, while white capitalists will incur a loss. These propositions will presently be proved.

White net labor incomes are given by

$$Y_{L_W}^{net} = \bar{L}_W(f_W^L - d_W^L), \qquad (A4:1)$$

where d_W^L is the discrimination coefficient per white worker employed in the white sector, that is the psychic cost per white worker of working with Negro counterparts.

Differentiating (A4:1) with respect to L_E gives us an expression which shows the impact on white net labor incomes of requiring a higher pecuniary wage for working with Negroes:

$$\frac{dY_{L_W}^{net}}{dL_E} = \bar{L}_W f_W^{LL} < 0. \tag{A4:2}$$

Discrimination is advantageous for white labor. The opposite, however, is true with respect to white capitalists. White capital income is

$$Y_{K_W}^{net} = \bar{K}_W f_W^K \tag{A4:3}$$

when it is assumed that capitalists hold no prejudice, when Negroes are paid the same wage as whites and when no capital is exported to the Negro sector. Discrimination affects these incomes negatively:

$$\frac{dY_{K_W}^{net}}{dL_E} = \bar{K}_W f_W^{KL} > 0. \tag{A4:4}$$

These results are, however, exactly the same as those which would obtain without the presence of any tastes.

Appendix 2: The Madden Model

In Appendix A of her book *The Economics of Sex Discrimination*, Janice Madden attempts to correct in Becker's analysis 'a simple specification error in a mathematical proof'.[1] The purpose is to show that white society as a whole may gain in net terms from discrimination. We recall from Chapter 3 that to measure white net incomes Becker employs

$$Y_W^{net} = (K_R + K_E)f_W^K + \bar{L}_W f_W^L, \tag{3:7}$$

that is he uses the fact that with discrimination

$$f_N^K(1 - d_W^K) = f_W^K, \qquad (3:5)$$

to measure the return to capital in both sectors with the aid of the marginal productivity of capital in the white sector.

Madden objects to this procedure on the grounds that due to discrimination, all white capital does not have the same marginal product. Instead she proposes the formulation

$$Y_W = K_R f_W^K + \bar{L}_W f_W^L + K_E f_N^K. \qquad (A4:5)$$

Two different interpretations can be made about this formulation. In the first place, Madden may mean that (A4:5) represents net white incomes, but then the formulation is clearly wrong since it violates Becker's condition (3:5). Instead of the last term on the right-hand side of (A4:5), we should have $K_E f_N^K(1 - d_W^K)$ or, as Becker has, its equivalent, $K_E f_W^K$.

The second interpretation is that Madden is only considering pecuniary incomes,[2] but then it is difficult to understand why she calls the Becker formulation a 'specification error'. At any rate, assuming that Madden is dealing with pecuniary incomes, since her (A4:5) corresponds to Krueger's (4:1) (in the present work), the result of discrimination should be the same in both models. This is, however, not the case. Madden derives

$$\frac{dY_W}{dK_E} = -K_E f_N^{KK} + f_W^{K_E} - f_N^K, \qquad (A4:6)$$

where it is stated that on the right-hand side the first term is positive (sign included), the second one is positive (sic!) and the last one negative (sign included), so that whites gain from discrimination if $-K_E f_N^{KK} + f_W^{K_E} < f_N^K$. This is an incorrect result. (A4:6) should read

$$\frac{dY_W}{dK_E} = K_E f_N^{KK} + f_W^{K_E} + f_N^K, \qquad (A4:7)$$

where the first right-hand side term is negative, the second is negative (and equal to $-f_W^K$) and the third is positive, and the condition for white gains is that $K_E f_N^{KK} + f_W^{KE} > f_N^K$, or if, as Krueger has chosen to do, it is assumed that no discrimination takes place at the outset,[3] so that returns to capital are equalized,

$$\frac{dY_W}{dK_E} = K_E f_N^{KK} < 0, \qquad (4:2)$$

that is, the Krueger result.

It is not correct to contend, as Madden does, that 'The problem with the Becker analysis lies in a simple specification error in a mathematical proof . . .'[4] Instead, the problem is one of changing preferences, as we found in Chapter 3.

Notes

1. Madden (1973), p. 47.
2. Cf. ibid., where reference is made to 'financial' losses.
3. This assumption makes sense in that it allows us to find out whether it pays for a non-discriminating white group to employ discrimination to raise group incomes, while it is harder to see why one would like to compare a situation where some discrimination is already present with one where the extent of discrimination has increased. If the white group can discriminate, it is likely that once the decision to discriminate is taken, the optimum level of discrimination is sought. To determine this level we maximize white incomes as given by (4:1), which yields

$$\frac{dY_W}{dK_E} = K_E f_N^{KK} - f_W^K + f_N^K = 0, \text{ or } f_W^K = f_N^K + K_E f_N^{KK},$$

that is a situation where the marginal product of capital is lower in the white than in the Negro sector.
4. Madden (1973), p. 47.

5 A TWO-GOOD MODEL WITH COMPLETE SPECIALIZATION

The analysis of Chapters 3 and 4 adhered strictly to the Becker framework in the sense that it was assumed that only one commodity was produced and that the production functions for this commodity did not differ between the two sectors. This may be a fruitful simplification if the two societies do not trade commodities to any large extent. Often, however, the assumption of a single, composite commodity is too restrictive since even if the two groups live and work in segregation, extensive commodity trade may take place between the sectors.

This is important from the theoretical point of view. 'Even intuitively it would seem that if there were more than one commodity the results of discrimination would definitely be altered.' writes Janice Madden in a critical comment on the Becker model.[1] Madden's proposition is of course as true for the economics of discrimination as for all other branches of neo-classical economics. The step from one to two commodities is an important one in that it allows us to deal with the implications of changes in relative commodity prices, caused by discrimination. Moreover, it opens the possibility of trade not only in factor services but in commodities as well between the two societies postulated by Becker. Hence, it constitutes a step towards increased realism.

In the present chapter, we will amend the models of Chapter 4 to allow for a second commodity and explore the implications of this change for the results derived previously. We will begin with a criticism of the one-commodity assumption and of the restrictiveness that this assumption entails. The second section deals with a two-commodity version of the Krueger model, where whites and Negroes are each completely specialized in the production of one commodity.[2] In the third section, the same type of extension is made for the model of labor market segregation, both for the (less likely) case where Negroes receive the same wage regardless of which sector they happen to work in, and for the (more realistic) case where all those who work in the white sector receive the same pay.

The analysis will show how the real incomes of different groups in society are affected by discrimination, that is we shall calculate income changes in terms of both commodities. It is demonstrated that both with capital and labor market segregation the results derived in the one-good setting may differ from those obtained when there is more than a single good.

The Limitations of the One-Good Model

As Joseph Stiglitz has pointed out, even if no commodity trade at all takes place, and even if the analysis is limited to the one-good case, complete factor price equalization will result as long as all but one of the production factors are mobile:

> Assume . . . that only unskilled workers have an aversion to working with members of the other group, but capital and skilled laborers do not. We have then a conventional 'regional' trade model with mobile factors. As long as all but one of the factors are mobile, there will be complete factor-price equalization even in the absence of any commodity trade. We would find all firms having completely segregated work forces, but there would be no wage discrimination. Wage discrimination requires 'interfactor' prejudices ([undiscriminated] employers not wanting to work with [discriminated] employees), not intrafactor prejudices. The latter can only explain segregation.[3]

With more than one good, other possibilities arise. The assumption of a single composite commodity has been criticized by Janice Madden on the grounds that this assumption disallows commodity trade, and consequently, the implications that follow from conventional trade theory:

> If there were differently specified production functions, then a labor-intensive F society would specialize in the production of the economy's labor-intensive commodities so as to raise the marginal productivity and the wages of F labor. F would export these commodities, rather than labor, to M, and M society would produce and export that economy's capital-intensive commodities. Discrimination against a factor would prompt a shift to greater commodity specialization and commodity trade.[4]

The most important implication that follows from the standard two-by-two-by-two model of international trade in the present case is that of factor price equalization between the sectors. With commodity trade present, factor price equalization may arise in the absence of any factor mobility:

> ... trade in commodities is a perfect substitute for trade in factors, provided factor endowments are not too different; that is from the factor price equalization theorem, there will be complete equalization of factor price ratios, even if the relative factor supplies differ. This, of course, requires that there be at least two commodities which are freely traded ...[5]

The employment of a two-good model does not, however, exclude the possibility of differences in factor prices between the two sectors. Madden has listed a series of conditions that may preclude factor price equalization from taking place when there are more commodities than one:

(1) No commodity trade is allowed.
(2) All products are produced with the same factor intensities.
(3) Whites have a preference function which successfully discriminates against Negro labor and against all goods produced by Negroes.
(4) Factor intensity reversals take place.
(5) Negroes are completely specialized in the production of labor-intensive goods or whites are completely specialized in capital-intensive commodities.
(6) There are increasing returns to scale.[6]

In the present chapter, condition 1 is ruled out by assumption[7] and it is extremely unlikely that condition 2 is fulfilled in practice. The form of discrimination postulated in condition 3 has been ruled out in the present work, beginning with Chapter 4. As regards the three remaining conditions, fulfilment of 4 or 6 creates difficulties not only for the analysis of economic discrimination but for trade theory in general, and hence belongs to a category of problems which is more general than those discussed in the present work. In addition, increasing returns to scale in one of the two lines of production may lead to complete specialization by either Negroes or whites in the production of that commodity and is then a special case of complete specialization (condition 5).[8]

This leaves the fifth condition, that of complete specialization of either Negroes or whites, which is not altogether unrealistic in the context of discrimination. The Becker model constitutes a framework for analyzing discriminatory practices in the presence of segregation. Society is divided into two parts, and production is assumed to take place separately in the two sectors. Frequently, however, segregation has a wider meaning, that is not only that different groups work in different firms or departments but in addition that they hold different occupations and hence produce different goods. Two prime examples of this are women, who are occupationally segregated in most countries, and foreign workers, for example in Western Europe, who are typically concentrated within a few occupations and industries.

If it is assumed that there is no factor mobility at all, as in most models of international trade, the establishment of the factor price equalization theorem is crucially dependent on the existence of only incomplete specialization.[9] If in the two-by-two-by-two model, factor endowments differ sufficiently between the two countries, complete specialization may arise and factor prices may differ between the countries even when trade takes place. This fact is of considerable interest in the context of discrimination. If, as is maintained above, discrimination is often accompanied by segregation, we may well have cases of complete specialization. In the absence of discrimination, the factor price equalization theorem will usually apply as long as one of the factors is mobile between sectors,[10] but as soon as mobility is impeded by discriminatory measures, factor price differences may arise between the sectors.

In the present chapter we will analyze the situation where there is complete specialization in the production of both goods to ascertain whether it is possible to state anything definite regarding the gains and losses from discrimination for different groups. We shall deal with both capital and labor market segregation. Let us begin with the former.

Capital Market Segregation

Let us assume that, as before, we have a society that consists of two groups: whites and Negroes. Both groups consume two goods, manufactured goods and agricultural products (M and A). Whites are completely specialized in the production of manufactured goods, and Negroes are completely specialized in the production of agricultural goods. Whites export capital to Negroes and receive an income from this export, while there is no mobility of labor between the sectors. Relative commodity prices are endogenously determined in a general equilibrium system. It is also assumed that perfect competition prevails in both commodity markets and that the two sectors trade with each other.

The production function for manufactures is

$$S_M = M(\bar{K}_W - K_E, \bar{L}_W) \tag{5:1}$$

and for agricultural goods

$$S_A = A(\bar{K}_N + K_E, \bar{L}_N). \tag{5:2}$$

These two production functions are assumed to be linearly homogeneous with signs of the first and second partial derivatives corresponding to those of the production functions employed in Chapters 3 and 4.

We assume in addition that both labor forces are fully employed and that the supply of labor in both sectors is fixed. The capital stocks owned by whites and Negroes, respectively, are given and must be fully employed.

Using P_M as the *numéraire*, the incomes of whites and Negroes, respectively, are given by

$$Y_W = S_M + P_A A^K K_E \tag{5:3}$$

and

$$Y_N = P_A S_A - P_A A^K K_E. \tag{5:4}$$

So far, our model corresponds to that of the one-commodity case. With two goods, however, the demand side must be introduced as well:

$$M_W = M_W(P_A, Y_W), \tag{5:5}$$

$$A_W = A_W(P_A, Y_W), \tag{5:6}$$

$$M_N = M_N(P_A, Y_N), \tag{5:7}$$

$$A_N = A_N(P_A, Y_N). \tag{5:8}$$

Equations (5:5), (5:6), (5:7) and (5:8) state that the white and Negro demand for the two goods depends on relative commodity prices and on the incomes of each group. It is assumed that the redistribution of incomes within each racial group that arises as a result of discrimination does not affect the demand pattern.[11] This simplifying assumption is made in order to focus on the distribution between whites and Negroes.

Finally, we need the equilibirium condition for one of the two commodity markets. Thus the total demand for manufactures must equal the supply of this commodity:

$$M_W + M_N = S_M. \tag{5:9}$$

Assuming Walras' law to hold, no corresponding equation is needed for the market for agricultural goods, since equilibrium in the market for manufacturing goods ensures that the market for agricultural commodities is also in equilibrium. Thus, we may omit the second equilibrium condition from our system, since it is not independent from (5:9).

We now have a general equilibrium system of nine equations and nine unknowns (M_W, A_W, M_N, A_N, S_M, S_A, P_A, Y_W and Y_N). Two of the equations, (5:6) and (5:8), may, however, be discarded immediately, since the unknowns defined by them (the demand for good A) do not appear anywhere else in the system. Assuming that a unique solution to the remaining system exists, we may proceed to solve this system for changes in real incomes that result from discrimination. Let us, however, begin by investigating how discrimination affects relative commodity prices. (This knowledge is required for the computation of real income changes.)

To derive an expression for dP_A/dK_E we differentiate the system (5:1)-(5:5), (5:7) and (5:9) totally and solve the differentiated system for dP_A/dK_E.

The desired expression is

$$\frac{dP_A}{dK_E} = \frac{1}{\Delta+}[M^{K_E} + (M_N^Y - M_W^Y)P_A K_E A^{KK}], \tag{5:10}$$

where

$$\Delta+ = M_W^P + M_N^P + M_W^Y A^K K_E + M_N^Y(S_A - A^K K_E). \tag{5:11}$$

Beginning with the denominator, $\Delta+$, of (5:10), it would seem that for a number of reasons its sign is not generally determinate. First, the two first terms on the right-hand side of (5:11) may assume either positive or negative values. Secondly, the third term will be positive in the absence of inferior goods. Finally, by the same token the fourth term should also be positive, provided that some of the value of the production of good A remains in the Negro sector. However, this is a purely superficial interpretation, since the underlying significance of expression (5:11) removes any doubt as to its sign.

The excess demand for good M is

$$M_E \equiv M_W + M_N - S_M. \tag{5:12}$$

Taking the partial derivative of M_E with respect to P_A yields

$$M_E^P \equiv M_W^P + M_W^Y Y_W^P + M_N^P + M_N^Y Y_N^P, \tag{5:13}$$

which, using (5:3) and (5:4), may be rewritten as

$$M_E^P \equiv M_W^P + M_N^P + M_W^Y A^K K_E + M_N^Y (S_A - A^K K_E) = \Delta +. \tag{5:14}$$

Thus, our denominator is nothing but the partial derivative of the excess demand for good M with respect to P_A. When composing the general equilibrium system employed to derive the expression for dP_A/dK_E, we assume Walras' law to hold:

$$(M_W + M_N - S_M) + P_A (A_W + A_N - S_A) \equiv 0. \tag{5:15}$$

Hence, an excess demand for manufactures corresponds to an excess supply of agricultural goods which has been created by the rise of P_A. This excess supply should be positive. Otherwise, our model will not be stable in the Walrasian sense. Hence, our denominator must have a positive sign.

The numerator of (5:10) is simpler than the denominator. The first term is negative (cf. (5:1)), and the entire numerator is negative if the marginal propensity to consume manufactures (the good produced in the white sector) is higher (or equal) among Negroes than among whites. Discrimination will then lead to a deterioration in the white terms-of-trade (improvement of Negro terms-of-trade).

The mechanism behind the change in the terms-of-trade is the following: When capital is withdrawn from the Negro sector and instead put to work in the white sector, the production of agricultural goods will fall and the production of manufactures will increase at given prices. Simultaneously white incomes will rise and Negro incomes will fall,[12] and if the marginal propensity to consume manufactures is higher among Negroes than among whites, the demand for manufactures will fall and cause an excess supply of manufactures and an excess demand for agricultural products. To clear the markets, the relative price of manufactures must fall. On the other hand, should the marginal propensity to consume manufactures be higher among whites than among Negroes, the demand for that good will fall rather than rise. Before the impact on relative prices can be determined, the magnitude of this fall will have to be compared to the magnitude of the increase of the supply of manufactures.

Effects on Real Incomes

Next, we want to find out how the introduction of discrimination affects the real incomes of the white and Negro communities, respectively. Beginning with white incomes, we differentiate (5:3) with respect to K_E. This yields

$$\frac{dY_W}{dK_E} = A^K K_E \frac{dP_A}{dK_E} + P_A K_E A^{KK}. \tag{5:16}$$

Expression (5:16) actually contains *three* different effects, and not two as one might believe. The first of these is a production effect. When capital is transferred from agriculture to manufacturing as a result of discrimination, the production of manufactures increases, with the marginal product of capital in that sector. At the same time, agricultural production declines, with the marginal product of capital in the agricultural sector. With a given price of agricultural goods, these two changes are equal but have opposite signs. Hence the two sum to zero and do not appear explicitly in (5:16).

The second effect is the one shown by the first term on the right-hand side of (5:16). This states that as the price of agricultural goods changes in relation to that of manufactures, the remuneration of the (pre-discrimination) stock of export capital will also change. The sign of this change is not determinate in the general case. However, we have already demonstrated that if $M_N^Y \geq M_W^Y$, dP_A/dK_E is negative. Consequently discrimination leads to a higher value of export capital in terms of our *numéraire* good.

The last effect — the last term of (5:16) — shows that discrimination induces a rise in the marginal product of agricultural capital. This raises white incomes from a given export capital at a given price of agricultural goods. Thus, we may conclude that capital market segregation raises total white incomes in terms of good M, provided that the marginal propensity to consume manufactures among Negroes is equal to or higher than that of whites, so that P_A rises in the process.

If Y_W increases in terms of good A as well, that is if Y_W/P_A rises, there will be an increase in real income. However, differentiating Y_W/P_A with respect to K_E and substituting the expression for dY_W/dK_E (expression (5:16)) it would appear difficult to derive simple conditions for such an increase. Instead we may work directly with the expression for Y_W with good A as the *numéraire*:

$$Y_W = P_M S_M + A^K K^E. \tag{5:17}$$

Assuming that factor prices are equal at the outset, differentiating (5:17) with respect to K_E gives

$$\frac{dY_W}{dK_E} = S_M \frac{dP_M}{dK_E} + K_E A^{KK}. \tag{5:18}$$

In (5:18) dP_M/dK_E is positive under the same conditions as our expression (5:16) is negative, that is when $M_N^Y \geq M_W^Y$. Thus, the first term on the right-hand side may be positive, while the second is always negative. These terms can easily be compared. It is then seen that a large volume of capital exports and a low production of manufactured goods, *ceteris paribus*, tend to make discrimination profitable in terms of good A for the white group. Discrimination brings about a fall in the price of manufactures when $M_N^Y \geq M_W^Y$. If, however, only small amounts of this commodity are produced, while simultaneously capital exports are large, the rising marginal productivity of capital in agriculture has a heavy impact on white incomes. The former effect is then likely to be swamped by the latter. (It is quite possible that S_M is low when K_E is high, since large capital exports may drain the manufacturing sector of capital.)

To derive the effects on Negro incomes we begin by differentiating (5:4) with respect to K_E. We then obtain

$$\frac{dY_N}{dK_E} = (S_A - A^K K_E)\frac{dP_A}{dK_E} - P_A K_E A^{KK}. \tag{5:19}$$

The last term of (5:19) shows that when the marginal productivity of capital in agriculture increases, due to discrimination, an increasing amount has to be paid to a given stock of export capital at a given P_A. This negative effect on Negro incomes may, however, be offset by the increase in the value of the share of agricultural production retained by the Negro community that is due to the change in agricultural prices. However, the latter only takes place when there is an increase in P_A and when this increase is sufficiently large to swamp the effect due to the change in the marginal productivity of capital.

Nevertheless, a strong terms-of-trade effect with a positive influence on Negro incomes does not guarantee an increase in Negro real incomes, since discrimination will always lead to a *fall* in Negro incomes in terms of agricultural goods. In order to demonstrate the latter, we differentiate Y_N/P_A with respect to K_E and substitute our expression (5:19). This yields:

$$\frac{d(Y_N/P_A)}{dK_E} = \frac{1}{(P_A)^2} \{[P_A(S_A - A^K K_E) - Y_N] \frac{dP_A}{dK_E}$$

$$- (P_A)^2 K_E A^{KK}\}, \qquad (5:20)$$

or, since

$$Y_N = P_A S_A - P_A A^K K_E, \qquad (5:4)$$

$$\frac{d(Y_N/P_A)}{dK_E} = -K_E A^{KK} > 0. \qquad (5:21)$$

Comparing (5:21) with (5:19) we see that calculating Negro income changes in terms of good A instead of in terms of manufactures, the first term on the right-hand side of (5:19) disappears, since the value of a unit of agricultural goods is now given and equal to one. For the same reason ($P_A = 1$), P_A disappears in the second term and only (5:21) remains.

With regard to factor incomes, white capitalist incomes, as in the one-good case, are composed of the sum of capital incomes in the white sector and incomes from capital exported to the Negro sector:

$$Y_{K_W} = M^K(\bar{K}_W - K_E) + P_A A^K K_E, \qquad (5:22)$$

which when differentiated with respect to K_E gives

$$\frac{dY_{K_W}}{dK_E} = -(\bar{K}_W - K_E)M^{KK} + P_A K_E A^{KK} + A^K K_E \frac{dP_A}{dK_E} \qquad (5:23)$$

Here the first term on the right-hand side is positive (sign included), the second one is negative and the third one depends on the sign of dP_A/dK_E. We cannot determine the sign of the sum of the two terms, since the production functions are no longer identical. The white capitalists suffer a loss from the reduction of the marginal productivity of capital in the white sector when capital is repatriated, but at the same time gain through the corresponding increase in marginal productivity in the Negro sector. Thus, the likelihood of a loss for white capitalists decreases, *ceteris paribus*, when the amount of capital originally exported to the Negro sector increases. The remuneration of that capital is increased by the increase in its marginal productivity and, provided that dP_A/dK_E is negative, also by the rise of the relative price of the good produced in the Negro sector. Simultaneously in the white sector the capital stock that is subject to diminishing returns becomes correspondingly smaller.[13]

Under the same conditions, white capitalists may also gain in terms of agricultural goods and consequently in terms of *real* income. With agricultural goods as the *numéraire*, white capital incomes amount to

$$Y_{K_W} = P_M M^K (\bar{K}_W - K_E) + A^K K_E. \tag{5:24}$$

Differentiation of this expression with respect to K_E yields:

$$\frac{dY_{K_W}}{dK_E} = -P_M(\bar{K}_W - K_E)M^{KK} + M^K(\bar{K}_W - K_E)\frac{dP_M}{dK_E} + K_E A^{KK}, \tag{5:25}$$

given that $P_M M^K = A^K$, initially.

In the case where dP_M/dK_E is positive ($dP_A/dK_E < 0$), the first two terms on the right-hand side of (5:25) are positive and the last one negative. However, *ceteris paribus*, the larger the capital exports, the more white capitalists will benefit from increased marginal productivity of capital in agriculture as capital is withdrawn from that sector. Moreover, the first two terms which denote respectively, the impact of the fall in the marginal productivity of manufacturing capital and the change in the value of manufacturing output accruing to capital, tend to shrink. Note, however, that in the second term an increased K_E is accompanied by an increased M^K. These two effects will tend to counteract each other. The argument that higher capital exports tend to increase the likelihood of a real income gain for white capitalists is a *ceteris paribus* argument and must not be given a general equilibrium interpretation.

The case of labor is much simpler:

$$Y_{L_W} = M^L \bar{L}_W, \tag{5:26}$$

and

$$\frac{dY_{L_W}}{dK_E} = -M^{LK}\bar{L}_W < 0. \tag{5:27}$$

White workers gain by discrimination, in terms of manufactures, due to the increased availability of capital in the white sector. This gain is, however, not necessarily preserved in terms of agricultural goods. Then the effect stemming from the increased marginal productivity of labor must be weighed against the possible negative effect of a decline in the value of labor's share of manufacturing output when $dP_M/dK_E > 0$ (that is when $dP_A/dK_E < 0$). This can be demonstrated in an analogous manner to the derivation of (5:25).

In the Negro sector,

$$Y_{K_N} = P_A A^K \bar{K}_N \tag{5:28}$$

and

$$Y_{L_N} = P_A A^L \bar{L}_N, \tag{5:29}$$

in terms of manufactures, so that

$$\frac{dY_{K_N}}{dK_E} = P_A A^{KK}\bar{K}_N + A^K \bar{K}_N \frac{dP_A}{dK_E} \tag{5:30}$$

and

$$\frac{dY_{L_N}}{dK_E} = P_A A^{LK}\bar{L}_N + A^L \bar{L}_N \frac{dP_A}{dK_E}, \tag{5:31}$$

respectively.

In (5:30), the first term on the right-hand side is negative, indicating a gain through the loss of competing white capital, as in the one-commodity case. If dP_A/dK_E is negative, the second term will also be negative. Improved terms-of-trade vis-à-vis manufacturing will then be added to increased marginal productivity of capital in the Negro sector. This gain is a *real* gain. Differentiating Y_{K_N}/P_A with respect to K_E and substituting (5:30) and (5:28) gives the impact of discrimination on Negro capitalist incomes in terms of agricultural goods:

$$\frac{d(Y_{K_N}/P_A)}{dK_E} = A^{KK}\bar{K}_N < 0. \tag{5:32}$$

With $P_A = 1$, only the effect on the marginal productivity of agricultural capital remains.

In (5:31), the first term on the right-hand side is positive, but the second term may be negative (when $dP_A/dK_E < 0$). The outcome is indeterminate. In terms of agricultural goods, on the other hand, Negro labor always makes a loss. Analogous to (5:32),

$$\frac{d(Y_{L_N}/P_A)}{dK_E} = A^{LK}\bar{L}_N > 0. \tag{5:33}$$

Hence the possibility of a positive terms-of-trade effect disappears.

The effects of discrimination on the real incomes of whites and Negroes are summarized in Table 5.1. The latter also provides a comparison with the one-commodity (Krueger) model. The table clearly

Table 5.1: Welfare Effects of Capital Market Segregation in the One- and Two-Good Models

Effects on incomes of:	One-good (Krueger) model	Two-good model $P_M = 1$	$P_A = 1$
Whites	gain	gain if $M_N^Y \geqslant M_W^Y$	?
White capitalists	loss	?	?
White labor	gain	gain	?
Negroes	loss	?	loss
Negro capitalists	gain	gain if $M_N^Y \geqslant M_W^Y$	gain
Negro labor	loss	?	loss

shows that the neatness of the one-good model is destroyed by the introduction of a second commodity into the analysis. The only result from the Krueger model that is reasonably well preserved is the one regarding Negro capitalist income. Negro capitalists always gain in the one-good setting, and if $M_N^Y \geq M_W^Y$, whereby discrimination leads to a rise in the relative price of agricultural goods, this will also be the case in the extended setting. In all the remaining cases, the conditions for a determinate outcome are more complicated in that opposing forces must be weighed against each other.

The most important findings of the present section are those regarding the impact of discrimination on white labor and capital incomes, respectively. Labor no longer necessarily makes a gain. For this to be the case, either manufacturing terms-of-trade must improve or the impact of the deterioration must be low in relation to the impact of the rise in labor productivity that results from the increased use of capital in the manufacturing sector.

The most interesting finding, however, is that white capitalists do not necessarily lose by resorting to discriminatory withdrawal of some of their capital from the Negro sector, as in the Krueger one-good model. They may even gain by this procedure if a large proportion of the white capital stock is exported in the absence of discrimination. *This finding provides a possible incentive for white capitalists to discriminate against Negroes, one which is absent in the one-commodity model.*

Labor Market Segregation

When we proceed to analyze the two labor market segregation cases, we find that the results differ from those of the capital case. Let us begin with the assumption that Negroes receive equal wages in both sectors.

Equal Negro Wages in Both Sectors

When labor is the mobile factor, the two production functions (5:1) and (5:2) change to

$$S_M = M_1(\bar{K}_W, \bar{L}_W + L_E), \tag{5:34}$$

and

$$S_A = A_1(\bar{K}_N, \bar{L}_N - L_E). \tag{5:35}$$

148 A Two-Good Model with Complete Specialization

Given that Negro wages are determined by the marginal productivity of labor in the Negro sector, the two income expressions (5:3) and (5:4) become

$$Y_W = S_M - P_A A_1^l L_E \tag{5:36}$$

and

$$Y_N = P_A S_A + P_A A_1^l L_E. \tag{5:37}$$

As above, we begin by solving for relative price changes. To find the expression of dP_A/dL_E, the system (5:34) - (5:37), (5:5) - (5:9) is employed. This system may be simplified and solved in the same manner as our previous system. This yields

$$\frac{dP_A}{dL_E} = \frac{1}{\Delta^{++}} \left[M_1^L + (M_N^Y - M_W^Y) P_A L_E A_1^{LL} \right], \tag{5:38}$$

where

$$\Delta^{++} = M_W^P + M_N^P - M_W^Y A_1^l L_E + M_N^Y (S_A + A_1^l L_E). \tag{5:39}$$

The sign of the denominator may be determined in the same way as with (5:11). Departing from (5:13) we now use production functions (5:34) and (5:35) and income expressions (5:36) and (5:37) instead. The expression corresponding to (5:14) then becomes

$$M_E^P \equiv M_W^P + M_N^P - M_W^Y A_1^l L_E + M_N^Y (S_A + A_1^l L_E) = \Delta^{++} \tag{5:40}$$

which must be positive if our model is to possess Walrasian stability.

In the numerator of (5:38), the first term is positive, and so is the second term provided that $M_W^Y \geqslant M_N^Y$. In this case the relative price of agricultural goods will fall as a result of discrimination. On the other hand, should the marginal propensity to consume manufactures be higher among Negroes than among whites, supply and demand effects will have to be weighed against each other in the same manner as in the discussion of (5:10). As a result of labor market segregation, the production of manufactures falls. At the same time (given relative commodity prices), white incomes increase by an amount that corresponds to the fall in Negro incomes. Then, if $M_W^Y \geqslant M_N^Y$, the demand for manufactures will increase as a result of the income changes. This creates an excess demand for this good (an excess supply of good A). As a result the relative price of good A falls in order to clear markets. If the inequality sign is reversed, supply and demand factors pull in opposite directions. The outcome with respect to price changes depends on the relative magnitude of these factors. Note that the sufficient condition for obtaining a determinate sign for the change in P_A is the opposite of the one obtained in the case of capital market segregation.

Turning to the effects of labor market segregation on *real* incomes, it can be easily demonstrated by differentiating expressions (5:36) and (5:37) that the white group may derive a gain in terms of manufactures:

$$\frac{dY_W}{dL_E} = P_A L_E A_I^{LL} - A_I^I L_E \frac{dP_A}{dL_E}. \tag{5:41}$$

Given that factor prices are equal at the outset, $M_W^Y \geq M_N^Y$, $dP_A/dL_E > 0$ and both terms on the right-hand side of (5:41) will be negative. The white community benefits from a falling marginal productivity of labor in agriculture as the entry of Negro labor to the white sector is restricted, since this tends to lower the wage rate that has to be paid to Negroes working in manufacturing as well. Whites also gain from the fall in the relative price of agricultural goods, since this also lowers the wage that has to be paid to Negro workers, both in agriculture and in manufacturing.

The gain obtained by the white community when $dP_A/dL_E > 0$ is a *real* gain, since with Y_W rising in terms of manufactures and P_A falling simultaneously, there will also be an inevitable increase in Y_W in terms of agricultural goods.

Differentiating (5:37) with respect to L_E we find that the Negro community loses in terms of manufactures when $dP_A/dL_E > 0$:

$$\frac{dY_N}{dL_E} = (S_A + A_I^I L_E)\frac{dP_A}{dK_E} - P_A L_E A_I^{LL}. \tag{5:42}$$

The first term on the right-hand side shows that the fall in the price of agricultural goods caused by discrimination lowers both the value of agricultural production in terms of manufactures and the wage paid to export labor. The second term demonstrates that this wage is further depressed by the decrease in the marginal productivity of labor in agriculture that results from the forced influx of labor into that sector.

150 A Two-Good Model with Complete Specialization

The Negro community always loses in terms of agricultural goods. Consequently it suffers a decline in *real* income (when $dP_A/dL_E > 0$). Differentiating Y_N/P_A with respect to L_E, substituting (5:42) and (5:37) yields:

$$\frac{d(Y_N/P_A)}{dL_E} = -L_E A_1^{LL} > 0. \tag{5:43}$$

The wage to export labor in terms of agricultural goods will always (regardless of what happens to P_A) fall since the marginal productivity of labor decreases in the agricultural sector when labor market segregation is practiced.

Proceeding to factor incomes, the two labor cases turn out to be fairly simple. For white labor,

$$Y_{L_W} = \bar{L}_W M_1^L \tag{5:44}$$

and

$$\frac{dY_{L_W}}{dL_E} = \bar{L}_W M_1^{LL} < 0. \tag{5:45}$$

White workers gain in terms of manufactures since the competition from Negro labor decreases. Moreover, if $dP_A/dL_E > 0$, discrimination lowers the price of agricultural goods. Hence there is a gain in terms of the latter commodity in *real* terms.

The incomes of Negro labor are given by

$$Y_{L_N} = P_A \bar{L}_N A_1^L \tag{5:46}$$

and

$$\frac{dY_{L_N}}{dL_E} = -P_A \bar{L}_N A_1^{LL} + \bar{L}_N A_1^L \frac{dP_A}{dL_E}, \tag{5:47}$$

which is positive when dP_A/dL_E is positive. Negro workers find their wages reduced both by a fall in the marginal productivity of labor and by a decrease in the price at which the marginal product of labor is valued in agriculture.

A Two-Good Model with Complete Specialization 151

In terms of agricultural goods, Negro labor loses regardless of what happens to P_A. Differentiating Y_{L_N}/P_A and substituting (5:46) and (5:47) yields

$$\frac{d(Y_{L_N}/P_A)}{dL_E} = -\bar{L}_N A_1^{LL} > 0. \tag{5:48}$$

The wage paid to Negro workers falls as the marginal productivity of labor in agriculture declines.

The results for capital incomes are less determinate. Beginning with Negro capital incomes,

$$Y_{K_N} = P_A \bar{K}_N A_1^K, \tag{5:49}$$

and

$$\frac{dY_{K_N}}{dL_E} = -P_A \bar{K}_N A_1^{KL} + \bar{K}_N A_1^K \frac{dP_A}{dL_E}. \tag{5:50}$$

Here the two terms on the right-hand side may be of the opposite sign. If dP_A/dL_E is positive, Negro capital incomes tend to fall in terms of manufactures since the valuation of the marginal product of capital in agriculture is lowered. This, in turn has to be weighed against the gain stemming from the influx of labor in the sector.

In terms of agricultural goods, the result is clear-cut. Differentiation of Y_{K_N}/P_A with respect to L_E, plus the insertion of (5:49) and (5:50) yields

$$\frac{d(Y_{K_N}/P_A)}{dL_E} = -\bar{K}_N A_1^{KL} < 0. \tag{5:51}$$

Negro capitalists gain from the increased use of labor in agriculture.

Finally, let us deal with the most complicated case, namely that of white capital incomes. If, as in Chapter 4, it is assumed that capitalists are simultaneously employers and that they are able to appropriate the difference in the marginal productivities of labor in the two sectors, these incomes may be expressed as

$$Y_{K_W} = \bar{K}_W M_1^K + L_E(M_1^L - P_A A_1^L), \tag{5:52}$$

Differentiating (5:50) with respect to L_E we obtain

$$\frac{dY_{K_W}}{dL_E} = \bar{K}_W M_1^{KL} + L_E(M_1^{LL} + P_A A_1^{LL}) - L_E A_1^L \frac{dP_A}{dL_E}, \qquad (5:53)$$

since wages do not differ between sectors in the absence of discrimination.

The first term on the right-hand side of (5:53) indicates that as labor leaves manufacturing the marginal productivity of capital, and hence the remuneration accruing to the owners of the white capital stock, falls. The second term shows that discrimination creates a difference between the marginal productivity of labor in manufacturing and agriculture. This is appropriated by white capitalists/employers who pay Negro labor a wage that is not commensurate with the higher marginal productivity in manufacturing but with the lower level that prevails in agriculture. The third and final term shows the impact of a change in the price of agricultural goods on the valuation of the marginal product of labor in that sector. In the case where dP_A/dL_E is positive ($M_W^Y \geqslant M_N^Y$), this term is negative (sign included). Thus, the outcome is indeterminate.

However, rewriting expression (5:53) somewhat makes it possible to identify some of the decisive forces. Since the production function for manufactures is linearly homogeneous, we know that

$$\bar{K}_W M_1^{LK} + (\bar{L}_W + L_E) M_1^{LL} \equiv 0. \qquad (5:54)$$

Hence (5:53) may be rewritten as

$$\frac{dY_{K_W}}{dL_E} = P_A L_E A_1^{LL} - \bar{L}_W M_1^{LL} - L_E A_1^L \frac{dP_A}{dL_E}. \qquad (5:55)$$

If L_E is high and $\bar{L}_W$ is low, that is if the labor force in manufacturing is dominated by Negro workers (when P_A falls), *ceteris paribus*, discrimination is likely to benefit white capitalists, since this allows them a more extensive use of the wage differential. This, in turn, compensates for the loss suffered by the reduction of the marginal productivity of capital in manufacturing as labor leaves the sector.

By differentiating Y_{K_W}/P_A with respect to L_E and substituting (5:55) it may be shown that under the same conditions white capitalists are also likely to gain in terms of agricultural goods (provided that $dP_A/dL_E > 0$) and hence in *real* terms.

Table 5.2: Welfare Effects of Labor Market Segregation in the One- and Two-Good Models with Uniform Negro Wages

Effects on incomes of:	One-good model	Two-good model $P_M = 1$	Two-good model $P_A = 1$
Whites	gain	gain if $M_W^Y \geq M_N^Y$	gain if $M_W^Y \geq M_N^Y$
White capitalists	indeterminate gain if $L_E > \bar{L}_W$	?	?
White labor	gain	gain	gain if $M_W^Y \geq M_N^Y$
Negroes	loss	loss if $M_W^Y \geq M_N^Y$	loss
Negro capitalists	gain	?	gain
Negro labor	loss	loss if $M_W^Y \geq M_N^Y$	loss

Table 5.2 provides a summary of the results regarding the effects of labor market segregation on real incomes given the somewhat unrealistic assumption that Negroes earn the same wage in both sectors. A comparison is also made with the one-good model.

If we begin by comparing the impact of discrimination on the incomes of the white and Negro communities as a whole with those derived in the one-good model, we find that the white community gains and the Negro community losses are no longer unconditional. As we now have two commodities, changes in relative commodity prices must be taken into account when calculating gains and losses. A sufficient condition for the application of the results of the one-good model to the two-goods case is that the relative price of agricultural goods falls as a result of discrimination. As we have demonstrated, this will always happen when the marginal productivity of the white community to consume manufactures is at least equal to that of the Negro community. Fulfilment of this condition also ensures that white workers gain and Negro workers lose in the two-good model.

More substantial differences between the two models appear when we come to capital incomes. Negro capitalists no longer necessarily gain from discrimination. Moreover white capital owners do not necessarily benefit from discrimination when the majority of the workers in the white sector are Negroes. In the case where the relative price of agricultural goods falls, however, the larger the size of the 'immigrant' relative to the white manufacturing labor force, the greater the likelihood, *ceteris paribus*, for a gain by white capitalists. This is due to the larger scope for exploiting differences in wages between whites and Negroes. Consequently, this gain is more likely to outweigh the fall in the marginal productivity of white capital that occurs when Negro labor is forced to leave manufacturing.

Uniform Wages in the White Sector

In the second and more realistic of the two cases of labor market segregation, where those Negroes who work in the white sector receive a wage which is equal to that paid to white labor, expressions (5:36) and (5:37) instead become

$$Y_W = S_M - M_1^L L_E \tag{5:56}$$

and

$$Y_N = P_A S_A + M_1^L L_E. \tag{5:57}$$

To derive an expression for relative price changes, we simply substitute (5:56) and (5:57) for (5:36) and (5:37) in the system used to derive (5:38). Solving the differentiated version of this new system gives a new expression for dP_A/dL_E:

$$\frac{dP_A}{dL_E} = \frac{1}{\Delta+++}[M_1^L - (M_N^Y - M_W^Y)L_E M_1^{LL}], \tag{5:58}$$

where

$$\Delta+++ = M_W^P + M_N^P + M_N^Y S_A. \tag{5:59}$$

To prove that the denominator $\Delta+++$ is positive, we once more depart from (5:13). With incomes as given by (5:56) and (5:57), the equivalent of (5:14) this time becomes

$$M_E^P \equiv M_W^P + M_N^P + M_N^Y S_A = \Delta+++, \qquad (5:60)$$

which is positive.

As long as $M_N^Y \geqslant M_W^Y$, the numerator of (5:58) will be positive. Changes in supply and demand will work in the same direction and ensure that the relative price of A falls in order to eliminate the excess supply of this good at constant relative commodity prices. With given commodity prices, the supply of agricultural goods increases and that of manufactures falls. At the same time income is transferred from whites to Negroes. Thus, if the marginal propensity to consume manufactures is higher among Negroes than among whites, an excess demand for this good (an excess supply of good A) will arise. In order to restore equilibrium, the relative price of good A must fall (rather than rise as in the case of capital market segregation).

Differentiating (5:56) gives the impact on white incomes:

$$\frac{dY_W}{dL_E} = -L_E M_1^{LL} > 0. \qquad (5:61)$$

The white group will lose in terms of manufactures by resorting to labor market segregation. The marginal productivity of capital falls when Negro labor is forced to leave manufacturing. There is, however, no guarantee that this loss is a real one, since provided that $M_N^Y \geqslant M_W^Y$, $dP_A/dL_E > 0$. Hence we cannot determine *a priori* the direction in which white incomes will change in terms of agricultural goods.

The opposite situation prevails for the Negro group. Differentiating (5:57) with respect to L_E gives the impact of discrimination in terms of manufactures:

$$\frac{dY_N}{dL_E} = L_E M_1^{LL} + S_A \frac{dP_A}{dL_E}, \qquad (5:62)$$

since factor price equalization prevails at the outset. As expression (5:62) reveals, the effect of the increased marginal productivity of labor must be weighed against the changed valuation of agricultural goods as P_A changes. The outcome is not determinate since, as has already been pointed out, dP_A/dL_E may be positive.

In terms of agricultural goods, matters are simpler. Measuring Negro incomes in terms of agricultural goods:

$$Y_N = S_A + P_M M_1^L L_E. \qquad (5:63)$$

Differentiating this expression with respect to L_E, noting that wages are equal at the outset, gives

$$\frac{dY_N}{dL_E} = P_M L_E M_1^{LL} + M_1^L L_E \frac{dP_M}{dL_E}, \qquad (5:64)$$

which is always negative when $dP_M/dL_E < 0$ ($M_N^Y \geqslant M_W^Y$). Here, the changing valuation of agricultural goods disappears, and a change in P_M occurs instead. Provided the latter is positive (when discrimination is introduced), Negroes gain in terms of agricultural goods.

White labor incomes are given by

$$Y_{L_W} = M_1^L \bar{L}_W. \qquad (5:65)$$

Differentiating (5:63) with respect to L_E yields

$$\frac{dY_{L_W}}{dL_E} = \bar{L}_W M_1^{LL} < 0. \qquad (5:66)$$

When Negro workers are forced to leave manufacturing, their white competitors gain in terms of manufactures. Provided that $dP_A/dL_E > 0$, the gain is also a real gain. The effect on the marginal productivity of white workers will then be reinforced by a fall in the relative price of agricultural goods.

In turn, white capital incomes are:

$$Y_{K_W} = M_1^K \bar{K}_W, \qquad (5:67)$$

and

$$\frac{dY_{K_W}}{dL_E} = \bar{K}_W M_1^{KL} > 0. \qquad (5:68)$$

White capitalists incur a loss in terms of manufactures when Negro labor leaves manufacturing, but this loss is not necessarily a real one since, if the price of agricultural goods falls simultaneously, this may offset the loss when agricultural goods are used as the *numéraire*.

Negro capitalists are in the opposite situation. Their incomes are given by

$$Y_{K_N} = P_A A_1^K \bar{K}_N, \tag{5:69}$$

so that

$$\frac{dY_{K_N}}{dL_E} = -P_A \bar{K}_N A_1^{KL} + A_1^K \bar{K}_N \frac{dP_A}{dL_E}. \tag{5:70}$$

Here, the positive impact on the marginal productivity of capital emanating from the addition of labor to agriculture may be offset by the lower valuation of the capital share in that sector if the price of agricultural goods falls.

In terms of agricultural goods no opposing forces are at work. Differentiating Y_{K_N}/P_A with respect to L_E and substituting (5:69) and (5:70) yields

$$\frac{d(Y_{K_N}/P_A)}{dL_E} = -\bar{K}_N A_1^{KL} < 0. \tag{5:71}$$

The gain is unequivocal.

Finally, we have to determine what happens to Negro labor incomes,

$$Y_{L_N} = P_A A_1^L (\bar{L}_N - L_E) + M_1^L L_E. \tag{5:72}$$

Differentiating (5:72) with respect to L_E gives

$$\frac{dY_{L_N}}{dL_E} = -P_A A_1^{LL}(\bar{L}_N - L_E) + A_1^L(\bar{L}_N - L_E)\frac{dP_A}{dL_E} + M_1^{LL} L_E, \tag{5:73}$$

since wages are equal in the two sectors when no discrimination takes place. In (5:73), the first term on the right-hand side is positive, the second is indeterminate and the last one is negative. The outcome is highly uncertain. The introduction of discrimination causes the marginal productivities of labor in the two sectors to move in opposite directions. Also, the re-evaluation of the share of labor in agriculture may be in either direction. However, in the case where $dP_A/dL_E > 0$, the likelihood of a loss increases, *ceteris paribus*, when the original number of Negro workers in manufacturing decreases. Differentiating Y_{L_N}/P_A with respect to L_E and substituting (5:72) and (5:73) it is evident that the same conclusion also holds in terms of agricultural goods.

The effects of labor market segregation on real incomes in the two-good model, with a uniform wage rate within the white sector, are summarized in Table 5.3, where they are also compared with the results derived in the one-good model.

Table 5.3: Welfare Effects of Labor Market Segregation in the Two-Good Model with Uniform Wages in the White Sector

Effects on incomes of:	One-good model	Two-good model $P_M = 1$	Two-good model $P_A = 1$
Whites	loss	loss	?
White capitalists	loss	loss	?
White labor	gain	gain	gain if $M_N^Y \geq M_W^Y$
Negroes	gain	?	gain if $M_N^Y \geq M_W^Y$
Negro capitalists	gain	?	gain
Negro labor	loss	?	?

Most of the neatness of the one-good model is lost in the two-good setting. The most interesting results are those for white factor incomes. In the one-good model, the capitalists incur an unconditional loss while the workers always gain. This is no longer certain when a second good is introduced. However, provided that the marginal propensity to consume manufactures is higher among Negroes than among whites, the change in relative commodity prices is always in the 'right' direction so that white workers can be certain to benefit from labor market segregation. Thus, *in the two-good model, it is also possible to identify a white group that is likely under certain circumstances to advocate discrimination. However, this group is not the capitalists.*

Conclusions

In this chapter we have worked with a two-good model to analyze the effects on incomes and welfare of different types of discrimination. The introduction of a second commodity in the analysis has made the results somewhat less clear-cut than in the one-good cases that were dealt with previously.

With two goods, we have to take into account changes in relative commodity prices when dealing with both income and welfare effects. Expressions for the change in relative prices as a result of capital or labor market segregation have been derived. The results have, however, not been unambiguous. Only by adding restrictions to the analysis has it been possible to determine the direction of the price changes.

In the first section, some criticisms against the one-good approach to discrimination were presented. In particular, it was stressed that when a two-by-two-by-two model of the type which is common in international trade theory is employed, the possibility of factor price equalization, even in the absence of factor mobility, arises. However, the case of complete specialization in both sectors emerges as a realistic possibility since discrimination and segregation often go hand in hand leaving whites and Negroes to produce different goods.

This case was analyzed in the remaining two sections, first in the context of capital market segregation and subsequently in models of labor market segregation assuming either that all Negroes received the same wage (determined by their productivity in the Negro sector) or that all workers in the white sector, whites or Negroes, receive the same pay.

The results obtained in the two-good setting generally differ from those derived with the aid of the one-good model. This is of great interest when it comes to identifying the group or groups that could gain by discriminatory practices. With discrimination taking the form of capital market segregation, the introduction of the second commodity provided a possible rationale for discrimination from the point of view of white capitalists — one which was not present in the one-good setting. (However, the workers may gain as well, as in the one-good model.) In the labor market segregation case, this rationale is weakened, compared to the one-good case, if Negroes earn the same wage in both sectors. Much weaker conditions were derived for white worker gains. Finally, in the most realistic case, that is a uniform wage in the white sector, the possibility of a white capitalist gain is even less likely. The group most likely to advocate discrimination in this setting are the white workers.

To conclude, the two-good model in the two most realistic cases — capital market segregation and labor market segregation with equal wages in the white sector — provide a better explanation than the one-good models of why white capitalists may advocate discrimination.

Nevertheless, white workers are at least as likely as the capitalists to be the group that forces discriminatory practices on the white economy.

Notes

1. Madden (1973), p. 50.
2. The second section of the present chapter incorporates some of the results derived in Lundahl & Wadensjö (1977), (1979).
3. Stiglitz (1973), p. 289.
4. Madden (1973), p. 50. Madden uses F (females) and M (males) instead of N (Negroes) and W (whites) as Becker does, to denote the labor-intensive and the capital-intensive societies, respectively.
5. Stiglitz (1973), p. 288.
6. Madden (1973), p. 51.
7. Also, as Madden points out (ibid.) it '. . . seems incongruous with the prior assumption that M and F are independent societies.'
8. Ibid., pp. 49, 54.
9. See e.g. Samuelson (1948), (1949). A critical view of the factor price equalization theorem is taken in Pearce (1970), Chapter 16.
10. We may of course have the case when a transfer of all the endowment of one of the factors into one sector does not suffice to equalize the returns to the other (immobile) factor between the two sectors, but this is not a realistic case.
11. We could, for example, assume the tastes within each racial group to be identical and homothetic.
12. Taking the partial derivatives of white and Negro incomes (keeping relative commodity prices constant) with respect to capital exports yields

$$\frac{dY_W}{dK_E} = P_A A^{KK} K_E < 0 \text{ and } \frac{dY_N}{dK_E} = -P_A A^{KK} K_E = -\frac{dY_W}{dK_E} > 0,$$

when the return on capital is equal between the two sectors at the outset.

13. The third effect of the repatriation of capital consists of the change in export capital multiplied by the original difference in rates of return on capital between the two sectors. However, the entire effect is zero since this difference is also zero when no discrimination takes place.

6 A CROWDING APPROACH TO LABOR MARKET SEGREGATION

The Beckerian approach to discrimination assumes that capital and labor are homogeneous production factors. However, this assumption is often of doubtful empirical validity. In many instances, labor market segregation typically takes the form where skilled labor from the discriminated group is forced into unskilled occupations by means of discriminatory legislation. Prime examples are of course South Africa, where Apartheid laws keep Negro labor in unqualified jobs while skilled and semi-skilled positions are in principle reserved for whites, and the Indian caste system, which is a hierarchically stratified system of occupational segregation.[1] Furthermore, this discrimination usually takes place in a setting where productive activities are integrated in a single economy rather than in a society of the Beckerian type where the two groups simultaneously constitute separate sectors of the economy.[2]

This case is not covered by the formulation where no difference is made between different types of occupation. Therefore the purpose of the present chapter and Chapter 7 is to adapt and reshape the Beckerian approach to labor market segregation in such a way that it may be applied to the case of differing job categories and labor skills in an integrated economy.

We will begin the present chapter with an examination of several criticisms against the type of approach that was used in Chapter 5, where Negroes and whites were assumed to produce in completely or partially segregated sectors and where only one category of jobs was assumed to exist. In the second section, we present a one-good model with two categories of labor, skilled and unskilled, which enables a comparison to be made between the consequences of discrimination in that model and those obtained in the models in Chapter 4. The main portion of the chapter extends this model to a two-by-two-by-two framework (two goods, two factors, two ethnic groups) comparable to those discussed in Chapter 5. A similar analysis is also presented.

Analogous to Chapter 5, we will investigate the welfare effects of discrimination for both racial groups. However, in order to do so in the two-good case, we must also know how the relative price of the two commodities changes. In order to determine the latter, we need, as

161

before, to find out what happens to the outputs of the two goods at constant prices.

Integration of the Economy. Disaggregation of the Labor Force

The Becker approach to economic discrimination is a 'trade' approach. It makes the assumption that society can be divided in principle into two subgroups that produce in one sector each, with white entrepreneurs organizing production in one of the sectors and Negro entrepreneurs in the other. The interplay between the sectors is limited to factor flows (the models of Chapters 3, 4 and 5) and trade of goods (the models presented in Chapter 5).

The case which probably comes closest to this representation is South Africa. Territorial separation is represented by the bantustan or 'homeland' policy which means that the European economy in principle is reserved for whites while the Africans have to live and work in areas denoted as African. In practice, however, this policy has not been consistently applied. Africans are being allowed into the European sectors as well and the discrimination against them takes place *inside* these sectors, via job reservation for whites by means of a color bar in skilled and semi-skilled occupations. (We shall come back to the South African case at some length in Chapter 8.)

In other contexts, the assumption of two separate societies does not correspond so well to reality. This is the case, for example, with racial discrimination in the United States:

> Applying the theory of tariffs to a world of perfect competition has serious limitations in a world where much of the impact of discrimination comes from the monopoly powers of the discriminator rather than from his ... [ability] to distort perfect competition with trade barriers. Some types of discrimination seem to fit Becker's model but many do not. Discrimination cannot be represented adequately by a model of two independent societies freely trading with each other over the barriers created by racial discrimination. Racial discrimination occurs in one society, not two.

Thus writes Lester Thurow.[3] Referring to Thurow, Ray Marshall stresses that to assume that blacks and whites are like separate countries trading is hardly compatible with a world in which blacks mainly work for white employers and where it is difficult to determine the skin color of the owners of capital.[4]

Finally, in the context of sex discrimination the analogy breaks down completely. In her study of discrimination against women, Janice Madden concludes that analyses of family structure, socialization processes, legal codes and female representation in the power structure all tend to refute the argument that males and females can be represented as two groups which are segregated from each other.[5] The family is a powerful vehicle for creating female inferiority on which discrimination can be based: 'Males and female alter their independent status through the institution of marriage. Women are the only minority in history to live with the master race.'[6] This dependence, according to Madden, is reinforced by all the other processes enumerated above.[7]

In a society where production is integrated in a single economy where both whites and Negroes (to continue to use our racial categories) work in the same subsectors and firms, it is not possible to contend that discrimination takes the shape of capital or labor market segregation in the manner described in Chapters 3–5, where for reasons of tastes or because of the opportunity for certain groups to make pecuniary gains, the discriminated factors were given only limited access to complementary factors. Other mechanisms must be employed. Frequently, these mechanisms involve the reservation of certain jobs for certain categories of people rather than the existence of wage differences for homogeneous labor:

> If I am right in assuming that job control and status are the main objectives of workers, and profits and status are the main objectives of employers, then discriminatory wage differentials for homogeneous labor in the same firms are not likely to be very significant forces in the real world. There is indeed no evidence that such differentials exist for workers who are perfect substitutes. Because of job specificity and on-the-job training, it would almost be necessary to show that blacks and whites in the same firms and occupations were paid different wages, and this seems to be a highly unlikely occurence.
>
> There is, however, considerable evidence of job segregation and the concentration of blacks in certain kinds of jobs. The larger supplies of blacks in these 'traditional' jobs undoubtedly tends to cause wages in these jobs to be lower than otherwise.

So writes Marshall.[8] Madden draws similar conclusions regarding sex discrimination:

Examination of the occupational pattern of female employment in other countries [than the United States] does indicate . . . that females are over-represented in the lower-paying, less prestigious jobs in all countries, regardless of cultural differences in the specification of the low rank jobs. This author finds the latter result to be an indication that some occupational differentiation may be based on occupational discrimination . . . The evidence clearly supports occupational differences as the most important contributor to the wage differential between the sexes.[9]

The works of dual labor market theorists have also shown that discrimination in integrated economies frequently takes the form of job reservation.[10] For example, Michael Piore describes the dualism of labor markets in the following way:

The basic hypothesis of the dual labor market was that the labor market is divided into two essentially distinct sectors, termed the *primary* and the *secondary* sectors. The former offers jobs with relatively high wages, good working conditions, chances of advancement, equity and due process in the administration of work rules and, above all, employment stability. Jobs in the secondary sector, by contrast, tend to be low-paying, with poorer working conditions, little chance of advancement; to have a highly personalized relationship between workers and supervisors which leaves wide latitude for favoritism and is conducive to harsh and capricious work discipline; and to be characterized by considerable instability in jobs and a high turnover among the labor force. The hypothesis was designed to explain the problems of disadvantaged, particularly black, workers, in urban areas, which had previously been attributed to unemployment.[11]

The primary sector may itself be segmented into subordinate and independent jobs. The former are of a routine character and encourage such personality traits as dependability, discipline and responsiveness to rules and authority. Both factory and office jobs are included in this category. Independent primary jobs on the other hand, have creative, problem-solving and self-initiating characteristics. They often have professional standards for work and there is a premium on individual achievements.[12]

Discrimination may be responsible for both these types of segmentation by confining certain workers to secondary and subordinate jobs, respectively, not because of the lack of innate or acquired capabilities but because these workers are identified with the majority of the workers holding such 'inferior' jobs on the basis of race, sex or other features that have nothing to do with labor productivity.[13] Thus, statistical discrimination, where the individuals of a particular group are elevated as if they all had the average characteristics of the group,[14] may be responsible for the segmentation of the labor market.[15]

On the other hand, as Michael Reich has pointed out, the statistical discrimination hypothesis requires that certain highly restrictive conditions regarding the unobservability of individual abilities must be fulfilled. Standard personnel data regarding the background of individual candidates for jobs belonging to the primary and independent categories are usually available. The applicants are interviewed. Trial or probationary periods are employed to collect information about the productivity of the individuals. Firms that fail to acquire the necessary information will in the long run be driven out of the market by firms with better screening and testing procedures.[16]

Segregation of the labor market in an integrated economy may, however, arise for other reasons as well. Crowding, not in the Becker-inspired sense of Bergmann, which, as we know from Chapter 2, is fraught with stability problems, but in the sense in which the word was used in the early British debate of discrimination, is a realistic possibility. In her 1917 article on 'The Position of Women in Economic Life', Millicent Fawcett points out that the maintenance of high wage levels has been a deliberate policy of certain trade unions in order to restrict the number of people who enter skilled occupations. She concludes that the action of excluding women from skilled jobs has had a prejudicial effect on female wages.[17] Five years later, Francis Edgeworth made the same observation:

> The pressure of male trade unions appears to be largely responsible for that crowding of women into a comparatively few occupations, which is universally recognised as a main factor in the depression of their wages . . . The exclusion of women from the better-paid branches of industry may be affected less openly than by a direct veto, such as the 'No females allowed' in the rules of an archaic society . . . Withholding facilities for the acquisition of skilled trades comes to much the same as direct prohibition.[18]

In the remainder of this chapter we will construct two formal models, containing one and two goods, respectively, of this type of discrimination. In these models, Negroes have to leave skilled occupations and are forced to take unskilled jobs instead. This can be either interpreted to mean that they are not allowed to acquire the skills that are necessary to hold the better-paid positions, for example through discrimination in the educational system, or that direct legislation, trade union action or other similar measures are brought to bear so that people who already have the skills are not allowed to use them.

A One-Good Model

Let us assume that we have an economy where only one good (Q) is produced with the use of two kinds of labor, skilled (S) and unskilled (U), but that no capital is needed. From the ethnic point of view, the economy may as before be divided into one white and one Negro community. The entire white labor force is employed in skilled jobs, while Negro labor works in both skilled and unskilled occupations. (This difference may be taken to be, for example, the result of differences in schooling.)[19] The following production function (homogeneous of the first degree) is assumed to hold:

$$Q = f(L^S, L_N^U), \qquad (6:1)$$

with $f^S > 0, f^U > 0, f^{SS} < 0, f^{UU} < 0$ and $f^{SU} = f^{US} > 0$.

Furthermore,

$$L^S = \bar{L}_W^S + L_N^S, \qquad (6:2)$$

that is the skilled labor force contains both whites and Negroes. The total (skilled and unskilled) supply of Negro labor is given by

$$\bar{L}_N = L_N^S + L_N^U, \qquad (6:3)$$

and is assumed to be fixed (as is the supply of white labor).

White incomes are given by

$$Y_W = f^S \bar{L}_W^S \qquad (6:4)$$

and Negro incomes by

$$Y_N = f^S L_N^S + f^U L_N^U. \tag{6:5}$$

When crowding is practiced, the number of Negro workers allowed to hold skilled positions diminishes, and some Negroes are forced into unskilled jobs instead.[20] Differentiating (4:3), keeping the total supply of Negro workers constant, we may express this change as the negative of

$$dL_N^S = -dL_N^U. \tag{6:6}$$

The effect of this measure on white incomes is given by

$$\frac{dY_W}{dL_N^S} = (f^{SS} - f^{SU})\bar{L}_W^S < 0. \tag{6:7}$$

White incomes will increase as a result of crowding, since the reduced supply of skilled Negro labor raises the skilled wage rate.

The impact on Negro incomes is

$$\frac{dY_N}{dL_N^S} = (f^{SS} - f^{SU})L_N^S + (f^{US} - f^{UU})L_N^U + f^S - f^U. \tag{6:8}$$

However,

$$L^S = \bar{L}_W^S + L_N^S. \tag{6:2}$$

Consequently, (6:8) may be rewritten as

$$\frac{dY_N}{dL_N^S} = (f^{SS} - f^{SU})(L^S - \bar{L}_W^S) + (f^{US} - f^{UU})L_N^U + f^S - f^U. \tag{6:9}$$

With a production function that is linearly homogeneous we obtain as before the following expressions:

$$f^{SS}L^S + f^{US}L_N^U \equiv 0 \tag{6:10}$$

and

$$f^{SU}L^S + f^{UU}L_N^U \equiv 0, \tag{6:11}$$

since, given a homogeneous production function, Euler's theorem applies.

Hence expression (6:9) reduces to

$$\frac{dY_N}{dL_N^S} = (f^{SU} - f^{SS})\bar{L}_W^S + f^S - f^U. \tag{6:12}$$

Assuming diminishing returns to skilled labor and positive cross derivatives, the first term on the right-hand side of (6:12) is positive. The wage rate received by skilled labor should also be expected to exceed that paid to unskilled workers so that $f^S > f^U$.

Hence, expression (6:12) is positive. The Negro group suffers a loss when some of its members are forced out of skilled occupations and have to take unskilled jobs instead. As shown by expression (6:8), (6:12) is actually composed of three changes:

(1) the change in incomes of skilled Negro workers as a result of an increased skilled wage rate that would have resulted, had the number of Negroes in skilled occupations remained constant,

(2) the change in incomes of unskilled Negro workers as a result of a fall in the unskilled wage rate that would have accrued, had the number of unskilled Negro workers not changed,

(3) the change in incomes for those transferred from skilled to unskilled occupations, had the original wage rates not changed.

By virtue of the linear homogeneity of the production function, the second of these changes corresponds exactly to the gain that would have accrued to the total (white plus Negro) skilled labor force, if this had remained constant. (In order to ascertain this conclusion, subtract (6:11) from (6:10).) Hence, the second change listed above must be more than enough to swamp the gains registered in the first change. Finally, the loss listed under (3) must be added to this net loss.

A Two-Good Model

The results obtained in the one-good case are neat and clear-cut. White workers gain and Negro workers lose from crowding — a result which corresponds exactly to the one obtained in the most realistic setting in Chapter 4. However, as we found in Chapter 5, results derived from simple models containing only one good or one factor often suffer from misplaced aggregation. Important facts and implications of the analysis may easily be concealed. In the remainder of the chapter we will investigate whether this is the case with the model presented in the foregoing section.

Instead of a single good, we now have two, manufactures and agricultural goods (M and A), the production functions for which are given by

$$M = M_*(L_M^S, L_M^U) \tag{6:13}$$

and

$$A = A_*(L_A^S, L_A^U), \tag{6:14}$$

(where superscripts S and U denote skilled and unskilled labor, respectively, as before) both of which are assumed to be linearly homogeneous and to have partial derivatives whose signs correspond to those of (6:1). It is also assumed that no reversals of factor intensities occur but that $L_M^S/L_M^U > L_A^S/L_A^U$ at all factor prices.

We also need the supply functions for the two goods, describing the choice of production point on the transformation curve:

$$S_M = S_M(P_A, L_N^S) \tag{6:15}$$

and

$$S_A = S_A(P_A, L_N^S), \tag{6:16}$$

where the price of good M is used as *numéraire*. Changes in the second argument show how the transformation curve shifts as a result of discrimination. Production and consumption of both goods take place under competitive conditions (excepting, of course, discrimination).

Next, we have the demand functions for both goods and racial groups. As in Chapter 5, demand is assumed to be a function of the relative price of the goods and of the total income of the group in question:

$$M_W = M_W(P_A, Y_W), \qquad (6{:}17)$$

$$A_W = A_W(P_A, Y_W), \qquad (6{:}18)$$

$$M_N = M_N(P_A, Y_N), \qquad (6{:}19)$$

$$A_N = A_N(P_A, Y_N). \qquad (6{:}20)$$

With profit-maximizing producers, each category of labor is employed up to to the point where the value of its marginal product equals its wage. Thus, white and Negro incomes are given by

$$Y_W = M_*^S L_{WM}^S + P_A A_*^S L_{WA}^S = M_*^S \bar{L}_W^S \qquad (6{:}21)$$

and

$$Y_N = M_*^S L_{NM}^S + P_A A_*^S L_{NA}^S + M_*^U L_{NM}^U + P_A A_*^U L_{NA}^U$$

$$= M_*^S L_N^S + M_*^U L_N^U, \qquad (6{:}22)$$

respectively.

Finally, we need an equilibrium condition, for example the one for the market for agricultural goods:

$$S_A = A_W + A_N. \qquad (6{:}23)$$

Assuming, as in Chapter 5, that Walras' law holds, no equilibrium condition for the market for manufactures is needed, but this market will always be in equilibrium as soon as the market for agricultural goods is. (The labor market and the equilibrium conditions for that market will be introduced below.)

The nine equations (6:15) - (6:23) describe the commodity side of the economy. However, these nine equations contain ten unknowns (S_M, S_A, M_W, A_W, M_N, A_N, Y_W, Y_N, P_A, and L_N^U). Thus, the system must be completed in order not to be underdetermined. This we do by adding five equations describing the factor side.

First, we have the use of skilled labor in agriculture as a function of the relative price of the two goods and of the number of Negroes allowed in skilled occupations:

$$L_A^S = L_A^S(P_A, L_N^S). \qquad (6{:}24)$$

(Since with linearly homogeneous production functions, a rise in the relative price of agricultural goods will always lead to a rise in the relative wage of unskilled labor — the factor used intensively in agricultural production — relative factor prices need not be explicitly included in the model. These automatically move in the 'right' direction when commodity prices change.)[21]

The use of skilled labor in manufacturing, in turn, is given by the full employment condition

$$L_A^S + L_M^S = L_N^S + \bar{L}_W^S \qquad (6{:}25)$$

(where the supply of white labor is assumed to be fixed). As before, it is assumed that all white workers belong to the skilled category. For unskilled labor, we use the corresponding two equations:

$$L_A^U = L_A^U(P_A, L_N^S) \qquad (6{:}26)$$

and

$$L_A^U + L_M^U = L_N^U. \qquad (6{:}27)$$

Finally, we know that the total (fixed) supply of Negro labor is divided between skilled and unskilled occupations:

$$L_N^S + L_N^U = \bar{L}_N. \qquad (6{:}28)$$

This completes our general equilibrium system. The five equations (6:24)-(6:28) add the four unknowns L_A^S, L_M^S, L_A^U and L_M^U. The number of equations now equals the number of unknowns. Assuming that the system possesses a solution, we may now proceed to find this solution.

Factor Use and Outputs at Constant Commodity Prices

The first thing that will be investigated is how the output of the two goods and the factor uses in each sector change when Negroes are forced out of skilled occupations and put into unskilled jobs instead. For this,

172 A Crowding Approach to Labor Market Segregation

we need not go into the entire general equilibrium system set out above, but five equations will suffice. Under competitive conditions, factor prices will be equalized between the two sectors, so that

$$P_A A_*^S = M_*^S, \qquad (6:29)$$

for skilled labor, and

$$P_A A_*^U = M_*^U, \qquad (6:30)$$

for unskilled labor. These two conditions together with the conditions that factor use must equal factor supply for both types of labor (6:25) and (6:27) provide five unknowns and four equations. To close the system we use (6:28).

Differentiating these five equations with respect to L_N^S while keeping relative commodity prices constant gives

$$0 = M_*^{SS} L_M^{SSN} + M_*^{SU} L_M^{USN} - P_A \left(A_*^{SS} L_A^{SSN} + A_*^{SU} L_A^{USN} \right), \qquad (6:31)$$

$$0 = M_*^{UU} L_M^{USN} + M_*^{US} L_M^{SSN} - P_A \left(A_*^{UU} L_A^{USN} + A_*^{US} L_A^{SSN} \right), \qquad (6:32)$$

$$L_A^{SSN} + L_M^{SSN} = 1 \qquad (6:33)$$

and

$$L_A^{USN} + L_M^{USN} = -1. \qquad (6:34)$$

It is assumed that those skilled Negro workers who are being excluded from holding skilled jobs are now forced into competing with unskilled labor instead.

We now have a simultaneous equation system with four equations and the four unknowns L_A^{SSN}, L_A^{USN}, L_M^{SSN}, and L_M^{USN}. To solve the system for these four unknowns we first make use of the fact that our production functions are linearly homogeneous. Then, according to Euler's theorem, the following identities hold:

$$A_*^{SS} L_A^S + A_*^{SU} L_A^U \equiv 0, \qquad (6:35)$$

$$A_*^{UU}L_A^U + A_*^{US}L_A^S \equiv 0, \tag{6:36}$$

$$M_*^{SS}L_M^S + M_*^{SU}L_M^U \equiv 0, \tag{6:37}$$

and

$$M_*^{UU}L_M^U + M_*^{US}L_M^S \equiv 0, \tag{6:38}$$

so that

$$A_*^{SS}\frac{L_A^S}{L_A^U} = -A_*^{SU} = -A_*^{US} = A_*^{UU}\frac{L_A^U}{L_A^S} \tag{6:39}$$

and

$$M_*^{SS}\frac{L_M^S}{L_M^U} = -M_*^{SU} = -M_*^{US} = M_*^{UU}\frac{L_M^U}{L_M^S}. \tag{6:40}$$

Substituting (6:39) and (6:40) into (6:31) and (6:32) gives

$$0 = M_*^{SU}\left(L_M^{USN} - \frac{L_M^U}{L_M^S}L_M^{SSN}\right) - P_A A_*^{SU}\left(L_A^{USN} - \frac{L_A^U}{L_A^S}L_A^{SSN}\right) \tag{6:41}$$

$$0 = M_*^{SU}\left(L_M^{SSN} - \frac{L_M^S}{L_M^U}L_M^{USN}\right) - P_A A_*^{SU}\left(L_A^{SSN} - \frac{L_A^S}{L_A^U}L_A^{USN}\right), \tag{6:42}$$

Together with (6:33) and (6:34) these two equations constitute a new general equilibrium system which may be solved for the four unknowns. After some algebraic manipulations the following solutions emerge with, *nota bene*, commodity prices constant:

$$L_M^{SSN} = \frac{1}{\Delta^*}\frac{L_M^S}{L_M^U}\left(1 + \frac{L_A^S}{L_A^U}\right) > 0, \tag{6:43}$$

$$L_M^{USN} = \frac{1}{\Delta^*}\left(1 + \frac{L_A^S}{L_A^U}\right) > 0, \qquad (6:44)$$

$$L_A^{SSN} = -\frac{1}{\Delta^*}\frac{L_A^S}{L_A^U}\left(1 + \frac{L_M^S}{L_M^U}\right) < 0 \qquad (6:45)$$

and

$$L_A^{USN} = -\frac{1}{\Delta^*}\left(1 + \frac{L_M^S}{L_M^U}\right) < 0, \qquad (6:46)$$

where

$$\Delta^* = \frac{L_M^S}{L_M^U} - \frac{L_A^S}{L_A^U} > 0, \qquad (6:47)$$

given that the production of manufactures is always more skill-intensive than the production of agricultural goods.

Expressions (6:43) - (6:46) also give us the signs of S_A^SN and S_M^SN at constant commodity prices. If the manufacturing sector is skill-intensive and the agricultural sector is intensive in the use of unskilled labor, the production of manufactures must contract in absolute terms while the output of agricultural goods expands.

This is a well-known result in the theory of international trade, although in a somewhat special setting. The Rybczynski theorem[22] states that in a two-by-two framework, the production of the commodity that uses the growing factor intensively must increase and that the production of the good using the non-growing or diminishing factor intensively must decrease, as long as the relative price of the two goods is kept constant.

Hence, $S_A^SN < 0$ and $S_M^SN > 0$ with fixed prices.

As the relative factor supply of the economy changes as a result of discrimination, the supply of skilled workers is reduced while that of unskilled labor increases. In order that relative commodity prices remain constant, the employment of skilled workers in the (skill-intensive) manufacturing sector must decline while the increase of unskilled workers must be absorbed in agriculture (which employs unskilled workers intensively). In this model, given linearly homogeneous production functions, relative factor prices depend solely on factor intensities. Hence, unless commodity prices are to change factor prices must remain constant. The only way of keeping factor intensities unchanged is to allocate the increased supply of unskilled workers to the sector where they are employed intensively, that is to agriculture. However, this also requires an increased use of skilled labor in agriculture. The latter, however, may be taken from manufacturing, together with some unskilled workers.

Conversely, in order not to disturb the relative commodity price relationship when the supply of skilled workers contracts, these workers must be obtained from the skill-intensive sector (manufacturing) together with some unskilled personnel. Hence, when discrimination alters the relative supply of the two categories of labor, the expansion of agricultural production and the reduction in the output of manufactured goods allows both factor intensities and relative factor prices, and consequently relative commodity prices, to be held constant.

The Development of Relative Commodity Prices

By differentiating the two equation systems (6:15) - (6:23)[23] and (6:24) - (6:28), using the two production functions (6:13) and (6:14), we obtain the impact of discrimination on relative commodity prices:

$$\frac{dP_A}{dL_N^S} = \frac{1}{\Delta^{**}}(S_A^{SN} - A_W^Y\alpha - A_N^Y\beta) \tag{6:48}$$

where

$$\alpha = \bar{L}_W^S\left[M_*^{SS}(1 - L_A^{SSN}) - M_*^{SU}(1 + L_A^{USN})\right], \tag{6:49}$$

$$\beta = \gamma(1 - L_A^{SSN}) - \delta(1 + L_A^{USN}) + M^S - M^U, \tag{6:50}$$

$$\Delta^{**} = A_W^P - A_W^Y\bar{L}_W^S(M_*^{SS}L_A^{SP} + M_*^{SU}L_A^{UP}) + A_N^P \\ - A_N^Y(\gamma L_A^{SP} + \delta L_A^{UP}) - S_A^P, \tag{6:51}$$

$$\gamma = L_N^S M_*^{SS} + L_N^U M_*^{US} \tag{6:52}$$

and

$$\delta = L_N^S M_*^{SU} + L_N^U M_*^{UU}. \tag{6:53}$$

The denominator (6:51) can be shown to be negative, since it represents the change in the excess demand for agricultural goods with respect to a rise in the price of that good. As long as we want our model to be stable in the Walrasian sense, this derivative must be negative.

Turning to the numerator of (6:48), it may be proved that $\alpha = 0$, and that β is positive. To do so, we divide (6:43) by (6:44) and (6:45) by (6:46) and rearrange. Then (noting that the changes in labor use have been derived with commodity prices constant), we find that

$$\frac{L_M^{SSN}}{L_M^S} = \frac{L_M^{USN}}{L_M^U} \tag{6:54}$$

and

$$\frac{L_A^{SSN}}{L_A^S} = \frac{L_A^{USN}}{L_A^U}. \tag{6:55}$$

Within each sector, both factors show the same (positive or negative) growth rate. Factor proportions remain constant in both sectors as long as the relative price of the two commodities is unchanged.

The assumption of linearly homogeneous production functions implies that all marginal productivities will also remain constant. Hence the two influences on the marginal productivity of skilled labor in manufacturing that stem from changes in the use of skilled and unskilled labor, respectively, cancel each other out. α is simply the change in white (skilled labor) incomes resulting from the change in the marginal productivity of skilled workers at constant factor and commodity prices. Thus, the two terms of (6:49) eliminate each other, so that $\alpha = 0$. White incomes do not change when the two production factors are reallocated at constant commodity prices.

By the same token, we know that the sum of the first two terms of

(6:50) must equal zero so that β (the change in Negro incomes) reduces to $M^S - M^U > 0$, and (6:48) to

$$\frac{dP_A}{dL_N^S} = \frac{1}{\Delta^{**}}\left[S_A^{S_N} - A_N^Y(M_*^S - M_*^U)\right], \qquad (6:56)$$

which must be positive as well. The relative price of agricultural goods must fall as a result of crowding. On the one hand discrimination gives rise to an increase in the supply of agricultural commodities and on the other hand it reduces the incomes of those Negro workers who are forced out of their skilled positions into unskilled jobs. Given that neither good is inferior, this reduction of incomes leads to a fall in the demand for agricultural goods. In order to eliminate this excess supply of agricultural commodities (and the corresponding excess demand for manufactures), the relative price of agricultural goods must fall.

Discrimination and Real Incomes

The next step of our analysis will be to investigate the impact of discrimination on the real incomes of different groups in society. From our analysis of the development of relative commodity prices we already know that at given commodity prices neither skilled nor unskilled wages will be affected, since factor intensities remain unchanged in both branches. The only change that takes place is that those Negro workers, who are forced out of skilled occupations into unskilled ones suffer a wage reduction which is equal to the difference between the skilled and the unskilled wage rate.

Relative commodity prices, however, change as a result of discrimination. The relative price of agricultural goods falls. This in turn affects real wages. To find the impact of relative commodity price changes on real wages we use the following system:

$$w^S = P_A A_*^S, \qquad (6:57)$$

$$w^S = M_*^S, \qquad (6:58)$$

$$w^U = P_A A_*^U, \qquad (6:59)$$

$$w^U = M_*^U, \qquad (6:60)$$

178   *A Crowding Approach to Labor Market Segregation*

$$L_A^U + L_M^U = \bar{L}_N^U, \tag{6:61}$$

$$L_A^S + L_M^S = \bar{L}_N^S + \bar{L}_W^S. \tag{6:62}$$

Wages equal the values of the marginal products of the two types of labor. In addition, the total supplies of the two types of labor must be allocated between the two sectors. It should be noted that the total supplies of both types of labor are now given. Some skilled Negro workers have already been transferred into unskilled activities. This has led to a commodity price change which, given the new supplies of labor, will affect wage rates.

Differentiating the system (6:57) - (6:62) totally, making use of the Euler relations (6:39) and (6:40) yields the following solutions for the changes in wage rates:

$$W^{SP} = -\frac{1}{\Delta^*}\left(A_*^U \frac{L_A^U}{L_A^S} + A_*^S\right)\frac{L_A^S}{L_A^U} < 0 \tag{6:63}$$

and

$$W^{UP} = \frac{1}{\Delta^*}\left(A_*^U \frac{L_A^U}{L_A^S} + A_*^S\right)\frac{L_A^S}{L_A^U}\frac{L_M^S}{L_M^U} > 0. \tag{6:64}$$

The change in the relative commodity price resulting from discrimination leads to an increase in the skilled wage rate and a fall in the unskilled wage rate, since manufacturing is the skill-intensive sector.

When the relative price of agricultural goods falls, producers react by decreasing the supply of these goods and increasing the supply of manufactures. Given that manufacturing is the skill-intensive line of production, relatively more skilled than unskilled labor will then be demanded by manufacturing producers than agricultural producers will release at given factor prices. Thus, skilled wages will rise and unskilled wages will fall before a new equilibrium can be reached.

The changes in skilled and unskilled wage rates derived in (6:63) and (6:64) represent changes in terms of manufactures. However, it may be shown that the skilled wage rate increases and the unskilled wage rate falls in terms of agricultural goods as well, so that the wage rate changes represent changes in *real* wages. In terms of agricultural goods (with given factor endowments), the change in skilled wages is

$$\frac{d(w^S/P_A)}{dP_A} = \frac{P_A w^{SP} - w^S}{(P_A)^2} < 0. \tag{6:65}$$

It is immediately evident that (6:65) is negative. When discrimination is introduced, the skilled wage rate rises not only in terms of manufactures but in terms of agricultural goods as well. To show that the unskilled wage also falls in terms of agricultural goods, we rewrite (6:59) as

$$\frac{w^U}{P_A} = A_*^U. \tag{6:66}$$

We then have that (with given factor endowments)

$$\frac{d(w^U/P_A)}{dP_A} = A_*^{UP}. \tag{6:67}$$

Given linearly homogeneous production functions, the marginal product of unskilled labor in agriculture is a positive function of the ratio of skilled to unskilled labor in that sector, so that

$$A_*^{UP} = \frac{dA_*^U}{d(L_A^S/L_A^U)} \frac{d(L_A^S/L_A^U)}{dP_A}. \tag{6:68}$$

We already know that in order to maintain full employment w^S must increase and w^U must decrease when P_A falls as a result of discrimination. Producers in agriculture thus reduce the skill intensity of production as P_A falls. In other words, $d(L_A^S/L_A^U)/dP_A > 0$. Consequently, expression (6:68) must have a positive sign.

The white group derives a real income gain by resorting to discrimination. Thus, *provided that the impact on real income is used as the criterion for determining whether or not to resort to discrimination, an economic rationale has been found which may serve to explain the existence of crowding.*

Going on to Negro incomes, we already know that at given commodity prices those who are transferred from skilled to unskilled jobs will suffer a loss of income. In addition, we find that commodity price changes affect different groups in different ways. Thus, those skilled Negro workers who are fortunate enough to remain in skilled jobs in the presence of discrimination will see their real incomes increased. Those who hold unskilled jobs regardless of whether discrimination is present or not will suffer a loss of real income. Altogether, we have two loser groups in the Negro community: unskilled workers and those who are transferred from skilled to unskilled jobs, and one 'winner' group: those skilled workers who are allowed to keep their jobs. Clearly, the first two groups will oppose discrimination. Presumably, the 'winners' will do so as well, unless we establish some criterion for selecting those to be thrown out of skilled jobs which unequivocally separates this group from the prospective 'winners' *a priori*.

To sum up: *In the one-good model of the present chapter, we found that a job reservation policy pursued by whites which forces Negroes out of skilled occupations into unskilled jobs will unequivocally result in a white gain and a Negro loss. The same type of conclusions also hold in the two-good setting.* Whites gain and Negroes lose. (Only those Negroes who manage to stay in skilled occupations both before and after the introduction of discriminatory practices gain.) Thus, both models provide a rationale for discrimination.

Conclusions

We began the present chapter by noting two criticisms of the models employed in Chapters 4 and 5. In the first place, one cannot always assume that the discriminated and favored groups constitute two separate 'societies' without a severe loss of realism. The two groups often work together in a unified economy, and discrimination takes place in this setting. Secondly, in an integrated economy, it is not possible to work with discrimination in the capital or labor market that requires segregation of sectors. Discrimination must take on a different form. We have now examined two different models within the crowding tradition in order to investigate the effects of discriminatory labor market segregation where skilled Negro workers are precluded from holding skilled jobs and are forced into accepting unskilled positions instead. This type of discrimination is common, for example, in South Africa.

In the simplest possible framework, where a single good is produced solely with the aid of skilled and unskilled labor, but without capital the discriminating (white) community can always improve its real income by resorting to discrimination, while the discriminated (Negro) community will always lose.

The second model employed is one where the two goods are produced with the aid of the same two factors as in the one-good case. Here, at constant relative commodity prices, discrimination always leads to an increase in the output of the good that uses unskilled labor intensively and to a fall in the production of the other good. Commodity prices will, however, not remain constant, but the relative price of agricultural goods will fall.

Turning to real incomes, discrimination will tend to raise the real incomes of whites (in analogy with the one-good case). The two losing groups in Negro society are the unskilled workers and those workers who are forced out of skilled occupations (who are not allowed to enter) into unskilled jobs, whereas those who manage to keep their skilled jobs will derive a gain.

Notes

1. An account of the Apartheid laws is given in Hepple (1971). Cf. also Hutt (1954) and Horwitz (1967). We will come back to an explicit analysis of South African discrimination in Chapter 8. For analyses of the caste system, see e.g. Berreman (1979), Dumont (1970) and Klass (1980).
2. South Africa represents a combination of these two cases.
3. Thurow (1969), p. 117.
4. Marshall (1974), p. 862.
5. Madden (1973), p. 55.
6. Ibid. Cf. also Chiplin & Sloane (1974), pp. 387-8 for a similar view.
7. Madden (1973), pp. 55-8.
8. Marshall (1974), p. 862.
9. Madden (1973), p. 92.
10. See Chapter 2 for a survey of the dual labor market theory.
11. Piore (1975), p. 126.
12. Gordon, Edwards & Reich (1982).
13. Marshall (1974), p. 856.
14. Cf. Phelps (1972:2), Arrow (1972:1).
15. Blau & Jusenius (1975), p. 23.
16. Reich (1981), pp. 103-7.
17. Fawcett (1917), pp. 194-5. See Chapter 2 for a more detailed presentation.
18. Edgeworth (1922), p. 439.
19. The latter differences may themselves be a result of discrimination. For an example, see Lundahl (1979), Chapter 10.
20. Note that this is a mere analytical device. In practice barriers of different types are created which makes it difficult for the discriminated group to hold skilled jobs.

21. Cf. Stolper & Samuelson (1941). This is shown explicitly in the section on real incomes below.
22. See Rybczynski (1955).
23. (6:15) (6:17) and (6:19) can be deleted, since S_M, M_W and M_N appear only in these three equations.

7 A MORE REALISTIC CROWDING MODEL

Chapter 6 contained the simplest possible model of crowding. The two categories of labor that form the core of the problem — skilled and unskilled workers — were employed to produce either a single commodity or two goods (manufactures and agricultural goods). The two-good case had the advantage of allowing us to pursue the analysis within the familiar context — central to the theory of international trade — of a two-by-two model. The main results derived were that the white community would be better off in terms of real incomes by resorting to job reservation and that everybody in the Negro community, except those skilled workers who manage to obtain skilled jobs, would suffer a loss from discrimination.

The advantage of being able to conduct the analysis within the scope of the traditional two-by-two model, however, has to be weighed against the desire to make the model a reasonably realistic one. It is hardly a true reflection of the real world to postulate that no capital is used by the manufacturing sector or no land by the agricultural producers. On the other hand, this will complicate the model. Departing from the framework of Chapter 6, we will therefore make the smallest possible addition of realism to each of the production functions by assuming that production does not only require skilled and unskilled labor but also capital in the manufacturing sector and land in agriculture. We will then examine to what extent this assumption changes the results of Chapter 6. In the one-good case, only capital is added.

This amended model is not a complete three-factor, two-good model where all the factors are mobile between the two sectors.[1] In principle, such a model could be constructed by employing the methodology to which we have adhered throughout the present work. Judged solely from the point of realism, this would be desirable. Where discrimination takes the form of crowding as sketched in Chapter 6, the producers not only have the option of using more or less of the two types of labor but in the long run, they can also make a choice with respect to the employment of capital which can then be reallocated between the two sectors. (Moreover, land should be added in agriculture.)

On another count, however, constructing a complete three-by-two model may make little sense. In the first paper to produce any patent results within the general three-by-two framework, Roy Ruffin makes the following reference to the state of arts within the theory of international trade:

> The general three-factor, two-good model of international trade has thus far resisted analysis. Kemp . . .[2] pointed out long ago that the relationship between commodity prices and factor prices involves complicated technical substitution terms between the various factors and, hence, simple Stolper-Samuelson-type results are impossible. Batra and Casas . . .[3] have pointed out that the relationship between factor prices and factor endowment is 'difficult to interpret' and 'not very intuitive' since, presumably, the notion of factor intensity in a three-factor model loses some of its sting.[4]

Thus, the main difficulty on the production side is that in the complete three-factor model, the properties of what Ronald Jones calls 'two-ness'[5] are lost, because 'in situations where more than two factors are involved, we cannot have a unique ordering of technologies according to relative factor intensity.'[6] On the demand side, things are complicated by the fact that when both sectors use three completely mobile factors, the reward to each factor (wages and interest) is affected by the change in three factors (via the second derivatives of the production functions) instead of by only two changes as in the traditional two-factor, two-good model.

More than any other area of economics, the theory of international trade has for a long time been dominated by two-by-two models. However, during the past fifteen years, the issue of dimensionality has been brought to the forefront, in attempts to generalize the more important standard theorems.[7] In this context, two different approaches have been chosen. In the first one, the procedure has been to start from the results of the two-by-two cases and to find the restrictive assumptions which allow the same conclusions to be produced in cases of higher dimensions.[8] As one can expect, such an approach yields results which are valid only under special circumstances, and in this sense dodges the question of to what extent the two-by-two models can be generalized.

The second approach to the dimensionality problem adopts the opposite route. It departs from the structure of higher dimension models and poses the question of which results are likely to emerge from the solution of such models without the imposition of, for example, such restrictions that make it possible to make 'unique one-to-one assignments of factors to commodities so that each commodity price rise leads to an increase in the real return to the factor uniquely assigned it ... and a decrease in all others ...'[9] Thus, the second approach is concerned with establishing general results regardless of whether these results happen to conform to those given by the two-by-two structure or not.[10]

Clearly, it is the second of the two approaches that is the more interesting one. Nevertheless, research along those lines does not abound in trade theory, and if the issue is considered from the point of view of applicability, the reason is perhaps not hard to find. Increasing the realism of the model frequently involves a departure from the neatness, simplicity and determinacy of the conclusions established in the simpler cases.

In the present chapter, a mix of the two research strategies sketched above will be employed. We will derive expressions for the general case, although the discussion of these expressions will be related to the results of Chapter 6 in order to find certain additional assumptions which make it possible to produce the same qualitative results in the extended model as in the restricted two-by-two framework. Before we proceed, however, let us examine the extended one-good model.

The Extended One-Good Model

The simple one-good analysis which was employed in Chapter 6 yielded clear-cut expressions both for white and Negro incomes. It was demonstrated that discriminatory labor market segmentation which restricts Negro entry to skilled occupations increases white incomes while the incomes of the Negro community fall under the same circumstances. The model was based on a production function which included only skilled and unskilled labor. In the present section, we will seek to find out whether the results still hold once we introduce capital as well into the production function.

The inclusion of capital changes the production function (6:1) to

$$Q = f_4(L^S, L^U, \bar{K}), \qquad (7:1)$$

with positive first derivatives, negative 'direct' second derivatives and positive cross derivatives. Assuming that the entire capital stock is owned by white capitalists, the incomes of the white group as a whole become

$$Y_W = f_+^S \bar{L}_W^S + f_+^K \bar{K}. \qquad (7:2)$$

When a fraction of the skilled Negro labor force is forced into unskilled jobs, these incomes change as follows:

$$\frac{dY_W}{dL_N^S} = (f_+^{SS} - f_+^{SU})\bar{L}_W^S - (f_+^{KU} - f_+^{KS})\bar{K}, \qquad (7:3)$$

since

$$\bar{L}_N = L_N^S + L^U. \qquad (7:4)$$

With diminishing returns to skilled labor and positive cross derivatives in the production function, the first term of expression (7:3) is always negative, but the sign of the second term depends on the relative magnitudes of f_+^{KU} and f_+^{KS}. For the white community as a whole to derive a secure gain from a job reservation policy, it is necessary that $f_+^{KU} > f_+^{KS}$, that is that on the margin the complementarity between capital and unskilled labor is stronger than the complementarity between capital and skilled labor. This implies that the 'capital-skill complementarity hypothesis' is incorrect, which may not be too plausible a condition.[11] Even if the hypothesis *is* correct, the whites may, however, still make a net gain by employing discrimination, namely when the gain of the workers exceeds the loss incurred by the capitalists, that is when

$$(f_+^{SS} - f_+^{SU})\bar{L}_W^S > (f_+^{KU} - f_+^{KS})\bar{K}. \qquad (7:5)$$

The introduction of capital into our one-good model does, however, not completely destroy the determinacy of the results with respect to the impact of discrimination on white incomes. The unconditional white labor gain in the one-good model without capital is preserved when capital is present as well. Although the capitalists may gain by discrimination against skilled Negro workers, given that the complementarity of skilled labor and capital is higher than that of unskilled labor and capital, they may also lose. Transfers from workers to capitalists may indeed become necessary if the capitalists are to be persuaded to continue with their policy of reservation of skilled jobs for whites.

The effect on Negro incomes, finally, is the same as that spelled out in Chapter 6. With due changes of notation, expression (6:12), which shows that the Negro community loses when the whites apply discriminatory practices, still remains valid when capital is introduced in the model.

We may now proceed to the extended two-good model.

The Extended Two-Good Model

The production functions that we are going to make use of in the present chapter include capital in manufacturing and land (T) in agriculture (both in fixed supply):

$$M = M_+(L_M^S, L_M^U, \bar{K}), \tag{7:6}$$

and

$$A = A_+(L_A^S, L_A^U, \bar{T}), \tag{7:7}$$

with positive first derivatives, negative 'direct' second derivatives and positive cross derivatives.

The commodity side of the economy is described by nine equations; two supply functions (the same as in Chapter 6):

$$S_A = S_A(P_A, L_N^S) \tag{7:8}$$

and

$$S_M = S_M(P_A, L_N^S), \tag{7:9}$$

with the price of manufactures used as *numéraire*, two demand functions for each racial group (also unchanged):

$$M_W = M_W(P_A, Y_W), \tag{7:10}$$
$$A_W = A_W(P_A, Y_W), \tag{7:11}$$
$$M_N = M_N(P_A, Y_N), \tag{7:12}$$

and

$$A_N = A_N(P_A, Y_N), \tag{7:13}$$

188 *A More Realistic Crowding Model*

one income expression for whites and one for Negroes (both modified):

$$Y_W = M_+^S L_{WM}^S + M_+^K \bar{K} + P_A A_+^S L_{WA}^S + P_A A_+^T \bar{T} = M_+^S \bar{L}_W^S \\ + M_+^K \bar{K} + P_A A_+^T \bar{T}, \qquad (7{:}14)$$

where it is assumed that whites own all capital and all agricultural land, and

$$Y_N = M_+^S L_{NM}^S + M_+^U L_{NM}^U + P_A A_+^S L_{NA}^S + P_A A_+^U L_{NA}^U \\ = M_+^S L_N^S + M_+^U L_N^U \qquad (7{:}15)$$

and, finally, the equilibrium condition for the market for agricultural goods

$$S_A = A_W + A_N. \qquad (7{:}16)$$

Assuming Walras' law to hold, as in Chapter 6, only one equilibrium condition is needed to describe the commodity market system.

The factor side of the economy is described by the same five equations as in Chapter 6. First we have two equations for skilled labor:

$$L_A^S = L_A^S(P_A, L_N^S), \qquad (7{:}17)$$

which expresses the employment of skilled labor in agriculture as a function of the relative price of agricultural goods and of the size of the skilled Negro labor force, and

$$L_A^S + L_M^S = \bar{L}_W^S + L_N^S, \qquad (7{:}18)$$

which shows that with a given supply of white skilled labor and the use of skilled labor in agriculture being determined by (7:17), the employment of skilled labor in manufacturing depends on the amount of skilled Negro labor available.

The employment of unskilled workers is described in a similar manner:

$$L_A^U = L_A^U(P_A, L_N^S)^{12} \qquad (7{:}19)$$

and

$$L_N^U = L_A^U + L_M^U. \qquad (7{:}20)$$

The latter equation determines the use of skilled labor in manufacturing, given the size of the unskilled (Negro) work force and its use in agriculture.

Finally, the markets for skilled and unskilled labor are connected via the distribution of Negro labor.

$$L_N^U + L_N^S = \bar{L}_N. \qquad (7{:}21)$$

The system is then complete.

Changes in Relative Commodity Prices

Assuming that a solution to our system (7:6) - (7:21) exists we may next proceed to solve this system for the impact of discrimination (the negative of an increase in L_N^S) on relative commodity prices. This solution is needed later in the discussion of changes in the real incomes of different groups.

However, to spare the reader some tedious algebra we will not present the solution in the main text. Those interested in the details are instead referred to the appendix to the present chapter. Here, we will only comment on the results.

The general conclusion is that *the result that the relative price of agricultural goods falls, established in Chapter 6, is not generally preserved in the model including capital and land.* It is not hard to see why. The conclusion in Chapter 6 hinges in a critical fashion on the one-to-one correspondence between relative commodity prices and relative factor prices. In order to keep the former constant, we also had in Chapter 6 to allow the latter to remain fixed. This meant that neither the skilled nor the unskilled wage could change. Since all whites remained in skilled occupations throughout the analysis, their incomes did not change either. Nor did the incomes of those Negroes who were not transferred from one skill category to the other. The only impact on incomes was the drop experienced by those who were down-graded from skilled to unskilled jobs. As neither good was inferior, this drop led to a decrease in the demand for both goods, whereas the supply of agricultural goods had risen and the output of manufacturing goods had fallen. Together, these events created an excess supply of agricultural goods (an excess demand for manufactures). The relative price of agricultural goods then had to fall to clear the markets.

In the present chapter, it is not possible to establish any analogous chain of reasoning. As demonstrated in the appendix, complications arise both on the supply and on the demand side. With regard to the former, the factor use of either sector is not determinate in the general case. We have, however, derived conditions which make it possible to duplicate the Rybczynski-type results derived in Chapter 6 which stated that when the supply of skilled labor shrinks and the supply of unskilled workers increases at constant relative commodity prices due to discrimination, the skill-intensive sector (manufacturing) will cut down on the use of both types of labor and hence decrease its output volume, while the sector employing unskilled workers intensively (agriculture) will increase its use of skilled and unskilled labor and consequently its production. These conditions are that the skill intensity of manufacturing should be high and that of agriculture low in order that a substantial difference should exist between the sectors.

Even if we postulate that the supply of agricultural goods does rise and that the output of manufactures contracts, no clear-cut solution, however, emerges. The demand side is also indeterminate. In the case of two goods and four factors, relative factor prices will generally change even when relative commodity prices remain unchanged. In models which are based on production functions that are homogeneous of the first degree, marginal productivities, and hence relative factor prices will be determined solely by factor combinations. Hence the proportions in which production factors are employed in the two sectors will have to be held constant in order not to change factor prices. However, in the extended model factor intensities change with given commodity prices, and only by chance will the changes in white and Negro factor incomes be such as to leave total white incomes unchanged and to make total Negro incomes fall.

However, the change in relative commodity prices may be determined in the special case when the marginal propensities to consume the two goods do not differ between the two racial groups. In that case it is total income, rather than the distribution of incomes between whites and Negroes that will affect demand. The use of discrimination leads to a drop in the total real income of the economy, and consequently to a drop in the demand for both goods. If in addition the supply of agricultural goods increases, the relative price of these goods must fall. In the general case we cannot, however, be certain as to the direction in which relative commodity prices will move when crowding is practised.

Effects on Real Incomes

We will next examine the effects of discrimination on white and Negro factor incomes. Once again we recall the conclusions arrived at in Chapter 6, where it was established that at constant commodity prices, the white community as a whole (consisting only of skilled workers) made no gain nor any loss in real terms, whereas the Negro community viewed as a whole incurred a loss. Those who were withdrawn from skilled occupations and put into unskilled jobs saw their incomes drop (whereas the real incomes of those Negro workers who remained in either category throughout were not affected). When relative commodity price changes were also taken into account, the whites derived a real gain while all Negroes, except those who managed to keep a skilled job when discrimination was present, lost in real terms.

The impact of discrimination on total white and Negro real incomes, respectively, may be obtained from the second terms of the denominator and numerator of (A7:1). The third term of the numerator and the fourth term of the denominator specify the impact on total Negro real incomes. Both the resulting expressions are highly indeterminate (and will not be spelled out).

Now that we have introduced capital and land in the model, we should, however, not be satisfied by examining only the total effects. The effects of discrimination on different factor rewards (incomes) should also be investigated. As has been stated, each factor receives the value of its marginal product:

$$w^S = P_A A^S_+, \qquad (7:22)$$

$$w^S = M^S_+, \qquad (7:23)$$

$$w^U = P_A A^U_+, \qquad (7:24)$$

and
$$w^U = M^U_{+.} \tag{7:25}$$

Solving a system consisting of (7:22) - (7:25) plus (7:18), (7:20) and (7:21) for (a) the impact of discrimination on the two wages at constant commodity prices, and (b) the impact of a change in P_A on the two wages, gives for (a):

$$w^{SSN} = -\frac{P_A}{\Delta''} \left\{ (A^{SU}_+ - A^{SS}_+) \left[M^{UU}_+ M^{SS}_+ - (M^{US}_+)^2 \right] \right.$$
$$\left. + P_A (M^{SU}_+ - M^{SS}_+) \left[A^{UU}_+ A^{SS}_+ - (A^{US}_+)^2 \right] \right\} \tag{7:26}$$

and

$$w^{USN} = -\frac{P_A}{\Delta''} \left\{ (A^{UU}_+ - A^{US}_+) \left[M^{UU}_+ M^{SS}_+ - (M^{US}_+)^2 \right] \right.$$
$$\left. + P_A (M^{UU}_+ - M^{US}_+) \left[A^{UU}_+ A^{SS}_+ - (A^{US}_+)^2 \right] \right\} \tag{7:27}$$

where Δ'' is (A7:23) in the appendix, which is positive.

By substituting (A7:14) and (A7:15) from the appendix, it can be proved that (7:26) is negative, while (7:27) is positive. At constant commodity prices, the skilled wage, and hence the real incomes of skilled workers (white and Negro), increases as a result of discrimination while the real wages and incomes of unskilled workers fall. As has been noted previously, this is necessary to clear the labor markets, since the supply of skilled labor contracts and that of unskilled labor expands.

Allowing P_A to change (with a given factor endowment) and substituting (A7:14) and (A7:15) from the appendix gives

$$w^{SP} = \frac{1}{\Delta''} \left[A^S_+ \lambda + P_A A^S_+ \frac{\bar{K}}{L^U_A L^S_M} M^{KS}_+ (\bar{T} A^{TU}_+ + L^S_A A^{SU}_+) \right.$$
$$\left. + P_A A^U_+ \frac{\bar{K}}{L^S_M} M^{KS}_+ A^{SU}_+ + \mu \right] \tag{7:28}$$

and

$$w^{UP} = \frac{1}{\Delta''} \left[A^U_+ \lambda + P_A A^U_+ \frac{\bar{K}}{L^S_A L^U_M} M^{KU}_+ (\bar{T} A^{TS}_+ + L^U_A A^{SU}_+) \right.$$
$$\left. + P_A A^S_+ \frac{\bar{K}}{L^U_M} M^{KU}_+ A^{SU}_+ - \frac{L^S_M}{L^U_M} \mu \right], \tag{7:29}$$

where

$$\lambda = \bar{K}\left[\frac{\bar{K}}{L_M^U L_M^S}M_+^{KU}M_+^{KS} + M_+^{SU}\left(\frac{1}{L_M^U}M_+^{KS} + \frac{1}{L_M^S}M_+^{KU}\right)\right] > 0 \quad (7{:}30)$$

and

$$\mu = P_A M_+^{SU}\left[\frac{\bar{T}}{L_A^U}\left(A_+^S \frac{L_M^U}{L_M^S}A_+^{TU} - A_+^U \frac{L_A^U}{L_A^S}A_+^{TS}\right) + \left(A_+^U + A_+^S \frac{L_A^S}{L_A^U}\right) A_+^{SU}\left(\frac{L_M^U}{L_M^S} - \frac{L_A^U}{L_A^S}\right)\right]. \quad (7{:}31)$$

In (7:28) the first three terms are positive, and the fourth (μ) is indeterminate. In the appendix we deduce conditions sufficient for P_A to fall. We also know that at constant commodity prices, the real skilled wage will rise as a result of discrimination. In order for this to continue to be true, when we allow the price of agricultural goods to fall, (7:28) must have a negative sign. A fall in P_A should lead to a rise in w^S. This, in turn takes place when the difference in skill intensities between the sectors is large, since then the fourth term becomes negative. As shown in the appendix, a low skill intensity in agriculture also tends to create a low degree of complementarity between skilled labor and land. Finally, a large difference in skill intensities ensures that the last term is large. If the difference is sufficiently high, the negative term will outweigh the first three positive ones. These are conditions which lead to a rise in w^S and a fall in P_A, in terms of manufactures. Consequently w^S must also increase in terms of agricultural goods, that is it increases in real terms.

This is an important conclusion, since it shows that *the magnitude of skill intensities may play an important role in the decision of skilled white workers of whether to advocate discrimination or not*. If the difference between the sectors is substantial, discrimination will increase the real incomes of this group, provided that discrimination also gives rise to a fall in the relative price of agricultural goods.

In (7:29), we find that all terms except the fourth one are always positive, given that manufacturing is the skill-intensive sector. If the skill-intensity difference is high, the fourth term, and thus the entire

194 A More Realistic Crowding Model

expression, will also be positive. Thus, relative skill intensities also play a crucial role in determining whether or not unskilled workers will lose in terms of manufactured goods when being subjected to discrimination. If the difference is large and discrimination leads to a fall in the relative price of agricultural goods, unskilled workers lose. However, there is no guarantee that this will also be true in terms of agricultural goods, since in this case P_A falls.

Finally, we have to look at the impact of discrimination on the returns to capital and land. The returns are given by

$$i = M_+^K \tag{7:32}$$

and

$$r = P_A A_+^T. \tag{7:33}$$

With commodity prices held constant we obtain:

$$i^{SN} = M_+^{KS} L_M^{SSN} + M_+^{KU} L_M^{USN} \tag{7:34}$$

and

$$r^{SN} = P_A(A_+^{TS} L_A^{SSN} + A_+^{TU} L_A^{USN}). \tag{7:35}$$

The real return to manufacturing capital will fall and the return to land will rise when employment of both types of labor falls in manufacturing and increases in agriculture. Drawing on our discussion of expressions (A7:18) - (A7:19) and (A7:24) - (A7:25) in the appendix, it can be shown that this is likely to happen, for example, when the difference in skill intensity between the two sectors is large.

The effects of commodity price changes on the returns to capital and land are in turn given by

$$i^P = M_+^{KS} L_M^{SP} + M_+^{KU} L_M^{UP} \tag{7:36}$$

and

$$r^P = P_A(A_+^{TS} L_A^{SP} + A_+^{TU} L_A^{UP}) + A_+^T. \tag{7:37}$$

These expressions both have determinate signs. In note 12 we mention that by solving the system that was used to determine the impact on wages for the impact of price changes on factor use as well, it can be shown that an increase in P_A is accompanied by an increase in the employment of both types of labor in agriculture, while employment falls in manufacturing. Hence, if discrimination produces a fall in the relative price of agricultural goods, manufacturing capitalists will derive a gain whereas agricultural landowners lose in terms of manufactures. It is easily verified, by dividing both sides of (7:32) and (7:33) by P_A and differentiating the resulting expressions with respect to the same price, that this is also true in terms of agricultural goods. Hence, a fall in the relative price of agricultural goods leads to an improvement in the real incomes of capitalists and to a fall in the real incomes of landowners.

These gains and losses, however, have to be weighed against the effects stated in (7:34) and (7:35). Neither capitalists nor landowners can thus be certain to gain by discrimination against skilled Negro workers.

Thus, in the same way as the one-good model that was used in the second section, *our extended two-good model of crowding fails to give white capitalists or landowners any unconditional rationale for advocating discrimination*. The outcome of discrimination for these two groups, in terms of real income, will remain uncertain, even when skill intensity differences between the sectors are large and when moreover discrimination leads to a fall in the relative price of agricultural goods.

Conclusions

In the present chapter the model introduced in Chapter 6 has been extended by allowing for the use of sector-specific factors both in the one-good and the two-good case. As a result the conclusions derived in Chapter 6 have been changed to a certain extent. In the one-good model outlined at the beginning of the chapter, it was shown that white workers continue to gain, although their gain may be outweighed by a possible loss on the part of the capitalists. The latter, however, also gain in the case where the capital-skill complementarity hypothesis does not apply to the economy.

In the two-good model, it was shown that the direction of the change in the relative price of agricultural goods and manufactures can no longer be generally determined. This in turn means that it is no longer possible to reach clear-cut conclusions with regard to changes in total real incomes for either racial group. One reason is that discrimination may affect different groups differently. Moreover, it becomes difficult to determine what will happen to each factor income. It is only in the case of a small, open economy, where commodity prices are not affected by crowding, that it can be shown that white workers will always stand to gain from crowding, since this measure reduces the extent of competition with Negroes. For capitalists and landowners, real returns could move in either direction.

Notes

1. For a critique of the assumption of intersectoral capital mobility, see Neary (1978), pp. 507–08.
2. See Kemp (1969), p. 51.
3. Batra & Casas (1976), esp. note, p. 21.
4. Ruffin (1980), p. 1. A generalization of results to the n × m case is found in Ethier (1982:1).
5. See the discussion in Jones (1979:2).
6. Vanek & Bertrand (1971). Cf. also Vanek (1968), p. 749 and the classical article by Samuelson (1953).
7. An overview of the costs and benefits of two-ness is given in Jones (1979:2). Ethier (1982:2) surveys the results obtained in higher-dimensional models.
8. This approach characterizes e.g. the works of Chipman (1969), Kemp & Wegge (1969), Uekawa (1971), Inada (1971) and Balkhy (1973). The approach has been criticized by Jones (1979:2).
9. Jones (1979:3), p. 53.
10. This is the course taken in e.g. Ethier (1974), Kemp & Wan (1976), Jones & Scheinkman (1977), Jones (1979:1), (1979:2), Ruffin (1980) and Ethier (1982:1). See Porter (1978), and in this connection also Fallon & Layard (1975), for a brief discussion of the problems of three-factor models in applications to discrimination.
11. Fallon and Layard formulate this hypothesis in relative terms, i.e. as $f_+^{SK}/f_+^S > f_+^{UK}/f_+^U$ (see Fallon & Layard (1975), p. 281). For our purposes, an 'absolute' formulation is more adequate, also when we come to the two-good model.
12. Factor prices are not needed in (7:17) and (7:19). Below we will first investigate what happens when L_N^S changes and P_A is kept constant. Thereafter (as a result of the change in L_N^S), P_A is allowed to change (keeping L_N^S fixed) and the effects of this change are traced. In the appendix we will derive the impact of changes in L_N^S on factor uses at constant prices. To find the impact of changes in P_A one can solve the system (7:22) – (7:25), (7:18), (7:20) and (7:21). Thus, it may be demonstrated that $L_A^{SP} > 0$, $L_A^{UP} > 0$, $L_M^{SP} < 0$ and $L_M^{UP} < 0$.

Appendix: The Development of Relative Commodity Prices

To solve the system (7:6) – (7:21) for the impact of crowding on

A More Realistic Crowding Model 197

relative commodity prices, we apply the same type of procedure as in Chapter 6.

Equations (7:9), (7:11), and (7:13), describing the supply of and demand for manufactures, may be omitted from the system, since these variables do not appear anywhere else. Differentiating the remaining equations and solving for dP_A/dL_N^S yields

$$\frac{dP_A}{dL_N^S} = \frac{1}{\Delta'} \left\{ S_A^{SN} - A_W^Y \left[(\bar{L}_W^S M_+^{SS} + \bar{K} M_+^{KS})(1 - L_A^{SSN}) \right.\right.$$

$$+ P_A \bar{T} A_+^{TS} L_A^{SSN} - (\bar{L}_W^S M_+^{SU} + \bar{K} M_+^{KU})(1 + L_A^{USN})$$

$$+ P_A \bar{T} A_+^{TU} L_A^{USN} \right] - A_N^Y \left[(L_N^S M_+^{SS} + L_N^U M^{US})(1 - L_A^{SSN}) \right.$$

$$\left.\left. - (L_N^S M_+^{SU} + L_N^U M_+^{UU})(1 + L_A^{USN}) + M^S - M^U \right] \right\}, \quad (A7:1)$$

with

$$\Delta' = A_W^P + A_W^Y \left[(P_A \bar{T} A_+^{TS} - \bar{L}_W^S M_+^{SS} - \bar{K} M_+^{KS}) L_A^{SP} \right.$$

$$+ (P_A \bar{T} A_+^{TU} - \bar{L}_W^S M_+^{SU} - \bar{K} M_+^{KU}) L_A^{UP} + A_+^T \bar{T} \right] + A_N^P$$

$$- A_N^Y \left[(L_N^S M_+^{SU} + L_N^U M_+^{UU}) L_A^{UP} + (L_N^S M_+^{SS} + L_N^U M_+^{US}) L_A^{SP} \right] - S_A^P$$

$$(A7:2)$$

The denominator Δ' of (A7:1) must be negative. Analogous to Chapter 5, it may be demonstrated that (A7:2) is the partial derivative of the excess demand for agricultural goods with respect to P_A. In order that the model possess Walrasian stability, this derivative must be negative so that equilibrium can be restored.

Going on to the numerator of (A7:1), we need to derive an expression of S_A^{SN} in order to find its sign. This can be done by adopting the same procedure as in Chapter 6. We depart from the conditions that skilled labor must fetch the same return in both sectors:

$$P_A A_+^S = M_+^S. \qquad (A7:3)$$

198 A More Realistic Crowding Model

The same holds for unskilled labor:

$$P_A A_+^U = M_+^U. \tag{A7:4}$$

The full employment conditions (7:18) and (7:20) must be included plus the requirement that the total supply of Negro labor must be distributed between skilled and unskilled positions, that is equation (7:21).

Differentiating these five equations while the relative commodity price P_A is kept constant, making use of the production functions (7:6) and (7:7) gives us

$$0 = M_+^{SS} L_M^{SSN} + M_+^{SU} L_M^{USN} - P_A \left(A_+^{SS} L_A^{SSN} + A_+^{SU} L_A^{USN} \right), \tag{A7:5}$$

$$0 = M_+^{UU} L_M^{USN} + M_+^{US} L_M^{SSN} - P_A \left(A_+^{UU} L_A^{USN} + A_+^{US} L_A^{SSN} \right), \tag{A7:6}$$

$$1 = L_A^{SSN} + L_M^{SSN}, \tag{A7:7}$$

$$L_N^{USN} = L_A^{USN} + L_M^{USN} \tag{A7:8}$$

and

$$L_N^{USN} = -1. \tag{A7:9}$$

These five equations can then be solved for the four unknowns L_A^{SSN}, L_M^{SSN}, L_A^{USN} and L_M^{USN}.

Since we are working with linearly homogeneous production functions, we may again make use of Euler's theorem to derive that with three production factors in each sector,

$$M_+^{SS} L_M^S + M_+^{SU} L_M^U + M_+^{SK} \bar{K} \equiv 0, \tag{A7:10}$$

A More Realistic Crowding Model

$$M_+^{UU} L_M^U + M_+^{US} L_M^S + M_+^{UK} \bar{K} \equiv 0, \qquad (A7:11)$$

$$A_+^{SS} L_A^S + A_+^{SU} L_A^U + A_+^{ST} \bar{T} \equiv 0, \qquad (A7:12)$$

$$A_+^{UU} L_A^U + A_+^{US} L_A^S + A_+^{UT} \bar{T} \equiv 0, \qquad (A7:13)$$

or, that

$$M_+^{SS} \frac{L_M^S}{L_M^U} + M_+^{SK} \frac{\bar{K}}{L_M^U} = -M_+^{SU} = -M_+^{US} = M_+^{UU} \frac{L_M^U}{L_M^S} + M_+^{UK} \frac{\bar{K}}{L_M^S},$$

$$(A7:14)$$

and

$$A_+^{SS} \frac{L_A^S}{L_A^U} + A_+^{ST} \frac{\bar{T}}{L_A^U} = -A_+^{SU} = -A_+^{US} = A_+^{UU} \frac{L_A^U}{L_A^S} + A_+^{UT} \frac{\bar{T}}{L_A^S}.$$

$$(A7:15)$$

Using (A7:14) and (A7:15), (A7:5) and (A7:6) may be rewritten as

$$0 = -\left(M_+^{SU} + M_+^{KS} \frac{\bar{K}}{L_M^U}\right) \frac{L_M^U}{L_M^S} L_M^{SS} N + M_+^{SU} L_M^{US} N$$

$$+ P_A \left[\left(A_+^{SU} + A_+^{TS} \frac{\bar{T}}{L_A^U}\right) \frac{L_A^U}{L_A^S} L_A^{SS} N - A_+^{SU} L_A^{US} N\right], \qquad (A7:16)$$

and

$$0 = -\left(M_+^{SU} + M_+^{KU} \frac{\bar{K}}{L_M^S}\right) \frac{L_M^S}{L_M^U} L_M^{US} N + M_+^{SU} L_M^{SS} N$$

$$+ P_A \left[\left(A_+^{SU} + A_+^{TU} \frac{\bar{T}}{L_A^S}\right) \frac{L_A^S}{L_A^U} L_A^{US} N - A_+^{SU} L_A^{SS} N\right] \qquad (A7:17)$$

A More Realistic Crowding Model

Following some algebraic manipulation, the solution of the amended system (A7:16) - (A7:17) and (A7:7) - (A7:30) for the changes in labor use at constant relative commodity prices yields

$$L_A^{SSN} = \frac{1}{\Delta''} \left\{ \epsilon + \zeta + P_A A_+^{TU} \frac{\bar{T}}{L_A^U} \left[M_+^{KS} \frac{\bar{K}}{L_M^S} + M_+^{SU} \left(1 + \frac{L_M^U}{L_M^S}\right) \right] + \eta \right\} \tag{A7:18}$$

$$L_A^{USN} = \frac{1}{\Delta''} \left\{ \frac{L_A^U}{L_A^S}(\epsilon + \zeta) - P_A A_+^{TS} \frac{\bar{T}}{L_A^S} \left[M_+^{KU} \frac{\bar{K}}{L_M^U} + M_+^{SU} \right. \right.$$
$$\left. \left. \left(1 + \frac{L_M^S}{L_M^U}\right) \right] - \eta \right\}, \tag{A7:19}$$

where

$$\epsilon = P_A M_+^{US} A_+^{US} (L_M^S + L_M^U) \frac{1}{L_M^S} \left(\frac{L_A^S}{L_A^U} - \frac{L_M^S}{L_M^U} \right) < 0, \tag{A7:20}$$

$$\zeta = P_A A_+^{US} \frac{\bar{K}}{L_M^S} \left(M_+^{KS} \frac{L_A^S}{L_A^U} - M_+^{KU} \frac{L_M^S}{L_M^U} \right) \tag{A7:21}$$

and

$$\eta = M_+^{SK} \frac{\bar{K}}{L_M^U} \left(M_+^{KU} \frac{\bar{K}}{L_M^S} + M_+^{US} \right) + M_+^{US} M_+^{KU} \frac{\bar{K}}{L_M^S} > 0, \tag{A7:22}$$

with the denominator

$$\Delta'' = P_A M_+^{US} A_+^{US} \frac{L_M^S}{L_M^U} \frac{L_A^U}{L_A^S} \left(\frac{L_M^U}{L_M^S} \frac{L_A^S}{L_A^U} - 1 \right)^2 - \left(M_+^{UU} + P_A A_+^{UU} \right)$$

$$\left(M_+^{KS} \frac{\bar{K}}{L_M^S} + P_A A_+^{TS} \frac{\bar{T}}{L_A^S} \right) + \left(M_+^{KU} \frac{\bar{K}}{L_M^U} + P_A A_+^{TU} \frac{\bar{T}}{L_A^U} \right)$$

$$\left(M_+^{US} \frac{L_M^U}{L_M^S} + P_A A_+^{US} \frac{L_A^U}{L_A^S} \right) > 0, \tag{A7:23}$$

and

$$L_M^{SS_N} = \frac{1}{\Delta''}\left\{\theta + \iota + P_A M_+^{KU}\frac{\bar{K}}{L_M^U}\left[A_+^{TS}\frac{\bar{T}}{L_A^S} + A_+^{US}\left(1 + \frac{L_A^U}{L_A^S}\right)\right] + \kappa\right\},$$

(A7:24)

$$L_M^{US_N} = \frac{1}{\Delta''}\left\{\frac{L_M^U}{L_M^S}(\theta + \iota) - P_A M_+^{KS}\frac{\bar{K}}{L_M^S}\left[A_+^{TU}\frac{\bar{T}}{L_A^U} + A_+^{US}\right.\right.$$

$$\left.\left.\left(1 + \frac{L_A^S}{L_A^U}\right)\right] - \kappa\right\},$$

(A7:25)

where

$$\theta = P_A M_+^{US} A_+^{US}(L_A^S + L_A^U)\frac{1}{L_A^S}\left(\frac{L_M^S}{L_M^U} - \frac{L_A^S}{L_A^U}\right) > 0,$$

(A7:26)

$$\iota = P_A M_+^{US}\frac{\bar{T}}{L_A^S}\left(A_+^{TS}\frac{L_M^S}{L_M^U} - A_+^{TU}\frac{L_A^S}{L_A^U}\right),$$

(A7:27)

$$\kappa = P_A^2\left[A_+^{TS}\frac{\bar{T}}{L_A^U}\left(A_+^{TU}\frac{\bar{T}}{L_A^S} + A_+^{SU}\right) + A_+^{US}A_+^{TU}\frac{\bar{T}}{L_A^S}\right] > 0.$$

(A7:28)

Differentiating the supply functions (7:8) and 7:9), the production functions (7:6) and (7:7) and substituting (A7:20), (A7:21), (A7:24), and (A7:25) yields the expressions for the changes in supplies (outputs) at constant commodity prices:

$$S_A^{S_N} = \frac{1}{\Delta''}\left\{(\epsilon + \zeta)\left(A_+^S + \frac{L_A^U}{L_A^S}A_+^U\right) + \eta(A_+^S - A_+^U) + P_A A_+^{TU}\frac{\bar{T}}{L_A^U}\right.$$

$$\left[M_+^{KS}\frac{\bar{K}}{L_M^S} + M_+^{SU}\left(1 + \frac{L_M^U}{L_M^S}\right)\right]A_+^S - P_A A_+^{TS}\frac{\bar{T}}{L_A^S}$$

$$\left.\left[M_+^{KU}\frac{\bar{K}}{L_M^U} + M_+^{SU}\left(1 + \frac{L_M^S}{L_M^U}\right)\right]A_+^U\right\}$$

(A7:29)

and

$$S_M^{SN} = \frac{1}{\Delta''} \left\{ (\theta + \iota)\left(M_+^S + \frac{L_M^U}{L_M^S}M_+^U\right) + \kappa(M_+^S - M_+^U) + P_A M_+^{KU}\frac{\bar{K}}{L_M^U} \right.$$

$$\left[A_+^{TS}\frac{\bar{T}}{L_A^S} + A_+^{US}\left(1 + \frac{L_A^U}{L_A^S}\right)\right]M_+^S - P_A M_+^{KS}\frac{\bar{K}}{L_M^S}$$

$$\left. \left[A_+^{TU}\frac{\bar{T}}{L_A^U} + A_+^{US}\left(1 + \frac{L_A^S}{L_A^U}\right)\right]M_+^U \right\}. \qquad (A7:30)$$

Let us now continue with the interpretation of these expressions. The first thing to note is that (A7:18) - (A7:19) and (A7:24) - (A7:25) are generalizations of the corresponding expressions in Chapter 6.[1] Next we note that, in the general case, none of these expressions is determinate.

Let us now see under which circumstances the results of Chapter 6 remain valid in the extended model. Given our assumption that manufacturing is the skill-intensive sector and agriculture the sector which makes intensive use of unskilled labor, so that $L_M^S/L_M^U > L_A^S/L_A^U$ at all relative factor prices, we derived the analogue of the Rybczynski theorem: $L_A^{SSN} < 0$, $L_A^{USN} < 0$, $L_M^{SSN} > 0$ and $L_M^{USN} > 0$, so that $S_A^{SN} < 0$ and $S_M^{SN} > 0$ (at constant commodity prices). When capital and land are introduced into the model, these results no longer necessarily hold.

Beginning with the common denominator (A7:23), it is easily seen that this is always positive. Then, the signs of (A7:18) - (A7:19) and (A7:24) - (A7:25) are determined exclusively by the sign of the respective numerators.

In (A7:18), the last two terms on the right-hand side are positive, while the first is negative and the second is not determinate. The latter plays a central role. For our result from Chapter 6 to remain valid the sum of the first two terms must be negative and large enough to outweigh the last two. The second term will definitely be negative, if $M_+^{KU} \geq M_+^{KS}$, that is when the complementarity of unskilled labor and capital is at least as high as that between skilled labor and capital. The 'capital-skill complementarity hypthothesis' must be false. This condition, however, only guarantees the sign of the sum of the first two terms but tells us nothing regarding the relative size of these terms and the last three terms. In order for the former to outweigh the latter, it is also essential, for example, for the difference in skill intensity to be large. Thus, a central role is played by the relative factor intensities. The results of Chapter 6 are also valid in the case where capital and land are used in production, provided that a further requirement is met. As has been previously stated, the skill intensity in manufacturing must exceed that in agriculture. However, it is also necessary to establish the magnitude of this difference.

Going on to the expression for the change in the input of unskilled labor in agriculture (A7:19), we find a somewhat different situation. Here, the last two terms on the right-hand side are negative. Hence it is sufficient to establish the conditions for the first term to be negative as well. ϵ is negative since manufacturing is the relatively skill-intensive sector. As far as ζ is concerned, the falsification of the capital-skill complementarity hypothesis is sufficient (given that manufacturing is skill-intensive).

Next, we have (A7:24), showing how the use of skilled labor in manufacturing changes as a result of discrimination when relative commodity prices are held constant. The last two terms on the right-hand side are positive and the first term is positive given that manufacturing uses skilled labor intensively. The condition for a positive second term is that $A_+^{TS} \geqslant A_+^{TU}$, that is that land is at least as complementary to skilled as to unskilled labor in agriculture (given the skill-intensity condition).

Finally, we must investigate the impact on the use of unskilled labor in manufacturing. The last two terms on the right-hand side of (A7:25) are negative, while the first one is indeterminate. We then have to establish a) the conditions for the first term to be positive, and b) the conditions required to have this term outweigh the last two. The skill intensity requirement is sufficient to establish the positive sign of θ. Together with a land-skill complementarity that is as high as the complementarity between unskilled labor and land, this makes ι positive as well. In order for the net effect to be positive, we are once again dependent, for example, on the size of the difference in factor intensities. The higher the difference in skill intensity between manufacturing and agriculture, the higher the probability that expression (A7:25) will be positive.

Thus, we have isolated three conditions which together are sufficient to extend the Rybczynski result regarding factor use to the model which contains one specific factor in each sector in addition to the two mobile labor factors. The first condition is the same as the one used in

Chapter 6, namely the requirement that manufacturing is relatively more skill-intensive than agriculture. The second condition is that the capital-skill complementarity hypothesis does not apply in manufacturing, but that the land-skill complementarity applies in agriculture. The third condition is that there should be a substantial difference in skill intensity between the two sectors.

Looking at the expressions for output changes, (A7:29) and (A7:30), which are simply the weighted sums of the changes in the use of the two types of labor, we again find that the difference in factor intensities and the applicability of the skill complementarity hypothesis in the two sectors are important in deciding whether or not agricultural production will expand and manufacturing output contract as a result of discrimination (when commodity prices are kept constant). Let us look at the economics behind these conditions.

Actually, the three conditions may be reduced to a single one, or rather to two conditions: that the skill intensity should be high in manufacturing and low in agriculture. When these conditions are fulfilled, the complementarity between skilled labor and land is high in agriculture, while the complementarity between skilled labor and capital is low in manufacturing. The opposite is true with regard to the complementarity between unskilled labor and land/capital. The impact of an addition of skilled labor to a given stock of capital or land in either sector on the marginal productivity of capital or land becomes successively smaller as the ratio of skilled to unskilled labor increases, *ceteris paribus*. On the other hand, the impact of an additional dose of unskilled labor increases, as the skill intensity rises. A single example may illustrate this case.[2]

Let us assume that the daily operations of the capital stock — the machines used in manufacturing — are handled by the unskilled workers, but that the machines need to be maintained and that maintenance is a complicated affair which can only be carried out by skilled workers. Given the number of machines and the unskilled labor force in the sector, some additional maintenance may improve the operation of the machines. Fewer rejects may be produced etc. With more maintenance, adding a machine will lead to a higher increase of output than if less maintenance is carried out. The work of the skilled workers, that is maintenance, should, however, be subjected to diminishing returns in the sense that the first 'units' of maintenance make a significant contribution towards the smoother running of the machines, whereas each further increase in the amount of maintenance will add successively less.

On the other hand, an increase in the number of unskilled workers handling the machines, while the amount of skilled labor remains constant, ought to make increased maintenance more efficient with regards to its ability to raise the marginal productivity of the machines. For example the addition of more unskilled labor may mean that the machines will have to run more hours each day or that the pace at which the machines run (for example, on an assembly line) can be increased. This in turn may necessitate more maintenance if the number of rejects is to be kept down etc.

A similar argument can be applied to land in the agricultural sector.

Thus, we ought to have that $M_+^{KSS} < 0$, $M_+^{KSU} > 0$, $M_+^{KUS} > 0$ and $M_+^{KUU} < 0$ and $A_+^{TSS} < 0$, $A_+^{TSU} > 0$, $A_+^{TUS} > 0$ and $A_+^{TUU} < 0$,[3] that is that the higher the skill intensity in manufacturing, the lower the value of M_+^{KS} and the higher the value of M_+^{KU} and the lower the skill intensity in agriculture, the higher the value of A_+^{TS} and the lower that of A_+^{TU}. Consequently, we can also explain the output changes that take place at given commodity prices.

The mechanism works in the following way. When discrimination sets in, the supply of skilled labor is forced to contract. This raises the skilled wage rate so that both sectors will cut down on their use of skilled workers. Thus, initially, both L_A^S and L_M^S must fall. At the same time, however, the released skilled workers are forced into unskilled occupations. The supply of unskilled labor expands, and the unskilled wage rate falls. Both sectors will start using more unskilled labor. L_A^U and L_M^U both increase.

Hence, a high skill intensity in the manufacturing sector makes M_+^{KU} larger than M_+^{KS}. If the difference is large enough the marginal productivity of capital will rise. At a given price of capital, the manufacturing producers will at this point attempt to substitute capital for skilled and unskilled labor. Thus, in the second round, the employment of both types of labor will fall in the manufacturing sector. The net result is a reduction of skilled employment in manufacturing, since the employment of skilled workers falls also in the first round. If the skill intensity of this sector is high enough, unskilled employment will also be subject to a net reduction, since in that case, the effect on the marginal productivity of capital caused by the initial substitution of unskilled labor for skilled will be so large that the secondary substitution of capital for unskilled workers caused by this substitution will more than outweigh the initial increase in unskilled employment in manufacturing. With a net reduction of both types of employment, the output of manufactures must fall.

In the agricultural sector, similar events take place. There as well, the initial substitution of unskilled for skilled labor will affect the marginal productivity of the fixed factor, in this case land. Given a low skill intensity in agriculture, A_+^{TU} will be so much smaller than A_+^{TS} that the marginal productivity of land will fall. Farmers will substitute labor (both skilled and unskilled) for land at given land prices. Skilled and unskilled employment increases. The net effect is a rise in unskilled employment in agriculture, since unskilled employment increased in the first round as well. Moreover, given a sufficiently low skill intensity, the secondary substitution of skilled workers for land will outweigh the initial fall in skilled employment. Hence the net effect on the employment of this category of workers will also be positive. Finally, with increased employment of both types of labor, agricultural output must rise.

Let us now summarize the above argument. *In Chapter 6 certain results were derived regarding changes in factor use and outputs at constant commodity prices. In order that these results should hold when a specific factor is introduced in each of the two sectors, it is sufficient that the skill intensity of manufacturing is high and that of agriculture is low.*

This, in turn, takes us back to expression (A7:1) for commodity price changes, this time to the demand side. In Chapter 6 we established that the relative price of agricultural goods had to fall since the increased supply of the latter was matched by a decrease on the demand side. Even given the conditions which make the supply of agricultural goods increase in the extended model, this conclusion does, however, not generalize to the present case.

At constant relative commodity prices, the effects on the demand for agricultural goods are given by the changes in the incomes of whites and Negroes and by the marginal propensities of these two groups to consume agricultural goods. We may begin by looking at the development of white incomes. This development is given by the sum of the terms within the first square brackets of (A7:1).

The first of the terms shows what happens to white labor and capital incomes when the use of skilled labor changes in manufacturing. We have already established the conditions for a positive value of L_M^{SSN}, which, according to (7:18), equals $1 - L_A^{SSN}$. However, it is still not possible to establish (without introducing further assumptions) whether the rise of skilled wages and incomes is sufficiently large to outweigh the fall in capital incomes that results when skilled labor leaves manufacturing. The second term tells us that, as the use of skilled labor in agriculture increases, landed incomes in that sector will increase accordingly. The third term shows that the decreased use of unskilled labor in manufacturing (equal to $1 + L_A^{USN}$, by (7:20) and (7:21)) must reduce both skilled incomes (in both sectors) and capital incomes in manufacturing. Finally, the fourth term shows that, as unskilled employment increases in agriculture, landed incomes will also increase in that sector. Hence, the impact on white incomes at given relative commodity prices remains indeterminate.

The same is true for Negro incomes — the expression within the second square brackets of (A7:1). There, the first term again points to a conflict between rising skilled incomes and falling incomes for unskilled workers when skilled labor leaves manufacturing. The second term reverses the fates of these two groups as the employment of unskilled labor falls in the same sector. The final two terms indicate the loss of Negro incomes arising from the transfer of people from higher-paid skilled jobs to lower-paid unskilled occupations at given wage rates. Once again, the net impact of these changes is not determinate.

It is thus seen that *the fall in the relative price of agricultural goods, established in Chapter 6, does not generalize to the model where capital and land is included, even in the case where the supply effects are the same.*

However, in at least one simplified case, it is possible to reproduce the result of Chapter 6. This is when the marginal propensities to consume the two goods are the same for both racial groups (provided that we also assume that the conditions leading to an increased output of agricultural goods and a contraction in the production of manufactures are fulfilled).

With

$$A_W^Y = A_N^Y, \tag{A7:31}$$

the interracial redistribution of incomes which arises when discrimination begins has no effect on demand, since the decrease in the demand of the losing group will always be matched by an equal increase in the demand of the gaining group. Hence, in this case, the demand for agricultural goods may be written solely as a function of total incomes (the sum of white and Negro incomes) and prices:

$$A_D = A_D(P_A, Y). \tag{A7:32}$$

Here, Y is the sum of (7:14) and (7:15):

$$Y = M_+^S L_M^S + P_A A_+^S L_A^S + M_+^U L_M^U + P_A A_+^U L_A^U + M_+^K \bar{K} + P_A A_+^T \bar{T}.$$

$$\tag{A7:33}$$

Differentiating (A7:33) with commodity prices constant, using the production functions (7:6) and (7:7), furnishes us with an expression which with the aid of (A7:10) - (A7:13) can be reduced to

$$Y^{SN} = M_+^S L_M^{SSN} + P_A A_+^S L_A^{SSN} + M_+^U L_M^{USN} + P_A A_+^U L_A^{USN}. \tag{A7:34}$$

With the aid of (7:18), (7:20), (7:21), (A7:3) and (A7:4), this expression may in turn be simplified to

$$Y^{SN} = M_+^S - M_+^U, \tag{A7:35}$$

which is a direct parallel to the final expression for the change in Negro incomes in Chapter 6. Expression (A7:35) shows that total incomes will be reduced by an amount equal to the difference between the original skilled and unskilled wage rates. Given our special assumption that the marginal propensities to consume agricultural goods do not differ between whites and Negroes, this fall also ensures that when neither good is inferior, the demand for both goods must fall. If in addition, as we have postulated, the conditions leading to an increase in the supply of agricultural goods are present, the desired excess supply of agricultural goods is again established, and the relative price of these goods must fall.

Notes

1. If all terms containing cross derivatives with respect to capital and land are deleted, only the terms containing ϵ and θ on the right-hand sides remain, and the expressions reduce to those of Chapter 6 which all had determinate signs.

2. Formally, neither the former nor the latter effect is necessary. Analogous to (A7:10) - (A7:13), we have that (in manufacturing)

$$M_+^{KS} L_M^S + M_+^{KU} L_M^U + M_+^{KK} \bar{K} \equiv 0.$$

Taking the partial derivative with respect to L_M^S (i.e. increasing L_M^S/L_M^U, since L_M^U remains constant) and rearranging terms yields

$$M_+^{KSS} L_M^S + M_+^{KUS} L_M^U + M_+^{KKS} \bar{K} \equiv -M_+^{KS} < 0.$$

Thus, in principle, the partial derivatives could be of either sign. (The same reasoning may be applied to a change in L_M^U with L_M^S held constant, i.e. to a fall in L_M^S/L_M^U.)

3. Cf. Becker (1971:2), note, p. 37: 'It seems plausible that [in the two-factor model f^{LKK}] ≤ 0.'

8 AN APPLICATION OF THE THEORY: RACIAL DISCRIMINATION IN SOUTH AFRICA

In the previous chapters of the present work, emphasis has been placed on the development of discrimination theory. Various approaches to the economics of discrimination were surveyed in Chapter 2. Beginning in Chapter 3, the properties of a number of neo-classically oriented models were then explored in some detail. This, however, leaves one question unanswered: 'Do neo-classical models of economic discrimination have any explanatory value when applied to concrete situations?'

Some authors have expressed considerable doubts regarding the applicability of neo-classical theories. Thus, Michael Reich has argued that they are not applicable to the analysis of problems of racial discrimination in the United States. In his view, the theories are either not logically coherent or their predictions are not empirically plausible. He writes: 'After more than two decades of effort and the development of a voluminous literature, neoclassical economists have failed to produce a satisfactory theory of racial discrimination.'[1]

We do not agree. In the present chapter we will show that neo-classical economics is indeed capable of shedding light on why discrimination is practiced in the case of South Africa. By using elements from the models discussed in Chapters 5-7, it is possible to construct a framework which can be used to explain the discrimination against Africans that has taken place in South Africa from the beginning of the European colonization up to the present time.[2]

We will begin with an account of some of the institutional realities of South Africa in a historical perspective in order to obtain some indication as to the kinds of elements that should be included in a model that is to capture the essential features of South African discrimination and their development over time. In the second section, the model itself will be set out in three different parts, each one corresponding to a particular period in the history of South Africa.

A Brief History of South African Discrimination[3]

The Traditional African Economy

When the European immigrants first clashed with the Africans in South Africa, land was the issue. In southern Africa, land was a relatively abundant resource, although the Africans were not prepared to part with it. The traditional African economy was based on land-intensive activities. The indigenous peoples in the area were mainly sheep farmers and extensive cultivators.[4]

Generally, land was owned collectively in a system based on descent or kinship. Households only had the right to use land for cultivation, for residential purposes, for grazing, for gathering and for hunting. The right to individual use of land was second to the rights of the social group: the clan or the lineage, which allocated usufruct rights to the households.[5]

Stock-keeping was the most important economic activity. Cattle, goats and sheep were kept throughout the region. Expansion of the size of the herds frequently led to overgrazing and armed conflicts between tribes over disputed land.[6] Agricultural production was based on shifting cultivation with fallow periods of varying length.

In sum, the 'original' economy in southern Africa built mainly on pastoral and agricultural activities. There was, however, no room for these activities in the policy of the intruding whites. The Africans were deprived of their most important resource — land — and the strain put on the traditional economy became too great. Soon, this economy began to display severe signs of degeneration. The traditional way of life could no longer support the population, and large numbers were forced into taking wage employment within the white economy.

White Expansion

The tendency of the white South Africans to drive the Africans off their land was manifest ever since the first years of European colonization. All measures to prevent direct contact between the Dutch settlers at the Cape and the native San (Bushmen) and Khoikhoi (Hottentots) proved to be utterly in vain. There was nothing that the officials of the Dutch East India Company could do to check the expansion of the *burghers* into African territory. Soon a process began which was not to end until all African tribes in South Africa had been reduced to a state of landlessness and concomitant deprivation.

Forces stronger than any legislation were at work. The territorial expansion was the result of economic factors. The pressure towards the interior had its main roots in the prevailing set of relative factor prices — as interpreted by the colonists. Capital was scarce, as was labor, given the small size of the colony.[7] Up to 1807 slaves were imported into the Cape colony to increase the labor supply.[8]

Nevertheless, relatively speaking, it was land that was cheap and plentiful — provided that the existing (African) property rights could be neglected.[9] In an economy dominated by subsistence considerations, land was the most important production factor,[10] and therefore a majority of the colonists were fully prepared to trample African rights under their feet, as their subsequent actions amply demonstrated. There was plenty of land in the interior to be taken over from the Africans. Gradually, cattle ranching — an eminently land-intensive activity — became the preferred livelihood, and with time, land also came to be regarded more or less as a birthright among the Dutch.[11] The *trekboers* pressed on, and the Africans were forced to retreat. The increasingly landless and impoverished Khoikhoi were employed to tend the cattle herds.

The same type of expansion pattern also persisted after the British had taken over the Cape colony around 1800. Already before the first British occupation of the Cape, the first two of the so-called Xhosa or Kaffir wars had been fought. There were to be seven more before the Xhosa were finally defeated and subjugated in 1878. At the same time, the situation of the Khoikhoi gradually worsened until all their lands had been transferred into white hands, leaving them with the unpalatable option of becoming low-paid workers in white service, going into a native reserve (the first of which was created in 1801) or moving into the territory of other African peoples.[12]

Within the colonized area, discrimination of the landless was legally sanctioned. In 1809, what amounted to the first pass law — the Hottentot Code — was promulgated to limit the mobility of the Khoikhoi, and passes were only granted to those who had entered into a labor agreement. Four years later, a law which made indenture ('apprenticeship') of Khoikhoi families possible was passed.[13] In this way, the combination of land alienation and the discriminatory legislation (based on it) helped to secure the labor supply for white farmers and cattle ranchers, among whom British had been added to Dutch after 1820.

This trend was temporarily reversed in the late 1820s and the early 1830s when the discriminatory laws were revoked and slavery was abolished (1834) in the entire British empire. From the white point of view, these measures created a labor problem,[14] and finally, a number of Boers decided that they would have no more to do with a British administration which provided too little help in the frontier skirmishes and gave too much protection to native interests — which, in short, interfered too much with their customary way of life. The Great Trek — the fan-shaped northward exodus of Boers — began in 1836.

It has repeatedly been pointed out that the *Voortrekkers* carried the eighteenth century into the nineteenth in terms of ideas and life style. This is true in an economic sense as well. The same motivation that underlay the eighteenth-century expansion from the Cape played an important role in the decision to trek northwards.[15] Both land and labor had become increasingly scarce in the Cape colony, and (given the other reasons for Boer discontent) this was enough to provoke a further expansion — this time on a larger scale than anything seen hitherto.[16] The Trek happened to coincide with a period of exceptional unrest among the Bantu tribes, caused mainly by the rise of the Zulu kingdom in the east.

The *mfecane* (crushing) or *difaqane* (forced migration) — a westward displacement of all the peoples in the area affected by the Zulu — had begun a few years before the first *Voortrekkers* packed their ox-wagons. Into this, the Boers now moved.

It took the *Voortrekkers* less than fifteen years to settle most of the best lands of South Africa. In this, they were aided by the *mfecane*, which had partially emptied large land tracts,[17] but when necessary, resort was made to violence. The two most powerful African kingdoms in the area, the Ndebele and the Zulu, were defeated (1837-40), and all the tribes in the area affected by the Trek lost large shares of land to the militarily superior Boers.

The treatment accorded to the Africans in the Boer republics was highly discriminatory. In the Natal Republic,[18] no Africans were allowed in 'settled' parts at all — except as servants. They were prohibited from owning land, and passes were required for movement. Resident Zulu were shared out as labor on white farms.[19] The Transvaal laws were modeled on those of Natal. White farmers were allowed up to four African squatter families whose labor could be used. Africans not settled on white lands were put into 'locations' nearby, administered by the government to secure the labor supply. Each location was subjected to taxes to be paid in cattle and to provision of manpower when requested. Here, as well, passes were required for movement.[20] In the Orange Free State, the government assumed no direct responsibility for controlling the supply of African labor, but the Boers were left to employ squatting arrangements and voluntary labor.[21]

Little had changed in the white economy of South Africa from the early days of the Dutch colony to the first half of the 1860s. Excluding the Cape colony with its more diversified economy, the whites essentially remained *trekboers* — and for good reasons. Land continued to be the abundant factor of production while capital and labor (especially skilled) were scarce.[22] African property rights were no more respected than two hundred years before, and as a concomitant, a supply of unskilled labor was forthcoming when the Africans were stripped of their land.

The Rise of Mining

The white farming and herding economy soon came under pressure. African labor became a scarce input, and land alienation increasingly became a prerequisite for the satisfaction of white demands for African labor. In 1867, diamonds were discovered at Kimberley, and in 1886, gold was found on the Witwatersrand. Following these discoveries, labor was no longer needed solely as a complement to land held by European farmers. An independent, 'almost insatiable'[23] demand for mining labor now arose. Most important was the demand emanating from the gold mines. The problem in these mines consisted in extracting the gold profitably from low-grade ore which was embedded in solid rock.[24] The price of gold could not be influenced by the producers, so the economic problem (given the mining technology of the day) could be reduced to one of securing sufficiently large amounts of human energy, that is unskilled labor, as cheaply as possible.[25] The mineral discoveries also had a secondary repercussion on the demand for labor in that it increased the demand for foodstuffs and thereby also for labor on the gradually developing white commercial farms.[26]

The increased demand for unskilled labor could not be satisfied without resort to measures based on further land alienation. The Africans were in the main opposed to wage employment with whites — provided that there were other ways of securing the necessary cash incomes.[27] To eliminate this resistance, three complementary measures were employed:

(1) crushing of the remaining African chiefdoms,
(2) crushing of the emerging African peasantry by discriminatory legislation,
(3) government supported monopsonistic recruitment of unskilled labor.

Around 1870, a number of African chiefdoms still maintained a comparatively autonomous position in their relations with Boers and Britons. Thirty years later, they had all been subjected to white rule, and consequently to white policies regarding labor and land.[28] These chiefdoms had been in contact with the Europeans earlier, but various forces had begun to erode the traditional structures. Missionaries were challenging customs and institutions. Traders were supplying new goods, creating an increased demand for cash incomes. Labor recruiters were looking for hands. White farmers had started to make land deals with chiefs and headmen. All these contacts were now intensified, and, with or without bloodshed, all the major chiefdoms fell to the Europeans: West Griqua, Southern and Natal Nguni, Zulu, Southern Sotho, Tswana, Mpondo and East Griqua. As the nineteenth century came to an end, autonomous African communities almost ceased to exist. The frontier was closed and the whites were free to implement their views regarding the role of the Africans in the economy across the entire South African territory.

As their land dwindled, the Africans developed new livelihoods. Those who could avoid it did not accept going to the mines or becoming laborers on white farms. Between 1830 and 1870, a black peasantry emerged in South Africa.[29] The primary response to the imposition of taxes and to the development of new wants requiring cash incomes was not work in the white ('modern') sector but rather the development of a commercially oriented agriculture in the reserves, on land rented from whites under squatting contracts (against labor or against a fee) and sharecropping contracts or on land bought on the market whenever this was possible. From the African point of view, the social opportunity cost of such an arrangement — with its greater similarity to pre-colonial life — was lower than that of acquiring the same amount of cash as miners or farmhands.

From the white point of view, the emergence of an African peasantry was undesirable. Its consequences were, however, not felt clearly until after the mineral discoveries. At that point, the demand for labor increased drastically in the white economy. In addition, the increased demand for food coming from the mining communities pushed up the value of land, which meant that the profitability of keeping squatters fell as compared to commercial development of the land.[30] This brought the peasantry under attack. When the value of land increased, so did rents, and squatters who could no longer pay were dislodged.[31]

The main weapon employed to crush the peasantry was, however, the legislative one. In the mid-1890s, both Boer republics issued a squatters' law which limited the number of African families on any white farm to five.[32] In the Transvaal, the 1908 Natives Tax Act provided for a higher tax on squatters than on labor tenants. In Natal, a number of laws were passed which made access to land difficult for Africans — in order to increase the supply of labor. Sales of Crown land to Africans were prohibited in 1904. In the Cape, Location Acts (1892,

1899, 1909) were used to tighten the pressure on squatters, and existing laws to this end were more scrupulously enforced.[33]

The decisive blow was the 1913 Natives Land Act which was applicable to the entire Union except the Cape province. The new act stated that no African (except by special permission from the Governor General) could purchase or rent land other than in areas 'scheduled' for Africans. By the time of the Union in 1910, some seven per cent of the entire South African territory was covered by African reserves. The extension of the areas scheduled was approximately equal to that of the existing reserves.[34] The Natives Land Act was a direct outcome of the need for cheap labor. Squatting and sharecropping arrangements provided the Africans with an alternative that was superior to wage employment. It appears that the main political pressure leading to the new act came from those white groups who stood to gain by the destruction of the peasant mode of production.[35]

The 'traditional' sector of present-day South Africa was created over a period of two and a half centuries by means of this type of land alienation imposed by force or by legislation rather than by the market. As early as the end of the nineteenth century, 'the prototype of the typical black South African of the twentieth century had emerged: the African who was born and reared in a "Native Reserve" or "Bantu Area", who spent the middle years of his life working intermittently for white employers in "White Areas", and who, when he was no longer employable, was constrained by economic necessity or by law to return to his "Reserve" and stay there until he died.'[36] Twenty years later, the African areas presented visible signs of overpopulation, with rural densities in the Transkei and in Natal almost in the same range as those of the highly urbanized Witwatersrand.[37] Too many people and too many cattle were concentrated in too small an area. Bush that would otherwise have been fallow was cleared to provide garden plots, and grazing land took over where trees and shrub had grown before — with the result that wind and water erosion began to take a heavy toll. The return to peasant farming fell when the existing factor proportions were disturbed. Indebtedness increased, and the pressure on the Africans to seek wage employment mounted.[38]

In the labor market, the Africans had to face increasingly strong attempts at monopsonization. These attempts were caused by the perceived difficulties to recruit unskilled workers in sufficient numbers at a low enough level of wages. This problem had been felt by the mine-owners at least since the late 1880s. Already in 1890, the Chamber of Mines tried to obtain government assistance to ensure a steady supply of labor, but failed.[39] During the years that followed, a policy where the outward façade was to identify the fate of the mining industry with that of the high-cost, marginal producer was adopted to press for government intervention to guarantee recruitment and fix maximum wages. In 1896, the Rand Native Labour Association was established to monopsonize the recruitment of African labor, but the effort did not prove successful. Competition among the mineowners (which at times was close to cut-throat) made breaches of the agreement frequent. Therefore, in 1900, the Chamber again suggested that the government take over the responsibility, but the proposition was turned down for the second time.[40]

Government assistance was secured in another area, however. The same year, the Witwatersrand Native Labour Association was established in a renewed attempt at monopsonization. Backed by the government, the WNLA obtained exclusive rights to recruit labor in Mozambique for the South African mines. From the point of view of the mineowners, Africans from Portuguese East Africa constituted a welcome addition to the domestic labor force.[41] The monopsonization effort failed, however, due to competition, for example, from Rhodesian employers.

Within South Africa itself, monopsonization was a difficult affair. Collusive agreements worked well only in times of abundant labor supply but had a tendency to break down as soon as the supply for some reason fell, as witnessed in 1905 and 1906, when the WNLA finally had to release its members from the agreement.[42] In 1911, however, a Native Labour Regulation Act was passed which licensed recruiting agents and which prohibited the breaking of labor contracts by offering higher wages. The following years, a monopsony was finally successfully established in the form of the Native Recruiting Corporation which subsequently managed to secure a reduction in the cost of unskilled labor.[43]

The Poor White Problem

From the First World War to the mid-1920s, the color bar was firmly established in the South African labor market. Skilled and semi-skilled jobs were now reserved for the Europeans, while the African majority were confined in their choice to unskilled jobs in the modern sector or to making a living in the impoverished 'traditional' sector which had emerged as a result of the white land alienation policy.

An important part of the background to the erection of the legally founded color bar may be found in the 'poor white problem' and its connection with increasing urbanization. For different reasons, pressure

Application of Theory: Racial Discrimination in South Africa 217

was exerted on approximately one out of eight of the white population to leave the countryside. Rural life had difficulties in adapting to increased population pressure. Agricultural methods were poor. Not only the Africans but the European farmers as well were facing a serious erosion problem. The system of inheritance as given by Roman-Dutch law made for an uneconomic subdivision of farms. Many failed to adapt to the changed requirements imposed by the increasing commercialization of agriculture following the mineral discoveries. Mining and land companies acquired vast holdings. The Anglo-Boer War, finally, led to outright destruction of a large number of farms.[44]

The poor whites (Afrikaners in their majority) were forced to leave the countryside to seek work in town.[45] However, lacking the education and training necessary for holding skilled positions, they had to face the stern competition of other racial groups, mainly the Africans, who were prepared to work at comparatively low wages — in a situation where labor costs were the dominating consideration in the mines and on the farms. As could be expected, this soon led to industrial unrest. The first trade unions (craft unions) had been founded by British immigrants in the late nineteenth century, and white trade unionism soon spread into the Rand mines. The mineowners strongly resisted these pressures which led to a clash between the two parties.

The white workers won a victory in 1911, when the Mines and Works Regulation Act established the color bar in mining, reserving the best jobs for Europeans.[46] However, the mineowners continued to oppose trade unionism, and a series of strikes in 1913-14 ended with military intervention and defeat for the unions.[47] In spite of this setback, attempts by the mineowners to minimize labor costs by substituting black labor for white was thwarted by the unions. A court decision had declared the color bar in the Mines Act *ultra vires*, but in 1918 a status quo agreement was concluded between the Chamber of Mines and the South African Industrial Federation whereby the color bar was maintained.[48]

Nevertheless, the conflict of interest between employers and white employees continued. After another strike in 1920, matters came to open revolt in 1922. During the First World War, depreciation of sterling had led to an increase in the price of gold. However, in 1922, the British government announced its intention of going back to the pre-war gold parity — a measure which amounted to a 35 per cent reduction of the gold price.[49] This put a considerable squeeze on the marginal mines. The Chamber made an attempt to renegotiate the status quo agreement, but the white miners (75 per cent of whom were Afrikaners) came out on strike.

The strike failed, and a Mining Industry Board concluded that the abolition of the status quo agreement was justified. Many whites lost their jobs, and a majority had to accept a cut in wages. Africans were promoted to higher levels and wage costs were cut in the mining industry. However, these effects were only short-lived. The white miners had not lost the battle. All of them had votes and used them, in 1924, to bring a joint Labour/Nationalist government into power. The Pact Government immediately passed three laws which definitely re-established the color bar. From 1924 on, the basic cleavage of the labor market was ensured.[50]

The most important act was the 1926 Mines and Works Amendment Act, which restored and reinforced the 1911 Act so as to legalize the color bar in mining. The second one was the Industrial Conciliation Act, which laid down the principle of collective bargaining, mediation and arbitration for industries with organized (white) labor. The definition of employees used in this act was such as to exclude the majority of Africans from the right to bargaining. The third and last act was the 1925 Wage Act, whereby a Wage Board was established to recommend minimum wages and working conditions (to be approved by the Minister of Labour) for unorganized labor.[51] In practice, the Wage Board turned into a mechanism to prevent wage increases for Africans:

> ... in one case only between 1925 and 1932, was the Wage Board directed to make a recommendation exclusively for unskilled workers; in five cases up to 1935 where the Wage Board found it could not recommend 'civilized standard' rates, it was directed to make no recommendation by the Minister of Labour; and in 1929 an amended regulation, requiring *all* persons supporting an application to the Wage Board for an investigation to sign it themselves, made it impossible for any large body of Africans, the least organized and the most illiterate, effectly to apply.[52]

Supplementary laws were passed as well. As early as 1922, two years before the advent of the Pact Government, an Apprenticeship Act had specified minimum educational standards plus requirements for technical school training for skilled jobs in such a manner as to preclude African entry and to train only white youths. Three years later, the Customs Tariff Amendment Act provided for special protection for industries employing a high proportion of 'civilized' labor.[53]

During the 1920s and 1930s European farming remained in a backward state, characterized by deficient methods and a lack of modern capital equipment. Soil erosion in particular proved to be a very serious problem, not only in the African reserves, but in European areas as well. Overstocking and indiscriminate burning of the vegetation in combination with the failure to protect the denuded soil from wind and water successively destroyed the natural resource basis for agriculture. 'Farming in South Africa had indeed degenerated into *Räuberwirtschaft*', writes Desmond Hobart Houghton.[54] Farmers lacked the necessary knowledge and were in addition unwilling to change their methods so as to reduce the extent of erosion.[55]

The consequence of the difficult situation in agriculture, which was further aggravated by price falls during the depression and a drought which killed thousands of livestock in 1932–33, was that more and more whites were forced out of the agricultural sector. After 1931, white farming employment started to decline in absolute terms.[56] The absorption of whites outside agriculture was, however, easy. In 1931, Great Britain abandoned the gold standard and devalued the pound. A world-wide wave of other devaluations followed. The result, for South Africa, was a strong stimulus both for gold mining and for manufacturing. The country was quickly lifted out of the depression and the whites who had been displaced from agriculture could be transferred into mining and industry. By the late 1930s, the poor white problem had been substantially reduced and by the end of World War II it had been almost entirely eliminated.[57]

The Post-World War II Period

During the period following World War II, white farming in South Africa underwent a profound transformation. The thirties and the war had brought an increased understanding of the importance of coming to grips with the erosion problem and in 1946, Parliament was finally able to pass a Soil Conservation Act.[58] A far-reaching technical change took place as well. Before the war very few farmers had used tractors, and combine-harvesters were almost nowhere to be seen. The predominant mode of traction was animal power. During the post-war period there was an extensive substitution of capital for farm labor.[59] The extent to which power-driven equipment was being used increased tremendously. Between 1937 and 1971 the number of tractors in white farming rose from 6,000 to 157,000 and the number of trucks from 8,600 to 94,600.[60] Today, white South African farmers are 'scientific and experimental in their approach . . .'[61]

In legal and political terms, the post-war period has seen a reinforcement of the race relation tendencies that have existed ever since the beginning of white hegemony in South Africa, with increased emphasis on geographical separation of whites and Africans.

After the triumph of the Nationalist Party in the 1948 elections, discrimination was given an elaborate ideological dress in the *Apartheid* doctrine as conceived by Hendrick Verwoerd and others.[62] It was also amply codified in a complicated set of laws, sometimes so intricate as to almost defy interpretation.[63] Basically, however, the system remained the same as before the war, with the best jobs reserved for whites and the Africans concentrated in unskilled and some semi-skilled occupations, the main difference being that the job reservation principle was extended to encompass other sectors of the economy.[64] The color bar, however, as we shall see below, has not been completely rigid.

The Apartheid plan contained three central elements. The number of Africans living in areas designed as 'white', that is the urban, industrialized districts, was to be reduced. The reserves were to be developed to provide a 'separate' livelihood for the Africans, outside the 'white' areas. Finally, white-owned industries were to be established on the borders of the reserves, to provide additional employment for the African population.[65]

In practice, only the first of these three points has been emphasized. Africans are allowed to enter urban districts only under special circumstances. According to the Bantu Urban Areas Act of 1945, no African may remain in an urban area for more than 72 hours, unless he or she can prove that he or she possesses certain qualifications:[66]

(1) continuous residence in the area since birth, or

(2) continuous legal residence in the area for at least fifteen years, or continuous work for the same employer for a minimum of ten years, or

(3) being the son under eighteen, the wife, or the unmarried daughter of someone who meets qualification 1 or 2, simultaneously residing with that particular person, having legally entered the area, or

(4) possession of a permit to remain in the area, issued by a labor bureau.

The law prohibits free movement of Africans between different urban areas and it is not possible to reside in one urban district and work in another. No employer may hire an African without permission from the local labor bureau. Ultimately, the right to remain in urban areas is dependent on the possession of a job. This means that Africans have to accept whatever jobs they can find. If not, they run the risk of being considered 'idle' and could be sent to a reserve or to a 'resettlement area'. Enforcement of the Urban Areas Act is guaranteed by the obligation for all Africans to carry a pass, without which they are immediately subject to prosecution. This pass, among other things, must contain an excerpt from the labor permit.

The Urban Areas Act and related legal codes[67] have been used to deport Africans from 'white' districts to the so-called bantustans or homelands. Between 1948 and 1962 the annual number of convictions for breaking the pass laws more than doubled, reaching a figure of 400,000 the latter year, or 3.4 per cent of the total African population.[68] During 1967-69 more than one million were prosecuted every year.[69] Between 1959 and 1969 some 900,000 Africans altogether were deported to the bantustans.[70] What has happened thereafter is not quite clear. *The Economist* in a 1980 survey of South Africa reported that since the late 1960s 2,115,000 people had been removed to the bantustans.[71] According to other sources, however, the figure dropped up to the mid-1970s but still remained significant.[72]

The second part of the Apartheid plan, envisaging the development of the bantustans, has not been realized. The Tomlinson Commission, appointed in 1951 to investigate what had to be done to develop the African reserves, reported in 1955 that some 100 million pounds would have to be invested and that some 50,000 jobs, including 20,000 in the manufacturing sector, would have to be created each year for Verwoerd's talk about 'separate development' to come true.[73] By 1970, however, only 2,000 industrial jobs had been created. In the Transkei (the largest of the bantustan areas) in 1968 only 32,700 jobs were available (excluding administration, teaching and subsistence agriculture), while 278,000 people had to find employment outside the reserve.[74]

The job situation has not improved in recent years. The Economic Development Programme for the 1974-79 period estimated that a 6.4 per cent annual growth rate would be necessary to provide enough jobs for the more than 200,000 Africans who entered the labor market every year. However, in 1976, the number of jobs created in the mining, manufacturing, construction and trade sectors was already 150,000 behind the EDP targets, and by the end of 1976, African urban unemployment was in the order of 220,000.[75]

In the bantustans, the situation was at least as bad. The total proportion of the land which has been reserved for Africans comprises a mere 13.7 per cent of the South African territory, while 86.3 per cent is reserved for whites.[76] This must be set against the fact that in 1970 69.8 per cent of the population consisted of Africans and only 17.7 per cent of whites.[77] The concentration of a disproportionally large segment of the population in areas that are too small and that lack natural resources leads to falling incomes over time in the bantustans.

Production statistics for the reserves speak very eloquently and unequivocally of stagnation and retrogression. Farm production per household appears to have fallen steadily from the early 1920s to the early 1970s. Cereal production per capita fell from 2.0 bags in 1918-23 to 0.55 bags in 1971-74. Livestock ownership per capita fell over the same period to barely more than a third of its original level. Thus, quite probably, per capita incomes generated in the reserves must have fallen as well.[78]

The failure of the government to provide enough jobs for Africans in combination with the inability of the reserves to absorb an increasing population leads unevitably to widespread unemployment for the black segment of the South African population. The South African government does not publish any statistics on this unemployment, but unofficial calculations indicate that in April 1971 almost 1.3 million people of all races were out of work. The Department of Labour at the same time reported that only 8,500 non-Africans were registered as unemployed, which means that one out of four Africans was without a job.[79]

More recent official estimates give much lower figures — around ten per cent in 1978[80] — but this is certain to be a gross underestimate. Unofficial calculations where adjustments for deficiencies in census data have been made, and where not only open unemployment but underemployment in the reserves has also been taken into account, point to some 2 million un- or underemployed at the end of the seventies. This corresponds to approximately 25 per cent of the African labor force — a figure that may very well be increasing over time.[81]

The bantustan policy changed character in the late 1960s. Beginning in 1968, recruitment of African labor for the European sectors of the economy was made primarily on a temporary basis. All Africans must be registered as looking for work with tribal labor bureaus. Nobody can leave a reserve without permission from one of these bureaus which are responsible for providing African labor to the white industrial areas. If permission is granted, it can be obtained for a maximum of one year. At the end of this period, the person holding the permit must return to his or her bantustan to sign a new labor contract before extension of the permission can be granted. This system makes it impossible for any African who has not already worked for the same employer for ten uninterrupted years or who has already lived in urban areas for fifteen years with official permission ever to qualify for permanent residence in these areas. In the long run an ever greater number of Africans will become temporary migrants to the cities instead of both living and working there. The system with migrant labor and short-term contracts means that it becomes easy to select the best labor. Only the most attractive part of the African labor force, the one with the highest productivity, is hired. The others have to remain in the reserves to take whatever jobs they can find there.[82]

Another part of the bantustan policy was to make it compulsory for Africans to hold citizenship in a homeland. Thus, Xhosa speaking Africans have been made Transkei or Ciskei citizens, Tswana speaking persons were linked to BophutaTswana, Zulus with KwaZulu, etc. Then, as the bantustans have been given nominal independence by the South African government, the Africans holding citizenship in these bantustans have automatically been stripped of their South African citizenship and thus of whatever rights they enjoyed as South African citizens.[83]

The policy of reserving the best jobs for whites during the post-World War II period has been practiced to a varying extent. The training of apprentices in skilled trades has by and large been limited to people of European descent.[84] In 1956, a new section was added to the Industrial Conciliation Act which gave great discretionary power to the Minister of Labour to prohibiting people from obtaining a certain job because of his or her race.[85] This provision ensured that white workers received enough skilled jobs to keep them fully employed.[86] In 1963, a color bar was erected in the engineering industry but was later suspended when employers and white trade unions undertook to apply a job reservation policy themselves. One year later (1964), racial quotas were introduced in the motor assembly industry.[87]

In practice, however, the demarcation lines were not always so straight. The small size of the white labor force led to problems of expansion for industry:

> ... white industrialists have put continued, concerted pressure on the South African government and white unions to allow them to use more black labour, and in more skilled jobs. They exert this pressure because, although they are affluent, they see this as a way of becoming more affluent. This increased affluence would come from increased production and from a reduction of the scarcity premium being paid white labour, that is it would be at least partially at the expense of the system of racial discrimination.[88]

The industrialists were at least partially successful in these endeavors.

A gradual reclassification of jobs took place in many industries, whereby whites moved into supervisory positions while Africans simultaneously took over the semi-skilled and skilled tasks previously performed by Europeans. The color bar was a 'floating' one.[89] Job 'dilution' was frequent, that is an employer hired Africans to do part of the job previously done by a white. The latter retained the most skilled, and hence best paid parts. In the process, the label of the job was changed to circumvent the regulations laid down by the laws.[90] Naturally, the extent of this type of manipulations was greatest in situations where an acute shortage of skilled workers threatened to choke the growth process.

Recent Developments

In 1979, a number of changes in the legislation governing the labor market were undertaken. The background to these changes is found in the changes that took place in the labor market itself during the seventies and especially in the increased industrial unrest among the Africans.[91]

In the early seventies, the South African economy entered a recession with a slowdown in the growth rate coupled with increasingly strong inflationary pressure.[92] The growth rate of GDP by and large just kept pace with the increasing population. In this situation, a series of African strikes commenced and these strikes proved to be successful in raising wage rates.

In the mid-seventies, African workers felt the effects that the world recession had on the South African economy. Declining growth rates fell short of the rate of population growth and food prices rose sharply. At the same time the threat of increased unemployment grew increasingly stronger. Strike activities continued intermittently and also combined with such events as the Soweto massacre in 1976 and the ensuing riots elsewhere. The Malawian decision to prohibit the recruitment of labor for the South African gold mines, following an airplane accident in 1974 which killed 74 such recruits, and the temporary drying up of the inflow of Mozambican immigrants to the same industry after the transfer of political power to FRELIMO in 1975 complete the picture.[93] White South Africa was becoming more dependent on recruiting African labor within its own borders — a situation which has been reinforced since the African take-over in Zimbabwe in 1980.

In addition, the changing overall political situation in Southern Africa has worked to the benefit of the Africans:

In the past any potential shortage in the supply of educated and sophisticated labour was met by increased White immigration, rather than by black advancement. However, with the growing political instability in Southern Africa, White immigration levels have been significantly reduced, so the potential for black advancement seems better now than in the past, particularly since there has been a rapid acceleration in State investment in black education at all levels.[94]

Between 1973 and 1977 public expenditure on African education increased at a rate of 26 per cent per annum — a figure that should be compared to a mere 5.5 per cent on average between 1948 and 1960. Thus, the situation is better than before. Still, it should be pointed out that for example in 1977 there were only 11,000 African children enrolled in the final school year — a figure corresponding to no more than 20 per cent of the white children enrolled in the same grade.[95]

Against this background, two government commissions were appointed in 1977 to examine the labor market. The Wiehahn Commission was to review the legislation administered by the Department of Labour and the Riekert Commission was to deal with legislation for improving the utilization of manpower. In 1979, the final report of the latter and the first report of the former were presented to Parliament and some changes in legislation were enacted.

Before 1979, the 1956 Industrial Conciliation Act had prohibited the creation of new racially mixed trade unions and had put the existing ones under strong pressure to reorganize along uni-racial lines. In addition, a number of severe obstacles to African unions had been created. The result of this legislation was that in 1977 less than one per cent of the entire African labor force was unionized. African workers had no influence by means of collective bargaining.[96]

Still, as we have seen in the foregoing, the Africans had managed to stage a number of successful strikes. In addition, the overall shortage of white skilled workers ensured that changes would take place in the job reservation policy. Thus, it was ruled that each trade union should be free to define its own requirements for membership, that unions thus constituted may apply for registration and that registered unions would have access to industrial conciliation procedures and industrial courts as well as the right to strike after 30 days' notice. The legal job reservation procedures were abolished. Simultaneously it was made a criminal offense for employers to hire Africans who do not have any residential rights in urban areas. Migrant workers are only allowed in if there is no 'suitable local labor' available.[97]

A Model of South African Discrimination

Equipped with the empirical knowledge of the preceding section we may now proceed to outline a model of discrimination in South Africa in a historical perspective.[98] We will then divide the analysis into three parts, roughly corresponding to three stages of the history of southern Africa. Throughout it will be assumed that the economy is 'small and open', so that events in South Africa do not have any effect on world market prices, and throughout real income will be used to measure welfare.

Stage I

The first of these stages, which extends from the first Dutch settlement in 1652 up to the discoveries of diamonds in 1867 and gold in 1886, is characterized by the intrusion of the white settlers into the African economy.[99] If we begin with the African part, we may express output (assumed to consist of products emanating from agriculture and cattle herding) as a function of labor and land:

$$X_N = f_N(L_N^B, T_N) \tag{8:1}$$

where X_N is output, L_N^B is the input of African labor, and T_N denotes the amount of land used in the sector. This production function is assumed to be linearly homogeneous with the first and second derivatives $f_N^L > 0, f_N^T > 0, f_N^{LL} < 0, f_N^{TT} < 0$ and $f_N^{LT} = f_N^{TL} > 0$.

Next, let us assume that people of European descent have arrived in southern Africa, and that they are producing the same goods as those produced in the African part of the economy. The production function for the European part can then be written as:

$$X_E = f_E(L^E + L_{E*}^B, T_E). \tag{8:2}$$

It is assumed that only one type of labor (unskilled) is employed. This labor can either be European or African. Europeans are recruited among immigrants and Africans from the African sector of the economy. (Neither herding nor agriculture at this stage demands any special skills. Supervisory activities are assumed to be unimportant.) The amount of capital employed is assumed to be negligible. This production function is also homogeneous of degree one and has first and second derivatives whose signs are identical to those of the derivatives of (8:1).

Application of Theory: Racial Discrimination in South Africa

The supply of African labor and of land is taken as given:

$$L_N^B + L_E^B = \bar{L}^B \qquad (8:3)$$

and

$$T_N + T_E = \bar{T}. \qquad (8:4)$$

Finally, we have an equilibrium condition which compares the wage offered in the European sector with the value of the marginal product of labor in the African economy (equality of factor rewards and values of marginal products is assumed for all factors throughout the chapter):[100]

$$f_E^L = f_N^L. \qquad (8:5)$$

This condition means that during the first stage African labor moves back and forth between the two sectors in response to wage differences.

During the first stage, the Europeans have two goals: increased numbers of Europeans, to establish hegemony in the area,[101] and increased incomes for Europeans from the land, or from land plus European labor (because the Europeans working in agriculture generally attempted to have their own farms).[102] To reach these two goals, the whites have two parameters that they can employ: immigration of more Europeans and alienation of African land.[103] (The latter corresponds to capital market segregation in the Becker model. The Africans are currently denied access to land. Hence the analogy.) Differentiating equations (8:1) – (8:5) totally and solving for the effects of immigration and land alienation on the goal variables yields the results shown in Table 8.1 (explicit solutions in Appendix 1). (The symbols w and r denote the wage rate and the return to land, respectively.)

Increased immigration of Europeans is simultaneously a goal and a means. It also increases the incomes of the Europeans, by contributing to increased output and by lowering the wage received by the Africans. This leads to a reduction in the number of blacks in the European sector. Land alienation from the Africans, in turn, also increases European incomes, provided that European agriculture is more land-intensive than production in the African sector. This would appear to be a reasonable assumption.[104] The last two conclusions also hold if we assume that the Europeans are basically landowners and that their main interest lies in increasing the return to land (r_E).

Table 8.1: Impact of White Policy Instruments on Target Variables and on African Incomes. Stage I

Target Variable	Goal	Parameter Change $dL^E > 0$	$dT_E > 0$
L^E	+	+	0
r_E	+	+	+[a]
$X_E - f_E^L L_E^B$	+	+	+[b]
w	–	–	–[a]
X_N/L_N^B	–	–	–[a]
r_N	+	+	+[a]

Notes: a. Iff $T_E/(L^E + L_E^B) > T_N/L_N^B$. b. If $T_E/(L^E + L_E^B) > T_N/L_N^B$.

Both wages and per capita incomes in the reserves are always negatively affected by European immigration and land alienation (given that the European sector is the relatively land-intensive sector). It is also possible that the European policy creates conflicts within the African sector since by increasing the man-land ratio both types of measures raise land rents (r_N). (The same kind of conflict may arise within the European sector, since wages to Europeans are also reduced.)

As Table 8.1 shows, the relative land intensity of the two sectors is central for the outcome of land alienation for various groups. When land is taken out of the African sector and transferred to the European one, factor prices are affected. Let us assume that we wish to maintain the original factor proportions in both sectors, reducing the African contribution and expanding the European one. If the latter is the relatively more land-intensive sector, this creates an excess supply of labor, since for each unit of land, more labor is released from the African sector than the European sector is willing to accept. Hence, the wage rate falls and both sectors increase employment. Land rents increase both in European and in African agriculture. In the African sector, each remaining worker has now less land at his disposal than before and hence produces less. Per capita incomes fall. In the European sector, those African workers who were present at the outset, produce as much as before with the aid of the original land endowment of the sector but receive a lower wage. The newly arrived workers with

Application of Theory: Racial Discrimination in South Africa 229

the newly alienated land, produce, in turn, a surplus above what they receive as wages. Consequently, there is an increase in European incomes.

Stage II

The second stage begins with the discoveries of diamonds and gold during the late nineteenth century and extends approximately up to the end of World War II, when the agricultural revolution began in South Africa and when the so-called poor whites had more or less ceased to be a problem for the white polity.[105] During this period, certain changes take place as compared to Stage I. The economy has become more complex. Instead of dealing with an entirely agrarian economy we must now analyze one where mining and industry (henceforth labeled 'industry' – I) play an import role. In addition, the land area alienated from the Africans has grown. Finally, European and African workers find themselves in a strongly competitive situation, which in turn changes the set of parameters employed by the whites.

The production function of the African reserves remains unchanged (equation (8:1)). For European agriculture (henceforth denoted by A), we have the production function

$$X_A = f_A(L_A^B, T_A) \tag{8:6}$$

and for industry,

$$X_I = f_I(L_I^B + \bar{L}_I^E, L_I^{BS} + \bar{L}_I^{ES}, \bar{K}_I). \tag{8:7}$$

Both these production functions are linearly homogeneous with conventional signs on the first and second derivatives. It is assumed that agriculture, in addition to land, only employs African labor, but neither Europeans nor capital. The assumption that no Europeans are employed in agriculture is made in order to focus attention on the poor white problem. All whites must be employed in the industrial sector. The no capital assumption is made to emphasize that farming methods in the European sector remained low-productive and technologically backward until World War II and its aftermath. Production in the industrial sector, on the other hand, required not only unskilled labor (Africans and poor whites) but also capital investment and the development of higher-skilled manpower (white or African), the latter denoted by S to distinguish it from unskilled workers (no superscript).

230 Application of Theory: Racial Discrimination in South Africa

The total supply of African labor must be divided between unskilled employment in all three sectors and skilled employment in industry:

$$L_A^B + L_I^B + L_N^B + L_I^{BS} = \bar{L}^B. \tag{8:8}$$

Land is divided between European and African agriculture:

$$T_A + T_N = \bar{T}. \tag{8:9}$$

The next equation introduces a new parameter at the disposal of the whites: job reservation, or 'civilized labor policy', as it was known at the time. When it is required that a certain fraction (c) of all unskilled jobs in industry must be reserved for whites we have the following equation:

$$\bar{L}_I^E = c(L_I^B + \bar{L}_I^E). \tag{8:10}$$

This equation determines the employment of African unskilled labor in industry. Finally, as before, the relative employment of Africans in European and African agriculture is regulated by the relative wages (actual or imputed) of these sectors:

$$f_A^L = f_N^L. \tag{8:11}$$

It is assumed that due to the job reservation policy, an insufficient number of unskilled workers are employed in industry to permit the equalization of unskilled wages between the latter and the other two sectors. Hence $w_I^L > w_A$.

During the second stage, whites have six different goals: increasing agricultural production, industrial output, land rents in European agriculture, the return on capital in industry, skilled and unskilled wages in industry. To reach these goals they make use of three parameters involving discrimination: land alienation and increased reservation of both skilled and unskilled jobs for whites in industry.[106] Differentiating the system (8:1), (8:6) – (8:11) and solving for the impact of changes in T_A, c and L_I^{BS} yields the results summarized in Table 8.2. (The explicit solutions are shown in Appendix 1.)

Land alienation can be used independently and efficiently by the landowners. It allows them to reach their goals without the creation of adverse side effects on other white groups. The remaining two

Application of Theory: Racial Discrimination in South Africa 231

Table 8.2: Impact of White Policy Instruments on Target Variables and on African Incomes. Stage II

Target Variable	Goal	Parameter Change $dT_A > 0$	$dc > 0$	$dL_I^{BS} < 0$
X_A	+	+	+	+
X_I	+	0	−	−
r_A	+	$+^a$	+	+
i_I	+	0	−	−
w^S	+	0	−	+
w_I^L	+	0	+	−
w_A		$−^a$	−	−
X_N/L_N^B		$−^a$	−	−
r_N		$+^a$	+	+

Note: a. Iff $T_A/L_A^B > T_N/L_N^B$.

measures are more interesting in that their use entails conflicts between different white groups. The 'civilized labor policy' mainly benefits unskilled white workers and landowners while industrial producers and skilled whites suffer from it. Reservation of skilled jobs for whites has with one exception similar effects; it benefits skilled whites and affects unskilled white workers negatively. Thus, the system contains conflicts both between agriculture and industry and between skilled and unskilled within the white community.

It is also interesting to note that the poor white problem has a direct connection with land alienation. The latter measure drives African workers out of the reserves and as long as the industrial job reservation ratio, c, remains unchanged all these workers must go into European agriculture. With a lower c, industrialists and skilled workers alike would benefit from land alienation, since the supply of unskilled labor in manufacturing would then increase. Hence, the efforts between World War I and the mid-twenties, referred to above, to substitute Africans for Europeans in industrial (mining) jobs.

Turning to the impact on African earnings we find that, given that European agriculture continues to be more land-intensive than African farming, all measures tend to reduce both agricultural wages and per capita incomes in the reserves (whereas land rents there tend to rise).

232 *Application of Theory: Racial Discrimination in South Africa*

Finally, the economics behind Table 8.2 is simple. Most of the table is more or less self-explanatory. The only point that requires comment is the factor intensity condition required for establishing the results with respect to European and African agricultural incomes. However, the mechanism is the same one as in Stage I.[107]

Stage III

Going into the third stage, the post-World War II period, we again find that the economy has undergone certain changes. The production function for the reserves remains the same as in the two preceding stages, but since a 'final' division of land between Europeans and Africans has been accomplished, the supply of land in the reserves is now given. We then have

$$X_N = f_N(L_N^B, \bar{T}_N). \tag{8:12}$$

In European agriculture, capital now plays an important role, so that

$$X_A = g_A(L_A^B, \bar{T}_A, \bar{K}_A). \tag{8:13}$$

At this stage of the analysis, we will assume that the capital stocks are given both in agriculture and industry. Later this assumption will be relaxed.

It is furthermore assumed that the poor white problem no longer exists but that all whites hold skilled jobs in manufacturing:

$$X_I = g_I(L_I^B, L_I^{BS} + \bar{L}_I^{ES}, \bar{K}_I). \tag{8:14}$$

The three production functions possess the same type of characteristics as in the first two stages.

During Stage III, the bantustan policy has been developed with the aid of a pass system regulating the influx of African labor into the white economy (L_E^B). The African workers allowed to enter the European sectors are divided between unskilled jobs in agriculture and industry and skilled positions in the latter sector:

$$L_A^B + L_I^B + L_I^{BS} = L_E^B. \tag{8:15}$$

Adding the Africans in the reserves to the former group gives the total supply of African labor:

$$L_N^B + L_E^B = \bar{L}^B. \tag{8:16}$$

With the introduction of influx control, the equality between agricultural wages in the European sector and the (imputed) wages in the reserves disappears. Instead, we have wage rate equalization between agriculture and industry in the European economy:

$$P_A g_A^L = P_I g_I^L, \tag{8:17}$$

where, without loss of generality, we choose to measure in such units that $P_A = P_I = 1$.

The whites have now two different discriminatory parameters at their disposal. As before, the number of Africans in skilled positions is restricted.[108] Secondly, the total number of Africans in the European economy is controlled. The goals remain essentially the same as during Stage II, except that, with no whites holding unskilled industrial jobs, the unskilled wage rate may be ignored.

Assuming that capital stocks remain fixed both in agriculture and in industry, the solutions summarized in Table 8.3 emerge. (See Appendix 1 for explicit expressions.)

Once again we find that one of the parameters cannot be used without creating conflicts within the white community. Thus, the farming community will be in favor of excluding Africans from skilled jobs, while industrialists will oppose it as they have done in practice. Industrial production will suffer, white workers will have to be paid more, and provided that the capital-skill complementarity hypothesis holds for manufacturing, the return to industrial capital will fall (since removing an African from a skilled position and giving him an unskilled job in industry instead will always lower the marginal productivity of capital). The incomes of those Africans who are living in the reserves will be unaffected, although unskilled Africans working in the European economy will be adversely affected by the reservation of skilled jobs for whites.[109]

However, the most interesting parameter to discuss is the second one: a change in the influx of African workers from the reserves to the white economy. As Table 8.3 demonstrates, an increase of the influx is beneficial for all white groups. This may appear to be a satisfactory

Table 8.3: Impact of White Policy Instruments on Target Variables and on African Incomes. Stage III

Target Variable	Goal	Parameter Change $dL_I^{BS} < 0$	$dL_E^B > 0$
x_A	+	+	+
x_I	+	$-^a$	+
r_A	+	+	+
i_A	+	+	+
i_I	+	$-^b$	+
w^S	+	+	+
w_E^L		−	−
x_N/L_N^B		0	+
r_N		0	−
w_N		0	+

Notes: a. If $g_I^S > g_I^L$, i.e. $w^S > w_E^L$. b. If $g_I^{KS} > g_I^{KL}$.

solution. However, an interpretation of the model which points to the desirability of increasing the number of African workers in the European economy may run contrary to the observed facts. In his discussion of the goals of the Apartheid system, Richard Porter interprets the latter among other things to mean that 'black labor should work separately from white labor . . .' due to 'labor's fear that white full employment is threatened and from a more profound fear of excessive white economic "dependence" on black labor which could eventually endanger the whites' political and social dominance.'[110] In his analysis of 'exploitation' of blacks by whites, on the other hand, he demonstrates that an inflow of African labor to the European sector of the economy will create a gain for white capitalists as compared to the situation where the two races are completely segregated, whereas under certain circumstances the white workers who compete with Africans for jobs may lose. This is part of 'the ultimate paradox of white policy; while the demands of internal politics evoke a rhetoric of "separate development", the continued exploitation of blacks requires . . . their integration . . .'[111] Here, according to Porter, we have 'the dilemma of white policy. While white policy seeks separation of the races, white living standards depend (to some extent at least) on their ability to extract gains from integration of the races.'[112]

Application of Theory: Racial Discrimination in South Africa 235

As both the Porter model and the present analysis demonstrate, it may thus very well be the case that the core of the segregation of blacks from whites should not be sought in economic rationality but in the fact that whites constitute a minority in South Africa and that this minority feels that it must somehow control the African majority if it is to survive. If white security is desired in the political situation which has prevailed in South Africa for many decades it may be a good idea not to have blacks living too close to the white community. It should be much easier in case of political or social turmoil to control the Africans if the latter are living in separate geographical districts where they can be isolated in limited areas. With this interpretation, the bantustan program constitutes a way of preserving white political dominance,[113] and as long as an African takeover is feared security considerations should dominate economic considerations. In this way a constraint is created within which the economy must work.

There is, however, also a second, *economic* reason behind the policy of concentrating the Africans in small, separate areas and restricting the influx into the European economy by means of pass laws. This policy has an important role to play in the system which, on the one hand, builds on geographical segregation of the races and, on the other, strives to ensure a supply of low-cost unskilled labor. By basing the mobility of Africans on the possession of a pass it can be ensured that only the 'right' kind of Africans are allowed to come into the white economy. Between 1960 and 1970, the composition of the African population in urban areas changed in the direction of more men of active age and fewer old people, children and women.[114] Thus, the bantustan policy and the pass laws can actually be employed to ensure that only African workers and not their dependents are allowed in white areas. The number of African workers in urban areas increased during the 1960s, while a massive removal of dependents took place.[115] As Table 8.4 shows, the

Table 8.4: Number of Temporary African Migrants Absent from the Rural Areas of South Africa on the Census Day

Year	Men	Women	Total
1946	415 000	122 000	537 000
1960	671 000	216 000	887 000
1970	1 035 000	260 000	1 295 000
1975	1 232 000	303 000	1 535 000

Source: Nattrass (1981), p. 41.

number of temporary migrants has increased during the entire post-war period.

If workers and dependents are viewed as a single group, the intention of Apartheid policy appears to be to reduce the number of Africans in white areas irrespective of their functions. However, if a distinction is made between workers and others, the policy may instead be interpreted as one of reducing the supply price of unskilled workers while at the same time avoiding all social costs connected with the presence of non-working African dependents in urban areas.

This process works in two different ways. First, the removal of Africans from the cities to bantustans (where in principle everybody works) of a given area reduces the wage and the per capita income in the latter and, accordingly, the supply price of unskilled labor to the white economy. This is both because of simple diminishing returns to labor and because the greater pressure on the productivity of the land will lead to a deterioration in its fertility. Secondly, earning opportunities for family members other than men who are not too old are likely to be fewer in the cities than on the African farms. Thus, a migrant worker who brings his family is likely to require a higher wage than one who does not.[116] In addition, social overhead costs for water, sanitation, health etc. will be higher the larger the number of Africans living in the cities, whereas such costs in the bantustans are not incurred by the white community. Thus, by employing a pass system which allows only single migrants to enter, the white economy reduces the wage that has to be paid. The conclusion drawn by Barbara Rogers indeed appears to be correct:

> The Bantustan policy has never been seriously intended to remove African labourers from the modern, white-owned sector of the economy. Instead, the system of native reserves was set up as part of the system whereby the African population was confined to a subsistence economy inadequate for their support, in order that the able-bodied men should come to the 'white' areas to sell their labour.[117]

At least, its validity has been confirmed by government representatives: '... the Bantu in the White area, whether they are born there or whether they were allowed to come there under our control laws, are there for the labour they are being allowed to perform'.[118]

Secondary Effects

Finally, it should be noted that the analysis of the third stage has built on the assumption that capital is sector-specific both in industry and in European agriculture, so that it is not shifted from one sector to the other in response to differences in the rate of return that arise from discrimination. The reason for this assumption is that capital resources are known not to move smoothly between these sectors. 'Finite values of ... [the speed of transferring capital from agriculture to industry or vice versa in response to interest rate differentials] are today more realistic in the Southern African context', writes Porter,[119] and S.P. Viljoen arrives at the same conclusion: 'those sectors of the economy between which the flow of resources can be expected to be comparatively mobile [are] ... manufacturing, commerce and services'.[120] The capital market is not perfect in the sense that rates of return are equalized between the sectors. This does, however, not necessarily mean that discrimination has no impact at all on the capital stocks of the South African economy. Reallocation of capital may in the longer run take place via the process of investment and disinvestment (depreciation). An increase in the rate of return in a sector may stimulate domestic or foreign investment there, whereas a fall may lead to a gradual depreciation of the capital stock without replacement.[121]

Discrimination may thus have secondary effects via changes in the two capital stocks even though these effects may be assumed to be smaller than the primary ones due to the sluggish response of investment to interest rate changes indicated in the Porter and Viljoen quotations above and because the bantustan policy tends to induce investment both in industry and in agriculture. Investment in one of these sectors counteracts the effects of investment in the other sector on target variables other than the return to capital. At the same time it acts as a brake on further investment in *both* sectors. For these reasons we should not expect the secondary effects that run counter to the primary ones to reverse the conclusions obtained above. To find these secondary effects we may solve our system for changes in K_I and K_A (which hitherto have been assumed to be constant). This yields the results shown in Table 8.5 (explicit solutions in Appendix 1).

If we assume that the industrial capital stock does not change, an increase in the agricultural capital stock, caused by either the reservation of skilled jobs for whites or by the bantustan policy, increases agricultural production and raises the return to agricultural land. It also draws unskilled labor to the sector and hereby exercises another

Table 8.5: Secondary Effects of Discrimination on Target Variables. Stage III. Change in Capital Stocks

Target Variable	Goal	$dK_A > 0$	$dK_I > 0$
x_A	+	+	−
x_I	+	−	+
r_A	+	+	−
i_A	+	−	−
i_I	+	−	−
w^S	+	−	+
w_E^L	+	+	+

positive influence on agricultural output and landowner incomes, raising the unskilled wage in the European economy in the process. This labor must come from the industrial sector. Thus, industrial production tends to fall as does the return to industrial capital and the skilled wage rate. Finally, an increased capital stock in agriculture can only be absorbed if the rate of return to capital in agriculture falls.

An increased inflow of unskilled labor to the European economy, as a result of the bantustan policy, also leads to an increase in the rate of return to industrial capital and hence to a possible increase in capital formation in the sector. The result of the reservation of skilled jobs for whites, on the other hand, is not determinate in the general case, but tends to reduce the industrial capital stock if the capital-skill complementarity hypothesis is valid for the industrial sector.

The effects of changes in the industrial capital stock are completely analogous to those of a change in the agricultural one. Let us assume that industrial investment increases while the agricultural capital stock remains constant. This increases industrial production and draws unskilled workers from agriculture to industry. Hence agricultural production falls and the remuneration of skilled labor increases, since these workers have both more capital and more unskilled labor at their disposal. By the same token, the rate of return to land and agricultural capital falls when unskilled workers leave that sector. The increased competition for unskilled workers increases their wages while the rate of return on industrial capital has to fall if the increased stock is to be fully employed.

Thus, the secondary effects of discrimination may create a conflict between agriculture and industry. If the agricultural capital stock increases, as we would expect it to, it is no longer certain that white workers will gain from discrimination. Their direct gains from the reservation of skilled jobs and from the increased influx to industry of unskilled workers may be lost as the unskilled wage increases in agriculture when investment takes place in that sector. Agricultural landowners, on the other hand, will see their gains increased. Thus, we see that in so far as agricultural capital stocks are responsive to interest rate changes, the common interest of white workers and landowners in racial discrimination on economic grounds may be weakened. Landowners continue to gain, but workers may lose. Disinvestment in industry, which might take place as a result of the reservation of skilled jobs for whites, has the same effects, while the bantustan policy stimulates both agricultural and industrial capital formation and hence produces some effects which are the opposite of those of agricultural investment.

The influence of discrimination on investment may also help us to interpret the phenomenon of job 'dilution', when Africans are allowed into skilled, or at least semi-skilled, positions. The primary effect of reservation of skilled jobs for whites is to increase the skilled wage rate. At the same time, however, there is a realistic possibility that the return to industrial capital falls. In this situation, it is not at all unlikely that workers and capitalists in the industrial sector reach an agreement. If the capitalists are given a tacit right to the dilution of skilled jobs, the white workers might possibly stand to gain. In the first place, job dilution increases the rate of return on capital in the sector and hence industrial investment and skilled wages as well. It also has the effect of lowering the rate of return to capital in agriculture. Capital stocks will decrease in the latter sector and unskilled workers will be attracted to industry with the result that the skilled wage rate rises even further.

The Interpretation of the 1979 Legislation

Finally, how are we to interpret the 1979 changes in labor legislation in economic terms? Beginning with the rights of African workers to organize, it is possible to argue that this is a measure which is intended to strengthen the bargaining position of the Africans — a measure which is the logical outcome of the disturbances in the labor market in the seventies. If the Africans are allowed to form trade unions they are more likely to respect peaceful settlements of labor conflicts as well, according to the principles laid down by the law.

This interpretation, however, is not plausible. It is not enough for the Africans to form unions and recruit members. These unions must also be able to back their demands with bargaining power. However, they will not be able to do this as long as unemployment figures continue to be high among Africans. It is not possible to discuss unionization without making reference to the bantustan policy at the same time.

At this point the trade union issue is connected with the decision to give preference in employment to urban Africans. Clearly, the same considerations as in the past are behind the recommendations delivered by the Riekert Commission. In the first place, influx control is necessary from the point of view of white security:

> Control over the rate of urbanisation is, in the light of circumstances in South Africa, an absolutely essential social security measure. Even though . . . the abolition of such control would lead to faster economic growth, the price to be paid for it in terms of direct and indirect social costs would be too high.[122]

This could be interpreted as a deliberate sacrifice of economic benefits in favor of civilian order and security, but at the same time the commission explicitly recognized the need for maintaining the inflow of African *workers*:

> The employment of labour must take place within the statutory framework created, and the necessary machinery must be used to ensure that the supply of and demand for black labour are brought into equilibrium.[123]

The strengthening of the influx control should be regarded as a *potential* measure rather than an actual one. Its importance from the economic point of view lies in the fact that it creates a way of controlling the emerging African trade union movement. By allowing African unions to be formed, on a superficial level Africans are granted increased rights. At the same time, the squeeze on African workers is maintained by increasing the degree of control over the inflow. Since Africans with urban residence are to be given preference in employment, it is always possible to get rid of undesirable elements by sending them back to the bantustans, should for example the unions become too militant:

> Against any black trade unionist, registered or unregistered, the government has weapons of quite overpowering force. Anyone involved in a dispute can find himself arrested for riotous assembly,

conspiracy, terrorism and breach of his labour contract. Any black dismissed in the course of a dispute could risk losing his or her rights of residence and be endorsed back to a homeland. A contract worker who goes on strike breaks his contract in doing so and may be offered only re-engagement not reinstatement afterwards, with a consequent loss of any accrued social security benefits. Besides, striking workers are regularly replaced by new migrants eager for work. Black strike leaders can be, and regularly are, banned.[124]

This strategy has already been employed. In late July 1980, the biggest single-employer strike in South Africa's history broke out in Johannesburg. Some 10,000 African municipal workers attempted to form a breakaway union and struck for higher wages and the reinstatement of fellow workers who had been fired for previous striking activities. The Johannesburg city council issued an ultimatum: return to work or be dismissed. Subsequently, some 2,000 Africans were fired and sent off to their respective 'homelands' by the police. The strike leaders were arrested.[125]

Events like this hardly lend any credibility to an interpretation that stresses the build-up of African power in the labor market. Rather, the tolerance of African trade unions seems a *divide et impera* strategy. By giving employment preference to those already in urban areas and by tightening the control over the inflow of Africans to these areas, it becomes possible to set unionized (and tolerated) African workers' interests against the interests of the Africans living in the bantustans who attempt to find work in the urban labor market. By 'co-opting black workers into trade unions that will operate according to the principles of the industrial conciliation system, and by providing a section of the African population with rather more secure residential rights in the urban areas than previously, the government [is] . . . promoting the growth of a black petite bourgeoisie with a stake in the system'.[126]

The removal of the legally sanctioned color bar, finally, appears to be without much practical importance. According to Jill Nattrass,

> . . . too much emphasis should not be put on the removal of the job reservation clasuses from the legislation, since not only did these clauses affect very few workers, but they were also never the key elements in the maintenance of the dominant position of the White workers. Far more important were the 'closed shop' agreements negotiated by the exclusively White trade unions.[127]

Leonard Thompson and Andrew Prior arrive at similar conclusions:

> Although the legal color bars in the work place have been repealed in all except a few mining jobs, the effects of custom plus the color bars in other aspects of South African society still pervade the work place. Education and technical training, mobility, and job security still correspond very closely with race, and there are still very few situations in which black workers have authority over Whites.[128]

As long as Africans are not given the same access to education as whites, no formal color bar is needed. Whites will continue to hold the best jobs by virtue of their superior schooling. A formal color bar simply constitutes an obstacle in certain situations. In the historical section of the present chapter the observation was made that employers, during the post-war period, devised a number of ways to circumvent the color bar in situations where no white workers were available. With the removal of formal restrictions, this was no longer required. The job reservation policy has become an education reservation policy which is more suited to today's needs than the old bureaucratic, time-consuming practices.

It is hard not to share the scepticism voiced by *The Economist* in its 1980 survey of recent South African developments: 'it is an open question whether, had the Wiehahn and Riekert commission advocated dismantling the apparatus of state labour control, they might have begun a genuine retreat from apartheid . . . But they do nothing of the sort. They supply the central framework for neo-apartheid.'[129]

Conclusions

The present chapter started by arguing that neo-classical theory could be employed to analyze discrimination in the case of South Africa. In the second section, we gave a historical outline of the development of racial discrimination in that country. It was shown how the expansion of the white settlers built on the alienation of land from the Africans — a measure which is a direct parallel to the withdrawal of white capital from the Negro sector in the Becker model. During a later period, when the competition of Africans threatened to create unemployment among the poor whites who had to leave the countryside to look for urban jobs, a 'civilized labor policy' was followed whereby a certain fraction of the urban as well as all skilled jobs were reserved for whites. Finally, during the post-World War II period, the fully-fledged *Apartheid* policy emerged. This policy aims at concentrating all Africans in bantustans or homelands allowing only African workers, but not their dependents, to enter the white economy, and then only on a temporary basis.

The historical section served as the starting point for the model presented thereafter, where the neo-classical apparatus was used to analyze the consequences of racial discrimination for various groups in South African society. The model contains three different stages, each one corresponding to a particular period of the history of South Africa. During the first stage, which extends from the first colonization in 1652 to the discoveries of diamonds and gold in the late nineteenth century, the main vehicles of discrimination, with the exception of outright slavery, were land alienation from the Africans in combination with immigration of Europeans to ensure political control. It was shown that both these measures increased European incomes, whereas there was a decline in both the wage received by the Africans working in the European part of the economy and in per capita incomes in the African sector.

During the second stage, which ended with World War II, land alienation continued to be an important parameter for the whites. In addition, a certain fraction of all unskilled industrial jobs was reserved for whites, and a policy where basically only Europeans were allowed to hold skilled jobs was pursued. It was seen that white landowners benefited from all three measures. Industrial capitalists, on the other hand, suffered a loss from job reservation policies. White skilled workers gained when Africans were kept out of skilled occupations, but lost from the policy of reserving a determined proportion of unskilled jobs in industry for whites. For unskilled whites, on the other hand, the effects were exactly the opposite. Unskilled Africans, both in the European and in the African sector, incurred a loss — that is all but those employees in industry who were able to keep their jobs and thereby gain from restrictions on entry to these jobs.

During the third stage, covering the post-World War II period, the policy of reserving skilled jobs for whites was continued to a varying extent. In the short run, when capital stocks can be regarded as fixed, white farmers and workers gain from such a policy. However, industrial capitalists will lose, provided that capital is more complementary at the margin to skilled than to unskilled labor in manufacturing. In the short run, African unskilled workers are hurt by this type of discrimination. In the longer run, when the possibility of capital formation or disinvestment is allowed for, the quantitative impact may be weaker, since the changes in capital stocks may counteract some of the primary effects. Moreover, if the long-run perspective is adopted, this allows us to advance a hypothesis which can explain the 'dilution' of skilled occupations with Africans, since in the long run, such a policy may be beneficial to both white workers and industrial capitalists.

The bantustan policy, whereby only African *workers* are allowed in white areas, turned out to be beneficial for *all* white groups in the short run, since it increases the supply of a factor which is complementary to all whites. This conclusion becomes weaker in the long-term perspective. The agricultural and the industrial capital stocks both tend to increase in the long run and this is likely to partly counteract the primary changes. However, the effects of these changes are diluted by the fact that investment in agriculture has effects that counteract the effects of industrial investment and vice versa.

The present chapter demonstrates that neo-classical models of the type developed earlier in the present work may be useful, if properly formulated, when it comes to analyzing economic discrimination in a given historical setting. The South African case includes all types of discrimination discussed in Chapters 5-7. There is a parallel to capital market segregation. Denying the Africans access to land represents the same type of discrimination as when, in the Becker and Krueger models, capital is withdrawn from the Negro sector. Labor market segregation (or rather its reverse) is also present. The bantustan policy of concentrating the Africans in the reserves and allowing only the workers proper in the white economy constitutes an example of this phenomenon. Finally, there is the policy of reserving skilled jobs for whites, that is the crowding discussed in Chapters 6 and 7.

All these measures have been analyzed in the present chapter in a model which is essentially of the 'cartel' type to use Reich's terminology.[130] In our case, the main difficulty with these models envisaged by Reich, that of policing the cartel, does not arise. In South Africa, racial discrimination of the type discussed here, has been entrenched in the legislation from the very beginning of white hegemony. The incentives that make white firms or farmers want to break the 'cartel' are counteracted, and in most cases nullified, by the law. Thus, it may be concluded that neo-classical models of discrimination, constructed in the proper way, may serve not only theoretical, but also empirical purposes.

Notes

1. Reich (1981), p. 108.
2. Curiously enough, Reich does not mention South Africa in his brief survey of discrimination in history (ibid., pp. 13-16).
3. This section incorporates some of the material of Lundahl and Ndlela (1980), pp. 107-16. Since that article was written the highly commendable works edited by Elphick & Giliomee (1979), Marks & Atmore (1980) and Lamar & Thompson (1981) have appeared. The reader is referred to these books for a more detailed picture of the period up to the mineral discoveries.
4. The exception to this rule were the San (Bushmen) who were neither cultivators nor sheep farmers but lived off game, fish and other collection from the veld. See e.g. Shapera (1930), Chapter 6, for a description.
5. Moyana (1975), p. 41, Bundy (1979), pp. 15-16, 20-2.
6. See the articles dealing with the pre-Dutch period in Wilson & Thompson (1969). Cf. also Shapera (1930), p. 288.
7. The number of colonists amounted to no more than 5,500 in 1740, 1,500 of whom were, however, officials (with families) in the service of the Company (Hobart Houghton (1976), p. 3).
8. Müller (1981), p. 153. In 1806 slaves outnumbered Europeans in the Cape, but four years later there were more Europeans than slaves (ibid., note, p. 153).
9. For some details see e.g. Katzen (1969), pp. 208-13.
10. On this point, cf. Horwitz (1967), p. 14.
11. The procedure for claiming land is described e.g. in Troup (1975), p. 65.
12. Davenport (1969), p. 293.
13. Troup (1975), pp. 83-4.
14. Davenport (1969), pp. 292-3.
15. Ibid., p. 292, Horwitz (1967), pp. 14-18. Marquard (1968), p. 118, Thompson (1969:2), p. 425.
16. Thompson (1969:2), p. 406.
17. Thompson (1969:1), p. 334.
18. This republic existed only from 1840 to 1845.
19. Thompson (1969:1), pp. 366-7.
20. Thompson (1969:2), pp. 435-9.
21. For a comparison with British policy, which differed little from that of the Boers, see Thompson (1969:1).
22. Hobart Houghton (1971), p. 1.
23. Hobart Houghton (1976), p. 12.
24. Horwitz (1967), pp. 167-8.
25. Ibid., p. 214.
26. Ibid., pp. 40-1, Wilson (1971), p. 114, Bundy (1972), p. 381.
27. Cf. especially Bundy (1972, 1977, 1979).
28. The details of this process are given in Thompson (1971).
29. See Bundy (1972), (1977) and especially (1979), for a discussion of the rise and fall of the African peasantry.
30. Bundy (1972), p. 382.
31. Ibid. Other factors were responsible as well. These are discussed in Bundy (1972, 1977, 1979).
32. Horwitz (1967), p. 44, Wilson (1971), p. 117.
33. Bundy (1972), pp. 384-6.
34. Horwitz (1967), p. 134. The 1936 Natives Trust and Land Act provided for another 6 per cent to be released for the African population, to be purchased

with government funds, but to date no more than a total of 8 per cent is owned by Africans (Stahl (1981), p. 20).

35. Wilson (1971), pp. 127-30. Wickins (1981) provides a detailed discussion of the causes of this legislation.
36. Thompson (1971), p. 284.
37. Horwitz (1967), p. 135. Cf. also Bundy (1977), p. 211.
38. Bundy (1972), p. 386, (1977), pp. 210-16, Horwitz (1967), pp. 136-8. Legassick (1977).
39. Jeeves (1975), p. 10.
40. Ibid., pp. 11-13.
41. Horwitz (1967), p. 66. The Portuguese Africans constituted almost 70 per cent of the total African labor force in the mines during the years before 1910. Subsequently, this figure dropped to 32 per cent in 1946 (Stahl (1981), p. 14).
42. Jeeves (1975), p. 27.
43. Ibid., p. 28, Horwitz (1967), pp. 27, 82.
44. Hobart Houghton (1971), pp. 25-6, Wilson (1971), pp. 126-36, Nattrass (1981), pp. 60-3.
45. Many of these were *bywoners* — 'not so fortunate relatives, who lived on the farms ...[of others, with] little or no obligation to their landlord' (Nattrass (1971), p. 61).
46. Horwitz (1967), pp. 82 ff.
47. Ibid., pp. 90-1.
48. Ibid., p. 176.
49. Hobart Houghton (1971), p. 26.
50. Horwitz (1967), p. 190.
51. Hobart Houghton (1971), pp. 30-1.
52. Horwitz (1967), p. 198.
53. Ibid., pp. 194, 197.
54. Hobart Houghton (1976), p. 58.
55. Wilson (1971), p. 137.
56. Ibid., p. 142.
57. Hobart Houghton (1971), p. 30. According to Nattrass (1981), p. 64, the problem 'was not effectively eliminated until the boom period of the 1960s'. This claim seems a bit exaggerated, however. The situation after World War II was in no way comparable to the situation after World War I.
58. Wilson (1971), p. 137.
59. Ibid., p. 153.
60. Hobart Houghton (1976), p. 66.
61. Ibid., p. 45.
62. For an account and a background, see Giniewski (1961) and Hepple (1967).
63. A survey is given e.g. in Hutt (1964), Horwitz (1967) and Hepple (1971). Cf. also Kane-Berman (1979). It has been estimated that some 2,000 laws and regulations have been required for the administration of the Apartheid system (*The Economist*, (1980:1), p. 5).
64. See Hepple (1971), pp. 36 ff.
65. Ibid., p. 7. For details, see Bell (1973). Changes during the 1970s are discussed in Ratcliffe (1979).
66. Hepple (1971), pp. 16-20. Kane-Berman (1979), pp. 85-91.
67. Hepple (1971), pp. 17-20, gives a sample.
68. Kane-Berman (1979), p. 86.
69. Hepple (1971), p. 18.
70. Rogers (1972), p. 39.
71. *The Economist* (1980:1), p. 20.

Application of Theory: Racial Discrimination in South Africa 247

72. Thus, Kane-Berman (1979), p. 80 reports that from 1968 to mid-1975 171,000 Africans from urban areas were resettled in the bantustans.
73. The report of the Tomlinson Commission is summarized in Van der Horst (1956).
74. Hepple (1971), pp. 7-8.
75. Kane-Berman (1979), pp. 48-9.
76. Rogers (1972), p. 11. No more than 8 per cent is, however, *de facto* used by Africans (Stahl (1981), p. 14).
77. Hepple (1971), p. 13.
78. Knight & Lenta (1980), pp. 161, 167.
79. First, Steele & Gurney (1973), note, p. 47.
80. Nattrass (1981), p. 56.
81. Knight (1978), p. 129, Thompson & Prior (1982), p. 65. The situation would have been even worse if the extent of temporary immigration of Africans from abroad had not decreased in the 1970s. On the one hand, it has been the deliberate policy of the South African mining industry to reduce its dependence on foreign labor in the face of the growing political instability in Southern Africa. In addition, for example, Mozambique and Malawi have strongly restricted the supply of labor to the South African mines. (See Stahl (1981), for details.) Thus, in the gold mines, the proportion of foreigners among the African workers fell from a maximum of 80 per cent in 1973 to 43 per cent in 1979 (ibid., p. 11). The total number of foreign African workers declined from 484,000 in 1964 to 327,000 in 1979 (ibid., p. 27).
82. Some details are given in Nattrass (1981), pp. 40-2.
83. Kane-Berman (1979), pp. 92 ff.
84. Hepple (1971), pp. 37-8.
85. This is analyzed at length in Piercy (1960).
86. Legassick (1977), pp. 192-3.
87. Hepple (1971), pp. 41-2.
88. Yudelman (1975), p. 93.
89. First, Steele & Gurney (1973), Chapter 4.
90. See ibid., pp. 71-7, for examples.
91. For details, see Johnson (1977), especially Chapters 5 and 9.
92. See Hobart Houghton (1976), Chapter 11 for the overall economic situation between 1970 and 1975.
93. Cf. Stahl (1981) for details.
94. Nattrass (1981), p. 49.
95. Ibid.
96. Jowell (1979), p. 373.
97. Nattrass (1981), pp. 289-92. Thompson & Prior (1982), pp. 161-2. *The Economist* (1980:1), pp. 14, 19-22.
98. The model, most of which is presented in Lundahl (1982), is an extension of the model in Porter (1976), 1978). A comparison with the Porter model is made in Appendix 2 to the present chapter.
99. Our main interest in the present chapter lies in the historical development of the present-day Apartheid system. From this point of view, the most interesting feature of Stage I is the alienation of land from the native Africans, rather than the introduction of slaves, although the latter undoubtedly has contributed to the shaping of contemporary race attitudes. Hence, the analysis of Stage I presented in the text is more valid for the post-1834 period than for the period before that date.

To analyze slavery in terms of the present framework is not difficult. If, for the sake of simplicity, we assume that the only labor used by the Europeans during the early part of Stage I was slaves, we have the production function

$$X_E = h_E(L, \bar{T}_E),$$

where L is slave labor and where the supply of land $\bar{T}_E$ is assumed to be given. This production function has the same characteristics as those in the main text (linear homogeneity, conventional signs of the partial derivatives).

It is then clear that the European landowners benefit from an introduction of more slaves, since this increases the return to land. If it is assumed that the slaves only receive enough to cover their subsistence and that this subsistence 'wage' is fixed, it pays the Europeans to obtain more slaves as long as the difference between the marginal product of slave labor and the subsistence 'wage' exceeds the marginal cost of obtaining the slaves.

100. Alternatively, one could argue that $f_E^L = X_N/L_N^B$, since it is possible that African workers may have lost their rights to tribal land when they immigrated into the European sector.

101. In practice this turned out to be difficult. 'Southern Africa had little to attract the Dutch in the early days of the settlement, except its value as a station on the way to the East', writes Hobart Houghton (1976), p. 8. This was true for two hundred years. As late as in 1815, there were only 35,000 whites in the colony (ibid., p. 11).

102. It may also be assumed that the Europeans strive to increase white per capita income. This is not necessarily accomplished by increased immigration, since this measure increases not only production but also the number of people who are to share white incomes. In that case we may interpret immigration mainly as a means for obtaining hegemony, while land alienation is used to increase incomes.

103. An alternative formulation would be to assume that whites *maximize* their incomes by choosing appropriate values of T_E and L^E. This would, however, be to attribute too much power to the whites. They were not in complete control either over immigration or over land distribution. Thus, it is more reasonable to assume that only marginal changes could be made and that the optimum was never reached in terms of either parameter.

104. With the land-grabbing policy employed by the Europeans, land should have been cheaper in relation to labor in the white sector than in the African part of the economy.

105. The dates given are of course only suggestive. The 'stage' concept, as employed presently, should not be interpreted too literally, but the use of 'stages' simply represents an effort to divide the history of South Africa into three separate periods with differing characteristics. It should also be pointed out that no effort is made to explain the transition of a particular stage into the subsequent one. The analysis only deals with what took place *within* each stage.

106. We will not deal with the impact of monopsonization of the labor market here. For an analysis of this, see Lundahl & Ndlela (1980).

107. Some of the effects shown in Table 8.2 may have been reinforced or mitigated by a reduction in investment (a reduction of the industrial capital stock). Thus, reducing the capital stock would increase the rate of return on capital and reduce the remunerations of the two complementary factors: skilled and unskilled labor. Industrial production would also fall. The agricultural sector and the reserves sector would not be affected, provided that the effect on w_I^L would not be large enough to reduce this wage below the level of w_A. However, this was not the case. These secondary effects, however, do not change the basic message conveyed by Table 8.2 — that of a conflict between different groups in the South African economy.

108. This can be regulated e.g. via the school system, via on-the-job training or via a color bar. During the 1960s and 1970s, the formal color bar moved upwards in the hierarchy of occupations (cf. Knight & McGrath (1977), p. 248), until it was finally abolished in 1979. A description of the techniques for this upward movement is given in First, Steele & Gurney (1973), Chapter 4.
109. See Bergsman (1982) for empirical estimates. According to Bergsman, in the mid-1960s, skilled wages were 10 per cent higher and unskilled wages were 39 per cent lower than they would have been in the absence of crowding.
110. Porter (1978), p. 749.
111. Ibid., p. 754.
112. Porter (1976), p. 34.
113. Thus, Africans who hold citizenship in an independent 'homeland' automatically lose their South African citizenship and hence all legal possibilities of exercising political influence.
114. See e.g. Rogers (1972), p. 39 and Kane-Berman (1979), Chapter 7.
115. Rogers (1972), p. 39.
116. Knight & Lenta (1980), p. 174. Cf. Berg (1966), p. 197.
117. Rogers (1972), p. 40.
118. Minister Blaar Coetzee in 1972, quoted by Jowell (1979), p. 390.
119. Porter (1978), p. 746.
120. Viljoen (1965), p. 304.
121. We are not assuming complete neo-classical flexibility here. Capital stocks are not mobile between sectors but if reallocation takes place it rather takes 'the form of a slowing down in the rate of replacement of depreciating capital goods in the declining sector, coinciding with a rechannelling of investment towards the expanding sector' (Neary (1978), pp. 507-8).
122. Quoted in *The Economist* (1980:1), p. 19.
123. Ibid.
124. Op. cit., pp. 21-2.
125. *The Economist* (1980:2), p. 34, Thompson & Prior (1982), pp. 208-9.
126. Thompson & Prior (1982), p. 207. Note also that registered unions are precluded from political association or political support (Jowell (1979), p. 379).
127. Nattrass (1981), p. 290.
128. Thompson & Prior (1982), p. 69. Cf. also Jowell (1979), pp. 381-6.
129. *The Economist* (1980:1), p. 22.
130. Reich (1981), pp. 88-97.

Appendix 1: Mathematical Solutions

In this Appendix we provide the explicit solutions of the systems (8:1) - (8:5); (8:1), (8:6) - (8:11) and (8:12) - (8:17).

A

Differentiating equations (8:3) - (8:5) and solving the resulting system for dL_E^B yields

$$dL_E^B = -\frac{1}{\Delta^A}\left[f_E^{LL}dL^E + (f_E^{LT} + f_N^{LT})dT_E\right], \qquad (A.8:1)$$

where

$$\Delta^A = f_E^{LL} + f_N^{LL} < 0. \tag{A.8:2}$$

European incomes are given by $X_E - f_E^L L_E^B$. Differentiating the latter, using (8:2) och (A.8:1) gives

$$d(X_E - f_E^L L_E^B) = \frac{1}{\Delta^A} \left\{ \left[\Delta^A f_E^L + L_E^B f_E^{LL} (f_E^{LL} - \Delta^A) \right] dL^E \right.$$
$$\left. + \left[L_E^B (f_E^{LL} f_N^{LT} - f_E^{LT} f_N^{LL}) + \Delta^A f_E^T \right] dT_E \right\}. \tag{A.8:3}$$

Since both production functions are linearly homogeneous, Euler's theorem applies so that

$$f_E^{LL}(L^E + L_E^B) + f_E^{LT} T_E \equiv 0 \tag{A.8:4}$$

$$f_N^{LL} L_N^B + f_N^{LT} T_N \equiv 0. \tag{A.8:5}$$

From these identities, expressions for f_E^{LL} and f_N^{LL}, respectively, can be derived. Insertion of these expressions into the last term of (A.8:3) shows that the expression within brackets is positive, provided that $T_E/(L^E + L_E^B) > T_N/L_N^B$.

Land rents in the European sector are given by $r_E = f_E^T$. Differentiating this, using (A.8:1), gives

$$dr_E = \frac{1}{\Delta^A} \left\{ f_E^{TL}(\Delta^A - f_E^{LL}) dL^E + \left[\Delta^A f_E^{TT} \right. \right.$$
$$\left. \left. - f_E^{TL}(f_E^{LT} + f_N^{LT}) \right] dT_E \right\}. \tag{A.8:6}$$

Using (A.8:4), (A.8:5) and

$$f_E^{TT} T_E + f_E^{TL}(L^E + L_E^B) \equiv 0, \tag{A.8:7}$$

it may be demonstrated that the expression within brackets is positive, provided that European agriculture is the relatively land-intensive sector.

Analogously, it may also be shown that rents in the African sector ($r_N = f_N^T$) are positively and wages ($w = f_E^L = f_N^L$) negatively affected under the same circumstances.

Per capita incomes in the reserves, finally, are given by X_N/L_N^B. Differentiating this, using (8:1), (8:3) and (A.8:1), noting that $L_N^B f_N^L - X_N = -T_N f_N^T$, gives

$$d\left(\frac{X_N}{L_N^B}\right) = -\frac{1}{\Delta^A (L_N^B)^2} \left\{ f_E^{LL} f_N^T T_N dL^E + f_N^T \left[T_N(f_E^{LT} + f_N^{LT}) \right. \right.$$
$$\left. \left. + L_N^B (f_E^{LL} + f_N^{LL}) \right] dT_E \right\}. \tag{A.8:8}$$

Developing the last term with the aid of (A.8:3) and (A.8:4) it may be demonstrated that this term is negative (including the sign) iff $T_E/(L^E + L_E^B) > T_N/L_N^B$.

B

Differentiating the system (8:1), (8:6) - (8:11) and solving for the impact of parameter changes on the goal variables yields

$$dX_A = \frac{1}{\Delta^B} \left\{ \frac{1}{c} f_A^L f_N^{LL} (L_I^B + \bar{L}_I^E) dc + \left[f_A^T (f_N^{LL} + f_A^{LL}) \right. \right.$$
$$\left. \left. - f_A^L (f_A^{LT} + f_N^{LT}) \right] dT_A - f_A^L f_N^{LL} dL_I^{BS} \right\}, \tag{A.8:9}$$

where

$$\Delta^B = f_N^{LL} + f_A^{LL} < 0, \tag{A.8:10}$$

$$dX_I = -\frac{f_I^L}{c}(L_I^B + \bar{L}_I^E) dc + f_I^S dL_I^{BS}, \tag{A.8:11}$$

$$di_I = -\frac{f_I^{KL}}{c}(L_I^B + \bar{L}_I^E) dc + f_I^{KS} dL_I^{BS}, \tag{A.8:12}$$

$$dw_I^L = -\frac{f_I^{LL}}{c}(L_I^B + \bar{L}_I^E) dc + f_I^{LS} dL_I^{BS}, \tag{A.8:13}$$

$$dw_I^S = -\frac{f_I^{SL}}{c}(L_I^B + \bar{L}_I^E) dc + f_I^{SS} dL_I^{BS}, \tag{A.8:14}$$

and, after substitution of f_A^{TT}, f_A^{LL} and f_N^{LL} from

$$f_A^{TT} T_A + f_A^{TL} L_A^B \equiv 0, \tag{A.8:15}$$

$$f_A^{LL} L_A^B + f_A^{LT} T_A \equiv 0, \tag{A.8:16}$$

$$f_N^{LL} L_B^N + f_N^{LT} T_N \equiv 0, \tag{A.8:17}$$

respectively,

$$dr_A = \frac{1}{\Delta^B} \left\{ \frac{1}{c} f_A^{TL} f_N^{LL} (L_I^B + \bar{L}_I^E) dc - f_N^{LT} f_A^{TL} \left(\frac{T_A}{L_A^B} - \frac{T_N}{L_N^B} \right) \frac{L_A^B}{T_A} dT_A \right. $$
$$\left. - f_A^{TL} f_N^{LL} dL_I^{BS} \right\} \tag{A.8:18}$$

Using (A.8:16) and (A.8:17) we may also derive the expressions for the changes in w_A and X_N/L_N^B:

$$dw_A = \frac{1}{\Delta^B} \left\{ \frac{1}{c} f_A^{LL} f_N^{LL} (L_I^B + \bar{L}_I^E) dc + f_N^{LT} f_A^{TL} \left(\frac{T_A}{L_A^B} - \frac{T_N}{L_N^B} \right) dT_A \right.$$
$$\left. - f_A^{LL} f_N^{LL} dL_I^{BS} \right\} \tag{A.8:19}$$

and, using $X_N - f_N^L L_N^B = f_N^T T_N$,

$$d\left(\frac{X_N}{L_N^B}\right) = \frac{1}{\Delta^B (L_N^B)^2} \left\{ -\frac{1}{c} f_N^T T_N f_A^{LL} (L_I^B + \bar{L}_I^E) dc \right.$$
$$\left. + f_N^T f_A^{LT} \left(\frac{T_A}{L_A^B} - \frac{T_N}{L_N^B} \right) L_N^B dT_A + f_N^T T_N f_A^{LL} dL_I^{BS} \right\}$$
$$\tag{A.8:20}$$

Finally, using (A.8:16) and

$$f_N^{TT} T_N + f_N^{TL} L_N^B \equiv 0 \tag{A.8:21}$$

we obtain

$$dr_N = \frac{1}{\Delta^B}\left\{\frac{1}{c}f_N^{TL}f_A^{LL}(L_I^B + \bar{L}_I^E)dc - f_N^{TL}f_A^{TL}\left(\frac{T_A}{L_A^B} - \frac{T_N}{L_N^B}\right)\frac{L_N^B}{T_N}dT_A\right.$$
$$\left. - f_N^{TL}f_A^{LL}dL_I^{BS}\right\} \qquad (A.8:22)$$

C

Solving the system (8.12) - (8.17) for the impact of changes in L_I^{BS} and L_E^B (remembering that factor rewards equal marginal value products so that for land: $r_A = P_A g_A^T$, for capital in agriculture: $i_A = P_A g_A^K$, for capital in industry: $i_I = P_I g_I^K$, for skilled workers: $w^S = P_I g_I^S$ and finally, for unskilled workers: $w_E^L = P_A g_A^L = P_I g_I^L$) yields:

$$dX_A = \frac{1}{\Delta^C}g_A^L\left[g_I^{LL}dL_E^B + (g_I^{LS} - g_I^{LL})dL_I^{BS}\right], \qquad (A8:23)$$

where

$$\Delta^C = g_I^{LL} + g_A^{LL} < 0, \qquad (A.8:24)$$

$$dX_I = \frac{1}{\Delta^C}\left\{g_I^L g_A^{LL}dL_E^B + \left[(g_I^S - g_I^L)g_A^{LL} + g_I^S g_I^{LL} - g_I^L g_I^{LS}\right]dL_I^{BS}\right\}, \qquad (A.8:25)$$

$$dr_A = \frac{1}{\Delta^C}g_A^{TL}\left[g_I^{LL}dL_E^B + (g_I^{LS} - g_I^{LL})dL_I^{BS}\right], \qquad (A.8:26)$$

$$di_A = \frac{1}{\Delta^C}g_A^{KL}\left[g_I^{LL}dL_E^B + (g_I^{LS} - g_I^{LL})dL_I^{BS}\right], \qquad (A.8:27)$$

$$di_I = \frac{1}{\Delta^C}\left\{g_I^{KL}g_A^{LL}dL_E^B + \left[g_I^{KS}g_I^{LL} - g_I^{KL}g_I^{LS} + g_A^{LL}(g_I^{KS} - g_I^{LL})\right]dL_I^{BS}\right\}, \qquad (A.8:28)$$

$$dw_E^L = \frac{1}{\Delta^C}g_A^{LL}\left[g_I^{LL}dL_E^B + (g_I^{LS} - g_I^{LL})dL_I^{BS}\right], \qquad (A.8:29)$$

$$d\left(\frac{X_N}{L_N^B}\right) = \frac{X_N - L_N^B f_N^L}{(L_N^B)^2}dL_E^B, \qquad (A.8:30)$$

$$dr_N = -f_N^{TL}dL_E^B, \tag{A.8:31}$$

$$dw_N = -f_N^{LL}dL_E^B \tag{A.8:32}$$

and

$$dw^S = \frac{1}{\Delta^C}\left\{g_I^{SL}g_A^{LL}dL_E^B + \left[g_I^{SS}g_I^{LL} - \left(g_I^{SL}\right)^2\right.\right.$$
$$\left.\left. + \left|g_I^{SS}g_A^{LL} - g_I^{SL}g_A^{LL}\right]\,dL_I^{BS}\right\}. \tag{A.8:33}$$

With the aid of

$$g_I^{SS}(L_I^{BS} + \bar{L}_I^{ES}) + g_I^{SL}L_I^B + g_I^{SK}K_I \equiv 0 \tag{A.8:34}$$

and

$$g_I^{LL}L_I^B + g_I^{LS}(L_I^{BS} + \bar{L}_I^{ES}) + g_I^{LK}K_I \equiv 0, \tag{A.8:35}$$

it can be shown that $dw^S/dL_I^{BS} < 0$.

D

Solving the system (8:12) – (8:17) for the impact of changes in K_A and K_I yields

$$dX_A = \frac{1}{\Delta^C}\left[g_A^L g_I^{LK}dK_I + (g_A^K\Delta^C - g_A^L g_A^{LK})dK_A\right], \tag{A.8:36}$$

$$dX_I = \frac{1}{\Delta^C}\left[(g_I^K\Delta^C - g_I^L g_I^{LK})dK_I + g_I^L g_A^{LK}dK_A\right], \tag{A.8:37}$$

$$dr_A = \frac{1}{\Delta^C}\left[g_A^{TL}g_I^{LK}dK_I + (g_A^{TK}\Delta^C - g_A^{TL}g_A^{LK})dK_A\right], \tag{A.8:38}$$

$$dw^S = \frac{1}{\Delta^C}\left[(g_I^{SK}\Delta^C - g_I^{SL}g_I^{LK})dK_I + g_I^{SL}g_A^{LK}dK_A\right], \tag{A.8:39}$$

$$dw_E^L = \frac{1}{\Delta^C}\left[g_A^{LL}g_I^{LK}dK_I + g_I^{LL}g_A^{LK}dK_A\right], \tag{A.8:40}$$

$$di_A = \frac{1}{\Delta^C}\left\{g_A^{KL}g_I^{LK}dK_I + \left[g_A^{KK}g_A^{LL} - (g_A^{KL})^2 + g_A^{KK}g_I^{LL}\right]dK_A\right\}, \tag{A.8:41}$$

Application of Theory: Racial Discrimination in South Africa   255

where with the aid of the Euler relations

$$g_A^{KK}K_A + g_A^{KT}\bar{T}_A + g_A^{KL}L_A^B \equiv 0 \tag{A.8:42}$$

and

$$g_A^{LL}L_A^B + g_A^{LT}\bar{T}_A + g_A^{LK}K_A \equiv 0 \tag{A.8:43}$$

it may be proved that di_A/dK_A (constant K_I) is negative, and

$$di_I = \frac{1}{\Delta^C}\left\{\left[g_I^{KK}g_I^{LL} - \left(g_I^{KL}\right)^2 + g_I^{KK}g_A^{LL}\right]dK_I + g_I^{KL}g_A^{LK}dK_A\right\} \tag{A.8:44}$$

where, using (A.8:35) and

$$g_I^{KK}K_I + g_I^{KS}(L_I^{BS} + \bar{L}_I^{ES}) + g_I^{KL}L_I^B \equiv 0,$$

it is easily demonstrated that $di_I/dK_I < 0$ (given K_A).

Appendix 2: The Porter Model of the South African Economy

Richard C. Porter has constructed a 'heuristic' model of what he calls the Southern African-type economy,[1] that is a model 'aimed primarily at understanding rather than empirical application,' of 'a market economy where market constraints and policy parameters are determined by whites and for whites'.[2] Within the framework of this model, Porter proceeds to analyze the effects on a number of goal variables of changes in four parameters at the disposal of the white policy makers: the white wage rate, the ratio at which jobs are reserved for whites in the industrial sector, the black wage and the price of manufactures in terms of agricultural goods.

The present Chapter 8 provides a model which is partly an alternative to, but mostly an extension of Porter's, one which lies closer to the historical reality of South Africa upon which Porter builds his model. The extension is twofold. In the first place, Porter concentrates his attention on the contemporary South African economy and does not deal with the historical sequence. In the present chapter, the development of the South African economy is split into three different stages, each corresponding to a particular period of South Africa's history. Secondly, Porter does not attempt any analysis of two of the historically most interesting parameters employed by the whites in southern Africa, namely the alienation of African land and the reservation of skilled jobs for whites. Our extension of Porter's model includes both of these.

Porter distinguishes three sectors in the Southern African-type economy: the reserves, (white) agriculture and industry. The reserves constitute an all-black sector, bantustans or homelands, where African labor works without access to capital, that is an economy where labor and land are the factors of prime interest. Land is, however, not explicitly introduced into the model although Porter assumes that 'labor and land are applied in fairly fixed proportions, and constant returns to labor is probably a satisfactory approximation'.[3] The reserves sector acts as a reservoir of labor for the white economy, the wage floor of black labor being given by the average standard of living in the reserves. The other two sectors in the Porter model form part of the white economy: agriculture and industry. Production in agriculture takes place with the aid of two factors, black labor and capital, the latter being owned solely by whites. Production in industry differs in that the labor input may be either black or white. Capital is mobile between the two white sectors and black labor can be moved between all three sectors.

The allocation of the (given) stock of capital takes place according to simple rules. The marginal revenue product of capital must be equal to the return on capital in each of the two white sectors. The supply of capital in each sector is, in turn, determined by the relative returns to capital in the two sectors. The allocation of labor is determined more by the chosen values of the policy parameters. In agriculture, the wage rate (of blacks) must be equal to the marginal revenue product of labor. In industry things become more complicated, since a job reservation policy is pursued whereby a certain proportion of all jobs must be reserved for whites. If the proportion is denoted by c, industrial firms will hire white (E) and black (B) labor in such a way that the marginal revenue product (X_I^L) of one worker becomes a weighted average of the two wage rates w^E and w^B:

$$X_I^L = cw^E + (1-c)w^B. \qquad (B.8:1)$$

The white (exogenously determined) labor force, finally, must be fully employed.

The present criticism is not directed towards the Porter model as such, conceived as a heuristic model which is not intended as a realistic description of the South African case but which rather serves as an illustration of the types of policy mechanisms that may be at work in a society where racial discrimination is a feature which pervades all economic life. Instead, the criticism emerges when we seek to increase the realism of the model in order to apply it to the actual historical sequence — in the present case South Africa. If this is the objective, the Porter model can be criticized in three respects:

(1) The model does not fit the historical sequence of the establishment of white supremacy in southern Africa in that it pays no attention to land alienation.

(2) The wage rates should be treated as endogenous variables.

(3) The model is too strongly aggregated in two senses:

    (a) It does not allow for any distinction between skilled and unskilled labor in the industrial sector.

    (b) It does not allow for any distinction between an earlier period in the history of southern Africa when the main (or only) white economic activity was agriculture and animal husbandry and the subsequent development of gold mining and industry whose production functions differ from those of early white agriculture.

With respect to the first point,[4] we have pointed out in the main text how the Boer expansion in South Africa built on land alienation from the Africans. It was the land alienation policy — the establishment of African reserves — which created what has later been interpreted as an 'unlimited' supply of labor (in the Lewis sense[5]) in the South African economy. By reducing the land area at the disposal of the Africans (the geographical area of the 'reserves' of the Porter model) the scope for white agriculture increased and the supply of African labor which was essential to the maintenance of the European standard of living in southern Africa could be increased in the white economy.

Land alienation took place in South Africa both during the period of agricultural expansion by the Boers up to the discoveries of diamonds in 1867 and gold in 1886 and during the ensuing expansion of the 'modern' sector of the economy up to World War I, when the demand for unskilled mining labor increased drastically.

By the same token, the assumption which Porter makes with respect to the production function of the reserves appears to be unrealistic. Postulating constant returns to labor amounts to assuming that land does not constitute a binding constraint on production in the reserves sector, so that when the population of the reserves increases there will always be unused land which may be put into production to ensure a constant standard of living in the reserves. This runs contrary to the observed historical pattern. As the African population grew, even more people were concentrated on a shrinking land area. Diminishing returns to labor were reinforced by increasingly denied access to the complementary production factor — with falling per capita incomes, overgrazing, and erosion in the reserves as patent results. This sequence should be included in any model which attempts to capture the historical reality.[6]

The second point where the Porter model appears not to coincide with historical reality is in its treatment of white and black wages. In a historical perspective, the point just made with regard to land alienation assumes some importance. The clue to the supply of African labor in the white economy, as well as to unskilled wages in the white sector, is to be found in the alternative prevailing for the Africans: that of remaining in the African part of the economy, that is in the reserves. A policy which dictates a wage rate that falls short of what the Africans can obtain by staying in the reserves would never have been successful. On the contrary, it would not have been necessary to offer a wage much higher than was available in the reserves.

We have worked with two alternative assumptions, the first being that unskilled wages in the white sector must equal the marginal value product of labor in the reserves and the second postulating that migration from the reserves into the white sectors is limited by means of pass laws so that unskilled wages in white agriculture and industry are determined by the marginal productivity of labor in these sectors and by the amount of African labor permitted to migrate from the reserves.[7] (Porter deals with the second of these mechanisms only.)

Turning to the wage rates of white workers, these are determined via a process of collective bargaining between trade unions and employer organizations — one which historically has not been without relation to the productivity of white labor. The case of mining is illustrative. In 1911, the Mines and Works Regulation Act laid down the principle of the color bar in mining and reserved jobs in the sector for whites. Nevertheless, the mineowners did their best to substitute Africans for Europeans, since black workers were willing to work for lower wages than whites. It was not until after a series of strikes organized by the white trade unions and the so-called Rand Rebellion that the white miners managed to vote out of power the government which refused to give legal sanction to the color bar. After 1924, a number of laws ensured white-worker domination in the labor market. Hence the significant point about the historical development of the South African labor market is that white wages should be regarded as a variable which is endogenously determined within a framework where restrictions on the supply of black labor play a central role.

Porter, whose discussion runs in terms of a single, unskilled category of labor, concentrates his analysis of discrimination on the job reservation technique. However, he points out that 'Empirically, the most important means of discrimination today is . . . through access to education, apprenticeship, or on-the-job training . . . black workers simply cannot acquire the education and training necessary to qualify for the more skilled and better paid jobs.'[8] This type of discrimination can be handled in a model which allows for two categories of labor: skilled and unskilled,[9] where discrimination is interpreted as a restriction upon the access of Africans to skilled positions. This restriction, given the demand conditions, decides the level of white skilled wages.[10]

Finally, it is desirable to distinguish, as we have done, between three different periods in the history of South Africa.

Notes

1. See Porter (1978). Cf. also an earlier discussion paper — Porter (1976) — for an attempt to link the model closer to the economy of South Africa.
2. Porter (1978), p. 743.
3. Ibid., pp. 743–4.
4. Porter States 'that the insight lost from the exclusion is small in comparison to the additional complexity caused by explicit consideration of land' (ibid., p. 744.)
5. Cf. the classic article by Lewis (1954).
6. A short account of these problems is given by Hobart Houghton (1976), pp. 70–82. Porter (1976), note, p. 3, quotes Horrell (1969), p. 43, for evidence as to the realism of his assumption of constant factor proportions and constant average productivity for labor in the reserves: '. . . the average yield of maize . . . is 3 bags per morgen [a measure of land area] . . . For over 30 years there has been little change . . .' However, he misinterprets this evidence. The constancy of yields per morgen could, of course, mean that the man/land ratio has remained fixed in the reserves, but in that case some of the black labor going into the reserves must be unemployed. Porter assumes that this is not the case. All black workers not absorbed by white agriculture or industry have to be employed in the reserves.

The alternative interpretation of Horrell's finding is that as more people move into the reserves, the fertility of the soil there falls but that the addition of labor approximately compensates for that in terms of yields per morgen. For constant average labor productivity we must in addition require that maize production per worker has remained constant, and this is not likely to have been the case in an economy where the increased population pressure has increasingly resulted in '*the creation of desert conditions*' (Hobart Houghton (1976), p. 72). As Knight and Lenta (1980) have pointed out (pp. 160-1), it appears that farm production *per household* in the reserves fell steadily from around 1920 to the early seventies.

7. This is more in line with the reasoning of Knight (1964), who in his model of the income distribution in South Africa lets African wages be determined by the income per head in the subsistence (reserves) sector and who stresses that wages are determined 'by the forces of demand and institutionally determined supply.' (Knight & McGrath (1977), p. 266.) 'White workers have the power to monopolise the high-skill, and possibly certain other occupations, so crowding Black workers into the remaining low-skill occupations and depressing wages in them' (ibid., p. 252).

8. Porter (1978), p. 744.
9. Cf. the first part of the third point of criticism above.
10. This is also more in line with the Knight model.

9 SUMMARY AND CONCLUSIONS

Main Conclusions

Discrimination and theories of discrimination have a long history. Despite this, discrimination has long stood on the periphery of neo-classical theory. In Chapter 1, we touched upon some possible explanations, among other things, that within neo-classical theory, income distribution and the existence of power has been neglected in comparison with allocation problems. The survey of the different theories of discrimination in Chapter 2 can also contribute towards an explanation of this situation.

Economic theories of discrimination are built on assumptions which in different aspects deviate from the basic assumptions of general equilibrium theory. This occurs either through the introduction of new arguments in the utility function (preferences for transactions with a certain group; social prestige), through persons having preferences concerning transactions which are made between other people, through different types of imperfections (incorrect or incomplete information, monopsony) or through explicitly taking into consideration the power relationships in society (the radical theory, bargaining models). Especially during the last decade, these types of relations have been dealt with more generally within economic theory. Such is the case for example with incomplete information and social customs, which are used in attempts to give macroeconomic theory a microeconomic foundation. This, together with the increased attention given to the position of blacks and women in the labor market in the United States and Western European countries, can explain the rapid expansion of research on economic discrimination.

Chapter 2 contains an overview of the research in this area. The starting point encompasses two different traditions: the British debate from the end of the last and the beginning of this century concerning the causes of low female wages and Becker's theory of discrimination.

In the British debate, several competing and complementary ideas were brought forth. Discrimination as a social tradition and monopsonistic discrimination are two of them. Another important explanation is the pressure exerted on firms from one group of employees to discriminate against another group, primarily in order to exclude the discriminated group from certain occupations. Occupational segregation depresses the wages in those occupations that are open to the discriminated group (crowding). It is characteristic of the British economists that they often combine different causes of discrimination, but also they they do not carry the analysis of the effects particularly far, with the exception of the case of monopsony.

Becker on the other hand based his theory on a single cause of discrimination — preferences for discrimination. Using this as his starting point, he analyzed the effects of discrimination. The strength of Becker's work lies in the uniformity of his approach and the skilfully made analysis, given the cause of discrimination. The analysis is carried out in both a microeconomic and a macroeconomic framework. There are, however, certain weaknesses in the Becker approach, primarily in the welfare-economic part, where Becker compares cases containing different preferences with each other. His theory has also invited criticism because its implications — chiefly that wage differentials due to discrimination cannot exist for a longer period of times — do not agree with the empirical studies that have been made. The conclusion drawn from this contradiction then is that preferences are not an important factor in explaining discrimination.

To solve this dilemma several attempts have been made to reformulate Becker's theory. Two examples are alternative specifications of the utility function and, in combination with employee discrimination, the existence of costs for hiring and firing. It is doubtful, however, if long-run wage differentials can be explained by these extensions of the theory.

Several alternative discrimination theories exist. The majority of these have originated during the last decade, but the bases for some of them revert back to the early British debate. This is the case with the theory of discrimination as a social custom and, to an even greater extent, with the monopsony theory where Joan Robinson's work from the 1930s still represents the obvious foundation. Other theories found in Chapter 2 build on prejudices or on statistical discrimination, on dividing and conquering (the radical discrimination theory) and on differences in bargaining power.

In Chapter 2 it was shown that the theories have in part different implications concerning wages, unemployment and segregation. The majority of the theories can explain the occurrence of short-term differentials. The only exception is employee discrimination between perfect substitutes where hiring and firing costs do not exist. In the case of long-run wage differentials the explanations differ even more. Several of

Summary and Conclusions 263

the theories cannot explain these divergences at all, and others can only account for small wage differences.

Segregation has different functions in the various theories. In some, it is a result of discrimination, in others a means. In yet another theory (the radical one), *integration* − the opposite of segregation − is the means whereby discrimination is achieved.

The distributional implications differ markedly among the various theories. They all share one element: the discriminated employee group does not gain. The conclusions regarding the capital owners and the non-discriminated employee group, however, vary from theory to theory. According to some theories, one or both of these two groups gain, according to others they lose.

In the survey, we have emphasized that the theories yield partly divergent results. This allows a direct comparison to be made when looking at empirical data. It should also be noted that the simultaneous occurrence of two forms of discrimination does not necessarily yield the same result as the sum of the two forms if they had appeared separately.

Segregation is important in several of the theories, although not in a uniform way. In several of the early British analyses, occupational segregation had great significance. Due to social tradition, pressure from employees, influence of trade unions or laws, women were excluded from certain occupations. In the recent discussion, this type of discrimination has been brought back into the debate. Our knowledge about the effects of such discrimination is, however, not particularly good. In Chapters 5-8 of this book, we have tried to make a contribution to this area. In the two immediately preceding chapters (3 and 4), we have taken up some unclear points in Becker's macroeconomic analysis. One thread which runs through Chapters 3-8 is the consistent use of the macroeconomic model, that is, the type of model employed traditionally within the theory of international trade.

In the welfare economic analysis, Becker compares a case without either preferences for discrimination or discrimination with a case containing both. By doing so, he violates one of the fundamental assumptions of welfare theory: that it is not possible to compare one set of preferences with another. In Chapter 3 we discuss this problem. One possible solution is to use a 'double' test, by first analyzing the effects of discrimination for the discriminating group assuming that preferences for discrimination exist and do not change, and thereafter performing the same operation assuming that the group does not have any such preferences. With this approach, unequivocal results are achieved only when both tests point in the same direction.

In Chapter 3 we analyze the case with constant preferences for discrimination. It is concluded that the discriminating society gains from discrimination, which is a result that reverses Becker's findings completely.

The basis of Becker's analysis is that those who discriminate do so because of aversion to the members of another group, and not because of benevolence (favoritism, nepotism) towards the members of their own group. The results differ in the two cases. If nepotism is the cause, the effect of changes in both preferences and discrimination is that the discriminating group gains. If preferences remain unchanged, however, this result no longer necessarily holds.

To measure the cost of discrimination, Becker uses the discrimination coefficient, which in the macroeconomic model is formulated as a certain percentage of the income received from the capital which is exported to the discriminated society. In Chapter 3 a somewhat more realistic formulation is attempted in which the cost is not dependent on capital income but rather on capital exports *per se*. The analysis shows that some of the results are influenced by this reformulation. In particular, in the case of nepotism the discriminating group always gains.

One way of continuing Becker's work is by retaining the macroeconomic approach but dropping the assumption that discrimination depends on preferences. Instead, it can be investigated whether there are any economic reasons for discrimination. This approach has been used by Anne Krueger, among others. In Chapter 4 this type of model is analyzed. (At the same time, this constitutes the second half of the double test in Becker's model of whether the group which has preferences for discrimination gains or loses.)

The main result of the Krueger model is that the discriminating society gains from discrimination. Within the discriminating society, however, capital owners lose. As it is the capital owners who discriminate in this model, this fact gives an unrealistic slant to the theory. A possible interpretation could be that the employee group in the discriminating society uses pressure and possibly reimburses the capital owners for the loss that the latter incur due to discrimination. Such a conclusion is in accordance with the results reached in bargaining models but does not appear as a very realistic one.

The Krueger model also agrees with the Becker one in that the labor force is fixed and capital is the mobile factor. Discrimination occurs in the form of reduced capital exports. It is, however, more realistic to imagine that discrimination occurs when labor is excluded from the discriminating society. On this basis, we have investigated two cases. In the

Summary and Conclusions 265

first one, wages for the discriminated employee group are assumed to be equal in both societies. (It is thus assumed that there are wage differences in the discriminating society.) In the other case, the wage is the same for both groups in the labor importing society.

The results diverge both for the discriminating society as a whole and for the capital owners within it. In the first case, the discriminating society gains, while in the second, it loses. In the second case, the capital owners in this society lose as well, while the result is indeterminate in the first case. In most instances, the second case is quite probably the more realistic one.

The common factor in the different models is that the employees in the discriminating society gain while the capital owners do so only under special and not particularly probable circumstances.

Becker's and Krueger's models are highly simplified. There is only one good in the model and one type of labor. This type of simplified assumptions can be justified for certain forms of analysis, but it precludes analysis of the effects of discrimination when a group may work only in certain occupations but not in others and produce certain goods but not others.

Chapter 5 is the first step on the road to increased realism. There, the model is a two-society, two-factor and two-good one. Both societies are completely specialized in the production of one good. The three cases dealt with in Chapter 4 are also taken up in Chapter 5. The results are negative in the sense that in many cases they are not clear-cut. In several instances, changes in relative prices make the effect on incomes indeterminate and furthermore dependent on which good is used as *numéraire*, which means that the effect on real incomes is uncertain. In order to extract more information from models of this type, further specifications of the production and demand functions are required.

In Chapter 6, the condition that the discriminating and discriminated groups live in segregated societies is eliminated. Instead, it is assumed that all live and work in a single society. Further, the analysis is extended to include the case where skills differ, that is where labor is no longer homogeneous. In this formulation, discrimination means that some members of the discriminated group who possess the necessary skills to get qualified jobs are not permitted access to them or are prevented from getting the necessary education through discrimination in the school system.

The analysis in Chapter 6 is made in the simplest possible manner with only two production factors — skilled and unskilled labor. The members of the discrimination group are all assumed to be skilled, while members of the discriminated group can be either skilled or unskilled. In the one-good case, the discriminating group gains and the discriminated group loses, as the latter is forced out of those jobs that require a greater degree of skill. The same type of conclusion is arrived at in the two-good case. The real income of the discriminating group increases and all the members of the discriminated group, with the exception of those who are able to retain better jobs even in the presence of discrimination, lose in real terms.

Thus, the analysis in Chapter 6 indicates a possible reason why members of a certain group discriminate against members of another. The model, however, is oversimplified in that it does not permit substitution between labor and other factors of production. In Chapter 7, this restrictive condition is removed by the addition of two further (sector-specific) production factors, one for each sector (in the one-good case, only one). This change proves to be sufficient to invalidate the results from Chapter 6. In the one-good model, the workers in the discriminating group gain, while the capital owners can easily lose. The discriminated group still loses. In the two-good case, the connection becomes even more complicated and it is no longer possible to draw any general conclusions about the effects of discrimination.

In the present book, we have consistently used a neo-classical approach in the analysis. In Chapter 8 this type of framework is applied to the analysis of discrimination in a specific case: South Africa. The South African case provides an opportunity to study the effects of discrimination in all the cases dealt with in the theoretical analysis in Chapters 5-7. The first part of the chapter recapitulates South Africa's economic history, placing special emphasis on how discrimination has changed over time. This survey is then used to divide the history of discrimination into three different periods.

During the first period, which extends from the arrival of the Dutch in 1652 to the important mineral discoveries at the end of the nineteenth century, the difference between the European and the African sectors of the economy was small. Both ethnic groups were occupied with agriculture and animal husbandry. During this period, excepting slavery, discrimination consisted primarily in the fact that when European immigration took place, the Africans were deprived of their rights to parts of the land that they had owned by tradition. The latter was a direct parallel to discrimination in the Becker model, in which the discriminated group is deprived of part of the capital stock that was available earlier. In the South African case both the European immigration and the transfer of land favored the Europeans,

Summary and Conclusions 267

while the influence on the average African standard of living was negative.

The second period covers the time from the discoveries of diamond and gold fields to the Second World War. Now, a mining and industrial sector sprang up which used capital and which required skilled workers in addition to the unskilled work force which was used in agriculture.

During this period, the Europeans continued to alienate African land, with consequent gains for the European farmers and losses for the African group. Two other forms of discrimination arose during the period. A certain percentage of all unskilled jobs were reserved for Europeans and African admittance to qualified jobs was limited by a color bar. Both of these measures influenced the standard of living of the Africans mainly negatively, while the influence on the real incomes of the Europeans was mixed. The farmers were favored in both cases, while the capital owners in industry saw their real incomes fall. The reservations of unskilled jobs for Europeans favored the unschooled European workers but not the skilled ones, while restrictions on qualified jobs had exactly the opposite effect.

The third phase, finally, covers the post World War II period. The major differences between this period and the immediately preceding one is that European agriculture now is using capital on a larger scale, and that in general, the European labor force has a higher standard of education. Discrimination has changed as well, The best jobs are still reserved for Europeans. Furthermore, the development of the bantustan policy means that admission to the European part of the economy is no longer free for Africans, but is regulated by pass laws. The effects of reserving jobs for Europeans are approximately the same as during the previous period, with the one difference that the standard of living for the bantustan inhabitants is not influenced because of the lack of free passage between these reserve areas and the European economy. On the other hand, a reduced inflow of Africans influences the real incomes negatively for all European groups. A model which takes into consideration that this migration is highly selective (where only male Africans of working age are allowed into the European economy and the remainder are left in the reserves), however, indicates that the results are favorable for the Europeans.

The above is valid as long as discrimination does not have any, or only a minimal, effect on capital formation. Capital is not mobile, in the neo-classical sense, between agriculture and industry. On the other hand, one may imagine that a falling return on capital in a given sector could in the long run lead to a failure to replace the capital stock, while an increased return stimulates investment. In that case, secondary effects arise through changes in the capital stocks, which, although quantitatively probably less important, gives rise to some possible conflicts among white groups. It is interesting to note that those conflicts may provide an explanation of the job dilution phenomenon: that jobs which are normally reserved for whites are offered to Africans as well. The explanation is to be found in an implicit contract between white capital owners and white workers. In order for the former to be able to hire Africans during periods of labor shortages, they undertake in return to maintain investments at a level which is sufficient to ensure a high wage level for the white labor force.

Theories of Discrimination and Anti-Discrimination Policies

It is evident from Chapter 2 that the effects of discrimination are inherently related to its causes. In addition, the analysis in Chapters 3-8 provided clear evidence to show that the effects of discrimination are also affected by slight changes in the assumptions of the model. Consequently, there is every reason to continue to analyze both the causes of discrimination and their institutional framework. Another argument in favor of continued study is that the effects of the various economic policy measures that are directed at ending discrimination are dependent upon what the causes are. A specific policy measure which is successful in dealing with the effects of a particular type of discrimination may only reinforce these effects when different causal factors are in operation. The differing choice of appropriate anti-discrimination policy measures will consequently be a reflection of the varying causes of discrimination.

It is not possible within the scope of this chapter to carry out a more detailed analysis of the effects of different types of anti-discrimination policy. However, we will briefly examine some of these effects in the light of the various theories of discrimination as well as discuss some of the principal measures which could be effective in relation to a particular causal factor.

For students of international trade it may come as a surprise to find that the use of tax-cum-subsidy policies to attain a first best optimum have hardly been discussed in the literature on anti-discrimination measures. A tax on employing members of the non-discriminated group could for example be used to subsidize the hiring of members of the discriminated community. Since presently we have chosen to limit the discussion to the most commonly advocated measures, we will not pursue this issue further here. (Cf., however, below, the discussion of measures to limit capital market segregation.)

We will first consider some of the most frequently recommended policy measures before going on to examine the impact of these measures, given the causes of discrimination.

Effects of Different Anti-Discrimination Policies

Equal Wages (Minimum Wages). One of the most frequently advocated and commonly used policy measures against discrimination involves some type of intervention into wage formation, such as wage equalization or minimum wage regulations. The former can be interpreted as a ban against wage discrimination while the latter, which may take the form of legislation or an agreement on minimum wages, seeks to raise wages and thereby reduce the opportunity for wage discrimination against low wage groups.

The effects of this type of legislation or agreements vary markedly according to the actual cause of the discrimination. If discrimination is due to preferences held by a firm, the result will be that the firm replaces wage discrimination with discrimination in hiring.[1] Instead of differences in wages there will be differences in unemployment between the discriminated group and other groups.[2] Consequently, the group that is the subject of discrimination may lose due to the equal wage regulations. The long-run effect that is derived from competition between different firms in the Becker model will not operate under equal wage conditions. Those companies that *have* discriminatory preferences do not lose economically compared with companies that do *not* have such preferences.

If equal wage (or minimum wage) laws do not encompass the total labor market this may lead to a crowding of discriminated groups in areas not covered by the law with a concomitant downward pressure on wages in these sectors.[3]

The results will be approximately the same if the propensity to discriminate depends on incorrect information – on prejudices – rather than on preferences. Equal wage regulations would once again give rise to differences in unemployment. However, in this instance, there is an adjustment mechanism that can be used: the distribution of information regarding the actual productivity of different groups. This adjustment mechanism will work less satisfactorily here than in the case where no wage equalization regulations exist. Discriminatory recruitment practices provide fewer employment opportunities for the discriminated group which in turn leads to a slower dissemination of knowledge regarding the relative productivity of various groups.

The same results are obtained in the case of statistical discrimination — greater uncertainty given the expected rate of productivity and the costs of uncertainty. Equal wage regulations will result in differences in wages being replaced by differences in unemployment.

Equal wage regulations may, however, be effective in relation to other types of discrimination. This applies particularly to those cases where discrimination is due to monopsony and where the male supply curve is more elastic than the female supply schedule. In such a case a wage equalization act may lead to both higher wages for women and a larger number of female employees. Equal wage regulations may, however, be without effect if firms can define equal work narrowly and allot the groups work tasks in such a way that formally they are not doing the same work.[4] In response to this, proposals have been made by advocates of equal wage legislation for a change from equal pay for equal work to equal pay for jobs (or work) of equal value.[5]

Legislation on wage equality may prove to be effective when wage differentials are based on a social custom maintained by different forms of social sanctions. The existence of such legislation provides support for those groups who, on economic grounds, wish to break this socially sanctioned discrimination but have not done so because of the risk of losing social standing or having sanctions imposed against them. The same argument can be applied within the framework of the 'bargaining model'. Equal wage legislation improves the position of some of the parties but weakens it for others. The principal beneficiaries of the legislation will be those groups who do not have an economic motive for discrimination.

According to the radical theory, companies are able to divide and rule by pitting the interests of different groups against each other. A necessary requirement in this case is the integration of the work force. Wage differentials are one means by which the company is able to increase its bargaining power. Equal wage legislation deprives employers of this instrument and weakens their negotiating position vis-à-vis the employees. However, this does not eliminate *all* the opportunities at the employer's disposal for playing the interests of different groups against each other.

A policy of wage equalization will have no effect when discrimination is aimed at the exclusion of particular groups from certain occupations (crowding) since legislation generally applies to comparisons within a given occupation.

Quotas (Affirmative Action). Another anti-discrimination measure which has been proposed and tested is the establishment of job quotas for certain groups. A quota system can take many different forms. For example, a quota may be based upon the discriminated group's share of the total population, of the economically active age groups or of the labor force in a particular region of the country. Quotas may also be defined in terms of the share of those in a particular occupation that belong to the discriminated group. In the latter case, the aim of the quota could be the removal of the effects of discrimination in order to obtain the distribution of occupations and work places that would have prevailed in the absence of discrimination. The intention behind the other types of quotas mentioned above is to counteract discrimination at an earlier stage, particularly within the educational system. This type of quota system can be viewed as a form of reversed discrimination — that is a type of discrimination which is of advantage to the (previously) discriminated group.[6] However, in the present context we shall be mainly concerned with the effects of quota systems that do not discriminate positively but instead seek to ensure that the relative proportions of groups of employees become equivalent to a non-discriminatory situation. A policy of this type would be effective in those cases where discrimination influences the composition of the labor force.

Segregation will not arise where every employer has the same preference or prejudice against a particular group, and quota regulations will consequently not have any effect in this case. However, the distribution on work places of a discriminated group can be affected by quotas if only certain employers have a preference for discrimination or prejudice. In those cases discrimination implies segregation and quotas may thus be effective. They may also weaken the cause of discrimination if the cause is prejudices. It can be assumed that such prejudices will disappear more rapidly as the employer becomes better informed by employing persons from the discriminated group. This will, however, not be the case where discrimination is due to preferences. Employers who hold preferences will continue in business and will in this case not be driven out of the market as a result of higher relative wage costs.

The most obvious case is where work places are segregated due to discrimination between groups of employees who are perfect substitutes in production. Effective quota regulations ought to lead to integration but should not affect wages. In this case, wages are initially equal according to the theory.

Employee discrimination against a group only when its members work in certain occupations as well as job competition combined with employer preferences for discrimination may both explain occupational segregation. Quota rules may in such cases be a way of obtaining integration.[7]

If discrimination is due to the existence of social customs that exclude certain groups from employment in certain occupations it would subsequently be possible to break these customs by means of quota legislation.[8]

In both the radical and monopsony theories, the work force is integrated. Nevertheless, quota regulations can still affect its composition, although the direction and the consequences of such a change are uncertain.

It has so far been assumed that the sole objective of quota regulations is to remove the effects of discrimination in the labor market but quotas can also be used to counteract the discrimination of previous generations, as well as discrimination that occurs prior to entry into the labor market. In this case, the effects will be the same with regard to the direction of change but will nevertheless vary in magnitude. This type of quota regulation has been criticized on the grounds that it will lead to a less satisfactory resource allocation (that is anti-discrimination policy imposes an additional cost) and that it may have negative consequences for the group that benefits formally from these regulations. All the members of a group covered by quota regulations may feel themselves accused as conspicuously subject to special treatment, since the hiring standard is lower for this group as a consequence of the quota. Although this argument can only be said to apply to a certain part of the group, it has been suggested that quota regulations may actively contribute towards the creation of prejudices.[9,10]

Measures to Increase Competition. According to Becker's theory, wage differentials that are a result of a firm's discriminatory preferences will tend to disappear over time. Firms that employ discriminatory practices will incur losses and gradually be driven out of the market by firms that do not have discriminatory preferences. Monopolistic firms will be taken over by non-discriminatory owners since these owners obtain larger economic gains from the ownership of a monopoly. According to this theory, countervailing measures against discrimination should be aimed at improving the operation of markets — both product and capital markets — in order to accelerate the effects of competitive forces. This recommendation also applies where prejudices (incorrect information) rather than preferences are the cause of discrimination. Increased competition raises the cost of being prejudiced.

An improvement in market operations may also lead to a reduction of other types of discrimination. Measures to remove labor market imperfections could be of considerable importance in this context. Increased labor mobility may lead to a reduction of discrimination if the cause of discrimination is monopsony in the labor market. The greater the opportunity for mobility, the greater is the extent to which wages are given for the individual firm.

However, it is not the case that all theories conclude that increased competition leads to reduced discrimination. An equilibrium with a social custom of discrimination does not disappear simply because of an increase in competition in the markets for goods or capital. The same is true of statistical discrimination. On the other hand, it is obvious that the removal of various labor market restrictions (that give rise to crowding effects) would lead to a lower level of discrimination.

A problem associated with measures that increase competition compared with the other measures dealt with earlier is that their effects are of a long-run nature. Hence, it is possible that, given a particular cause of discrimination, the effectiveness of various measures will vary over time. Consequently, an optimal strategy consists of a mixture of different measures. That particular question, however, lies outside the framework of our present discussion.

Causes of Discrimination and Anti-Discrimination Policy

An examination of the various types of anti-discrimination policy can also be conducted by considering each theory separately in order to see which type of policy, in the context of a given theory, can be expected to have an impact on discrimination. We will now continue with this aspect of anti-discrimination policy.

Preferences. Measures that increase competition in product and capital markets may have a positive effect if the cause of discrimination is preferences held by firms against a particular group. Competition in product or capital markets will force the discriminating firm out of the market or lead to a take-over, respectively. There are a large number of well-established policy measures that can exert an impact on the level of competition, for example anti-trust legislation and deregulatory actions. The relevant questions in this context concern the degree of effectiveness and the length of time required by any given policy measure that seeks to improve the operation of competitive forces.

Another form of discrimination due to preferences is employee discrimination of another group of employees. If the groups are perfect substitutes, discrimination will lead to work place segregation but not to wage differences. If, on the other hand, the groups of employees are complementary factors of production, discrimination will give rise to wage differentials.

The segregation of work places may be affected by the imposition of quotas. Equal wage regulations may have a short-run impact on wage differentials that are caused by discrimination between groups of employees who are complementary factors of production. In the long run, wage differentials may be influenced by measures that seek to increase the representation of the discriminated group in all occupations. This could lead to the elimination of wage differentials but also to a complete segregation of work places.

Policy measures such as increased competition, quota regulations and equal wage legislation are considered here as a means of eliminating the effects of discrimination. However, it remains uncertain whether they actually eliminate what is according to the theory the fundamental cause of this discrimination, namely the preferences for discrimination. According to Becker, these are dependent upon the degree of contact between the groups. Either a great deal of contact or no contact at all between the groups will lead to the disappearance of discriminatory preferences. The alternatives available for the elimination of discriminatory preferences would be either a complete division of society along ethnic lines, that is an *Apartheid* solution, or substantially increased integration. The latter solution would (at least in the case of employee discrimination) support the argument in favor of quota regulations. It is, however, important to emphasize in this context that an analysis of the causes of discriminatory preferences is an area of Becker's theory that has not been properly developed. Thus, it is, for example, not very likely that the institution of an *Apartheid* system leads to the disappearance of preferences for discrimination.[11]

Prejudices. The effects of prejudices, that is incorrect information among firms regarding the relative productivity of different groups, may be affected, as in the case of discriminatory preferences, by the degree of competition. Increased competition raises the cost of acting on the basis of incorrect information.

In contrast to the case of discriminatory preferences, several other types of policy measures can, however, also be expected to exert an influence on the effect of prejudices. Quota regulations that give rise to increased employment opportunities for the discriminated group may lead to an improvement in employer information regarding this group. Different types of information channels may provide firms with a more accurate description of the actual productivity performances.

Statistical Discrimination. The theory of statistical discrimination is based on two assumptions:[12]

(1) Given an individual's expected rate of productivity, an employer faces greater uncertainty in his assessment of individual productivity if the person who is being considered for recruitment comes from one particular group rather than from another.

(2) The discrepancy between actual and expected productivity gives rise to certain costs. The employer therefore has risk aversion.

The reason for this greater degree of uncertainty in the assessment of individual productivity may be due to the fact that the person who is responsible for recruitment belongs to a specific group (a certain ethnic group) and finds it easier to make a more accurate assessment of individuals who belong to his own group. Another possibility is that tests that have been used in the recruitment process provide more accurate results in relation to a particular group (less variance around the expected value).

The policy measures that are likely to have an effect in this context are, in the first place, measures that affect the recruitment of those individuals who actually do the hiring and, secondly, measures that increase the reliability of the tests in relation to individuals from different groups. Quota regulations may make these measures more profitable for the firms as they force the firm to search among the discriminated groups for new employees:

> Eliminating statistical discrimination is difficult, for its requires that employers and other screening agencies refrain from using objective and efficient information. It can only be done by some type of affirmative action that requires institutions to hire or admit women and members of minorities, and thus forces them to search among these groups for individuals who have the characteristics they desire. Unless they are under affirmative action pressures, all of their incentives will lie in the direction of practicing statistical discrimination.[13]

Discrimination as a Social Custom. Theories related to social customs have demonstrated that a stable equilibrium may be accompanied by discrimination if individuals have discriminatory preferences regarding the transactions that take place between other individuals and are prepared to adopt sanctions. Alternatively, the inclusion of social standing in preference functions may also create sufficient conditions for a stable social equilibrium accompanied by discrimination if the inclusion affects the individual's willingness to accept a given norm (in this case, the norm to discriminate). Measures to increase competition will in this case not bring the economy from an equilibrium position that is accompanied by discrimination to a non-discriminatory equilibrium. However, a change has taken place in the size of the minimum coalition that is required for making a violation against a given norm profitable.

If discrimination is a prevailing social norm, various measures that have a possible effect on this norm will in turn exert an influence on the level of discrimination. Legislation may have a direct impact. Equal wage legislation and quota regulations may succeed in moving the economy from an equilibrium position that is characterized by discrimination to a non-discriminatory equilibrium. If there is a comprehensive legislative framework which requires that individuals be recruited from the discriminated group, social sanctions against those who hire persons from that group will have no effect. Furthermore, the social standing of those who do not discriminate will be similarly unaffected. However, a more detailed analysis would require an accurate description of both the different forms that discriminatory customs may take (wage discrimination, discriminatory recruitment practices) and of the actual formulation of the legislation directed against discrimination.

Monopsonistic Discrimination. The preferred measures against both monopsony in general and monopsonistic discrimination in particular, are those that increase the wage elasticity of labor supply, particularly that of the discriminated group. A firm's monopsonistic position is inversely related to wage elasticities. The greater the wage elasticity, the weaker the position of the monopsonistic firm. By definition an infinitely elastic supply of labor eliminates monopsony.

An important group of measures that can affect wage elasticities seeks to influence the level of competition in the labor market, for example measures to reduce the costs of migration and commuting. Another group of measures is directed at reducing the influence of strong local employer bargaining power on the wage level. Examples of the latter would be national wage agreements and laws or agreements on equal wages. Minimum wage legislation may under certain conditions have the same effects.

The Radical Theory of Discrimination. According to the radical theory of discrimination, employers are able to divide and rule (achieve lower wage levels) by pitting one group of wage earners against another. In order to achieve this objective the work force has to be integrated. It is possible, but not necessary, that the maintenance of wage differentials between different groups of workers for the same work is one of the measures adopted by employers in order to play the interests of one group against another.

Equal wage legislation is a measure that could be used in this model in order to reduce the scope for discrimination. Another policy measure that can, however, for obvious reasons hardly be recommended is that of workplace segregation.

Measures related to an improvement in the organization of employees across group boundaries have been the principal form of proposal put forward by those who support the radical theory of discrimination. In this way, employers would not be able to divide up their labor force nor to achieve lower wage levels and, possibly, wage differentials:

> ..., it should be possible to mobilize a coalition against racism that encompasses broad segments of American population. To succeed, however, such efforts must indicate to whites that the achievement of racial economic equality need not occur at their cost.[14]

Bargaining Models. The bargaining models are the least well developed of the models of discrimination. Consequently, it is difficult to be precise about the likely effects that various measures might have, according to these models. In general terms, intervention can have an effect on the relative bargaining power of the various parties. Equal wages and quota regulations may for example strengthen the position of a discriminated group of workers as well as that of firms that do not have discriminatory preferences or prejudices. Changes in competitive conditions in the markets for goods, capital or labor may also influence negotiating positions. However, a more detailed analysis would require a fuller specification of the bargaining model.

This analysis of the effects of various types of anti-discrimination policy measures has not been particularly extensive. We have not dealt with all of the theories and measures utilized to combat discrimination. Nevertheless, it can be concluded that the effects of different policy measures are ultimately bound up with their causes, both in the sense that the same measure will not be equally effective in all cases and in the sense that a measure that is effective against one type of discrimination may have a completely different effect in an instance where the causes of discrimination are different.

Ending Discrimination: The First Best Solution

Having concluded the general discussion, the next step will be to examine the most suitable methods for removing discrimination in the cases that were analyzed in detail in Chapters 4-8. The question we have to answer for each of these cases is: 'How are we to put an end to discrimination in a way which creates no by-product distortion?'[15]

Beginning with the models of Chapters 4 and 5, it is obvious that very much depends on the relative political strength or bargaining power of white workers and capitalists. In the Krueger model, where capital is the mobile factor, and where discrimination takes the form of reducing capital exports below the level prevailing in the perfectly competitive situation, we must focus on the capitalist group, that is on the group which is the agent of discrimination. As Krueger has shown, the capitalist group will suffer a loss from discrimination, whereas white workers make a gain. This gain, in turn, is larger than the loss incurred by the capitalists. Thus, the result of discrimination from the capitalist point of view depends on whether the workers compensate the capitalists for their losses or not. If they do *not*, it is unlikely that the capitalists will resort to discrimination at all. On the other hand, if the capitalists receive sufficient compensation in order to make discrimination an attractive alternative, some type of measure is needed.

It is obviously not feasible to make legal provisions which ensure that white capitalists 'export' enough capital to Negro society to ensure equality of returns between the white and Negro sectors. A combination of taxes and subsidies can then be used. As the rates of return to capital begin to diverge, because of discrimination, investments in the white sector can be taxed and the proceeds can be used to subsidize investments in the Negro sector.

The second case in Chapter 4 is the one where labor is mobile and Negro workers receive the same wage in both sectors. This case is more difficult in the sense that both white workers and white capitalists may gain from discriminatory practices. Since the economy does not contain any other groups, they simultaneously constitute the polity. This case is, however, unlikely to arise, since every employer will always gain

Summary and Conclusions 279

from hiring the cheapest type of labor — Negroes, and this will go on until the Negro wage rate equals the white one.

In the third case analyzed in Chapter 4, discrimination no longer pays for white capitalists. This group makes a loss which cannot be compensated by any transfers from the workers, since the net result for white society as a whole is negative. It is thus unlikely that white capitalists by themselves will entertain the idea of resorting to discrimination.

Nevertheless, discrimination may arise if the workers are politically strong enough to pass laws which limit the outflow of capital (when capital is the mobile factor) or the inflow of Negro workers. This means that there exists no internal force which is powerful enough to impose anti-discriminatory measures on the white sector. In the discussion below of Chapter 8 we will return to the possibility of bringing outside sanctions to bear on this type of situation.

The same type of conclusions are applicable to the models of Chapter 5. The only difference is that with two commodities it is no longer so easy to determine gains and losses, but once this is done, the solutions are the same as in the one-good case.

In Chapters 6 and 7, discrimination takes on another shape: crowding. Here, Negroes are excluded from holding skilled jobs, either because they have been excluded from the type of training that makes skilled employment possible or because, even though they possess this training, skilled jobs to some extent are being reserved for whites. The most clear-cut case here is the one dealt with in Chapter 6, where only labor is employed, and no capital or land. Here, whites gain and Negroes lose, both in the one-good and in the two-good setting. The solution here is a legislative one. Schools must be integrated so that whites do not receive a better education than Negroes and, to ensure that Negroes receive on-the-job training and promotion according to skill, resort should be made to equal opportunity legislation. Again, however, this solution presupposes that a polity exists which is strong enough to override the objections of those who stand to gain from discrimination.

If, finally, we go on to the concrete case discussed in Chapter 8, South Africa, which (presently) represents a mixture of the two types of discrimination we have just dealt with, it is not difficult to outline the principles for putting an end to discrimination. The difficult part is that here we are dealing with a society where the polity does not wish to end discrimination. In that case, what can be done? The most commonly suggested remedy has been the imposition of a trade and investment boycott. Let us proceed to look at the effects of this measure.

Economic Effects of a Trade and Investment Boycott against South Africa[16]

The South African economy has for a very long time been characterized by the presence of large amounts of foreign capital. Almost from the very beginning of the mining industry, in the late nineteenth century, foreign investors were drawn to the country, and South Africa has continued to wield a considerable power of attraction on European and American capital:[17]

> The inflow of foreign capital into South Africa has been associated at every stage of the country's economic growth with the opening of new and vital sectors of the economy, which could never have been launched without the capital, and even more, the expertise, of overseas investors. The South African industrial and mining economy is at its present stage of prosperity because of the massive intervention of foreign capital at crucial stages in the country's history. This is true of gold, uranium, platinum, and other mining, the manufacturing sector, and emerging sectors such as 'defense' industries, the auto industry, and nuclear power. After the initial, pioneering stage, the foreign enterprise tends to take on a local coloration and becomes more identified with the general economic interests of the South African white community.[18]

From 1887 to 1934 60 per cent of the capital formation in the gold-mining industry was due to an inflow from abroad. Between 1946 and 1955, 35 per cent of all new investment in the South African economy was of foreign origin. Subsequently, this share has decreased, so that between 1966 and 1975 only 17 per cent was due to the direct inflow from the outside. This figure is, however, somewhat misleading, since it does not take into account that part of the earnings retained by South African companies actually must be considered the property of foreign shareholders.[19]

Most of the foreign capital has been absorbed by the mining industry, but recently the manufacturing sector has assumed increased importance. Thus, according to the 1973 census of foreign investment, the latter sector accounted for 40 per cent of the total while the figure for mining was much smaller, approximately 15 per cent. During the seventies, a new trend has also emerged. To an increasing extent, foreign capital is going into the public sector. While the inflow into the private sector of the economy grew by an annual average of 13.3 per cent per annum in 1973-78, the flow into government and banking and public corporations grew twice as fast, at the rate of 26.5 and 28.9 per cent per annum, respectively.[20]

South Africa has also been highly dependent on the capacity of its export sectors to generate foreign exchange. At the beginning of the century, imports were mainly of two kinds: on the one hand, a wide variety of consumer goods and mining machinery and other capital goods on the other.[21] The industrialization process of the past fifty to sixty years had reduced the country's dependency on consumer goods imports and has also increased the extent to which South Africa can supply its own capital goods. However, it still has a long way to go in the latter respect.[22] Had it not been for the country's 'unique role in the international division of labor as the capitalists world's main gold producer',[23] the development of the manufacturing industry in particular would have suffered. The investment funds amassed via gold mining have played a strategic role in the over-all economy. Jill Nattrass summarizes the role of gold for capital formation and growth:

> Had South Africa not had its very profitable mining sector, progress in manufacturing would have been limited to the level of the industry's own ability to produce capital goods, together with what it could buy abroad with the proceeds from exports. What is more, continued economic development in ... [the] country is still heavily reliant upon the mining industry's ability to earn foreign exchange.[24]

Ever since its beginnings, the gold industry has often accounted for more than 50 per cent of South Africa's total exports. In 1978-79, the figure was 61 per cent.[25] The price of gold is of enormous importance here. The seventies witnessed a strongly rising trend. By 1980, the real price of gold was about 15 times as high as in 1970. In the same year South Africa most likely had the highest growth rate in the world. When the price fell in 1981, the economy, on the other hand, entered a recession.[26]

Gold and other mining products are, however, not South Africa's only export goods. Both manufactures and agricultural products — sugar, corn, wool, processed fruits etc. — are of considerable importance, accounting in 1975 for 31 and 10.5 per cent, respectively, of the total export value.[27] This must be kept in mind later when we discuss against which products trade sanctions should be directed.

If South Africa is highly dependent on gold on the export side, it is even more dependent on oil on the import side. Oil is the only important mineral resource not found inside the country. In 1980, oil provided some 90 per cent of South Africa's liquid fuel requirements. Liquid fuels, in turn, accounted for 21 per cent of the country's total energy consumption in 1977. After the imposition of the OPEC embargo on oil deliveries to South Africa, in the early seventies, the country has had to buy petroleum products on the international spot market at high prices. It has thus attempted to cut down as much as possible on its use of oil, to the point where it may be close to 'the irreducible minimum'.[28]

Because of the high dependency of South Africa on foreign capital, exports and oil imports, it has freqently been suggested that a suitable way to put pressure on the white polity to reduce the extent of racial discrimination in the economy is to curtail trade and reduce foreign investment in the country.[29] The General Assembly of the United Nations has repeatedly passed resolutions for a trade and investment boycott against South Africa by its member countries. As is well known, this boycott has, however, been inefficient. The Western states have vetoed it in the Security Council. Besides,

> ... [the] resolution was not mandatory, and it has not been strictly observed by some of the Afro-Asian countries which initiated it, while it has been largely ignored by the countries which opposed it, notably Britain, France, the United States, and South Africa's other principal trading partners.[30]

Compliance has left a lot to desire, Sporadic actions against South African goods have, however, been carried out in many countries. In the case of investments, even less has been achieved.[31]

Even if a trade and investment boycott had been effective in the sense that the member states of the United Nations had followed a resolution taken by the General Assembly to reduce trade with and investment in South Africa it is, however, by no means certain that a boycott would have lead to a reduction in the extent to which Apartheid is practiced, for example, in the labor market. Using the model of Stage III from Chapter 8 we will in the present chapter discuss the possibility of successfully carrying out a trade and investment boycott against South Africa.[32] We will then examine the effects of, on the one hand, the imposition of import restrictions on South African export goods and on the other, a gradual reduction in the amount of foreign capital invested in the country. The effects of these measures will be compared with those of a reduction of racial discrimination in the South African labor market.[33] The analysis, tracing the effects of these two sets of measures on the real incomes of different groups in the white South African community, assumes that the most favorable outcome for the polity decides the course of action taken. (We will return to the question of whose interests the polity represents towards the end of the chapter.)

Economic Effects of a Boycott

With the aid of the Stage III model spelled out in Chapter 8 we may investigate the impact of a trade and investment boycott on the real incomes of different groups in the white South African community: landowners, agricultural and industrial capitalists and skilled workers. We will also determine how these measures affect the incomes of unskilled Africans working in the European sectors. Before we can do that, however, the two production functions (8:13) and (8:14) must be changed somewhat.

The new production function for the European agricultural sector (A) is

$$X_A = h_A(L_A^B, \bar{T}_A, K_A, t), \qquad (9:1)$$

and the production function for industry (I) is

$$X_I = h_I(L_I^B, L_I^{BS} + \bar{L}_I^{ES}, K_I, t). \qquad (9:2)$$

The only difference between these two production functions and (8:13) and (8:14), respectively, is the parameter t which is a shift parameter used to capture the effects of a reduction of oil imports. We will return to this parameter below.

Besides agricultural and industrial goods, import goods are implicit in the model. These are mainly capital goods and other goods not produced in South Africa. In the absence of any boycott, South Africa's terms of trade, (that is, the terms on which the country can exchange industrial and agricultural products for other goods with the rest of the world) are given. It is assumed that South Africa itself cannot influence these terms. When a tariff or a quantitative restriction is imposed by the rest of the world on South Africa's exports of industrial or agricultural products, the price received by South African producers for their goods decreases, while the price of goods imported but not produced by South Africa remains unchanged. In the tariff case, South African producers have to lower the price offered internationally to be able to continue to compete in the world market. If the tariff is prohibitive, exports will cease altogether and the formerly exported quantity must be disposed of at home. This is, however, not possible unless the price asked in the domestic market is reduced. A quota has the same effect, that is it reduces the price received by the producers for exactly the same reason. (The quota may also be 'prohibitive', i.e. it can be put equal to zero.)

An embargo on oil exports to South Africa has effects that are analogous to those of technological retrogression, both in agriculture and in industry. When the supply of oil is reduced, substitutes are to a certain extent developed, but this both takes time and should be expected to be only incompletely successful. The result is that with given inputs of land, labor and capital, less of both types of goods is produced. A negative shift in the production functions (9:1) and (9:2) takes place, symbolized by dt $<$ 0. It is assumed that this shift leads to a fall in the marginal productivities of all factors, *ceteris paribus*.[34]

An investment boycott, finally, will lead to gradual depreciation of the South African industrial capital stock without replacement, unless domestic capitalists take over.[35]

The effects of an investment boycott, an imposition of import restrictions on South African goods and an embargo on oil exports to South Africa are summarized in Table 9.1 (explicit solutions in the Appendix). It is assumed that the South African polity retains the same targets as in Chapter 8, which comprised on the one hand the real incomes of various groups in the white community and on the other, increased production both of agricultural and industrial products. In Table 9.1, these goals for the South African economic policy are compared with the effects of the boycott.

Beginning with the impact of import restrictions abroad on South African industrial goods, we find that as the price paid to South African exporters is reduced, a shift from industrial to agricultural production takes place and the degree of industrialization falls. Landowners and agricultural capitalists gain by this, since in the process, unskilled workers are transferred from industry to agriculture. By the same token, skilled workers (Africans as well as whites) incur a loss since their marginal productivity is reduced when unskilled workers leave the sector. Industrial capitalists also suffer in real terms provided that the interest rate on industrial capital is elastic with respect to changes in the price of manufactures. Finally, unskilled workers can only be absorbed in agriculture, at a lower wage in terms of agricultural goods. Hence, if the wage elasticity with respect to changes in the price of industrial goods exceeds one they suffer a loss in terms of manufactures as well.[36]

Table 9.1: The Impact of a Trade and Investment Boycott on the South African Economy

Target Variable	Goal	$dP_I < 0$	$dP_A < 0$	$dt < 0$	$dK_I < 0$
X_A	+	+	−	−c	+
X_I	+	−	+	−d	−
r_A	+	+	−b	−c	+
i_A	+	+	−b	−c	+
i_I	+	−a	+	−d	+
w^S	+	−a	+	−d	−
w_E^L	+	−a	−b	−	−

Notes: a. For the factor reward to fall not only in terms of agricultural goods and import goods but also in terms of industrial products, its elasticity with respect to P_I must exceed one. b. For the factor reward to fall not only in terms of industrial goods and import goods but also in terms of agricultural products, its elasticity with respect to P_A must exceed one. c. If $h_I^{Lt} < h_A^{Lt}$. d. If $h_I^{Lt} > h_A^{Lt}$.

If the restrictions are instead directed against exports of South African agricultural products, exactly the opposite results apply, *mutatis mutandis*, with the single exception of unskilled wages. A fall in the domestic price of agricultural products leads to a dismissal of agricultural workers. The latter can be absorbed in industry only at a lower wage rate in terms of manufactures. (If the unskilled wage is elastic with respect to changes in P_A, there is a fall in terms of agricultural goods as well.)

It must also be kept in mind that there is a relation between export earnings (foreign exchange earnings) and capital formation. More than half of South Africa's imports consist of machinery and equipment.[37] To the extent that a boycott reduces export earnings, it will therefore have repercussions on capital formation in industry as well as agriculture.

Next, let us examine the probable effects of reduced oil imports. As Table 9.1 indicates, neither the effects on agriculture nor the effects on industry are determinate, but it is possible to find a simple condition which leads to a clear-cut impact in one of the sectors.

An oil embargo has two effects. In the first place, it lowers the marginal productivities of all production factors, *ceteris paribus*. This tends to lead to a fall in both agricultural and industrial production and in addition tends to lower the remuneration paid to all factors. By lowering marginal productivities, however, the oil embargo also leads to a reallocation of the mobile factor: unskilled labor. The direction taken by this reallocation will depend on whether the marginal productivity of unskilled labor in industry suffers more than the marginal productivity in agriculture.

If this is the case, $h_I^{Lt} > h_A^{Lt}$, which means that unskilled workers will move from industry to agriculture. This reinforces the negative *ceteris paribus* effects on industrial output, the return to industrial capital and skilled wages, due to the complementarity of capital and skilled labor with unskilled labor. It also gives rise to a fall in the unskilled wage. Since the marginal productivity of unskilled workers in agriculture (and industry) is lower than before the embargo, these workers will not be absorbed in agriculture unless the wage rate falls as well.

What will happen in the agricultural sector is not clear in this case. If unskilled labor moves to this sector, this tends to increase agricultural output and the return to agricultural land and capital. These effects have to be weighed against the negative *ceteris paribus* effects in order to arrive at the net outcome. On the other hand, if unskilled workers move *out of* the sector ($h_I^{Lt} < h_A^{Lt}$) agricultural production, land rents and the return to agricultural capital all decrease, while what happens in industry becomes indeterminate. Note finally, that insofar as export production is dependent on oil, an oil embargo may have a negative effect on exports and hence capital formation in both sectors.

An investment boycott that leads to a reduction in the industrial capital stock has effects similar to those of import restrictions abroad on South African industrial goods for all parties concerned except industrial capitalists. When the industrial sector is forced to work with less capital, both production in the sector and the rewards to the complementary factors, skilled and unskilled workers, fall, while the return to the remaining capital in the sector increases. Unless this stimulates domestic capital formation, unskilled workers have to move into agriculture at a lower real wage. As a result, agricultural production increases and the returns to land and capital in that sector increase in real terms.

Thus, we find that it is mainly landowners and agricultural capitalists who stand to gain from an imposition of a boycott of South African industrial (mineral) exports and investment in South Africa, while white workers may incur a loss from both measures. Industrial capitalists, insofar as they raise their capital inside South Africa, derive a gain when foreign capital is removed but may lose when trade restrictions are imposed. An investment boycott will always hurt the majority of the Africans working in the European sector of the South African economy, and so could trade restrictions. A boycott of agricultural exports, on the other hand, is more likely to hurt agricultural interests while skilled workers and industrialists gain. The effects of an oil embargo are uncertain.

The Effects of Reduced Discrimination

However, knowledge of the economic effects of the boycott is not in itself sufficient to determine whether a threat to restrict investment and export and import trade with South Africa will lead to a reduction of discrimination in the labor market. These effects have also to be compared with the effects of a reduction in the extent of discriminatory practices. The latter effects are illustrated in Table 8.3 (explicit solutions in Part C of Appendix 1 to Chapter 8 with $dL_I^{BS} > 0$).

We recall that discrimination in the labor market is of two kinds. In the first place, the access of Africans to skilled jobs is limited and, secondly, the entry of blacks into the European sector of the economy is regulated by the pass system. A softening of the Apartheid policy in the skilled labor market, for example by allowing Africans to be trained either formally or on the job, leads to an increase of industrial output, since industry is the only sector that makes use of skilled workers, and skilled workers have a higher wage than unskilled. Hence agricultural production will fall and the degree of industrialization will increase.

By the same token, landowners and capitalists in the agricultural sector incur a loss. The same is true with respect to those workers who hold skilled jobs in the presence of discrimination. They now have to face the competition of additional labor. Unskilled workers, on the other hand, gain, since their number is reduced. Finally, the effect on the rate of return on industrial capital will depend on whether skilled or unskilled workers are more complementary to capital at the margin. When the employment of skilled workers is increased and the employment of unskilled labor is reduced by the same amount in industry, the marginal productivity of industrial capital will also rise as long as capital is more complementary to skilled than to unskilled labor at the margin. Consequently, in the same case the rate of return to capital increases in industry.

An increase in the number of Africans allowed in the European economy has a striking impact on the white economy. As we know, *all* groups in the white community benefit from this measure. An increased influx of Africans, given the number of Africans allowed in skilled positions, will increase the marginal productivity of all 'white' production factors, since all the new Africans will have to take unskilled jobs and unskilled labor is complementary to all 'white' factors. Those unskilled Africans who are already working in the two European sectors, on the other hand, will make a loss, because of the increased competition for jobs. Finally, this measure has also an impact on the economy of the reserves. As people leave the bantustans, per capita incomes there will rise due to the existence of diminishing returns to labor in that sector. The (explicit or implicit) wage rate will also rise, whereas the return to land will fall, since fewer people than before will be working on the land.

Thus, no white group stands to lose in economic terms from allowing more Africans to enter the European economy.[38] Allowing Africans to acquire higher skills, on the other hand, is a different matter. Here, as we have seen, agricultural interests and white industrial workers may raise objections, while industrial capitalists possibly gain, unless the boycott is directed against agricultural exports. Hence, a comparison of these findings with the consequences of a trade and investment boycott, shows that farming interests may very well advocate skill discrimination on economic grounds, even though a boycott is imposed on South Africa, although not on a boycott against agricultural products. Moreover, to the extent that their capital is raised within South Africa, an investment boycott will not affect them. Those who depend on international financial markets for capital, on the other hand, may find that they encounter difficulties in obtaining funds if an international investment boycott is enforced. The white workers, finally, are faced with a difficult decision. On the one hand, they are likely to lose from an investment boycott or a boycott against industrial exports, but they will also be worse off if Africans are allowed to compete more extensively for skilled jobs.[39] Their strategy should be to offer to accept a more liberal inflow of unskilled labor from the bantustans while trying to maintain racial segregation in the school system, with Africans in low-quality schools, and skill segregation along color lines within firms.

Thus, to conclude, if South Africa is faced with the threat of an *efficient* trade and investment boycott, the most likely outcome of the political bargaining process among the white interest groups will be that the country offers to allow more Africans to work in the European parts of the economy instead of in the bantustans, since everybody in the white community will be economically better off by this measure.[40]

Secondary Effects

Our analysis has rested on the assumption that the capital stocks of agriculture and industry are given and are sector-specific, so that capital is not shifted from one sector to the other in response to the differences in returns that arise from the parameter changes investigated. The reason for this assumption was that resources are known not to move smoothly between these sectors.[41] However, this does not necessarily mean that for example the capital stock in agriculture would not be affected by a boycott or by a reduction in the extent of discrimination in the longer run via the process of investment and disinvestment (depreciation).

The *most likely* secondary effects on the capital stocks of changes in the five parameters are summarized in Table 9.2. Three of the four types

Table 9.2: Probable Secondary Effects of a Trade and Investment Boycott and of Reduced Racial Discrimination on the South African Economy

Effect on	$dP_I < 0$	$dP_A < 0$	$dt < 0$	$dK_I < 0$	$dL_I^{BS} > 0$	$dL_E^B > 0$
K_A	−	−	−[a]	−	−	+
K_I	−	−	−[a]	−	+[b]	+

Notes: a. If $h_I^{Lt} > h_A^{Lt}$. b. If $g_I^{KS} > g_I^{KL}$.

of boycotts tend to work in the same direction. Provided that a fall in the price of exports can be brought about, this will reduce South Africa's imports of machinery and equipment. This will hamper the production capacity of the domestic industry, including the capital goods industry. Hence, in the long run we should expect capital stocks in both cases to be reduced. An oil embargo may work in the same direction, by reducing industrial production (although not necessarily), and so does an outright investment boycott.

The secondary effects of a boycott affect both the industrial sector and agriculture negatively. We already know the effects that a change in the industrial capital stock may have. Changes in agricultural capital have exactly the opposite impact. A fall in agricultural investments reduce agricultural output, both *ceteris paribus* and by expelling labor from the sector, reducing the unskilled wage rate in the process. This labor moves into industry, where production will consequently tend to rise. Thus, the degree of industrialization increases. The loss of capital in agriculture will tend to lead to a fall in the return to land, since the two factors are complementary at the margin. Likewise, as unskilled workers leave agriculture, the wages of skilled workers and the rate of return on industrial capital increase.

If we go on to examine the secondary effects of reduced discrimination, we find that allowing more Africans to hold skilled jobs draws people holding unskilled jobs out of the agricultural sector and thus depresses the return to capital. This in turn, acts as a brake on investment in that sector. The same is true for industry, but here there is a countervailing effect as well, due to the increase of the skilled labor force. If the marginal complementarity of the latter group with industrial capital is higher than that of unskilled labor, the return to capital will increase and industrial investment may be stimulated. Finally, allowing more unskilled workers from the bantustans into the white economy increases the return to both types of capital and hence should stimulate capital formation in both sectors.

As argued in Chapter 8, however, the secondary effects are not likely to be very important quantitatively, both because investment may respond sluggishly to differences in the rate of return and because agricultural and industrial investments tend to have effects which counteract each other.

Who Decides?

In the foregoing, we have shown that economic boycotts of South Africa are likely to have different effects on different groups in the white section of society. The question then inevitably arises as to which of these groups carry most weight in political decisions. If we know this, we may be able to judge whether a boycott is likely to be successful or not.

The basic fact regarding white South African society is the cleavage between Afrikaners (Afrikaans-speaking, of Dutch descent) and people of British origin. Of these groups, the former dominates political life almost completely:

> ... the process of interest articulation in South Africa is dominated for the most part by the overriding ethnic interest of the bulk of the Afrikaner community; in fact, the associational interest groups

within that community are all dedicated to the proposition that the political summum bonum is the welfare of the Afrikaner community.

For English-speaking communtiy groups, and for white caste groups that stand in opposition to Afrikaner community groups, effective access to governmental decision-makers is much more difficult.[42]

The National Party after its triumph in the 1948 elections, when it won 73 seats in the House of Assembly, has gradually increased this number to 131, in 1981, whereas the combined opposition has been reduced from 65 to 34 seats over the same period.[43] Thus, Afrikaner dominance is virtually complete.

The second important fact to keep in mind is that the Afrikaner community has strong rural roots. 'The great grandfathers of nearly every living Afrikaner were farmers,' write Leonard Thompson and Andrew Prior in their excellent book on South African politics.[44] This is of tremendous importance also among the politicians. Thompson and Prior checked the background of the twenty cabinet ministers and six deputy ministers in the government that was formed after the 1981 elections. Nineteen of the twenty cabinet ministers and all six deputies were Afrikaners. What is more,

. . . Most were born on farms or in country towns; the leadership is overwhelmingly of rural origin.

The Afrikaner leaders are the product of a community that is more egalitarian than most industrial societies. Insofar as there was an Afrikaner elite a half-century ago, it was an elite of achievement, consisting of predikants, politicians, lawyers, teachers, and successful capitalist farmers. Nearly all the present generation of cabinet ministers are sons of men who practiced one of these occupations; two-thirds of them were landowners or farmers, pure and simple. Notably absent from the list are industrial occupations, on both the management and the labor sides. Sixty years ago nearly all the successful entrepreneurs and skilled artisans of South Africa were members of the English-speaking white community. Afrikaner penetration into commerce and industry, which accelerated dramatically after 1948, has still to be felt in the upper echelons of political leadership.[45]

Before entering politics, six of the twenty-six ministers were farmers and many of the others combined farming with some profession.[46]

The rurality of the National Party is, however, gradually diminishing. Many of the leading national politicians have entered the business world as company directors after having entered politics:

> As the Afrikaner share of industrial, commercial and financial management has increased, the leaders of the National party, not withstanding their rural origin and their anti-capitalist traditions, have become personally involved in the capitalist interest.[47]

A couple of generations ago, Afrikaner interests in industry were very small. Today, this is no longer the case. In 1975 the share of exclusively Afrikaner enterprise in the private sector of South Africa's economy was estimated to be 27.5 per cent, a share which if present trends continue will increase to 34 per cent around the year 2000.[48]

The conclusion to be drawn from this is clear. Although the rurality of the dominant National Party has diminished during the past couple of decades, the interests of the white rural community are likely to continue to play an important role in political decision making in the immediate future. Thus, in the short run, an attempt to reduce racial discrimination in South Africa by means of international economic sanctions mainly calls for action against South African agricultural exports. Those hurt by the other types of boycotts are by and large more likely to belong to the industrial community than to the agricultural one. In the longer run, things may be slightly different. As Afrikaner interests in industry increase in importance the South African polity may become more sensitive to economic pressure applied on the industrial sector from abroad.

The above analysis demonstrates that, if the effects of a trade and investment boycott are mainly of a comparative static nature, a boycott does not appear to be an infallible weapon against discrimination. Then, the strategy of change has to be mainly political; that is, one of more passive support to groups who are advocating a transition to a nondiscriminatory society — reformist or revolutionary, depending on one's convictions. It is not easy to do away with discrimination as long as the legislators and administrators are not prepared to do so, while the more violent solutions may also fail. Given the military potential of the country, 'In the final resort, South Africa would be a tough nut to crack by force.'[49] This leaves only the slow road of political reformism.

Notes

1. See e.g. Demsetz (1965) and Landes (1968).
2. For a criticism of this conclusion see Flanagan (1978). Flanagan argues that this effect is outbalanced by the fact that those in the discriminated group who get a higher wage rate quit to a lesser extent than previously. As a result their unemployment is reduced.
3. See e.g. Lloyd & Niemi (1979), p. 301.
4. See Madden (1973), p. 95.
5. See Chiplin & Sloane (1982) and Treiman & Hartmann (1981).
6. An account of the development of anti-discrimination policy in the United States from equal opportunity to positive discrimination (affirmative action) is found in e.g. Jain & Pettman (1976).
7. For an analysis of the effects of quotas (and different bonus systems) in the case of job competition and employer preferences for discrimination, see Bell (1971).
8. See Masters (1975), pp. 158-9.
9. See e.g. Sowell (1976), Roberts (1979) and several of the articles in Block & Walker (1982).
10. If pre-market discrimination or discrimination of earlier generations has occured according to several characteristics (sex, race, social class), reversed discrimination according to one of them may lead to increased discrimination according to another. See Adelson (1978). For a thorough analysis of some of the arguments against reversed discrimination, see Sher (1975).
11. See e.g. Hampel & Krupp (1977) who compare prejudices (including preferred social distance) among whites in South Africa and Great Britain. The prejudices are, according to the psychological tests used by these authors, much higher in South Africa and highest among the non-British group there.
12. We follow the more rigid definition proposed by Aigner & Cain (1977).
13. Thurow (1975), pp. 205-6.
14. Reich (1981), p. 311.
15. By-product distortion is 'the by-product of a government policy designed to correct, or partially correct, a divergence [between private and social cost] of some kind . . .' (Corden (1974), p. 14).
16. This section builds on the material in Lundahl (1984).
17. See e.g. Frankel (1938), du Plessis (1970), Mackler (1972). First, Steele & Gurney (1973), Rogers (1976) and Seidman & Seidman (1977) for facts and analyses regarding the presence of foreign capital in South Africa.
18. Rogers (1976), p. 93.
19. Nattrass (1981), p. 85.
20. Ibid., pp. 85-6.
21. Houghton (1976), p. 175.
22. Thompson & Prior (1982), p. 62. The development of the manufacturing sector is dealt with in some detail in Marais (1981).
23. Milkman (1979), p. 262. In the mid-seventies, South Africa accounted for seventy per cent of total world output of gold outside the Soviet Union (Hobart Houghton (1976), p. 102). Cf. also Thompson & Prior (1982), p. 59.
24. Nattrass (1981), p. 146.
25. Ibid., p. 125.
26. Thompson & Prior (1982), pp. 57-8.
27. Nattrass (1981), p. 146. South Africa's comparative advantages are discussed by Ariovich (1979).
28. Thompson & Prior (1982), p. 238. Oil problems are discussed e.g. in Dagut

(1978). The country's foreign trade policy is debated e.g. in Ratcliffe (1975), Main (1975), Zarenda (1975), Reynders (1975) and Bell (1975).

29. Cf. e.g. Segal (1964), Spandau (1978), Botha (1978) — a review of Spandau's book, Bailey & Rivers (1978), Liff (1979), Porter (1979), Bailey (1980), and Uys (1980) for a discussion.

30. Thompson & Prior (1982), p. 14.

31. Some details are given in Rogers (1976), Chapter 8. Cf. also Thompson & Prior (1982), pp. 229 ff. The most far-reaching measures have been taken by Sweden (cf. SOU (1978)).

32. A conceptual discussion of this problem is given in Hansson & Lundahl (1984).

33. This is usually not done in discussions of economic sanctions against South Africa. The effects of the sanctions are established but these could, *nota bene*, by preferred to the effects of reducing discrimination by the decison makers.

34. That is, that h_I^{Lt} and h_A^{Lt} are both positive.

35. Note that foreign investment in South Africa is concentrated in industry and mining. The extent to which foreign investment acts as a substitute for domestic capital formation is discussed in Suckling (1975) and Gulati (1976). An investment boycott would presumably lead South Africa to retain dividends that otherwise would be exported in the country. This would help in maintaining the capital stock.

36. The reasoning builds on the assumption that South Africa can be regarded as a 'small and open' economy that cannot influence its terms of trade with the rest of the world. South Africa is, however, not 'small' with respect to gold. This means that if substantial import restrictions are imposed abroad on South African gold, this could lead to an increase in the world market price of gold, i.e. the measure could be partly self-defeating. This has to be taken into account when the relative attractiveness of a boycott against gold is considered.

In the *model* used here (and in Chapter 8), on the other hand, gold is lumped with other mining products and with manufactures under the common heading of 'industry'. In 1979, gold accounted for 74 per cent of the value of total mining output (Nattrass (1981), p. 149) and mining accounted for 34 per cent of the combined output value of mining and manufacturing (ibid., p. 25). Thus, the proportion of gold in the value of our 'industry' was around 25 per cent. This in turn means that output changes in 'industry' should affect gold only to approximately this extent. Taking the composite character of the 'industrial' sector into consideration it has therefore been deemed reasonable to treat it as a 'small and open' sector which cannot influence world market prices.

37. UNCTAD (1980), p. 147.

38. Note, however, that this assumes that no additional costs are imposed on e.g. white tax payers as more Africans are allowed in European areas. This is not necessarily the case, since housing, water, sanitation, health etc. must be provided for.

39. At least in the short run, with sanctions, there would be a necessity for South Africa to build up internal defense production, which is intensive in skilled white labor. This would to some extent mitigate the consequences of a boycott.

40. The present analysis does not deal e.g. with white security considerations.

41. Viljoen (1965), p. 304; Porter (1978), p. 746.

42. Thompson & Prior (1982), p. 164.

43. Ibid., p. 103.

44. Ibid., p. 40.

45. Ibid., p. 130.

46. Ibid., p. 131.

47. Ibid., p. 133.
48. Ibid., p. 157.
49. Ibid., p. 242.

Appendix: Mathematical Solutions

To obtain the impact of changes in P_I, P_A, t and K_I on the variables listed in Table 9.1, we proceed in an analogous manner with the method presented in Appendix 1 to Chapter 8, Part C, keeping in mind that (9:1) and (9:2) have been substituted for (8:13) and (8:14), respectively. This yields the following solutions:

$$dX_A = \frac{1}{\Delta^D}\left\{h_A^L h_I^{LK} dK_I + h_A^L h_I^L dP_I - (h_A^L)^2 dP_A \right. \\ \left. + \left[h_A^t \Delta^D + h_A^L(h_I^{Lt} - h_A^{Lt})\right] dt\right\}, \quad (A.9:1)$$

where

$$\Delta^D = h_I^{LL} + h_A^{LL} < 0, \quad (A.9:2)$$

$$dX_I = \frac{1}{\Delta^D}\left\{(h_I^K \Delta^D - h_I^L h_I^{LK})dK_I - (h_I^L)^2 dP_I + h_I^L h_A^L dP_A \right. \\ \left. + \left[h_I^t \Delta^D - h_I^L(h_I^{Lt} - h_A^{Lt})\right] dt\right\}, \quad (A.9:3)$$

$$dr_A = \frac{1}{\Delta^D}\left\{h_A^{TL} h_I^{LK} dK_I + h_A^{TL} h_I^L dP_I + (h_A^T \Delta^D - h_A^{TL} h_A^L)dP_A \right. \\ \left. + \left[h_A^{Tt} \Delta^D + h_A^{TL}(h_I^{Lt} - h_A^{Lt})\right] dt\right\}, \quad (A.9:4)$$

$$di_A = \frac{1}{\Delta^D}\left\{h_A^{KL} h_I^{LK} dK_I + h_A^{KL} h_I^L dP_I + (h_A^K \Delta^D - h_A^{KL} h_A^L)dP_A \right. \\ \left. + \left[h_A^{Kt} \Delta^D + h_A^{KL}(h_I^{Lt} - h_A^{Lt})\right] dt\right\}, \quad (A.9:5)$$

$$dw^S = \frac{1}{\Delta^D}\left\{(h_I^{SK} \Delta^D - h_I^{SL} h_I^{LK})dK_I + (h_I^S \Delta^D - h_I^{SL} h_I^L)dP_I \right. \\ \left. + h_I^{SL} h_A^L dP_A + \left[h_I^{St} \Delta^D - h_I^{SL}(h_I^{Lt} - h_A^{Lt})\right] dt\right\}, \quad (A.9:6)$$

$$dw_E^L = \frac{1}{\Delta^D} \left\{ h_A^{LL} h_I^{LK} dK_I + h_A^{LL} h_I^L dP_I + h_I^{LL} h_A^L dP_A \right.$$
$$\left. + \left[h_A^{Lt} \Delta^D + h_A^{LL} \left(h_I^{Lt} - h_A^{Lt} \right) \right] dt \right\} > 0 \qquad (A9:7)$$

and

$$di_I = \frac{1}{\Delta^D} \left\{ \left[h_I^{KK} h_I^{LL} - (h_I^{KL})^2 + h_I^{KK} h_A^{LL} \right] dK_I \right.$$
$$+ (h_I^K \Delta^D - h_I^{KL} h_I^L) dP_I + h_I^{KL} h_A^L dP_A$$
$$\left. + \left[h_I^{Kt} \Delta^D - h_I^{KL} (h_I^{Lt} - h_A^{Lt}) \right] dt \right\}. \qquad (A.9:8)$$

Since we are working with linearly homogeneous production functions, Euler's theorem applies so that

$$h_I^{KK} K_I + h_I^{KS} (L_I^{BS} + \bar{L}_I^{ES}) + h_I^{KL} L_I^B \equiv 0 \qquad (A.9:9)$$

and

$$h_I^{LL} L_I^B + h_I^{LS} (L_I^{BS} + \bar{L}_I^{ES}) + h_I^{LK} K_I \equiv 0. \qquad (A.9:10)$$

Deriving expressions for h_I^{KK} and h_I^{LL} from (A.9:9) and (A.9:10) and substituting these expressions in (A.9:8) it may easily be proved that di_I/dK_I (constant P_I) is negative.

BIBLIOGRAPHY

Adelson, Joseph (1978) 'Living with Quotas', *Commentary*, Vol. 65, pp. 23-9
Aigner, Dennis J. & Cain, Glen G. (1977) 'Statistical Theories of Discrimination in Labor Markets', *Industrial and Labor Relations Review*, Vol. 30, pp. 175-87
Akerlof, George A. (1976) 'The Economics of Caste and of the Rat Race and Other Woeful Tales', *Quarterly Journal of Economics*, Vol. 90, pp. 599-617
— (1980) 'A Theory of Social Custom, of Which Unemployment May Be One Consequence', *Quarterly Journal of Economics*, Vol. 94, pp. 749-75
— (1983) 'Loyalty Filters', *American Economic Review*, Vol. 73, pp. 54-63
Alchian, Armen A. & Kessel, Reuben A. (1962) 'Competition, Monopoly and the Pursuit of Money', in *Aspects of Labor Economics* (Princeton: National Bureau of Economic Research), pp. 157-83
Alexis, Marcus (1973) 'A Theory of Labor Market Discrimination with Interdependent Utilities', *American Economic Review*, Vol. 63, Papers and Proceedings, pp. 296-302
— (1974 'The Political Economy of Labor Market Discrimination: Synthesis and Exploration' in George M. von Furstenberg; Ann R. Horowitz & Bennet Harrison (eds.), *Patterns of Racial Discrimination. Volume B: Employment and Income* (Lexington, Mass.: D.C. Heath), pp. 63-83
Ariovich, G. (1979) 'The Comparative Advantage of South Africa as Revealed by Export Shares', *South African Journal of Economics*, Vol. 47, pp. 188-97
Arrow, Kenneth J. (1972:1) 'Models of Job Discrimination', in Anthony H. Pascal (ed.), *Racial Discrimination in Economic Life* (Lexington, Mass.: D.C. Heath), pp. 83-102
— (1972:2) 'Some Mathematical Models of Race in the Labor Market' in Anthony H. Pascal (ed.), *Racial Discrimination in Economic Life* (Lexington, Mass.: D.C. Heath), pp. 187-203
— (1973) 'The Theory of Discrimination' in Orley Ashenfelter & Albert Rees (eds.), *Discrimination in Labor Markets* (Princeton: Princeton University Press), pp. 3-33
Bailey, Martin (1978) 'Oil Sanctions: South Africa's Weak Link', New York: UN Centre Against Apartheid, No. 12, June
— & Rivers, Bernard (1980) 'Oil Sanctions Against South Africa', New York: |UN Centre Against Apartheid, No. 15, April
Baldwin, Robert E. (1980) 'The Political Economy of Protectionism', *mimeo*, National Conference on Import Competition and Adjustment: Theory and Policy, May 8-11, 1980, Cambridge, Mass.
Balhky, Hassan| O. (1973) 'International Trade and Income Distribution: A 3 × 3 Model', Ph.D. Dissertation, University of New Mexico, Alberquerque
Baron, Harold M. (1975) 'Racial Domination in Advanced Capitalism: A Theory of Nationalism and Division in the Labor Market' in Richard Edwards, Michael Reich & David M. Gordon (eds.), *Labor Market Segmentation* (Lexington, Mass,: D.C. Heath), pp. 173-216
Batra, Raveendra N. & Casas, Francisco R. (1976) 'A Synthesis of the Heckscher-Ohlin and the Neoclassical Models of International Trade', *Journal of International Economics*, Vol. 6, pp. 21-38.
Beacham, A. (1974) 'Competition Policy in Britain and South Africa', *South African Journal of Economics*, Vol. 42, pp. 118-26

Becker, Gary (1957) *The Economics of Discrimination* (Chicago: The University of Chicago Press)
— (1959) 'Union Restrictions on Entry' in P. Bradley (ed.), *The Public Stake in Union Power* (Charlottesville, Va.: The University of Chicago Press)
— (1971:1) *Economic Theory* (New York: Alfred A. Knopf)
— (1971:2) *The Economics of Discrimination.* 2nd ed. (Chicago: The University of Chicago Press)
Bell, Duran (1971) 'Bonuses, Quotas and the Employment of Black Workers', *Journal of Human Resources*, Vol. 6, pp. 309–20
— (1974) 'The Economic Basis of Employee Discrimination' in George M. von Furstenberg; Ann R. Horowitz & Bennet Harrison (eds.), *Patterns of Racial Discrimination. Volume B: Employment and Income* (Lexington, Mass.: D.C. Heath) pp. 121–35
Bell, Trevor (1973) *Industrial Decentralization in South Africa* (Cape Town: Oxford University Press)
— (1975) 'Productivity and Foreign Trade in South African Development Strategy', *South African Journal of Economics*, Vol. 43, pp. 476–515
Berg, Alan, portions with Muscat, Robert (1973) *The Nutrition Factor. Its Role in National Development* (Washington, D.C.: The Brookings Institution)
Berg, Elliot (1966) 'Major Issues of Wage Policy in Africa' in Arthur M. Ross (ed.), *Industrial Relations and Economic Development* (London: Macmillan) pp. 185–208
Berger, Suzanne & Piore, Michael J. (1980) *Dualism and Discontinuity in Industrial Societies* (Cambridge: Cambridge University Press)
Bergmann, Barbara R. (1971) 'The Effects on White Incomes of Discrimination in Employment', *Journal of Political Economy*, Vol. 79, pp. 294–313
— (1974) 'Occupational Segregation, Wages and Profits when Employers Discriminate by Race and Sex', *Eastern Economic Journal*, Vol. 1, pp. 103–10
Bergsman, Joel (1982) 'Apartheid, Wages, and Production Costs in South Africa: An Application of the Crowding Hypothesis', *Journal of Human Resources*, Vol. 17, pp. 633–45
Berreman, Gerald D. (1960) 'Caste in India and the United States', *American Journal of Sociology*, Vol. 66, pp. 120–7
— (1979) *Caste and Other Inequities* (Meerut: Folklore Institute)
Blau, Francine & Jusenius, Carol (1976) 'Economists' Approaches to Sex Segregation in the Labor Market: An Appraisal' in Martha Blaxall & Barbara Reagan (eds.), *Women and the Workplace* (Chicago: The University of Chicago Press) pp. 181–99
Bliss, Christopher & Stern, Nicholas (1978) 'Productivity, Wages and Nutrition', *Journal of Development Economics*, Vol. 5, pp. 331–98
Block, Walter & Walker, Michael (eds.) (1982) *Discrimination, Affirmative Action and Equal Opportunity* (Vancouver, B.C.: The Fraser Institute)
Bloom, Gordon F. (1941) 'A Reconsideration of the Theory of Exploitation', *Quarterly Journal of Economics*, Vol. 55, pp. 413–42
Bluestone, Barry (1970) 'The Tripartite Economy: Labor, Markets and the Working Class', *Poverty and Human Resources*, July–August, pp. 15–35
Borjas, George J. (1982) 'The Politics of Employment Discrimination in the Federal Bureaucracy', *Journal of Law and Economics*, Vol. 25, pp. 271–99
— & Goldberg, Matthew S. (1978) 'Biased Screening and Discrimination in the Labor Market', *American Economic Review*, Vol. 68, pp. 918–22
Boskin, Michael J. (1973) 'The Economics of Labor Supply' in Glen G. Cain & Harold Watts (eds.), *Income Maintenance and Labor Supply* (Chicago: Rand McNally) pp. 163–81

Botha, D.J.J. (1978) 'An Economic Boycott of South Africa?' (Review Article), *South African Journal of Economics*, Vol. 46, pp. 271-81
Bronfenbrenner, Martin (1939) 'The Economics of Collective Bargaining', *Quarterly Journal of Economics*, Vol. 53, pp. 535-61
— (1956) 'Potential Monopsony in Labor Markets', *Industrial and Labor Relations Review*, Vol. 9, pp. 577-88
Bundy, Colin (1972) 'The Emergence and Decline of a South African Peasantry', *African Affairs*, Vol. 71, pp. 369-88
— (1977) 'The Transkei Peasantry c. 1890-1914: Passing Through a Period of Stress' in Robin Palmer & Neil Parsons (eds.), *The Roots of Rural Poverty in Central and Southern Africa* (London: Heinemann) pp. 201-20
— (1979) *The Rise and Fall of the South African Peasantry* (London: Heinemann)
Butler, Richard J. (1982) 'Estimating Wage Discrimination in the Labor Market', *Human Resources*, Vol. 17, pp. 606-21
Cain, Glen G. (1976) 'The Challenge of Segmented Labor Market Theories to Orthodox Theory: A Survey', *Journal of Economic Literature*, Vol. 14, pp. 1215-57
— & Watts, Harold (eds.) (1973) *Income Maintenance and Labor Supply* (Chicago: Rand McNally)
Cannan, Edwin (1914) *Wealth* (London: P.S. King & Son)
Cassel, Gustav (1918) *Theoretische Sozialökonomie* (Leipzig: C.F. Wintersche Verlagshandlung)
— (1923) *The Theory of Social Economy* (London)
Cherry, Robert (1977) 'Economics Theories of Racism' in David M. Gordon (ed.), *Problems in Political Economy: An Urban Perspective*, 2nd ed. (Lexington, Mass.: D.C. Heath)
Chiplin, Brian & Sloane, Peter J. (1974) 'Sexual Discrimination in the Labour Market', *British Journal of Industrial Relations*, Vol. 12, pp. 371-402
— (1976) *Sex Discrimination in the Labour Market* (London: Macmillan)
— (1982) *Tackling Discrimination at the Workplace: An Analysis of Sex Discrimination in Britain* (Cambridge: Cambridge University Press)
Chipman, John (1969) 'Factor Price Equalization and the Stolper-Samuelson Theorem', *International Economic Review*, Vol. 10, pp. 399-406
Chiswick, Barry R. (1973) 'Racial Discrimination in the Labor Market: A Test of Alternative Hypotheses', *Journal of Political Economy*, Vol. 81, pp. 1330-52
Collet, Clara E. (1891) 'Women's Work in Leeds', *Economic Journal*, Vol. 1, pp. 460-73
Corden, W. Max (1974) *Trade Policy and Economic Welfare* (Oxford: Oxford University Press)
Dagut, M.D. (1978) 'The Economic Effect of the Oil Crisis on South Africa', *South African Journal of Economics*, Vol, 46, pp. 23-35
Davenport, T.R.H. (1969) 'The Consolidation of a New Society: The Cape Colony' in Monica Wilson & Leonard Thompson (eds.), *The Oxford History of South Africa, Vol. 1, South Africa to 1870* (Oxford: The Clarendon Press) pp. 272-333
Demsetz, Harold (1965) 'Minorities in the Market Place', *North Carolina Law Review*, Vol. 43, pp. 271-97
Doeringer, Peter B. & Piore, Michael J. (1971) *Internal Labor Markets and Manpower Analysis* (Lexington, Mass.: D.C. Heath)
Du Plessis, J.C. (1970) 'Foreign Investment in South Africa' in Isaiah A. Litvak & Christopher J. Maule (eds.), *Foreign Investment: The Experience of Host Countries* (New York: Praeger)
Dumont, Louis (1970) *Homo Hierarchicus: An Essay on the Caste System* (Chicago: University of Chicago Press)

The Economist (1980:1) 'The Great Evasion. South Africa: A Survey', 29 June, Special Supplement

— (1980:2) 'Botha Beset', 16 August, p. 34

Edgeworth, Francis Y. (1922) 'Equal Pay to Men and Women for Equal Work', *Economic Journal*, Vol. 32, pp. 431-57

Edwards, Richard C.; Reich, Michael & Gordon, David M. (eds.) (1975) *Labor Market Segmentation* (Lexington, Mass.: D.C. Heath)

Elphick, Richard & Giliomee, Hermann (eds.) (1979) *The Shaping of South African Society* (Cape Town: Longman)

Ethier, Wilfred (1974) 'Some of the Theorems of International Trade with Many Goods and Factors', *Journal of International Economics*, Vol. 4, pp. 199-206

— (1982:1) 'The General Role of Factor Intensity in the Theorems of International Trade', *Economics Letters*, Vol. 10. pp. 337-42

— (1982:2) 'Higher Dimensional Issues in Trade Theory', Seminar Paper No. 218, Institute for International Economic Studies, University of Stockholm

Fallon, P.R. & Layard, P. Richard G. (1978) 'Capital-Skill Complementarity, Income Distribution, and Output Accounting', *Journal of Political Economy*, Vol. 83, pp. 279-301

Fawcett, Millicent (1876) *Political Economy for Beginners*, 4th ed. (London: Macmillan)

— (1892) 'Mr. Sidney Webb's Article on Women's Wages', *Economic Journal*, Vol. 2, pp. 173-6

— (1904) 'Review of "Women in the Printing Trades: A Sociological Study",' ed. by J.R. Macdonald. With a Preface by Professor F.Y. Edgeworth', *Economic Journal*, Vol. 14, pp. 295-9

— (1917) 'The Position of Women in Economic Life' in W.H. Dawson (ed.), *After-War Problems* (London: Allen & Unwin) pp. 191-215

— (1918) 'Equal Pay for Equal Work', *Economic Journal*, Vol. 28, pp. 1-6

First, Ruth; Steele, Jonathan & Gurney, Christabel (1973) *The South African Connection: Western Investment in Apartheid* (Harmondsworth: Penguin)

Flanagan, Robert J. (1978) 'Discrimination Theory, Labor Turnover, and Racial Unemployment Differentials', *Journal of Human Resources*, Vol. 13, pp. 187-207

Florence, P. Sargant (1931) 'A Statistical Contribution to the Theory of Women's Wages', *Economic Journal*, Vol. 41, pp. 19-37

Frankel, S. Herbert (1938) *Capital Investment in Africa: Its Course and Effects* (London: Oxford University Press)

Freeman, Richard B. (1974) 'Alternative Theories of Labor Market Discrimination. Individual and Collective Behavior' in George M. von Furstenberg; Ann R. Horowitz & Bennet Harrison (eds.), *Patterns of Racial Discrimination. Volume B. Employment and Income* (Lexington, Mass,: D.C. Heath) pp. 33-49

Friedman, Milton (1953) *Essays in Positive Economics* (Chicago: The University of Chicago Press)

— (1962) *Capitalism and Freedom* (Chicago: University of Chicago Press)

von Furstenberg, George M. (1972) 'A Model of Optimal Plant Integration in the Presence of Employee Discrimination', *Review of Regional Studies*, Vol. 2, pp. 72-85

—; Horowitz, Ann R. & Harrison, Bennet (eds.) (1974) *Patterns of Racial Discrimination. Volume B: Employment and Income* (Lexington, Mass.: D.C. Heath)

Gilman, Harry J. (1965) 'Economic Discrimination and Unemployment', *American Economic Review*, Vol. 55, pp. 1077-96

Giniewski, Paul (1961) *The Two Faces of Apartheid* (Chicago: Henry Regnery)

Goldberg, Matthew S. (1982) 'Discrimination, Nepotism and Long-Run Wage Differentials', *Quarterly Journal of Economics*, Vol. 97, pp. 307-19

Gordon, David M. (1972) *Theories of Poverty and Underemployment. Orthodox, Radical, and Dual Labor Market Perspectives* (Lexington, Mass,: D.C. Heath)
—; Edwards, Richard & Reich, Michael (1982) *Segmented Work, Divided Workers. The Historical Transformation of Labor in the United States* (Cambridge: Cambridge University Press)
Gordon, Nancy M. & Morton, Thomas E. (1974) 'A Low Mobility Model of Wage Discrimination — with Special Reference to Sex Differentials', *Journal of Economic Theory*, Vol. 7, pp. 241-53
Gulati, U.C. (1976) 'Foreign Investment and Domestic Savings — A Comment', *South African Journal of Economics*, Vol. 44, pp. 442-5
Hampel, Rainer & Krupp, Burkhard (1977) 'The Cultural and the Political Framework of Prejudice in South Africa and Great Britain', *Journal of Social Psychology*, Vol. 103, pp. 193-202
Hansson, Göte & Lundahl, Mats (1984) 'A Social Clause Against Discrimination in the Labor Market', *Journal of Development Economics*, Vol. 14, pp. 395-405.
Harrod, Roy F. (1952) *Economic Essays* (London: Macmillan)
Hepple, Alexander (1967) *Verwoerd* Harmondsworth: Penguin)
— (1971) *South Africa: Workers under Apartheid*, 2nd ed. (London: Christian Actions Publications)
Hobart Houghton, Desmond (1971) 'Economic Development 1865-1965' in Monica Wilson & Leonard Thompson (eds.), *The Oxford History of South Africa, Vol. 2, South Africa 1870-1966* (Oxford: The Clarendon Press), pp. 1-48
— (1976) *The South African Economy*, 4th ed. (Cape Town: Oxford University Press)
Horrell, Muriel (1969) *The African Reserves of South Africa* (Johannesburg: South African Institute of Race Relations)
Horwitz, Ralph (1967) *The Political Economy of South Africa* (London: Weidenfeld & Nicholson)
Hutt, William H. (1964) *The Economics of the Colour Bar* (London: André Deutsch)
Inada, Ken-ichi (1971) 'The Production Coefficient Matrix and the Stolper-Samuelson Condition', *Econometrica*, Vol. 39, pp. 219-40
Jain, Harish C. & Pettman, Barrie O. (1976) 'The American Anti-Discrimination Legislation and Its Impact on the Utilization of Blacks and Women', *International Journal of Social Economics*, Vol. 3, pp. 109-34
Jeeves, Alan (1975) 'The Control of Migratory Labour on the South African Gold Mines in the Era of Kruger and Milner', *Journal of Southern African Studies*, Vol. 2, pp. 3-29
Johnson, R.W. (1977) *How Long Will South Africa Survive?* (London and Basingstoke: Macmillan)
Johnstone, Frederick A. (1976) *Class, Race and Gold: A Study of Class Relations and Racial Discrimination in South Africa* (London: Routledge & Kegan Paul)
Jones, Ronald W. (1979:1) 'The Structure of the General Production Model in Trade Theory', in *International Trade: Essays in Theory* (Amsterdam' North-Holland) pp. 57-83
— (1979:2) '"Two-ness" in Trade Theory: Costs and Benefits', in *International Trade: Essays in Theory* (Amsterdam: North-Holland) pp. 289-326
— (1979:3) *International Trade: Essays in Theory* (Amsterdam: North-Holland)
— & Scheinkman, José (1977) 'The Relevance of the Two-Sector Production Model in Trade Theory', *Journal of Political Economy*, Vol. 85, pp. 909-35
Jowell, Kate (1979) 'Labour Policy in South Africa', *South African Journal of Economics*, Vol. 47, pp. 369-96

Kane-Berman, John (1979) *South Africa. The Method in the Madness* (London: Pluto Press)
Katzen, M.F. (1969) 'White Settlers and the Origin of a New Society, 1652-1778' in Monica Wilson & Leonard Thompson (eds.), *The Oxford History of South Africa, Vol. 1, South Africa to 1870* (Oxford: The Clarendon Press) pp. 187-232
Kemp, Murray C. (1969) *The Pure Theory of International Trade and Investment* (Englewood Cliffs: Prentice Hall)
— & Wan, Henry (1976) 'Relatively Simple Generalizations of the Stolper-Samuelson and Samuelson-Rybczynski Theorem' in Kemp, Murray C., *Three Topics in the Theory of International Trade* (Amsterdam: North-Holland) pp. 49-59
— & Wegge, Leon (1969) 'On the Relation Between Commodity Prices and Factor Rewards', *International Economic Review*, Vol. 10, pp. 407-13
Klass, Morton (1980) *Caste. The Emergence of the South Asian Social System* (Philadelphia: Institute for the Study of Human Issues)
Klitgaard, Robert E. (1972) 'Institutionalized Racism: An Analytical Approach', *Journal of Peace Research*, Vol. 9, pp. 41-9
Knight, John B. (1964) 'A Theory of Income Distribution in South Africa', *Bulletin of the Oxford University Institute of Economics and Statistics*, Vol. 24, pp. 289-310
— (1978) 'Labour Allocation and Unemployment in South Africa', *Oxford Bulletin of Economics and Statistics*, Vol. 40, pp. 93-129
— & Lenta, G. (1980) 'Has Capitalism Underdeveloped the Labour Reserves of South Africa?', *Oxford Bulletin of Economics and Statistics*, Vol. 42, pp. 157-201
— & McGrath, Michael D. (1977) 'An Analysis of Racial Wage Discrimination in South Africa', *Oxford Bulletin of Economics and Statistics*, Vol. 39, pp. 245-71
Kock, Karin (1938) 'Kvinnoarbetet i Sverige (Female Work in Sweden)', Appendix 1 to SOU 1938:47, *Betänkande angående gift kvinnas förvärvsarbete m.m.* (Report on the Gainful Employment of Married Women), pp. 351-470
Kosters, Marvin & Welch, Finis (1972) 'The Effects of Minimum Wages by Race, Age and Sex' in Anthony Pascal (ed.), *Racial Discrimination in Economic Life* (Lexington, Mass.: D.C. Heath) pp. 103-18
Koutsoyiannis, Anne (1979) *Modern Microeconomics*, 2nd ed. (London: Macmillan)
Krueger, Anne O. (1963) 'The Economics of Discrimination', *Journal of Political Economy*, Vol. 71, pp. 481-7
Lamar, Howard & Thompson, Leonard (eds.) (1981) *The Frontier in History. North America and Southern Africa Compared* (New Haven: Yale University Press)
Landes, William M. (1967) 'The Effect of State Fair Employment Laws on the Economic Position of Nonwhites', *American Economic Review*, Vol. 62, pp. 578-90
— (1968) 'The Economics of Fair Employment Laws', *Journal of Political Economy*, Vol. 76, pp. 507-52
Legassick, Martin (1977) 'Gold, Agriculture, and Secondary Industry in South Africa, 1885-1970: From Periphery to Sub-Metropole as a Forced Labour System' in Robin Palmer & Neil Parsons (eds.), *The Roots of Rural Poverty in Central and Southern Africa* (London: Heinemann) pp. 175-200
Leibenstein, Harvey (1957) *Economic Backwardness and Economic Growth* (New York: John Wiley & Sons)
Leijonhufvud, Axel (1976) 'Schools, "Revolutions" and Research Programmes' in

Spiro Latsis (ed.), *Method and Appraisal in Economics* (Cambridge: Cambridge University Press) pp. 65-108
Lewis, W. Arthur (1954) 'Economic Development with Unlimited Supplies of Labour', *Manchester School of Economic and Social Studies*, Vol. 22, pp. 139-91
Liff, David M. (1979) *The Oil Industry in South Africa* (Washington, D.C.: Investor Responsibility Research Center)
Little, Ian M.D. (1957) *A Critique of Welfare Economics*, 2nd ed. (Oxford: Oxford University Press)
Lloyd, Cynthia B. & Niemi, Beth T. (1979) *The Economics of Sex Differentials* (New York: Columbia University Press)
Lundahl, Mats (1979) *Peasants and Poverty: A Study of Haiti* (London: Croom Helm; New York: St. Martin's Press)
— (1982) 'The Rationale of Apartheid', *American Economic Review*, Vol. 72, pp. 1169-79
— (1984) 'Economic Effects of a Trade and Investment Boycott against South Africa', *Scandinavian Journal of Economics*, Vol. 86, pp. 68-83.
— & Ndlela, Daniel B. (1980) 'Land Alienation, Dualism, and Economic Discrimination: South Africa and Rhodesia', *Economy and History*, Vol, 23, pp. 106-32
— & Wadensjö, Eskil (1977) 'Economic Discrimination in a Two-Good Model: *Zeitschrift für Nationalökonomie*, Vol, 37, pp. 407-16
— & Wadensjö, Eskil (1979), 'Economic Discrimination in a Two-Good Model: Addendum', *Zeitschrift für Nationalökonomie*, Vol. 39, pp. 189-90
Mackler, Ian (1975) *Pattern for Profit in Southern Africa* (New York: Atheneum)
Madden, Janice F. (1973) *The Economics of Sex Discrimination* (Lexington, Mass,: D.C. Heath)
— (1977:1) 'A Spatial Theory of Sex Discrimination', *Journal of Regional Studies*, Vol. 17, pp. 369-80
— (1977:2) 'An Empirical Analysis of the Spatial Elasticity of Labor Supply', *Papers*, Regional Science Association, Vol. 39, pp. 157-71
— & White, Michelle J. (1980) 'Spatial Implications of Increases in the Female Labor Force: A Theoretical and Empirical Synthesis', *Land Economics*, Vol. 56, pp. 432-46
Main, T.R.N. (1975) 'The Reynders Commission and the Mining Industry', *South African Journal of Economics*, Vol. 43, pp. 92-110
Marais, G. (1981) 'Structural Changes in Manufacturing Industry 1916 to 1975', *South African Journal of Economics*, Vol. 49, pp. 26-45
Marks, Shula & Atmore, Anthony (eds.) (1980) *Economy and Society in Pre-Industrial South Africa* (London: Longman)
Marquard, Leo (1968) *A Short History of South Africa* (New York & Washington: Praeger)
Marshall, Ray (1974) 'The Economics of Racial Discrimination: A Survey', *Journal of Economic Literature*, Vol. 12, pp. 849-71
— (1977), 'Black Employment in the South' in Phyllis A. Wallace & Annette M. La Mond (eds.), *Women, Minorities and Employment Discrimination* (Lexington, Mass.: D.C. Heath), pp. 57-81
— & Christian, Virgil Jr. (1978) 'Economics of Employment Discrimination' in Ray Marshall & Virgil Christian, Jr. (eds.), *Employment of Blacks in the South. A Perspective on the 1960s* (Austin: The University of Texas Press) pp. 205-36
Masters, Stanley H. (1975) *Black-White Income Differentials: Empirical Studies and Policy Implications* (New York: Academic Press)
McCall, John J. (1972) 'The Simple Mathematics of Information, Job Search, and

Prejudice' in Anthony Pascal (ed.), *Racial Discrimination in Economic Life* (Lexington, Mass.: D.C. Heath) pp. 205-24
— (1973) *Income Mobility, Racial Discrimination, and Economic Growth* (Lexington, Mass.: D.C. Heath)
Milkman, Ruth (1979) 'Contradictions of Semi-Peripheral Development: The South African Case' in Walter L. Goldfrank (ed.), *The World System of Capitalism: Past and Present* (London: Sage Publications) pp. 261-84
Mill, John Stuart (1848) *Principles of Political Economy* (London: Parker & Co.)
Moyana, H.V. (1975) 'Land Apportionment in Rhodesia', Ph.D. Thesis, Columbia University, New York
Mueller, Dennis C. (1979) *Public Choice* (Cambridge: Cambridge University Press)
Müller, A.L. (1981) 'Slavery and the Development of South Africa', *South African Journal of Economy*, Vol. 49, pp. 153-65
Myrdal, Gunnar (1929) *Vetenskap och politik i nationalekonomin* (Stockholm: P.A. Norstedt & Söner)
— (1939) *Monetary Equilibrium* (London: W. Hodge & Co.)
— (1944) *An American Dilemma. The Negro Problem and Modern Democracy* (New York: Harper & Row)
— (1953) *The Political Element in the Development of Economic Theory* (London: Routledge & Kegan Paul)
— (1968) *Asian Drama. An Inquiry into the Poverty of Nations* (New York: Pantheon)
— (1978) 'Institutional Economics', *Journal of Economic Issues*, Vol. 12, pp. 771-83
Nath, S.K. (1969) *A Reappraisal of Welfare Economics* (London: Routledge & Kegan Paul)
Nattrass, Jill (1981) *The South African Economy. Its Growth and Change* (Cape Town: Oxford University Press)
Neary, J. Peter (1978) 'Short-Run Capital Specificity and the Pure Theory of International Trade', *Economic Journal*, Vol. 88, pp. 488-510
Nelson, Richard R. (1956) 'A Theory of the Low-Level Equilibrium Trap in Underdeveloped Economies', *American Economic Review*, Vol. 46, pp. 894-908
Olson, Mancur (1982) *The Rise and Decline of Nations* (New Haven: Yale University Press)
Oshima, Harry T. (1967) 'Food Consumption, Nutrition, and Economic Development in Asian Countries', *Economic Development and Cultural Change*, Vol. 15, pp. 385-97
Pearce, I.F. (1970) *International Trade* (London: Macmillan)
Phelps, Edmund S. (1972:1) *Inflation Policy and Unemployment* (New York: W.W. Norton)
— (1972:2) 'The Statistical Theory of Racism and Sexism', *American Economic Review*, Vol. 62, pp. 659-61
Phelps Brown, E. Henry (1949) 'Equal Pay for Equal Work', *Economic Journal*, Vol. 59, pp. 384-98
— (1977) *The Inequality of Pay* (Oxford: Oxford University Press)
Piercy, Mary V. (1960) 'Statutory Work Reservation in the Union of South Africa (Concluding Article)', *South African Journal of Economics*, Vol. 28, pp. 206-33
Pigou, Arthur Cecil (1952) *Essays in Economics* (London: Macmillan)
Piore, Michael J. (1970) 'Jobs and Training' in Samuel H. Beer & Richard S. Barringer (eds.), *The State and the Poor* (Cambridge, Mass.: Winthrop Publishers) pp. 53-83

— (1974) 'Labor Market Stratification and Wage Determination', *mimeo*, Massachusetts Institute of Technology
— (1975) 'Notes for a Theory of Labor Market Stratification' in Richard C. Edwards; Michael Reich & David M. Gordon (eds.), *Labor Market Segmentation* (Lexington, Mass.: D.C. Heath) pp. 125-50
Porter, Richard C. (1976) 'A Model of a South-African-Type Economy', Discussion Paper No. 60, Center for Research on Economic Development, The University of Michigan, Ann Arbor
— (1978) 'A Model of the Southern African-Type Economy', *American Economic Review*, Vol. 68, pp. 743-55
— (1979) 'International Trade and Investment Sanctions. Potential Impact on the South African Economy', *Journal of Conflict Resolution*, Vol. 23, pp. 579-612
Q & A on Equal Pay, (1947) (London: Trade Union Council)
Ratcliffe, Anne E. (1975) 'Export Policy in Perspective', *South African Journal of Economics*, Vol. 43, pp. 74-91
— (1979) 'Industrial Development Policy: Changes during the 1970s', *South African Journal of Economics*, Vol. 47, pp. 397-421
Rathbone, Eleanor (1917) 'The Remuneration of Women's Services', *Economic Journal*, Vol. 27, pp. 55-68
Reder, Melvin W. (1974) 'Comment on Arrow' in Orley Ashenfelter & Albert Rees (eds.), *Discrimination in Labor Markets* (Princeton: Princeton University Press) pp. 34-42
Reich, Michael (1981) *Racial Inequality. A Political-Economic Analysis* (Princeton: Princeton University Press)
—; Gordon, David M. & Edwards, Richard (1973) 'A Theory of Labor Market Segmentation', *American Economic Review*, Papers and Proceedings, Vol. 63, pp. 359-65
Reynders, H.J.J. (1975) 'Export Status and Strategy', *South African Journal of Economics*, Vol. 43, pp. 123-31
Roberts, Lance W. (1979) 'Some Unanticipated Consequences of Affirmative Action Policies', *Canadian Public Policy*, Vol. 5, pp. 90-6
Robinson, Joan (1933) *The Economics of Imperfect Competition* (London: Macmillan)
Roemer, John E. (1979) 'Divide and Conquer: Micro Foundations of A Marxian Theory of Wage Discrimination', *Bell Journal of Economics*, Vol. 10, pp. 695-705
Rogers, Barbara (1972) *South Africa: The 'Bantu Homelands'* (London: Christian Action Publications)
— (1976) *White Wealth and Black Poverty. American Investments in South Africa* (Westport: Greenwood Press)
Rosenstein-Rodan, Paul N. (1961) 'Notes on the Theory of the "Big Push"' in Howard S. Ellis assisted by Henry C. Wallich (eds.), *Economic Development for Latin America* (London: Macmillan) pp. 57-78
Rothenberg, Jerome (1961) *The Measurement of Social Welfare* (Englewood Cliffs: Prentice Hall)
Royal Commission on Equal Pay (1946) *Appendix IX to Minutes of Evidence Taken before the Royal Commission on Equal Pay* (London: HMSO)
Rubery, Jill (1978) 'Structured Labour Markets, Worker Organisation and Low Pay', *Cambridge Journal of Economics*, Vol. 2, pp. 17-36
Ruffin, Roy J. (1980) 'Trade and Factor Movements with Three Factors and Two Goods', Paper presented to the Trade Theory Workshop at the Institute for International Economic Studies, Stockholm, 4-15 August 1980

Rybczynski, T.M. (1955) 'Factor Endowments and Relative Commodity Prices', *Economica*, N.S., Vol. 22, pp. 336-41
Samuelson, Paul A. (1948) 'International Trade and Equalisation of Factor Prices', *Economic Journal*, Vol. 58, pp. 163-84
— (1949) 'International Factor-Price Equalisation Once Again', *Economic Journal*, Vol. 59, pp. 183-97
— (1953) 'Price of Factors and Goods in General Equilibrium', *Review of Economic Studies*, Vol. 21, pp. 1-20
Schapera, I. (1930) *The Khoisan Peoples of South Africa. Bushmen and Hottentots* (London: Routledge & Kegan Paul)
Segal, Ronald (ed.) (1964) *Sanctions Against South Africa* (Harmondsworth: Penguin)
Seidman, Ann & Neva (1977) *US Multinationals in Southern Africa* (Dar es Salaam: Tanzania Publishing House)
Sen, Amartya (1980) 'Personal Utilities and Public Judgements: Or What's Wrong with Welfare Economics' in Karl W. Roskamp (ed.), *Public Choice and Public Finance* (Paris: Editions Cujas) pp. 19-41
Schlicht, Ekkehart (1982) 'A Robinsonian Approach to Discrimination', *Zeitschrift für die gesamte Staatswissenschaft*, Vol. 138, No. 1, pp. 64-83
Schoeffler, Sidney (1952) 'Note on Modern Welfare Economics', *American Economic Review*, Vol. 42, pp. 880-7
Sher, George (1975) 'Justifying Reverse Discrimination in Employment', *Philosophical & Public Affairs*, No. 2, pp. 159-70
Shoup, Carl S. (1965), 'Production from Consumption', *Public Finance*, Vol. 20, pp. 173-206
Siebert, W. Stanley & Sloane, Peter J. (1980) 'Shortcomings and Problems in Analyses of Women and Low Pay' in Peter J. Sloane (ed.), *Women and Low Pay* (London: Macmillan, pp. 223-52)
Sloane, Peter J. (1980) 'The Structure of Labour Markets and Low Pay for Women' in Peter J. Sloane (ed.), *Women and Low Pay* (London: Macmillan) pp. 127-64
Smith, Barton & Newman, Robert (1977), 'Depressed Wages Along the US-Mexico Border: An Empirical Analysis', *Economic Inquiry*, Vol. 15, pp. 51-66
SOU (1978) Betänkande av Sydafrikautredningen. *Förbud mot investeringar i Sydafrika* (the Swedish Government Offical Reports, 1978:73, Findings of the South African Commission. *Ban on Investment in South Africa*) (Stockholm: Ministry of Commerce and Industry)
Sowell, Thomas (1975) *Race and Economics* (New York: David McKay)
— (1976) '"Affirmative Action" Reconsidered', *The Public Interest*, No. 42, pp. 47-65
— (1981) *Markets and Minorities* (Oxford: Basil Blackwell)
Spandau, Arndt (1975) 'Competition Policy in South Africa: Further Comments', *South African Journal of Economics*, Vol. 43, pp. 322-39
— (1977) 'Towards a New South African Competition Policy' (Review Article), *South African Journal of Economics*, Vol. 45, pp. 299-308
— (1978) *Economic Boycott against South Africa: Normative and Factual Issues* (Cape Town: Juta)
Spence, A. Michael (1974) *Market Signaling* (Cambridge, Mass.: Harvard University Press)
Stahl, Charles W. (1981) 'Migrant Labour Supplies, Past, Present and Future; With Special Reference to the Gold-Mining Industry' in W. Roger Böhning (ed.), *Black Migration to South Africa. A Selection of Policy-Oriented Research* (Geneva: International Labour Office) pp. 7-44
Stiglitz, Joseph E. (1973) 'Approaches to the Economics of Discrimination', *American Economic Review*, Vol. 63, Papers and Proceedings, pp. 287-95

— (1974), 'Theories of Discrimination and Economic Policy' in George M. von Furstenberg; Ann R. Horowitz & Bennet Harrison (eds.), *Patterns of Racial Discrimination. Volume B: Employment and Income* (Lexington, Mass.: D.C. Heath) pp. 5-26

Stolper, Wolfgang F. & Samuelson, Paul A. (1941) 'Protection and Real Wages', *Review of Economic Studies*, Vol. 9, pp. 58-73

Suckling, John (1975) 'Foreign Investment and Domestic Savings in the Republic of South Africa, 1957-1972', *South African Journal of Economics*, Vol. 43, pp. 315-21

Swan, Trevor W. (1962) 'Circular Causation', *Economic Record*, Vol. 38, pp. 421-6

Swinton, David H. (1977) 'A Labor Force Competition Theory of Discrimination in the Labor Market', *American Economic Review*, Vol. 67, Papers and Proceedings, pp. 400-4

Thompson, Leonard (1969:1) 'The Zulu Kingdom and Natal' in Monica Wilson & Leonard Thompson (eds.), *The Oxford History of South Africa, Vol. 1, South Africa to 1870* (Oxford: The Clarendon Press) pp. 334-90

— (1969:2) 'Co-operation and Conflict: The High Veld' in Monica Wilson & Leonard Thompson (eds.), *The Oxford History of South Africa, Vol. 1, South Africa to 1870* (Oxford: The Clarendon Press) pp. 391-446

— (1971) 'The Subjection of the African Chiefdoms 1870-1898' in Monica Wilson & Leonard Thompson (eds.), *The Oxford History of South Africa, Vol. 2, South Africa 1870-1966* (Oxford: The Clarendon Press) pp. 245-86

— & Prior, Andrew (1982) *South African Politics* (New Haven & London: Yale University Press)

Thurow, Lester C. (1969) *Poverty and Discrimination* (Washington D.C.: The Brookings Institution)

— (1975) *Generating Inequality* (New York: Basic Books)

Toikka, Richard S. (1976) 'The Welfare Implications of Becker's Discrimination Coefficient', *Journal of Economic Theory*, Vol. 13, pp. 472-7

Treiman, Donald J. & Hartman, Heidi I. (eds.) (1981) *Women, Work and Wages: Equal Pay for Jobs of Equal Value* (Washington D.C.: National Academy Press)

Troup, Freda (1975) *South Africa. An Historical Introduction* (Harmondsworth: Penguin)

Uekawa, Yasuo (1971) 'Generalization of the Stolper-Samuelson Theorem', *Econometrica*, Vol. 39, pp. 197-218

UNCTAD. *Supplement 1980. Handbook of International Trade and Development Statistics* (New York: United Nations)

Uys, Stanley (1980) 'Prospects for an Oil Boycott', *Africa Report*, September-October, pp. 15-18

Van der Horst, Sheila T. (1956) 'A Plan for the Union's Backward Areas: Some Economic Aspects of the Tomlinson Commission's Report', *South African Journal of Economics*, Vol. 24, pp. 89-112

Vanek, Jaroslav (1968) 'The Factor Proportions Theory: The *n*-Factor Case', *Kyklos*, Vol. 21, pp. 749-56

— & Bertrand, Trent J. (1971) 'Trade and Factor Prices in a Multi-Commodity World' in Jagdish N. Bhagwati; Ronald W. Jones; Robert Mundell & Jaroslav Vanek (eds.), *Trade, Balance of Payments, and Growth. Papers in International Economics in Honor of Charles P. Kindleberger* (Amsterdam: North-Holland) pp. 49-75

Viljoen, S.P. Du T. (1965) 'Investment in the Private Sector of South Africa', *South African Journal of Economics*, Vol. 33, pp. 298-309

Wachter, Michael L. (1974) 'Primary and Secondary Labor Markets: A Critique of the Dual Approach', *Brookings Papers on Economic Activity*, pp. 637-80

Wadensjö, Eskil (1975) 'Remuneration of Migrant Workers in Sweden', *International Labour Review*, Vol. 112, pp. 1-14

War Cabinet Committee on Women in Industry (1919:1), *Report* (Cmd. 135) (London: HMSO)

— (1919:2), *Minority Report* (Beatrice Webb) (Cmd. 135) (London: HMSO)

— (1919:3), *Appendix II. Evidence from Economists* (Cmd. 135) (London: HMSO)

Webb, Beatrice (1919) *The Wages of Men and Women: Should They be Equal?* (London: Fabian Society and Allen & Unwin)

Webb, Sidney (1891) 'The Alleged Differences in the Wages Paid to Men and Women for Similar Work', *Economic Journal*, Vol. 1, pp. 635-62

Welch, Finis (1967) 'Labor Market Discrimination: An Interpretation of Income Differences in the Rural South', *Journal of Political Economy*, Vol. 75, pp. 225-40

Wickins, P.L. (1981) 'The Natives Land Act of 1913: A Cautionary Essay on Simple Explanations of Complex Change', *South African Journal of Economics*, Vol. 49, pp. 105-29

Wilson, Francis (1971) 'Farming 1866-1966' in Monica Wilson & Leonard Thompson (eds.), *The Oxford History of South Africa, Vol. 2, South Africa 1870-1966* (Oxford: The Clarendon Press), pp. 104-71

Wilson, Monica & Thompson, Leonard (eds.) (1969) *The Oxford History of South Africa, Vol. 1, South Africa to 1870* (Oxford: The Clarendon Press)

Women in Industry, (1930) 'A Study of the Factors Which Have Operated in the Past and Those Which are Operating Now to Determine the Distribution of Women in Industry', Cmd. 3508) (London: HMSO)

Yudelman, David (1975) 'Industrialization, Race Relations and Change in South Africa. An Ideological and Academic Debate', *African Affairs*, Vol. 7, pp. 82-96

— (1977) 'The Quest for a Neo-Marxist Approach to Contemporary South Africa (Review Note)', *South African Journal of Economics*, Vol. 45, pp. 201-5

Zarenda, H. (1975) 'Tariff Policy: Export Promotion versus Import Replacement', *South African Journal of Economics*, Vol. 43, pp. 111-22

Zellner, Harriet (1972) 'Discrimination Against Women, Occupational Segregation, and the Relative Wage', *American Economic Review*, Vol. 62, Papers and Proceedings, pp. 157-60

INDEX

ad valorem coefficient 99
affirmative action 271-2, 275
African economy, traditional 209-10; see also South Africa
Africans in S. Africa models 226-59, 266-8, 283-90
Afrikaners, effect of boycott on 290-2
agriculture: and manufacturing in 2-good model 137-58, 169-81; in S. African economy 210-15, 217; in S. African models 226-58, 266-7, 283-7, 291-2
Aigner, Denis 44
Akerlof, George 37, 38-40, 52, 59, 66, 71
Alchian, Armen 29
Alexis, Marcus 33
alienation of African land 227, 230, 242, 243, 256, 257, 266-7
'Alleged Differences in the Wages Paid to Men and to Women for Similar Work' (Webb) 8-9
allocation problems 261, 272
altruism 117
American Dilemma, An (Myrdal) 8, 16-18, 53
Anglo-Boer War 217
anti-discrimination policies 268-92; causes of discrimination and 273-8; effects of 269-70; governmental 56-7, 68, 268-92
Apartheid policy 220-5, 234, 236, 242, 243, 274, 282, 287
Apprenticeship Act (1922) 218
Arrow, Kenneth 27, 32, 33, 34, 43, 111

bantustan policy 221-3, 232, 235-44, 267
Bantu Urban Areas Act (1945) 220-1
bargaining: collective 225, 258; deprivation of rights 218, 225; model 38, 55-7, 72, 261, 262, 264, 270, 277-8; reduction of employers' power 276; strengthening of rights 239-41
Batra, Raveendra N. 184

Becker, Gary 3, 4-5, 6, 8, 13, 18, 20-40 *passim*, 42, 47, 49, 52, 55, 59, 68, 69, 71, 81-104 *passim*, 109-13, 117, 118, 122, 123, 131, 132, 161, 162, 165, 244
Becker model 83-9, 162, 262-5, 266, 269, 272, 274; conclusion 103-4; DC and 97-103; flaw in 91-8; nepotism and 94-7; as one good model 135-7; pecuniary version of 109-29; reformulation of 91-4; as 'trade' approach 162
Bell, Duncan 48
Bergmann, Barbara 165
black(s): advancement of in S. Africa 224-5; peasantry in S. Africa 214-15; workers as protagonists in economy 56-7; see also Negroes; racial discrimination
Boers 211-14, 257
boycott against S. Africa 280-92; economic effects of 283-7
British Equal Pay Controversy 8
British in S. Africa 211, 290
Bronfenbrenner, Martin 13-14, 18, 19, 20, 47, 55
Brown, Henry Phelps 15
Bushmen, S. African 210

Cain, Glen 44
Cannan, Edwin 10-11
capital: in crowding model 183-208; foreign, in S. Africa 280-92; -intensive commodities 135; market segregation 117-28, 137-47, 244; reduced export of 22, 86, 88, 89, 115, 264, 278; in S. African model 232-9, 267; supply of 83-104, 114-17
Capitalism and Freedom (Friedman) 111
capital owners: discrimination by 71, 72, 82-104, 109-29, 131, 152-4, 162, 263-8, 278-9; effects of S. African boycott on 284-90; negro 151, 153-4, 162; and white workers 110
Casas, Francisco R. 184

Index

Cassel, Gustav 9, 11, 12, 57
caste system 38–41, 160
cattle herding in S. African model 226
causes of discrimination 3–6, 59–67; and anti-discrimination policy 273–8
changing preferences 89–91, 94, 103
chiefdoms, crushing of S. African 213–14
civilized labor policy 230, 231, 242
class factors 53
closed shop policies 24, 241
codes of behavior 39–40
coefficient, discrimination (DC) 4, 20–6, 27, 31, 82, 84, 89, 93, 94, 111, 131, 264; interpretation of 97–103; specific *vs.* ad valorem 99–102
colonization, white 112; in S. Africa 209–59
color bar 162, 216–44, 258–9, 267
commodity prices: changes in 189–91, 206; constant 171–5, 194, 206, 208; development of 196–208; relative 175–7, 184–5
commuting costs, reduction of 276
competition: as anti-discrimination measure 272–3, 274, 276; and discrimination 23–4, 27–9, 45, 54, 69, 111–12, 150, 269, 221–2; as effect of reduced discrimination 287–8; and prejudice 71, 110; in S. African model 229, 238, 242; in white sector 123
constant preferences 91–4, 95, 103; nepotism and 95–7, 102
consumer discrimination 24–5
conventions and pressure 10, 15, 18, 19, 37; *see also* social custom
crowding 8, 11–12, 19, 34, 70, 262, 270, 273, 279; approach to labor market segregation 161–81; more realistic model 183–208; in S. Africa 244
cultural differences 67
cumulative process 16–18
Customs Tariff Amendment Act (1925) 218

DC (discrimination coefficient) *see* coefficient, discrimination
Demsetz, Harold 29
difaqane 212

dilution, job 224, 239, 244, 268
dimensionality 184–5
disaggregation of labor force 122–6
discrimination, economic theory of: alternatives to Becker 37–57, 113–29, 262–3; application of 209–59; background 8–72, 261; Becker's 20–6, 81–104, 262–4; conclusion 261–96; critique of Becker 109–33; crowding approaches 161–81, 183–208; development of Becker 26–37; pecuniary 109–33; pre-Becker 8–20; S. African model 209–59; summary 261–96; two-good model 134–60
distribution of incomes 3–4, 66, 71, 263
distributive coalition 40–1
disutility 97–8
dual labor market theory 38, 49, 52–5, 164, 180; and bargaining models 55
Dutch East India Company 210
Dutch settlers in S. Africa 210–12, 266
dynamic theory 16–18, 21, 27–30

Economics of Discrimination, The (Becker) 3, 4–5, 8, 20, 81, 94
Economics of Imperfect Competition, The (Robinson) 12–13, 46
Economics of Sex Discrimination, The (Madden) 131
economy, integration of 161, 162–6, 180
Edgeworth, Francis 11, 13, 16, 19, 55, 81
education, discrimination in 67, 166, 265, 271, 279; in S. Africa 225, 242, 259, 267
effects: of anti-discrimination policies 269–73; of discrimination 68–70, 262; of reduced discrimination 287–9; secondary 289–90
employee discrimination 24, 27–9, 72, 261–3, 273–4; and monopsony 47–9, 57, 68; and workplace segregation 68, 71, 262
employer discrimination 23, 29, 32, 37, 53, 277; and monopsony 47–9, 57, 58
ending discrimination 278–9
endowments, factor 136, 137

equal opportunity legislation 279
equal wages 269-70, 274, 276, 277
Europeans in S. Africa model 226-43, 266-8, 280, 283-92
exploitation of blacks by whites 234
export(s): of capital, reduced 22, 86, 88, 89; S. African 281-2

factor: flows 162; mobility 135-7, 147; -price equalization 36, 91, 118, 135-6, 137, 155, 159, 172; use and outputs 171-5, 206
family structure 163
farming in S. Africa 212-15, 217-19, 222, 267; effect of boycott on 291-2
favoritism 82, 94, 164, 264; *see also* nepotism
Fawcett, Millicent 10, 11, 13, 19, 55, 165
Florence, Sargent 11-13, 14, 18, 19, 47-8
foreign workers in W. Europe 137
Friedman, Milton 111-12

Gilman, Harry 30
gold, S. African production of 213, 217, 219, 224, 243, 281
Goldberg, Matthew 32
Gordon, Nancy 48
government: anti-discrimination policy by 56-7, 68, 268-92; discrimination 25, 215-44
Great Trek, The 211-12

Harrod, Roy 15, 19
hegemony, European in S. Africa 227, 244
Henderson, Hubert 15
Hobart Houghton, Desmond 219
'homeland' policy 162
Hottentots (Khoikhoi) 210; Code 211
housing market, discrimination in 66-7

immigrants: black 54, 117, 122-3; European into S. Africa 227-9, 243, 266-7
imports, S. African 281-2
incentives to discriminate 116
income: distribution of 3-4, 261; 'net' and 'money' 84-94; real 141-7, 150, 153, 158-60, 177-80, 181, 183, 191-5, 226, 265
Indian caste system 161
individual aspects of discrimination 55
Industrial Conciliation Act 218, 223, 225
industrial unrest in S. Africa 217-18, 224-5
industry in S. Africa: effects of boycott on 280-92; model 229-44, 253, 256-9, 267
institutional discrimination 3-4, 70, 208, 268
integration: as anti-discrimination measure 274; of economy 161, 162-6; of workforce 277; of workplace 277
interest, conflict of 2, 3
interest rate changes 237, 239
international trade, theory of 1, 4, 26, 31, 34-7, 71, 135, 137, 159, 183, 184-5, 263, 268-9
investment in S. African industry and agriculture 237-9, 244, 268; boycott against 280-92

job(s): dilution 224, 230, 244, 268; reservation of 6, 162-4, 180, 183, 186, 216, 220, 223-5, 230, 231, 233, 238, 239, 241-4, 256, 259, 267
Jones, Ronald 184

Kaffir wars 211
Kemp, Murray 184
Kessel, Reuben 27
Khoikhoi (Hottentots) 210, 211
Klitgaard, Robert 39
Krueger, Anne 6, 34, 59, 91, 113, 264; model 113-18, 122, 127-8, 132, 147, 244, 264-5, 278

labor: force, disaggregation of 162-6; -intensive society 135; as mobile factor 109, 117; in Porter model 256
labor market: conflicts in 13, 217, 239; discrimination in 9, 25, 31, 43, 83-104 *passim*; dual 49, 52-5, 166, 180; radical 49-52; relations 56; segregation 5, 6, 59-72, 117, 121, 134-5, 147-60,

labour market: (*cont.*)
  161–81, 183–208, 227, 263;
  S. African 215, 244, 259
land: in crowding model 183–208;
  -owners in S. Africa 284; in
  Porter model 260; rents 230;
  and S. African discrimination
  210–15, 227, 242, 243, 266–7
legislation: anti-discriminatory
  268–92; discriminatory 70,
  211, 214–16, 263; interpretation
  of 1979 239–42; in S. Africa
  219–25
Location Acts 214–15

macroeconomic analysis 21–2, 261,
  262, 263, 264
Madden, Janice 131, 134, 135–6,
  163; model 131–3
managers 56
manufacturing: and agriculture in
  2-good models 137–58, 169–81,
  183; in S. Africa 221, 280–2,
  285
marginal productivity 83–104, 118,
  120–2, 125, 126, 132, 142–58,
  204–6, 227, 258, 286–8
market discrimination coefficient
  21–4, 31, 111
Marshall, Ray 33, 56–7, 162, 163
Marxist approaches 1
mfecane (crushing) 212, 213,
  214–15
microeconomic analysis 22–5,
  57–8, 261, 262
migrant labor in S. Africa 222–3,
  235–6
migration costs, reduction of 276
Mines and Works Amendment Act
  (1926) 218
Mines and Works Regulation Act
  (1911) 217, 258
minimum wages 269–70, 276
mining: and boycott against
  S. Africa 280–2; and poor
  whites 217–19; rise of S. African
  213–16; in S. African model
  229–31, 243, 267
mixed work force 111
mobility: between labor sectors
  54–5, 69, 137, 237, 273, 278–9;
  lower of blacks 66–7; of production factors 135–7; restriction
  of S. African blacks 235–6, 242

monetary analysis *see* pecuniary
  model
Monetary Equilibrium 16
monopolies 23, 27–9, 111–12, 162,
  272
monopsony 8, 12–14, 18–20, 37,
  46, 52, 59, 66, 69, 71–2, 261,
  262, 272, 273, 276; and employee
  discrimination 47–9, 57, 58, 68;
  in S. Africa 213, 215–16
Morton, Thomas 48
Myrdal, Gunnar 1, 2, 8, 16–18, 19,
  21, 53, 59

National Party (S. Africa) 291–2
Native Labour Regulation Act (1911)
  216
Native Recruiting Corporation
  (1912) 216
Natives Land Act (1913) 215
Natives Tax Act (1908) 214
Nattrass, Jill 241, 281
negative vs. positive discrimination
  21, 82
Negroes, discrimination against
  82–104, 109–29, 130–3, 134–60,
  166–80, 185–208, 278–9; *see
  also* blacks; racial discrimination
neo-classical theory 69, 89, 208,
  242–4, 260, 266
neo-Marxist theory 49
nepotism 5, 21, 31–2, 71, 82, 92,
  100, 264; in Becker-Toikka model
  94–7, 102–4; removal of 110

occupational discrimination 164
occupational segregation 10, 21, 23,
  24, 27–9, 32–4, 49, 51, 58, 59,
  61, 63, 65, 70, 108, 161, 163,
  220–2, 261–2
occupational status 33–4
oil imports to S. Africa 281–2;
  embargo on 284–6, 289
Olson, Mancur 40–1
one-good models 6; Becker's model
  as 134; in crowding approach
  158–60, 166–8; extended 185–7;
  limitations of 135–7, 262–5; and
  two-good model 153–4, 158–60
overpopulation, rural 215, 217,
  221–2, 258

Paretian analysis 1, 2
pass laws 235–7, 287

peasantry, S. African black 214-15
pecuniary model 109-29
Phelps, Edmund 43
Pigou, Arthur Cecil 11
Piore, Michael 52-4, 164
poor white problem 216-19, 229, 231, 242
Porter, Richard 234-5, 237; model of S. African economy 255-9
positive discrimination 82; vs. negative 21
preferences for discrimination 13, 19, 26, 47, 48, 53, 59, 66, 71, 261-4, 269, 271, 273-4, 276, 277; changing 89-91, 94, 103; constant 91-4, 95, 103, 264, 276, 277
prejudices 42-3, 52, 53, 59, 67, 262, 269, 271, 272, 274-5, 277; competition and 71, 110; by employers 111
primary labor market 52-5, 164
Prior, Andrew 242, 291
productivity 41, 59, 67; marginal 83-104, 118, 120-2, 125, 126, 132, 142-58, 204-6, 227, 258, 286-8
psychic costs: as factor 82-104; removal of 109-10; for white labor 131

quotas, as anti-discrimination measure 271-2, 274-7, 284

racial discrimination 5, 14, 16-18, 24, 38, 39; in S. Africa 209-59
radical labor market theory 38, 49-52, 67-9, 72, 262, 263, 270, 272; and bargaining models 55, 56, 59, 261, 277
Rathbone, Eleanor 9, 10, 11, 19
real incomes: effect of boycott on S. African 283-7; effect of discrimination on 141-7, 150, 153, 158-60, 177-8, 181, 183, 191-5, 226, 265, 267
reduced discrimination in S. Africa: effects of 287-9; secondary 289-90
Reich, Michael 51-2, 112, 165, 244
reservation of jobs 6, 162-4, 183, 216, 220, 223-5, 230, 231, 233, 238, 239, 241-4, 256, 259, 267
reserves (sector of S. African economy) 256-8
residential discrimination 25
reversed discrimination 271
Riekert Commission 225, 240, 242
Robinson, Joan 12, 13, 14, 16, 18, 19, 20, 46, 47, 55, 262
Roemer, John 50-2
Rogers, Barbara 236
Royal Commission on Equal Pay 14, 15, 16, 19
Ruffin, Roy 183-4
Rybczynski, T.M. 190, 202, 203

Samuelson, Paul A. 185
sanctions against discrimination 276; in S. Africa 280-92
secondary effect of discrimination in S. Africa 237-9, 268
secondary labor market 52-5, 164-5
segregation: and employee discrimination 68, 71; occupational 10, 21, 23, 24, 27-9, 32-3, 34, 49, 51, 58, 59, 61, 63, 65, 70, 108, 161, 163, 220-2; residential 25, 220-1; in school system 288; sexual 163; in S. Africa 220-44; workplace 69, 274, 277; *see also* labor market segregation
separate development (Apartheid) 221, 234
skilled labor 135, 265-6; in crowding models 165-80, 183-208; effects of S. African boycott on 284-90; in S. Africa 216, 223, 224, 279; in unskilled jobs 161, 165-80
skill-intensity 190, 193-5, 202-6
slavery 210, 211, 266
social costs in S. Africa 236, 240
social custom, discrimination as 36, 38-41, 59, 66, 69, 71, 242, 261, 263, 272, 273, 275-6
South Africa: boycott against 279-92; conclusions 242-4; economic effects of boycott 283-7; history 209-25; legislation 239-42; model 226-42; poor white problem in 216-19; Porter model 255-9; post WWII 219-24; recent developments 224-6; reduced discrimination 287-9; secondary effects 289-90; Stage I 226-9; Stage II 229-32;

South Africa: *(cont.)*
　Stage III 232-6, 282, 283;
　traditional economy 209-10;
　white expansion 210-13
Sowell, Thomas 28
specialization, complete 136-7, 159
specific coefficient 99-102, 104
Spence, Michael 43
squatters, S. African white 212, 214-15
statistical discrimination 37, 43-6, 53, 59, 67, 69, 70, 72, 165, 262, 270, 273, 275
'Statistical Theory of Racism and Sexism, The' (Phelps) 43
status and discrimination 56
Stiglitz, Joseph 36, 135
Stolper, Wolfgang F. 184
strikes, industrial 241, 258-9
Swan, Trevor 18
Sweden, immigration to 122-3
Swinton, David 56

tariff on S. African exports 283-4
taste for discrimination 82, 84, 89, 90, 104; income gains and 92; and nepotism 94-5, 96, 99; problems with approach 109-13, 127; welfare effects caused by 101-2; among white labour 130-1
taxation, as anti discrimination measure 278
technical training, discrimination in 242
technological progress 98-100, 104, 219
terms of trade 140-1, 147
territorial expansion 210-13
Thompson, Leonard 242, 291
three-factor model 184
Thurow, Lester 34-6, 81, 162
Toikka, Richard 31, 94-6, 102, 103
trade: approach to discrimination 162; and investment boycott against S. Africa 280-92
trade unions: and bargaining models 55-6; discrimination and 10-13; 16, 18, 19, 24, 30, 70, 263; and radical theory 51-2; in S. Africa 217-18, 223, 225, 239-41, 258-9; and women 47, 165
traditional African economy 209-10

training: on the job 279; technical 242
tribal conflict 210
two-good model 6, 134-60, 265-6; capital market segregation 137-47; conclusions 158-60; in crowding model 168-81, 183, 184, 187-208; extended 187-208; effects on real incomes 141-7; labor market segregation 147-54; limitation of one-good model 135-7; uniform wages in white sector 154-8

uncertainty, discrimination under 37, 41-6, 70, 270, 275
unemployment 30-1, 59, 61, 63, 65, 68, 69, 222-4, 240, 242, 262, 269
United Nations General Assembly 282
United States, discrimination in 112, 117, 123, 162, 209, 261
unskilled labor 135, 265-6, 267; in crowding models 166-80, 183-208, 279; effects of S. African boycott on 284-90; in S. Africa 213, 220, 226-44
urbanization 216-17
utility functions 32-4, 37, 39, 71, 261, 262

Verwoerd, Hendrick 220, 221
Viljoen, S.P. 237

Wage Act (1925) 218
wage(s): differentials 5, 8-9, 20-1, 25, 27-9, 31, 32, 45, 51, 53, 58, 59, 66, 68, 163, 262, 265, 270, 274, 277; elasticity 31, 34-6, 48, 49, 276, 285; equal, as antidiscrimination measure 269-70, 274, 277; equal, in 2-good model 147-58; long term differences 61, 63, 65, 68, 262-3; in pecuniary model 118-27; rigidity 45, 71; short-term differences 60, 62, 64, 68, 261; in S. Africa model 227-39; and women 8-16
War Cabinet on Women in Industry 10
Webb, Sidney 8-9, 11, 17, 19, 59
welfare economic analysis 5, 31, 32, 34, 263; of capital market

segregation 146-7; comparisons 90-1; effects 70-2, 84-9, 90-104, 112, 262-3; in Krueger model 113-17; of labor market market segregation 117-27, 153-4

Western Europe, foreign workers in 137

white(s): discrimination by 82-104, 109-29, 130-3, 134-60, 166-80, 185-208; effect of boycott on 283-90; expansion in S. Africa 210-13; labor, as protagonist in economy 56-7; taste for discrimination by 130-1; and white capitalists 110, 278

Wiehahn Commission 225, 242

Witwatersrand Native Labour Association 216

women: and discrimination 8-16, 19-20, 38, 46-7, 54, 55, 66, 163-4, 261, 263, 270; segregation of 137

Wootton, Barbara 14, 15, 19

workplace segregation 69, 274, 277

world recession 224

youths 54

Zulu Wars 212